A

HALF-CENTURY

OF THE

UNITARIAN CONTROVERSY,

WITH PARTICULAR REFERENCE

TO ITS ORIGIN, ITS COURSE, AND ITS PROMINENT SUBJECTS AMONG THE CONGREGATIONALISTS OF MASSACHUSETTS.

WITH AN APPENDIX.

BY

GEORGE E. ELLIS.

BOSTON:
CROSBY, NICHOLS, AND COMPANY.
1857.

CAMBRIDGE:
METCALF AND COMPANY, PRINTERS TO THE UNIVERSITY.

CONTENTS.

APPENDIX.

INTRODUCTION.

The seven Essays which occupy the substantial part of this volume have already appeared in print, in recently published numbers of the Christian Examiner. They are now issued in this present form in compliance with the wishes of many readers. An opportunity is thus afforded to the writer of them of laying aside the plural pronoun used in his late editorial capacity, and of writing an Introduction to them in his own proper name.

For the many and earnest expressions received through public and private channels, conveying to me grateful evidence that I have not spent labor on an unprofitable service, I would here make a most thankful return. To have contributed even in the humblest measure to a peaceful discussion of subjects too often associated with malignant feelings and offensive language, is a source of pleasure to me. If, beyond that, I have in the slightest degree simplified or relieved some themes which all former discussions have helped to confuse or perplex, I shall have realized the highest object which I dared to propose to myself as attainable.

I have been dealing with matters of controversy, and yet I have had in view no controversial design. If no better purpose had moved me than that of adding yet another to the endless and exhaustless reiterations of dogmatical disputation about the Gospel of Jesus Christ,

I am certain that I should have found more congenial employment for my time and my pen. I have endeavored wholly to avoid what is heating and bitter in writing upon controverted subjects. Too much that has been dictated in that spirit has necessarily passed under my notice, to give me any other feeling than that of sheer disgust toward it. I have believed that it is possible for intelligent persons to treat with rigid candor and with passionless feelings such matters of variance between them as those who claim alike to be Christians find to be grounds of division in faith and sympathy. If, notwithstanding my sincere purpose and my avowed resolution on this point, friendly or unfriendly readers should still detect in these pages any tokens of misrepresentation, or ill-feelings, or controversial unfairness, I make here a humble apology for the offence, and beg that my error may be accounted in part to the contagious influence of much unwholesome matter which I have been compelled to peruse, and in part to something still left incomplete in the process of my own conversion. I would use controversy with another rather as a means for discovering wherein my own views may be wrong, than as a means of triumphing over his errors. There is a wholesome discipline of mind in fair controversy, where both parties are alike interested in the subjects under discussion. Nor where truth is the only end in view, and where the search for it is but the first stage of full loyalty and deference to it, need controversy have any harmful effect on the heart.

It seemed to me that the best way to redeem what, in the retrospect, might appear to call for regret in the origin or conduct of the controversy among the descendants of a Congregational lineage in New England, was to seek for something among its results which would either justify it to Christian men, or be available as showing that a conciliation of old strifes was attended by an approximation of sentiments between the two extreme parties. My object, therefore, was to subordinate the controversial to the historical, and to make a sketch of the past strife between the parties a point from which to trace any subsequent modifications of opinion on either side, as now exhibited in the views advanced by their successors. A Christian minister who continues his professional studies in the quiet hours rescued from routine duties, enjoys all the means for testing the Gospel in the substance of its speculative and its practical elements. A critical or antiquarian student of the Bible and of ecclesiastical history, who is not brought daily into a religious relation with others, becomes either a dreamer or a sceptic. He will either work out some fanciful conceit or worthless theory of his own, and so add another to the already annoying tasks through which plain minds must make their way to truth; or he will yield himself to speculative doubts about facts which he has studied as barren theories. But a working student, who is searching for truth on its practical side, that he may carry it out from his study as the material for living appeal from the pulpit, or as strength, wisdom, guidance, or consolation to those who need it for such uses, will never be a dreamer or a sceptic. Still he may be a bigot, narrow-minded, prejudiced, and but half furnished for his high offices. His security against these vices and limitations of his profession must be found in catholic studies and in a well-disciplined heart. Considering the oracular authority which for ages has been assigned to Christian ministers, the more oracular, too, according to the narrowness of their sphere and the mystifications of their utterances, we may well regard their incessant controversies as, on the whole, valuable as mutual restraints and correctives of each other's narrowness.

But our own age affords opportunities for something

better than mere controversy. When we consider what treasures are heaped for our use, the fruits of toiling brains and of earnest hearts, gathered from the briery fields of truth, the least that we can do to prove our gratitude for them is to use them so as to vindicate their value. There is no drearier view of the application of the dismal sentence of "Vanity" to all human pursuits, than that which would persuade us that it has a special force when assigned to the tasks of mind and soul in search of speculative and theoretical truth. Most forlorn and dispiriting would be the conviction, that the way which we fondly believe is a progress onward, is only a circular path over the trodden ways of doubt, uncertainty, and error. Nor does it satisfy us that the yield of knowledge should only be larger in the sense of increase in the world's grain-harvests, as feeding more minds. We want our increase of knowledge to be also an increase in the relative amount of truth in it.

The influences which now prevail in the religious literature of the age are such as are highly favorable to the harmonizing and the conciliating of many old strifes. The Christian student, while pursuing the largest culture of his mind and the serious training of his heart, is disposed to seek out affinities, rather than alienations, from among the leading thinkers in a distracted Christendom. Our old controversies come back to us not merely to be reviewed, but to be sifted, and that we may select from them the largest seeds of the truth or error in them for trial by the new and improved processes of dialectics and criticism. The conservative theologians, who insist upon clinging to the old doctrinal tenets, as a part of their inheritance from ages of faith, may be allowed to take that stand as a position, if they will only indulge themselves in a good outlook from it. They love to quote the counsel of the Lord spoken by the prophet, "Stand ye in the way, in the old paths";

but they do not heed the advice which bids them *ask* for "the good way," — a question which implies a doubt whether they are already in it. It may be too much to expect that the old formulas and symbols to which have been attached the traditional piety of long centuries, and through the help of which we interpret the religious life of the great saints of Christendom, should be allowed to pass into oblivion. But we know that these are often cherished now-a-days rather for their associations, than as adequate exponents of the faith of men who hold the foremost places of religious influence. The attempt to run new truth into the old moulds, involves a great deal of that mystification of language, and that obscurity of thought, which, together with an evident and most vigorous independence of mind, characterize most of the writers in the school of progressive theology.

It is with the persuasion that many of the most earnest ministers and scholars of our own time, encouraged by the sympathy of practical reformers, are breaking away from the old stereotyped formulas of Orthodoxy, that I have sought to trace some of the results of their noble efforts in these pages. Such changes as a "Liberal Christian" hopes to see realized must necessarily be very slow in their progress, and they will be most grudgingly allowed by those who feel bound to resist them. Taking the space of fifty years, covered by the discussions which are here reviewed, and remembering what stupendous changes have transpired under the general name of progress and improvement, in most of the interests of human life, would an intelligent theologian of any party be willing to admit that his own professional pursuits had been stationary? The annotations added to new editions of our old histories often have the effect of discrediting the text above them, and of entirely reversing the judgment founded upon it. When the old themes of controversy are reconsidered, may we not expect that a comparison of the views of the extreme parties will help us, with the aid of new materials, to find reconciling processes for harmonizing some of them, and positive conditions for deciding others of them to be true or false?

The terms *Unitarian* and *Orthodox* occur much too frequently in these pages. My pen has written them so often that I have become wellnigh disgusted with them. As they have come back to me in the proof-sheets, strewn all over the paragraphs of each of the following essays, I have wished that I had agreed with printers and readers upon some symbol or cipher which, like an algebraical sign, should express the unknown element signified by each of them. Of course I have had to use the terms under their popular signification. Some one may ask, Why object to their use in all necessary discussions, if they have a well understood and definite meaning? The difficulty is, that they have not such a distinct and self-interpreting signification. Each of them, to the majority of those who use them, means a great deal more or a great deal less than is positively essential to the two sides of the issue which they represent. The term *Orthodoxy* covers the whole faith of the one party; the term Unitarian is at best but a definition of one of the doctrinal tenets of the other party. The associations connected with both the terms have also overborne their simple meaning as originally used. It may be well to remember that the title Unitarian was forced upon those who now bear it, and that, after objecting to have it assigned to them, finding that for some purposes they, like everything else in heaven or earth, must have a designation in the speech of men, they tried to make it as intelligible as possible. As I shall soon have occasion to explain, however, only a small minority of those who really come under the definition have ever consented to be known by the title. The inequality towards the two respective parties which was thus introduced into the controversy, by claiming for one of them a comprehensive and honorable designation, and by assigning to the other an epithet which but vaguely expressed one tenet of their distinctive faith, has had a bad influence all through the course of the controversy. Opportunity was thus given to the Orthodox, of which they have always availed themselves, to represent the faith of Unitarians as simply a negative system. Another wrong has been done to the Unitarians, by the attempt to monopolize the use of the phrase *Evangelical Christians* for the designation of Trinitarians. Thus the smart of unjust reproach and of misrepresentation has been added to the unavoidable burden of a conscientious dissent from distinctive orthodox dogmas. The real merits of the controversy have often been wholly obscured by side issues. If, therefore, the heaped-up materials of the past discussions cannot be made serviceable for some real progress towards the harmonizing of differences, it will be better to begin the task all anew, and to begin it by the largest literary bonfire whose flames ever rose up to heaven. Much of this controversial literature would take the fire most kindly. It has almost the property of spontaneous combustion.

A very remarkable phenomenon presents itself to the notice of one who is interested in Unitarianism, whether as a friend or as an opponent of it. It is this, that the large majority of those who really come under its substantial definition, and actually receive Christian truth in that interpretation of it, cannot be brought into a sectarian acknowledgment of it, still less into any active association for its defence or extension. The apathy, the indifference of "Liberal Christians," their lack of zeal in any measures of proselytism, their willingness to remain quietly in other communions, indulging their own convictions, and never inviting attention upon their real dissent from their own nominal associations, are characteristics peculiar to this class of Christians. All other sects draw in a far larger proportion, if not the whole, and sometimes even more than the whole, of those who accept their distinctive views. Persecution and reproach have been found to be among the strongest forces of attraction for consolidating other sects out of all those really in sympathy with them. Nearly every Christian sect bears a name which was first given to it in contempt. Yet this never hindered any one who held its distinctive tenets from yielding himself up to the name, or taking it voluntarily upon him at the time when the name was most opprobrious, the date of its first use. The title *Christian* was first given to the disciples in scorn; but all to whom it belonged were glad to accept it, till they made it so honored that it became an object to bear it, and many then and ever since have received it without any just title to it. The epithets Reformers and Protestants, instead of being assumed, were visited as insults upon the heretics of the first age in which the Roman Church was assailed; but they were cheerfully accepted as names to be answered to by all who were entitled to them, and were thus very soon lifted into honorary definitions for public documents and solemn confessions. So, also, the epithet Puritan was as much a term of contempt from the lips of enemies as was the title Quakers; but they kept off no disciples through fear of the scorn that went with them. Indeed, these reproachful designations may justly be regarded as the very watchwords, or spells, which called out the sturdy disciples of each successive sect, and hardened their convictions, or at least confirmed their allegiance. But such reproach as is conveyed in a contemptuous epithet attached to unpopular opinions has not availed to call out Liberal Christians into the ranks of avowed and aggressive Unitarianism. Nor has the dread of this reproach, working in an opposite direction, had the effect of leading all to whom it might attach to rest quiet under a silent enjoyment of their own opinions. The fear of persecution or of popular odium is by no means the most efficient cause which has suppressed their denominational zeal. The phenomenon has another explanation. The following pages bear witness to the sharpness and pertinacity with which some of the earlier Unitarians have been censured for a concealment of their heresies. But it is a matter for surprise that Unitarianism has not received much sharper rebukes on the score of the apathy of the great majority of its real disciples in not assuming an antagonistic or sectarian, or at least an avowed, position in Christendom. The fact must be granted, it must even be proclaimed, that from the opening of the controversy, both here and in Great Britain, the majority of the Liberal party refused to come into a sectarian organization bearing the name Unitarian. Especially in our own country was this fact observable; and so strange is it to many, both friends and opponents, as to be worthy of particular notice here. Some of the scholarly and able men who wrote most effectively against Calvinism and in defence of Liberal Christianity in our periodicals and essays, some of the most devout and earnest ministers, whose pulpits rang with their denunciations of the exclusive system and with eloquent expositions of our views, and whole classes of laymen in the professions and in the common walks of life, with noble women not a few, utterly refused to have anything to do with a Unitarian Association. Such dissentients were the majority from the first, and have ever since been the majority. We should not err if we set the proportion between them and the sectarian Unitarians at the rate of ten to one.

Those who are embraced in this large majority have never joined the Unitarian Association, nor attended its meetings. It has been affirmed, on excellent authority, that far more copies of Orthodox periodicals and newspapers and books are circulated among Unitarians, and subscribed for by them, than of their own sectarian publications. Unitarians have given millions to colleges, academies, libraries, philanthropic and charitable institutions, from whom it would have been impossible to draw a single dollar for the "Association." Even the Association itself is one of the least antagonistic of all sectarian organizations. Its dignity, calmness, caution, and moderation keep down the fervors of its zeal, and temper the ardor of its proselytism. It has from the first been rather a philanthropic than a sectarian agency. Its "book fund" has proved its most popular measure, and one of the most acceptable of its publications is a volume of essays from liberal Orthodox writers.

And now, what is the explanation of the fact, that, from the first antagonistic manifestation of Unitarianism to the present hour, the majority of those who really accept the substance of it, including many of its very foremost disciples, would not and will not come under any association bearing the name, or engage in any direct sectarian assault upon views which they reject? There have been two reasons — reasons, I must add, of very great force and cogency — assigned by such persons, by word of mouth, or in their writings, in explanation (they would not have said, in justification) of their course. As these reasons operate so strongly in my own mind as to repress in me any intenseness of sectarian zeal, in spite of my having written this book, I shall state them in a way to manifest my own accordance with them.

The first of these reasons was a strong objection, amounting to an absolute repugnance, to assuming the name *Unitarian* as defining what was peculiar in the faith of dissenters from Orthodoxy. The epithet was objectionable to them alike on positive and on negative grounds. There were some who insisted that the Trinitarian theory about the Godhead was to them a matter of no importance whatever. The theory, under the form of a modal or historical Trinity, like that which Dr. Bushnell has within a few years developed, was so far from being offensive to them, that they might even be willing to accept it. Trinitarians, too, might insist that they also were Unitarians. At any rate, the epithet, whether ill-chosen or significant as far as related to the one point on which it designated a doctrinal belief, expressed dissent from only the least offensive of all the five points of Calvinism. The doctrine, that God visited the guilt of Adam's personal sin upon the unborn millions of his posterity, or at any rate subjected them on his account to an undiminished responsibility though with an impaired ability, was infinitely more objectionable to some Liberal Christians than the Trinitarian theory. If they must needs bear any sectarian name, they should prefer to choose one which would express their protest against the doctrine of the entailed corruption and condemnation of human nature. Others laid the stress of their repugnance to Orthodoxy to the account of the old notion of an atonement made to God by the vicarious sufferings of an innocent victim. There was something so hideously heathenish in this dogma, that they regarded a contention about the mode of the Divine existence to be relatively of no importance whatever when compared with a notion so revolting to their moral sense. The objection, therefore, was, that the epithet Unitarian was neither significant, comprehensive, nor distinctive enough to serve as a designation of their protests against Orthodoxy. It was a name that did not carry with it a definition. It would as well befit a

Mohammedan or a Jew, as a Christian. It carried with it so small a part of a liberal Christian's creed, and conveyed so slight a portion of the grounds of his dissent from prevailing views of religion, that it was rather an evasion than an announcement of the antagonistic position assumed by him. It would need to be explained whenever it was used. If those who assumed it did not fill it out by some complementary definitions, they would need to apologize for making a proclamation which defined neither their foes nor their friends. The opponents of Unitarians, it was added, would supplement the epithet by additional definitions of their own, and it would soon appear that those who had been willing to assume the title would have to take with it a creed about other doctrines fabricated for them by others, because they had promulgated none of their own.

As a part of this objection, too, many of the liberal party protested against the introduction into common usage among Christians of any other sectarian name. There were too many such names already. They were simply mischievous and alienating in their effects. The disciples were called Christians first at Antioch; and it was a pity that they had ever been called anything else anywhere else. It should be one of the most desirable objects of zeal and effort among Christians, to get rid of the sectarian names now in use. He was a seditious and troublesome person, who invented or was willing to bear any new designation of the kind. We, at least, was the closing plea, will not consent to have this label attached to us. We may agree with the generally understood views of Unitarians, we may sympathize with their objects, and pray for such reforms in faith and the methods of true piety as they favor, and we are in heart, mind, and soul utter foes of Calvinism. But do not compel us to bear the epithet Unitarian. We will not join an association bearing that epithet. We advise you not to form such an association, for the moment you do so, you will raise new enemies, and concentrate new opposition, and check the progress of the very views which you are aiming unwisely to advance.

The second reason urged as an objection to the banding together of a new sect under the title of Unitarianism was, and is, that it is impossible to construct a platform, as the word is, which will include all who really come under the designation, and exclude all undesirable associates who might claim to attach themselves to the party. Those who have protested as earnestly as have Liberal Christians against the setting up of religious tests, or the imposition of creeds, would find it very difficult to fashion or to impose a creed of their own. Yet they must have a creed. They may have a very stringent and definite one in their own minds, as a statement of their own Christian faith, and as a virtual test for deciding whether their neighbors are fairly entitled to be called Christian believers. But this private creed will not admit of publication. They must have another for use, for announcement, as the basis of fellowship, as the first article in the Constitution of an Association. This must necessarily be very loose and free, in order not to be inconsistent with their ultra Protestantism. But if thus loose and free, it will invite in all sorts of loose believers, all unsettled, visionary, sceptical persons and unbelievers who want to have the name of a home, if only as a fiction for satisfying them that they are not living absolutely out of doors. Unitarianism will thus become virtually responsible for all the eccentric speculations and absurdities that may be rife in a community. We have no idea of being mixed up with any such miscellaneous oddities as these, said the objectors, so we will not join your Association, nor identify ourselves with your sectarian name or measures.

These objections furnished good reasons to a large

number of intelligent and serious persons for keeping aloof from a Unitarian sect. They admit of a great variety in the modes in which they would influence fastidious, timid, or conscientious persons. The most thoughtful and best informed of those who felt and yielded to their force, reminded themselves of the conditions under which Liberal Christianity had manifested itself in different places and fellowships, and of the sort of minds and hearts with which it had proved its congeniality. They knew very well from these conditions that it admitted of no forcing process, that, to be healthfully cherished, it must be spontaneously recognized. They loved to feel the power of that sympathy which united them with such men as Grotius, LeClerc, Locke, Milton, Newton, Whitby, and Lardner. They believed that all that was excellent and true in what was known as Unitarianism would be fostered even in Orthodox communities, by influences which work deeper and more effectively than any sectarian measures. They were assured that Liberal Christianity would be checked in its progress by the formation of a Unitarian sect. Were they wrong or right in this their honest judgment?

Right or wrong, there are those among the living who accord with their views, and who hold them with even a firmer conviction, if possible, because, as they interpret the facts of past and present experience, they find such strong confirmations of these views. While Unitarianism, as a form of sectarian Christianity, finds a few very earnest and active friends, it is compelled to acquiesce in the seeming lukewarmness of the greater portion of its real disciples, and to be content with claiming hosts of unavowed friends in all other communions. These have been, and they are still, the conditions under which the sect exists and manifests itself. Its zealous, outspoken champions justify their own sectarian earnestness, by declaring their convictions that Orthodoxy is so harmful a thing, so unfair an exponent of true Christianity, so chargeable with the blame of promoting a wide-spread infidelity, as to demand of every one emancipated from its bonds, not only a rejection of it, and an implied testimony against it, but an active opposition to it by assault and a continuous warfare. Those who are called lukewarm or indifferent in this cause, who, though virtually Unitarians, will do nothing under the machinery of a sect for its advancement, are perfectly well qualified to vindicate their position. They have an intense dislike to sectarian strife, to party organizations in religion, to the working of all the agencies requisite for such enterprises. Their own views of Christian truth do not excite in them any warm sympathies with a cause which involves an assault upon the views of others. They shrink from being implicated in votes, *resolutions*, and measures, which may be carried by a majority, in a meeting that may not fairly represent those who are claimed as its constituents. They have strong private friendships, and many affectionate relations with members of other Christian communions, and prefer not to subject these heart-ties to the rude trials of controversy. More than all, these "lukewarm" Unitarians have satisfied themselves that, in our intelligent communities, so abundantly supplied with the means of information, and so divided by sects to each of which there is a right and a left extreme, true views have so free a field that they ought to be expected to advance themselves by their own inherent energies.

The fact that Unitarianism was developed in this community out of Orthodox Congregationalism, has virtually committed it to the church order and mode of worship which are distinctive of Congregationalism. If any one, who, by education, association, or a strong preference of his own, is attached to the Episcopal ritual and mode of worship, becomes a Unitarian, he must renounce religious usages which are very dear to him, if he would worship where the doctrines preached are perfectly congenial with his own views. This fact has suggested to many the belief that Episcopal Churches throughout the land contain quite a large number of those who are doctrinally Unitarians, but who cling to a ritual service.

And one more admission is to be recognized. Unitarianism, in the largest and most comprehensive exposition that can be made of it, as a form of sectarian Christianity, does not make an exhaustive statement of the doctrinal substance of the Gospel. The only essential characteristic which it can claim, by the laws of etymology, as going with its title, is a belief in the undivided unity of the Supreme Being, and a rejection of the doctrine of the Trinity. Unitarianism commits itself to the emphatic denial that the whole internal doctrinal system of the Gospel takes its start from a metaphysical dogma, which parts the Godhead into three Personalities. Everything else that is understood to go with a profession of Unitarianism, is rather inferential, than of the positive essence or substance of it. True, usage and the general understanding of things which establish themselves as a standard for popular judgment have attached to Unitarianism the responsibility of committing itself to assertions, or at least to negations, touching three other doctrines, — the nature and rank of Christ, the moral state and condition of human beings at birth, and the doctrine of reconciliation or atonement. But even as regards these three doctrines, the moment that Unitarianism is made responsible for a belief or a denial about either of them, we have to encounter professions and protests which prove that a supposed sect contains almost as many creeds as individual members. There is something in the very name Unitarian which seems to commit every one who bears it to the obligation of being himself a *unit* in some or most of the elements of his creed. Thus it comes to pass that Unitarians will not consent to be held responsible for such definitions as the Orthodox may attach to our speculative faith about the three doctrines just referred to, nor will Unitarians allow their own brethren to fix for them any shapings or forms of dogmatical definition of those doctrines.

As regards a speculative opinion about the nature and rank of Christ, Unitarians by no means hold themselves bound to define and hold a dogma on that profoundly mysterious subject. They may agree in the belief that Christ, in every relation and office in which he is presented to us, is subordinated to God. They may all admit that the practical ends of Christian piety, faith, obedience, and full redemption, are not made dependent, even most remotely, upon a correct speculative view of the nature and rank of Christ. But further than this, Unitarians do not think alike or believe alike, and they protest against being classified under or committed to any view which one of them or any number of them may advance. They insist upon being left individually free to their speculations, and as free to attach what value they may judge right to these speculations, while in the spirit of fidelity and docility they search the Scriptures.

As regards the natural state and condition of men at birth, Unitarians would refuse to be held accountable for any theory which would attempt to probe the mystery of sin, to account for its power over all human beings, or to indicate the dividing line between the infirmity coming from a guiltless misfortune, and the blameworthiness which is punishable as iniquity, — these being the phenomena pointed at in the doctrine of the Fall of Man. Unitarians may admit that sin in one generation will transmit hereditary tendencies to sin in other generations, just as diseases are transmitted.

They may allow that we are morally placed at disadvantage, and made to suffer on account of the disobedience of our first progenitor. But Unitarians in general would balance this allowance of theirs by an expression of their belief that the Divine demand upon us is reduced in exact proportion to the entailed infirmity, or to the impaired ability of human nature. A just scale and balance are the Lord's, and God requires just so much less of virtue and filial service of each individual as each has lost of the original rectitude of humanity. On the record book of heaven each one of us is charged with his obligations; but the scale of those obligations is graduated by ability and opportunity, and allows abatements for all original disadvantages. Not one whit more than this will Unitarianism accept, either as essential to its positive doctrine, or as logically following from its antagonism to Orthodoxy. All those cheap charges visited upon it, as that of making light of sin, or flattering human nature, or lowering the demands of God's law, are but poor stratagems of controversy.

As regards the doctrine of the Atonement, Unitarianism can fairly be made answerable only for a denial of that constructive and inferential view of the death of the Redeemer, which represents it as regarded by God as a substitute for our sufferings, and as an essential condition for the exercise of Divine mercy towards the penitent. Those who repudiate the dogma of Orthodoxy on this subject, do not hold themselves bound to give an exhaustive theory as to the actual relation between the death of the Redeemer and the exercise of God's grace towards sinners. They may advance inferences and constructive views of their own. They may admit a mystery about it without attempting its solution; they may propose various solutions of the mystery; or they may affirm that there is no mystery about it, and may proceed to define at every point the mode in which men are converted and redeemed and saved by the mediatorial agency of Christ. But it would be difficult to make Unitarians, as a body, responsible for any positive dogma on this subject.

Thus we see that, even as regards the three great themes of controverted divinity, about which Unitarianism is generally regarded, not only as in most direct antagonism with Orthodoxy, but as most positively committed to theories of its own, there is room for the widest possible range of speculation. Hence arises the difficulty of drawing out a Unitarian creed. But these three themes of Christian divinity constitute but a portion of its whole substance and materials. There is a whole field of speculation still left filled by doctrines not appropriated exclusively to Orthodoxy or Unitarianism. There are metaphysical and spiritual themes opened in the pages of Scripture, about which Unitarians may speculate and believe very differently, and about which their respective views may have such influence upon their sympathies as to alienate them farther from the Orthodox, or almost to reconcile their differences with them. Such doctrinal themes as these: the presence of Christ with his Church, and the relation between him and the disciple, his office as Intercessor and Advocate; the doctrine of the Holy Spirit; the method and test of regeneration; the doctrine of justification, i. e. of being brought into a right and reconciled state with God, through the efficacious working of a living internal energy of faith, rather than by fulfilling the conditions of an external law; the doctrine of the sacraments; the retributive sanctions and penalties connected with the Gospel rule of accountability; — such doctrinal themes as these, and many more that might be mentioned, offer themselves as wholly and alike unprejudiced by a belief or a denial of the doctrine of the Trinity. Unitarians claim a full share with other Christians in the prerogatives of free inquiry and free belief on all these themes. Their differences of speculative opinion and of devotional sentiment in reference to these themes do virtually divide them into many schools and fellowships, or rather prevent their consolidation into a sect.

Here, then, is evidence enough that there may be views of Christian doctrine, and of the law and method of Christian life, which may be distinguished from Unitarianism by the title of "Liberal Christianity." And yet more and further, there are such views of Christian truth which are in irreconcilable hostility with Orthodoxy, but which refuse to recognize themselves even under this latter designation, of "Liberal Christianity." For though some have preferred this to Unitarianism, others regard it as vague, assuming, and offensive to good taste.

In view of all these facts, I can well conceive that one whose zeal for Orthodoxy prompts him to assail Unitarianism, may raise the reasonable objection, that it is almost impossible to define and identify his foe. This is indeed the case. I do not know that I can relieve his perplexity, except by suggesting to him the expediency of giving over his hostile purpose. If he does not know against what to aim, his blows may fall where he would not have them strike. He may hit some of his own friends. There will always, however, be enough to assume the Unitarian name, and to avow its sectarian zeal, to serve as a mark for Orthodox championship. My own personal interest does not go with the controversy in any of its details or subordinate elements. The theme of the seventh of the following Essays is the one which carries with it my heart and hope. The New Theology has, as I believe, dealt a mortal blow upon the old Orthodoxy. It will cause me but little regret if it can establish the truth for which it is seeking in the place which sectarian Unitarianism has sought, thus far in vain, to plant itself.

A HALF-CENTURY

OF THE

UNITARIAN CONTROVERSY.

A HALF-CENTURY

OF

THE UNITARIAN CONTROVERSY.

THE caption of these remarks will be a summons that may stir the memories of a few of the eldest of our readers. The era referred to is longer far than our own remembrances will cover, and therefore we say at the outset, that we are to write upon the theme with the help of records, and principally for that other class of our readers who must also trust to records for their knowledge of what transpired a half-century ago.

It is now just fifty years since a controversy still in progress was opened in this Commonwealth between two parties who were held by a relation of mutual interest, because they constituted together the old Congregational body, and who were brought into a relation of painful antagonism because they were divided by a serious issue in matters of Christian doctrine. The suggestion presses itself upon us with something like the solemnity of a religious obligation, that we ought to sum up for present use the best lessons we can gather from a review of that space of years. A vast amount of time and thought and zeal has been spent upon the controversy which then arose. A mass of literature, in newspapers, pamphlets, periodicals, and solid volumes, has accumulated, presenting both sides of the controversy in all its details, in every possible light. The present relation between the parties to that strife, though it may still preserve some painful remembrances of mutual wrongs, and is still in many respects a relation of opposition, is, on the whole, highly favorable to a fair reconsideration of the points on which they are intelligently and conscientiously divided.

In reviewing, as in a series of papers it is our purpose to do, some of the more important elements of that controversy, we wish to avoid every matter of acrimony and strife. If we know our own intention, it is one that looks beyond any narrow, sectarian aim. We extend the hand of reconciliation, and address the word of fraternal friendship, to any member of the other fellowship of our divided household, who is ready to listen to what we may be able to say, in a spirit becoming a Christian, concerning the present aspect of our ancient strife. We believe that some approach to harmony may be made in defining the points of difference between us as they now stand, cleared from former animosities, and tested by the trial made of them by a generation of departed champions. For the sake of convenience and brevity, we shall freely use the terms *Unitarian* and *Orthodox* to designate the two parties. Our own sense of perfect justice to our predecessors would dispose us to use the word *Calvinist* instead of the word *Orthodox*, for it was Calvinism, the real concrete system of the Genevan Reformer, and not the vague and undefined abstraction entitled Orthodoxy, which our predecessors assailed. We might also plead, that a due respect for the strong preferences of many of the early advocates of our views dictated the application to them of the name of *Liberal Christians*, rather than that of Unitarians. But we shall content ourselves with saying just what we have said on the matter of names, and with saying no more. The terms Unitarian and Orthodox, which we have just accepted, may be used without the offence of allowance, of assumption, or of censure, to designate the parties to the controversy. That controversy in its early and midway stages was connected with many irritating and embittering circumstances, which we must recognize only as matters of history, dealing with them as with the ashes that are cooled, and will not admit of being kindled again. Much of the mutual misrepresentation, and many of the extreme measures and statements on both sides, are to be charged upon the acrimony involved in the controversy. Thus the real issue opened in the controversy as agitating simply and only the question, What are the doctrines of the Gospel as taught in the Bible? was to many minds hopelessly perplexed and obscured. We are to review the strife of fifty years solely to learn what that real issue was, and how it stands between us now. We can put aside all mean partialities, all unchristian animosities, all heats of temper kindled by collisions which embittered the relations of neighbors and households, which referred themselves for adjudication to the highest tribunals of the State, and even assailed the integrity of the decisions there pronounced upon them.

An opinion or sentiment which has found an extensive prevalence, and has been gratefully entertained by members of both parties, recognizes some present signs of concilation between them. This welcome recognition makes account not only of buried animosities and an oblivion of some old strifes, but discerns a tendency to modify and harmonize our respective creeds, and to come together at some point that lies between us. Our own opinion on that question, if given at all, will be expressed only through inferences. We are aware that to many persons an individual opinion in such a case is without value, because it can have no positive authority; while those who would allow it any weight would regard it as cast into the right or the wrong scale, according as it coincided or clashed with their own opinion. We certainly hope, however, that after we have exhibited in these papers the present aspect of the controversy, as defined by the principal points now at issue cleared of all irrelevant matter, we shall have furnished some means to help an intelligent decision on the opinion just referred to. At the close of this introductory sketch we shall state three great doctrinal positions, which, in our view, constitute the essence and substance of our side of the controversy, and which it is our intention to treat in subsequent papers. Under the epithet of *Unitarianism* have been classed a great many individual speculations, eccentric notions, extreme views and opinions on various religious matters, which are not essential to the substance of Unitarianism as a method of defining the doctrinal system of the Gospel. There was also left between the parties a middle ground, embracing much of the doctrinal and evangelical substance of our religion, which was open to the free enjoyment and use, to the belief or the denial, the speculations or the dogmatism, of either side, and concerning which a member of either party might hold the same opinions, or might be wholly at issue with a member of his own or of the other party, without involving the distinctive creed of Unitarianism or Orthodoxy. We shall have a word to add on this point before we close.

When the controversy opened, no one knew to what result it would lead. But so far as either party had formed any definite expectations, founded on their own wishes, as to what it would bring to pass, we may venture to say that both parties have been disappointed. The Unitarians expected that the change of opinion which had long been gradually working, and which had been brought to a crisis on the opening of the controversy, would advance more rapidly through discussion and division, till, before the interval of fifty years had, as now, elapsed, Orthodoxy would have become a thing of the past, while Unitarianism would be the prevailing type of religion. Unitarians did expect this rapid success, this form of a triumph, and they have been disappointed. The Orthodox, on their part, expected that they should succeed in putting down and utterly extirpating Unitarianism, by identifying it with infidelity, and by discrediting all its show of argument from Scripture and Christian history, if not from reason. This was really the purpose and the aim of Orthodoxy; but the purpose has been thwarted, the aim has not been attained.

It may, however, be affirmed, with a good show of plausibility, that while neither party has realized its expectation in the length and breadth of the full statement just made, both parties have in fact approximated to the substantial results which they had in view; both have realized their aims in a qualified form. The Unitarian may say that the old Orthodoxy has been extirpated, as the modern shape and temper of it are greatly unlike the old Calvinism that we assailed when it was nominally believed and theoretically defended. The dissensions which have divided that once united party into *schools*, (a very kindly name for them,) and the ingenious evasions, devices, and speculations which have essayed to abate the offensive qualities of Orthodoxy, might be turned to great account in proving that the Unitarian controversy has accomplished its main intent. On the other hand, the Orthodox party may affirm, that Unitarians have received, and been compelled to listen to, a warning, — a real warning, not without visible tokens of its painful penalties; that, if Unitarianism consistently and logically followed out what seemed to be some of its first principles, they would lead it to infidelity, would manifest the lack of the Gospel element in declining churches and in a wasting of the life and energies of true Christian piety. Whether certain results which have been reached by some who were once Unitarians should serve as a satisfactory demonstration of the truth of predictions uttered fifty years ago, will be considered by some of the Orthodox as a question not admitting debate, but as decided in the affirmative by facts that have transpired in this community. Candor, however, will plead that this decision be arrested, till the appearance of *infidelity* in other places, and apart from all the agencies of Unitarianism, and in the closest connection with Orthodoxy, has been fairly accounted for. Transcendentalism — that hard word for expressing an unwholesome fog — was not a native emanation from New England or from Unitarianism.

We have read over many wearisome and painful, as well as many most instructive pages, on both sides of this half-century of controversy. As we have read the history backwards, its earlier pages are for the hour most fresh in our thoughts, and these are unfortunately its most offensive and irritating pages. As we have perused some of these sharp and bitter documents, we have been tempted to impugn the truth of a thousand essays and of ten thousand commonplaces about the value of the press in diffusing light and in dispelling error, and to yield to a profound regret that the world contains such things as types and printing-ink. In this frame of mind, we ask ourselves if the documentary part of the controversy did not, on the whole, do more harm than good? Did it not minister to strife? Did it not sharpen pens with passion and dip them in gall? Did not the taking of sides as writers addressing a larger circle than embraced the real disputants, tempt to an intense, acrimonious, and exaggerated way of treating the views of opponents? Would not the ordinary methods of dealing with religious topics in preaching and in pastoral intercourse have relieved the controversy of much of its bitterness, and have served far better the ends of truth, and have left the relations of parties now in a more desirable position? Would not the controversial preaching of the time of strife, which also was very heating and offensive, have been much less so had it not been envenomed by the poisonous matter of a thousand malignant little pamphlets? It cannot but have been that these documents aggravated the controversy. Even when former friends, who have fallen out by the way, begin to write letters to each other concerning their variances, they generally cease from that time forward to hold any intercourse. Our first "religious newspapers," and some other journals, were established to aid in this controversy; and farmers and mechanics in the interior of this State, instead of being served with an agricultural or scientific sheet, were solicited to work themselves up into a theological rancor. Those who were the least informed about the real issue that was opened, thus became often the most excited about it. Their acquaintance with the controversy was confined to the hardest terms and the most irritating incidents in it, and their inquiries, such as they were, made as they were, and met as they were, resulted only in misinformation. A sober second-thought, which transfers all the blame of these hostilities and embitterments from the types to the tempers of those who used them, draws us away from these irritating pamphlets, with all their personalities, scandals, and misrepresentations. We can but express an emphatic regret that they will always lie at the threshold of this controversy for those who may concern themselves with its history. The very intermeddling with them, even with a kindly intent, makes one feel, as probably the most pacific visitor to Sebastopol will feel for years to come, as he walks over that mined and powder-impregnated citadel, that, though the great batteries are silenced, some unexploded engine or some petty fuse may still be rendered dangerous at his touch, and may go off and hit him.

The question very naturally presents itself to the mind of one who calmly and candidly reviews this controversy, Why was there so much of acrimony and passion, so much of bitterness and animosity, manifested in the conduct of it? Why was there such mutual hostility, misrepresentation, and uncharitableness? Why did any of these odious and wicked elements mingle in the strife? Considering the subject-matter of the controversy as neither financial, social, nor political, but as simply a matter of religion, where there was no establishment, no inquisition, no prize of power, connected with it, — considering the end which both parties had in view, the attainment of truth on matters of Scriptural and spiritual interest, — considering the character and standing of the chief parties to it, men of education, culture, refinement, and piety, friends, classmates, members of the same profession, and that a sacred one, — considering all these things, why was the controversy so bitter and passionate? One might say that the points of difference could have been discussed in perfect amity. The parties to it should have patiently aided each other to discover the truth; they should have corresponded as friends; they should have differed as brethren. Each might have taught the other; each might have learned from the other. Some portion, more or less, of their mutual ill-feeling would have been abated by this course, as certainly the most offensive elements were introduced into the controversy by the opposite course. It ought to have been thus, but it was not. Whether the questions then agitated *could have been* debated in the spirit we have indicated, is one of those contingencies which we must decide according to our view of human nature. A phrase which we have just used as to "differing as brethren," reminds us that this is generally the worst kind of difference. Either party in this controversy would have debated its differences with Mahometans in a much better spirit than that in which they discussed their differences with each other.

What we have thus written, as if reflecting upon the value of the press, because it was turned to the service of misrepresentation and passion, must not silence our grateful recognition of its noble service to the cause of truth and charity, when its potent agency was used by wise and good, by calm and moderate men, on either side. There are some noble and precious documents called out by the controversy, which will have a permanent value as contributions to our Christian literature, illustrative of the historical, the doctrinal, and the experimental elements and evidences and working forces of our religion.

It is observable, that when the successors to the parties in an old feud, after the lapse of many years, review the strife, if it has been cleared of the personalities and the acrimony and the rivalries of interest which originally embittered it, their readiness to reconsider the issue in a spirit favorable to charity and wisdom will often be accompanied by marked relentings of feeling. Sometimes, however, these revulsions which follow when all exciting passions have been quieted are attended with some weaknesses of concession, and with a tendency to depreciate what was once exaggerated. The two opposing parties did contend most hotly. The Orthodox measured their responsibility for zeal and opposition by the obligation laid on them to defend the Gospel, in all its essential truths, against an insidious and specious influence, which was undermining its foundations and destroying all its power to redeem souls and to save the world. The Unitarians defined the duty imposed on them to be a purification of the prevailing theology from all those inventions and corruptions of ages of superstition, which had impaired the power of the Gospel and were at the time making at least three sceptics or unbelievers for each single believer in this community. An additional motive prompted the Unitarians, namely, that of vindicating their own right to the Christian name, while they exercised a liberty that lay within the broad terms of Protestantism. The issue thus raised between the parties was a momentous and an exciting one. They mutually inflamed each other; while embarrassments growing out of a sundered fellowship, and hostilities raised by questions of rights in former joint property, aggravated the strife. These embitterments of the controversy have for the most part ceased to affect us. We must carefully distinguish between them and the doctrinal questions that were agitated. We must do this in order that we may not under-estimate the importance of the real issue, or fail of justice to the original parties to it.

The paramount object recognized by both those parties was to ascertain and defend the essential doctrines of the Gospel of Jesus Christ. A view of those doctrines conformed to the system of Calvinism had long prevailed here, and according to terms of law, that system might claim by right of possession, and by established authority, and by a thousand incidental results of its ancient tenure, to hold a place of power by well-certified and almost unquestioned warranties of Scripture and custom. The natural course of things would have indicated that any dissent from that system should declare itself by an open dispute, a frank, bold, and spontaneous challenge of its truth, its consistency with reason, or its authority in Scripture. We might have expected that the dissentients from Calvinism would have been the attacking party. But it was not so. The dissentients were put on the defensive at the opening of the controversy. We should insist upon this view of the case, even if we admitted all that the Orthodox party alleged as to the insidious and covert way in which Unitarianism undermined Calvinism. The plea of the defenders of the old system is, that by an artful course of measures, which included silence, concealment, a gradual and steady modification of the tone and substance of preaching, and a sort of tacit understanding among the leaders in the manœuvre, Orthodoxy was assailed with a vast deal more of effect than would have attended an open declaration of hostilities against it. But *this* issue is one which it does not belong to open and avowed Unitarians to assume as lying between them and the Orthodox. Fairly understood, the issue lies between two sections of the Orthodox party, and reaches far back into the last century. The first men who swerved from Calvinism, who relaxed their faith in the stern system, and broke the covenant of rigid conditions into which they had entered, were men who would have shrunk with dread from Unitarianism. We do not see, therefore, that we are bound to assume their cause. Some of them were precisely where tolerated and honored champions of Orthodoxy stand now. We may claim them, in one sense, as brethren, so far as they were dissentients from rigid Orthodoxy, and so far as they fostered the spirit of true religious freedom. But if any question of conscientiousness or candor is raised by the modern Orthodox as to the first incomings of a latent and unacknowledged heresy, and as to suspicions of an adroit or calculating management in connection with it, we submit that they must argue the question within their own fellowship, in much the same way in which the champions of their various schools are arguing it now. The first stages of dissent from Calvinism were the most difficult and venturesome to make, the most alarming in their foreshadowings of consequences; and those who

2

consciously passed through them were most responsible to their covenants and to their brethren. The later stages of that dissent were more easy and less accountable to any insulted or violated pledges, simply because they were taken under a relaxed state of doctrinal sentiment, and by men who, never having pledged themselves to Calvinism, had inherited a license in speculation and opinion. The reason, then, why the first dissent from Calvinism did not declare itself in open attack, but was reserved till, in a later generation, it was compelled to assume the defensive under the charge of being just hunted out from its disguises, — the reason of the fact seems to be, that the godfathers of infant Unitarianism would have insisted upon their own orthodoxy, while they were entertaining the first misgivings about Calvinism. When a man begins to doubt his own views, he does not assail them, but he modifies them. It would be hard to hold his son or grandson, who inherits his modification of opinions, responsible, not only for consistently following them to their ultimate consequences, but also for the original breach of covenant which the parent had to make in entertaining a heresy. But the reiterated charge, designed to convey a great reproach, while it accounts for a marvellous disclosure, is this: "Unitarianism came in privily." So it did. So did the Reformation come into Europe privily. So did Puritanism come into Great Britain privily. "What!" — we hear one of our modern echoes of the old charge ask, — "What! did not Luther and Knox and Baxter and their bold brethren make an honest avowal of their dissent from the old systems, and of their hearty and pledged allegiance to new heresies?" Most certainly they did. But the "Reformers before the Reformation" did not. And so have Unitarians in various places and under most exciting and painful consequences made the avowal of their Unitarianism. We contend, and we stand prepared to prove, that as soon as Unitarianism recognized its own features, it avowed itself; and as soon as Unitarians understood themselves as such, they practised no concealment. For Unitarianism not only "came privily" into this community, but it also came privily into the minds and hearts of its first disciples here. We do not deny that there were men who, at the crisis of the controversy, for reasons which weighed with their own consciences or sentiments, assumed under Unitarianism the same position — an equivocal one to others — which Erasmus assumed to the Reformation. Yet we think that most of these men remained with the Orthodox, as Erasmus did with the Romanists. We know also that there were men of unquestionable integrity and piety whose acknowledged views certainly classed them with Unitarians, who still utterly refused to bear or answer to the name. Still we assert, that from the first moment that the presence and the discipleship of Unitarianism were here fully recognized by those most concerned in it, it was fully avowed, and never showed any unwillingness to define and defend its positions. That it did not at once recognize itself by a sectarian name — especially at a time when that name in England was suggestive rather of offensive political and philosophical than religious opinions — is no marvel to a candid mind.

Even in the papers emanating from the Orthodox party, one may find scattered, at wide distances, sentences that will explain in a kindly way facts upon which that party sought to put the harshest construction. Thus in the "Spirit of the Pilgrims" (Vol. II. p. 66) a very severe witness to the insidious incomings of the heresy says: "The change has been, not sudden, but gradual. It has been long in preparation and in progress. It has been accomplished, in some of its stages, by slow and scarcely perceptible degrees. A variety of causes have contributed to produce it." Dr.

Beecher, in a letter to Dr. Woods, incidentally made a most frank admission, when he charged "the great defection from Evangelical doctrine in this city and region" to "the carelessness and negligence of former generations of ministers and churches." (Spirit of the Pilgrims, Vol. V. p. 393.) These words afford a most lucid and explanatory, as well as a most exculpatory, recognition of the development of Unitarianism, — a key to the whole mystery, a release from all insinuations and censures. The simple truth is, that the change of sentiment which resulted in Unitarianism may be traced distinctly, in three prominent stages of its progress, through three generations of ministers. When this fact is taken in connection with another important fact, — namely, that before the full development many ministers at their ordination had claimed, and the ordaining councils had yielded to them, an exemption from such a profession of doctrinal opinions as would have pledged them to Calvinism, — we have the means of relieving this subject of a great deal of mystery, and, what is more, of vindicating the moral honesty of a class of men who have often been severely misjudged.

The charge brought against the early Unitarians here, of having practised an adroit concealment of a change of opinions through which they had passed, also assigned a motive in policy for such concealment. It had been practised "to deceive an unsuspecting and confiding people," by secretly undermining the prevailing faith, and by working under covert towards a result which the deceivers had strengthened themselves to meet when it could no longer be hidden from exposure. This charge was reiterated in every shape and form, according to the taste in the choice of language and the private moral standard of those who uttered it. It was wrought in with all the arguments from logic, history, or Scripture which were brought to bear upon the heresy. "The poison had been working in secret." "Artful disguises had been assumed." "Guilty silence had been practised." "Insinuating methods had been used." "Heretical books from England had been covertly circulated; and others had been published here on no apparent responsibility but that of the bookseller." "Some men who would now be called Unitarians, when charged with being such, indignantly denied it, or prevaricated about it." Phrases and sentences like these are found on nearly every page of the controversial documents of one of the parties in this controversy. A seemingly convincing proof of the truth of such assertions was furnished in the private letters, the admissions, or the forced acknowledgments of the culprits themselves. Belsham, in his Memoirs of Lindsey, had published some private letters from this quarter which recognized the unannounced presence and prevalence of Unitarian views among us. Dr. Morse, of Charlestown, selected out and republished here, in 1815, this explosive matter, and then the war indeed opened as on the tented field.

It is easy for us to understand that this charge of concealment, with all its severity of censure, might have been made in entire sincerity, and with a show of evidence to support it, by the one party; while, at the same time, it does not fix the slightest stain upon the characters of those who were the subjects of it. A champion of that generation of Unitarians would now undertake a needless and a futile task, if he should set himself to vindicate them from the charge;— needless, because a simple knowledge of the facts of the case is a complete relief for them; and futile, because those who would censure them in view of these facts would not yield to the cogency of any other plea. Not for their vindication, then, but merely as a matter of explanatory history, will we briefly advert to these facts.

First of all stands the one, self-sufficient fact, that

those whom this charge involves were Independents, New England Independents. We are very well aware of the admissions and assertions which were made in the old Platform, and by some of the fathers of New England, down to the time of Cotton Mather, to rid their churches of the title of Independency. A deference to the prejudices of their friends in Scotland, and to an old odium connected with that epithet in England and in Holland, led to an awkward rejection of it here. We are aware, too, that a show of relationship, intercommunion, responsibility, and right of advice or expostulation, was set up as impairing the Independency of our churches. But none the less were our churches Independent; if they were not, the ministers, at least, were Independent ministers. They were not the subjects of a Papacy, a Prelacy, or a Presbytery. They inherited a right to form their own faith by the Bible, and in the Bible. They inherited it by their nature and from their lineage, and from their Master. They were not amenable to any ecclesiastical tribunal, nor to any covenant, except as in their own judgment they considered that tribunal or covenant as conformed to Scripture. They were not held to hang their minds out, like thermometers, on their pulpits or door-posts, to indicate the degree of their daily rise or fall in spiritual heat. They were free to yield every day and every hour to the workings of thought, the processes of study, the experimental tests and trials of opinion. They were bound to receive truth as it came to them, and to declare it as it would edify.

Another of these simple historical facts to be had in view is, that no one generation of ministers or laymen made the whole way of transition from Calvinism to Unitarianism. The responsibility of announcing the whole result, therefore, did not lie with those who were responsible for effecting but one stage in it. There is no denying, no candid student of our history can presume to deny, that, for a whole century before the full development of Unitarianism, there had been a large modification, a softening and toning down of the old theology, an undefined but recognized tempering of the creed, a relaxing of the strain upon faith, and *a compliant acquiescence in that state of things.* We must, indeed, go even farther back than the preceding century to find the real beginnings of that free spirit which, when reverently, but fearlessly and intelligently, exercised upon the Scriptures, introduced Unitarianism. Our fathers brought with them the Bible, to be interpreted by the principle of Protestantism. Their great doctrine was larger than their own minds, and they had to grow to it. We, their children, are still growing to it, so great is the doctrine, so full of developments, so sound and yet so undefined in its methods, so alarming sometimes, and yet so safe always in its issues. All that troubled and annoyed those noble men, all that they did wrong, as restrainers and persecutors of free opinion in its successive developments, is to be traced to their ignorance of the expansiveness, their dread of the consequences, of their own principle. They did not understand, they shrunk from applying, their own theory. The truth is, there never was a perfect accordance in doctrinal opinion even among the first company of exiled Christians. The colleague pastors of the first church in Boston made rival catechisms for the babes of their flock, and took opposite sides in the painful strife of the great Antinomian controversy. Those men and women, too, were all inquirers, all thinkers, all pupils. They felt that they had the key to truth, but they were all their lives long seeking to fit it thoroughly to the wards of that golden lock which guards its mysteries. An unbroken succession of heretics, a steady succession of heresies, are recorded on the pages of our history. The Browns of Salem were shipped back to England almost immediately after land-ing. The Episcopalian Maverick of East Boston was, in 1635, forbidden "to entertain strangers," lest they should be of an heretical turn, and Blackstone moved off from Boston from dislike of "the Lord's brethren." Roger Williams, Mrs. Hutchinson, and Samuel Gorton, Antinomians, Baptists, and Quakers, were successive trials of temper and of Protestantism. Independent thinkers, sectaries, dissentients from "order," in doctrine and rule, sprang up with each passing year. There must also have been much smothered thought, and unuttered dissent. Did not the good gossips and staid matrons, when, in the safety of a very small circle, the spinning-wheel ceased its hum, and the last sermon was rehearsed, occasionally try their honest logic upon the snarled web of their theology? Did not the husbandmen sometimes lean upon their hoes, or rest awhile from their labors in the forest, and seat themselves upon a log, to discuss something of the whole problem of Calvinism?

But our Orthodox brethren remonstrate, if, in asserting what we have just intimated, we imply that there were any germs or foreshadowings of Unitarianism in the latent or acknowledged ventures of free thought during the first century of our history. But why should we be forbidden to look so far back for the seeds of what was afterwards found to have so vigorous a growth? Unitarianism is really no such monstrous conception, no such terrible and malignant device of a godless heart and a perverted mind, as some of its dismayed opponents have represented it to be. If they only understood it, as it lies in the serious convictions and the earnest faith of one who believes with all his heart and soul and mind that it is the true statement of the doctrine of Christ, they would not boast of having so keen a discrimination that they can distinguish it by a mark of its own from all other heresies. In the year 1650, the General Court of Massachusetts Bay "convented" before it Mr. William Pynchon, the distinguished magistrate of Springfield, on account of some "false, erroneous, and heretical" notions, broached by him in a volume from his pen that had been published in London. His heresies related to the method of atonement through the death of Christ, and he showed no disposition to retract all his "errors," though "the elders" conferred with him, and the Rev. John Norton was appointed to answer his book. A little more than a century afterwards, the Rev. John Rogers of Leominster came under suspicions of "unsoundness in respect to the doctrine of original sin and the Deity of the Lord Jesus Christ," and was driven from his office. That, between the dates of these two official proceedings against heresy, the distinctive views of Unitarianism were presenting themselves with a cogent though an unwelcome earnestness to several ministers and laymen, we have no more doubt than we have of our own existence. "Moderate Calvinism," a very vague term, indeed, but all the more significant because of its vagueness, was the convenient shelter of the early stages of our heresy. Strange to say, this term never seems to have been a bugbear or a fright, though it expresses the agency of all the mischief. A very slight glance at our ecclesiastical history will show how this stage of heresy was reached, and how heresy passed on farther upon a very smooth and easy road.

By a law enacted in this colony in 1631, it was "ordered and agreed that for time to come noe man shalbe admitted to the freedome of this body pollitick, but such as are members of some of the churches within the lymitts of the same." No man, therefore, could hold any civil office, or vote in civil affairs, except he were a communicant. This ecclesiastical condition of citizenship had, of course, two most injurious and harmful consequences. Undesirable members united themselves to a church for the sake of securing their civil rights and reaching office. Worthy men who would not make the required profession, even for the sake of securing their civil rights, were rendered hostile to the prevailing type of religion. Those who were thus disfranchised in Massachusetts and Plymouth Colonies petitioned the respective Courts for relief, in 1646, and afterwards laid their complaint before Parliament. In deference to an intimation in a letter from the king of England, this odious statute was repealed in 1664; but even in the substitute enacted, "a cirtifficat of being orthodox in religion," signed by the minister, was necessary to qualify a citizen who was not a communicant. The relative number of church-members had begun to diminish, with the increase of the population, after the year 1650. About the time of the repeal of the statute just noticed, a measure was adopted from virtual necessity which the prospective emergencies of the case had been long foreboding. As the children of church-members only were considered proper subjects of baptism, there was growing up from year to year an alarmingly increasing number of "heathen infants," who, of course, were outside of the covenant. A remedy was sought in a half-way measure, — half demand, half concession, — called in modern times a compromise. Parents who had themselves been baptized, "if not scandalous in their lives," though still unfit for the Lord's Supper, were by this measure permitted, on owning the covenant which *their parents* had made for them, to secure baptism for their children. As a matter of course, again, the relative proportion of communicants continued to diminish all the more. Then came another relaxing change. The Rev. Solomon Stoddard of Northampton, who lacked but little of being the pope of his county, as he was of his town, so great was his influence and so fully did he exercise it, was the mover in this alarming innovation. He advocated, with wonderful success over the country, the theory that the Lord's Supper is among the appointed means of regeneration; that persons who regard themselves as unconverted are bound to avail themselves of the aid and benefit of the rite; and that a profession of piety ought not to be required of those who with that intent should offer themselves for communion. His theory was widely put into practice, and the avidity with which it was seized upon is one of those significant intimations of latent discontent with the prevailing usage, which reveals more of the workings of heresy than some dim eyes are willing to recognize. By that innovation not only did church-members come into communion, but ministers also acceded to pulpits, without reaching in spiritual stature the high mark of Calvinism. These certainly were not guilty of hypocrisy in gradually yielding to liberal tendencies. They came in through a door which the spiritual watchmen had left open.

President Edwards dates in 1734 the beginning "of the great noise in this part of the country about Arminianism," another of those vague terms of which we may truly say, that not one person out of each ten who used it knew the real meaning or the scope. This term was a real bugbear to the timid; and if they had known how much of unnamed and unlabelled heresy it signified, they would have dreaded it more than they did. It covered an indefinite amount of disloyalty to Calvinism. Whitefield's first visit to New England, in 1740, with his full record of experiences among friends and opponents, furnishes abundant proof that all the elements of Unitarianism were then at work here. The imported writings of Samuel Clarke and Thomas Emlyn probably favored the first direct Anti-Trinitarian speculations in this neighborhood. President Edwards wrote his work on the Freedom of the Will, in opposition to the heresies of Whitby, and his work on Original Sin, in opposition to those of Taylor. President John Adams affirmed that in 1750 his own minister, Rev. Lemuel Bryant, Dr. Jonathan Mayhew of Boston, Shute and Gay of Hingham, and Brown of Cohasset, were Unitarians. The famous Dr. Hopkins published, in 1768, a sermon on Hebrews iii. 1, upon "The Importance and Necessity of Christians considering Jesus Christ in the Extent of his high and glorious Character." The author says that he wrote the sermon "with a design to preach it in Boston, under a conviction that the doctrine of the Divinity of Christ was much neglected, if not disbelieved, by a number of the ministers of Boston." Nor were ministers the only heretics. President Adams adds to his statement just given: "Among the laity how many could I name, lawyers, physicians, tradesmen, and farmers. I could fill a sheet," &c. The "confiding people," among whom the Unitarians are charged with having secretly fostered their views, appear in some measure to have anticipated their teachers. Indeed, it is altogether probable that some societies, instead of having had their faith slowly undermined by an heretical minister, had, even under the teachings of sound Orthodoxy, liberalized their own opinions, and, after waiting patiently for a superannuated pastor with whom they did not accord to subside, had intelligently selected a successor with a view to his growth in an expanded creed. As this successor at his ordination resolutely refused to be catechized doctrinally, and as his church and council sustained him in his prerogative, the way was free to him, from the vague terms of opinion on speculative points under which he had been educated, to real Unitarianism as the result of his own mature thought. Still, he might not know his opinions by that name, or the associations and adjuncts of that epithet might make him unwilling to assume it, as many to whom it really applies are unwilling to assume it now. But to visit upon the ministers at that crisis the whole odium of the progressive heresy of three generations, and then to seek to increase that odium by aggravating the prejudice connected with an ill-sounding epithet, was neither just nor kind.

Still another of those simple facts which a candid mind would find or use to relieve a class of honored men from the charge of an insidious inculcation and a wicked concealment of their opinions, now forces itself upon our notice. It was from the first, and always has been, an element of that general view of Christianity, which goes by the name of Unitarianism, that the substance of the Gospel and the materials for effective preaching are not found in the speculative points of theology, — the doctrines that were modified by the change of creeds. As this is one of the most characteristic and vital of the principles of Liberal Christianity, its disciples had a right to regard it and to act by it. The Orthodox party could not fairly hold them bound to throw contempt on their own most prominent principle by direct controversial preaching. The distinction between the two parties, as drawn by the stress laid by one of them and the disparagement cast by the other upon the importance of a class of doctrines, is a most fundamental distinction between them. If one who had entered the ministry as a Unitarian should become a decided Calvinist, the peculiar cast of his new views would more than modify, it would wholly alter, the tone and style of his preaching. But a minister who had begun his official course as a "moderate Calvinist" might gradually become a Unitarian, and the only indication of the change that would appear in his preaching might be that it was less *doctrinal* and more *practical*, in the technical sense of those words. Within the knowledge of most of us, of mature observation, are examples of Orthodox preachers who indicate their heretical liberality, not by asserting Unitarian views, but by their silence upon the offensive peculiarities of Calvinism. Those wavering men of whom we are speaking had many secret struggles in their own privacy. The papers of several of them, examined after their death, have revealed how the writers went through the Bible to select and balance texts bearing upon disputed points. There are many affecting evidences of the reluctance with which they yielded to convictions pressing for recognition, as well as of the reluctance with which they yielded up tenets stamped with the authority of prescription, and tenderly associated with their own training in piety. That such men did not seek to stir a strife in their congregations, or to open another of those terrible feuds of faith which they knew to be so prejudicial to true religion, may be a token of their wisdom or a sign of their timidity, as their critics shall judge them. Still, the course which they pursued is not only consistent with sincerity, but was in itself one of the most essential elements, one of the most significant results, of the change through which they had passed. Attempts were indeed made by the Orthodox to prove that the doctrines which were renounced were of an eminently practical power. We can conceive that, if some of the doctrines of Calvinism were *believed* as we apply the word *belief* to common facts of life, they would have a tremendous practical influence; as, for instance, they would forbid any thorough disciple of them to become a parent, and would fill his heart with dreadful anticipations of the doom of some who are nearest to him. We can conceive, also, that if what the creed teaches of the fate of heathens were held with an intense conviction, the poor annual pittance raised by all Orthodox Christians for their relief, and which is not a thousandth part of the sum spent upon their luxuries and pleasures, would be increased a hundred-fold. Indeed, if the sincerity of the statement may relieve its apparent want of kindness, we will venture to say that the *practical power* theoretically attaching to the peculiarities of the Calvinistic creed does not seem to produce its practical *effects*. Charity, therefore, suggests, that there is something in the theory itself which averts or hinders the practical consequences that might be expected to result from it. Its believers do not appear and act, as we should feel obliged and impelled to appear and act, if we *believed* it. "Is it of no importance," asked one who was arguing against us on this point, (Spirit of the Pilgrims, IV. 359,) "whether the God we worship exists in three persons or in one?" We answer, there is no possible way in which a man can make a Trinitarian belief on this subject appear in his character or his life. He must content himself with such a display of it as he can make in words,—in words, too, that must necessarily indicate confused and vague ideas. The truth is, that, in the most heated stage of the controversy, the Unitarians were considered by the Orthodox as bound to renounce Christianity, and to make proclamation that they had renounced it. This the Unitarians had no intention of doing. Nor were they swift to proclaim specifically and in terms, that in accepting a purer Christianity they had renounced former corruptions. For in doing the latter, they would be subjected by zealots, as the event proved, to the imputation of having done the former. They preached in favor of what they believed, rather than against what they rejected. Their concealment was mainly a concealment of strife.

In connection with the charge of artful concealment, numerous essays were written by the Orthodox in the early as well as in later stages of the controversy, to account for the origin and the extensive reception of Unitarian views. Some of the reasons given were ingenious, and more or less pertinent. But it is a singular fact, that we have never found a single statement on the Orthodox side of what was really *the* reason, the effective and sufficient reason, of the new heresy, — the reason which any intelligent Unitarian would have given if questioned by an Orthodox friend. The reason for the adoption and prevalence of Unitarianism was simply and solely the failure of Orthodoxy to satisfy the hearts and minds of a large number of serious-minded and religious persons in this community. This failure was a marked fact. Our brethren of the other party will never treat our predecessors justly, to say nothing of ourselves, till they make a manly and a candid recognition of this fact. Their controversy properly began among themselves. The poison whose alarming introduction they marvelled and mourned over, was an acrid humor generated by disease and decay in their own system. Orthodoxy failed to retain the confidence, to feed the piety, to satisfy the hearts, of many of its own disciples. It failed to stand the test of a trial by the Scriptures, *instituted with a bias in its favor*, in all sincerity, earnestness, and ability, by competent men. Orthodoxy, to the dismay and regret of many of these anxious inquirers, was discovered to be unscriptural, — a human scheme, not a divine system of doctrine. We must insult all the usual features and evidences of sincerity, if we do not allow for this fact. To have recourse to other explanations of the revival and re-adoption of Unitarian views among Christians, while this fact is wholly blinked, is disingenuous in the extreme.

Doubtless the new sect embraced its full proportion of the superficial, the light-minded, the unregenerate, and the irreligious. The derogatory way in which its lax and tolerant features were drawn by some of its early enemies, led many to assume the name who were wholly destitute of faith and piety. But the new sect had also its men and women of sterling excellence, of real piety; cultivated, thoughtful, conscientious, cautious of judgment, slow of decision, but firm and well grounded in their conclusions. Multitudes of these from out of the very bosom of Orthodox churches, admitted to have been saints while within their covenants, have testified to the inexpressible relief which they found in Unitarian views, and to the deep and living impulses of devotion which they derived from them, after having faithfully, but in vain, tried to live in Orthodoxy. And this failure of Orthodoxy to retain its own domain, and to keep its own disciples, is the more remarkable, when we consider what advantages it had on its side. The whole prestige of existing institutions, forms, order, and authority was with it. Tradition, historical associations, living bonds of love, sacred ties to the departed, household affections, and the memories of early religious training, were with it; but all were insufficient to retain an allegiance which had been discredited by the failing confidence of its disciples. If no other solution of the fact can be found, we must conclude that God has so constituted some who wish to love him, and to understand his Word, and to comply with its demands, and to share its promises, that they cannot, while they are sane and honest, accept the Calvinistic scheme. Calvinists reason as if they were sure that the Gospel offers no alternative between their system and actual infidelity, — as if there were no other possible form of the Christian faith but that of the Genevan. But, thank God, we are sure that they are wrong.

If it be asked why this exposure of the insufficiency and the unscriptural character of Orthodoxy was deferred to our age in the Christian era, we must content ourselves with dropping two suggestions in answer, — suggestions that might be dwelt upon at some length and proved satisfactory in meeting the case. First, for long centuries after the Augustine theology had established its sway, as a corruption of the simple Unitarianism of the primitive Church, attention was not concentrated upon the doctrinal constitution of Christianity, but was withdrawn to other aspects of it. Rome had exalted the hierarchical element and the extra-Scriptural element of tradition. The Reformers were chiefly engaged upon strictly ecclesiastical issues; they assailed the Pope, *the Church*, with its councils, its inventions, its tyrannies, and its corruptions. The English Puritans were brought into hostility with the sacerdotalism and the ritualism of Episcopacy. Independency both here and in England first brought the Gospel to a simple but severe trial by textual criticism of its doctrinal system. From the close of the fourth century this searching test had not been applied to it by this method. The second suggestion, bearing on the question just asked, reminds us of a fact very familiar to all Christian scholars, that Unitarianism has lain latent in all the ages of the Church; there have always been intimations of its presence and of its secret workings; it has cropped out here and there always. The names of an unbroken line of men linking together like a chain may be selected even from our scanty records, whose sympathies might be claimed for what is called Liberal Christianity. They are the names of men in Poland, Italy, Switzerland, Holland, Austria, Germany, France, and England,—men whose characters and attainments will bear a favorable comparison with those of any class associated by doctrinal belief or Christian sympathy. Unitarianism had its martyrs before the discovery and the colonization of these parts of the world. Its main and strong position in conviction and argument always has been, not that it is simply a rational faith, but that it is the express, the positive, the literal exhibition of the doctrines taught in the Scriptures. Indeed, there are, to our minds, no more significant or recommendatory features about Unitarianism, than are found in the occasions and the manner of its presence, and in the class of men who have embraced it, and in the method of its advocacy by them through all the ages of Christian history. It would require a subsidiary revelation to convince us that Jesus and his Apostles ever taught Calvinism. We can easily trace the incomings and the progress of Orthodoxy, and we know that it has been dissented from and protested against, under just such circumstances, and by just such men, and for just such reasons, and in just such ways, as accord with all the harmonies of history and reason.

Our sympathy does not go wholly with all of those who on our side carried on this controversy when it waxed fiercest. Positions were assumed which could not be sustained. Measures were adopted which we will not justify. Pamphlets were written which reflect shame on their authors, and to some extent on their cause. Leaving to candid reviewers on the Orthodox side to visit such censures upon the proceedings and the spirit of their own party as they may see reason to utter, we will not assume their office for them, but will pass our judgments only on our side. For ourselves we do not accord with much of the incidental argument used on our side of the controversy, and we regret the unchristian, the unfraternal spirit of the strife. We would not undertake to defend all those views of Scripture, nor all those assertions or negations of doctrine, advanced even by some leading Unitarians. We do not feel perfectly satisfied with the legal decisions in two cases bearing upon the ownership of church property, though we admit that the issue raised was quite a perplexing one.

One who candidly reviews this controversy, even with his prejudices and convictions strongly on the liberal side of it, can hardly fail to be impressed with the seeming coolness, we might almost say the *nonchalance*, or the superciliousness and effrontery even, with which some Unitarians took for granted that the great change in religious opinions and methods advocated by them could perfect and establish itself in this community as a matter of course. Some Unitarians wrote and talked as if in utter amazement that Orthodoxy should presume to say a word for itself in arrest of judgment, or as a plea for continued right of possession where it had lived and ruled so long. The most assured and confident and intolerant of the new party did not scruple to declare that Orthodoxy was past apologizing for, and ought to retire as gracefully as possible, with the bats and owls. It was only after some considerable surprise and mortification, that such supercilious disputants were induced to entertain a reconsideration of the whole issue, as the adherents to the old system rallied to its defence, and, in the lack of sufficient champions here, imported a Philistine giant from Connecticut. Other Unitarians, who did not fully yield themselves to the conceit of an easy and unchallenged victory, were more or less alive to the fact that there must at least be death-struggles on the part of Orthodoxy, even if more formidable manifestations did not give proof of its tenacity of life and of its unabated vigor. These more considerate judges of the strength and the alliances of long-established views, were secured from those exhibitions of arrogance and unconcern which were especially galling to the serious-minded among the Orthodox. This spirit of contempt to which we have referred would have alleged, in its justification, the prevailing indifference, the lethargy, the disgust, that attached to Orthodoxy in this community. It would have pleaded, that what so many had outgrown, and discredited, and despised, and what others still believed was spreading an alarming amount of infidelity over the land, deserved no courtesy or forbearance of treatment. The coarseness and virulence and dogmatism of some of the Orthodox champions would doubtless be made, indeed they were made, the justification of some of our own partisans whom we cannot honor. The petty and vexatious artifices, the gnats and wasps of controversy, evidently were very provocative of ill passions among the Unitarians. The arrogant denial to them of the Christian name; the attempt to confound them by putting quotations from their writings into parallelisms from the writings of Tom Paine; the mean effort to foreclose the issue by a monopolizing of the epithet *Evangelical*, and by a constant use of the phrase "the peculiar doctrines of the Gospel," as if by simply insisting upon their identity with Calvinistic doctrines the question might be decided by being begged; — these offences, together with sundry shocking perversions of Scripture, as in the wicked application to Unitarians, for denying the Messiah to be God, of those words of Peter which refer to the faithless deceivers of the first age, "denying the Lord that bought them," — these offences were strong provocations to some of our predecessors. One of our own editors was moved to write the remonstrating words: "Let our characters be spared. We are not infidels. We are Christians, with the most sincere conviction of the truth of our religion, and with a deep sense of its inestimable value. We do not deny the Lord who bought us," &c.*

These irritating and odious strokes of bigotry, which were not intended for argument, but as evasions and substitutes for it, addressed to prejudice and designed to foreclose an issue that should have been calmly and seriously debated, excited much acrimony. We can estimate the force which these aggravations then had by the occasional recourse which is even now made to the same unworthy arts to help in giving Unitarianism a bad name. That some of its early advocates should have been put out of temper by this ill usage is but natural. Still, candor compels us to say that some prominent advocates of Unitarianism conceived too lightly

---

* Christian Disciple, for 1819, p. 139.

of the resistance they might expect to meet, and were not sufficiently aware of the revolutionary character of their own views. For Unitarianism did in fact involve a radical change of opinion and practice as to the true theory of the Gospel and the method of its dispensation. Only as one carefully and in detail compares the views, the usages, the tone, and the measures connected with religious offices by the two now existing parties among the Congregationalists, will he really appreciate the matter and the amount of this change. Orthodoxy is more intense, systematic, and pointed in its whole substance and in all its methods, than is Unitarianism, when under their respective organizations they represent types of religious belief or modes of religious action. Orthodoxy has sharp, well-defined, elaborate, and systematic standards for its disciples. Unitarianism is loose, vague, general, indeterminate in its elements and formularies. Orthodoxy commits the charge and the direction of its institutions to those pledged believers who, as communicants, constitute the avowed and available strength of its doctrinal fellowship. Unitarianism, conceiving that in a nominally Christian community all its respectable members may be considered as in a degree influenced by Christian convictions and purposes, extends its trusts and responsibilities through a whole religious society or congregation. Orthodoxy makes account of crises and temporary devices and periodical excitements. Unitarianism wishes to avoid all schemes and spasmodic action. Orthodoxy bands its disciples, assesses them, sets them at work, appoints committees to inquire after new-comers, in many places confines its patronage within its own communion, is apt to know "the faith" of applicants for schools, and will not always divide its sympathies and honors among those from whom it asks money and other aid. Unitarianism dislikes such agencies and intrigues. Orthodoxy is sacrificial. Unitarianism is moral. The intensity which characterizes the Orthodox system, and the laxity which is manifest in the Unitarian system, might be traced in all their respective doctrines and methods. The difference, though in some points trifling and hardly distinguishable, appears in others to be of exceeding importance. It could hardly be possible, therefore, for the milder system to displace the more rigid system in any community, without the visible tokens of a revolution. If the processes and results of this change should be followed up through its effects on feelings, habits, prejudices, interests, and cherished convictions, it will at once appear that it must have been burdened with dislikes and pointed with pains for many excellent persons. This fact, we say, some of the Unitarians made too light of. They did not estimate it and allow for it as they ought to have done. They did not try to soften, soothe, or conciliate the sufferings which it involved, and the opposition which it aroused. Some Unitarians did not treat, as became Christians, with respectful tenderness and with filial reverence, the faith and convictions which had been rooted in the hearts and honored in the churches of New England.

Nor is it to be disguised that the type of character formed by unrelieved and unqualified Orthodoxy, when it intensified its peculiarities, was not attractive to a Unitarian. Puritanism always was an uncomfortable neighbor to all who were not Puritans. We can admire and respect, almost to the border of a reverential homage, the heroic virtues, the dauntless spirit, and the enthralling soul of piety in our orthodox ancestry. But we feel that they need some set-off or concomitant from persecution, exile, or romance, some hill-side lurkings, some ocean risks, some wilderness trials, some prison straits, to fix our attention upon the severities of their lot that it may be withdrawn from the severities of their creed. We love Puritanism while it is in its process of purification by fire, prison, or banishment, and the sharper its pains, the softer and sweeter is its spirit. Nor can it be gainsaid that the Puritan creed needs such methods to secure disciples, to make them genial and of high soul while they live, and the subjects of an admiring reverence when they enter into stories of the past. All Puritanical persons ought to be pioneers and missionaries, and the more remote their sphere, and the harder their work, the worthier they would be, and the better we should like them. But living Puritans in prosperous, quiet times, are something different. When, after the softening influences of a quiet course of life, the strain of early zeal was relaxed, and the tenets of a severe creed were keenly examined, then it was manifest that there were Christian men and women here who could no longer come up to the rigid standard of the old piety. The fact presented itself in many little signs and tokens, as well as in some very serious exhibitions of a modifying influence that had long been at work in this community. When the effects of this change were brought together and commented upon, they admitted of being very easily exaggerated and misrepresented, as well as of being very severely censured by those who wished to retain the old forms and methods. The tone and phraseology of public prayers were changed. The old custom of supplicating the Deity in specific and almost dictatorial terms for the sick, the convalescent, the afflicted, and those going on journeys, was greatly modified. Children ceased to be taken directly from the womb into the meeting-house for baptism, and parents began to shrink from a public return of their thanks for such blessings, and a public supplication for more. The style of sermon-writing yielded to the weariness which impugned the old fashion, — of turning over the leaves of the Bible from beginning to end in what was little more than a culling of texts, — and brought in the modern fashion of writing after the manner of an essay on a Scripture or religious theme. The mode of keeping Sunday was relaxed. Extra meetings and evening lectures, which old persons in both parties equally objected to, were adopted first by the Orthodox, and then, after fruitless complaint, by the Unitarians. The custom of making a severe inquisition into the religious experience of candidates for the communion was set aside. Church discipline for heresy and private sin was less frequent. Some discriminations were adopted in the way of using and quoting from the Bible, — discriminations which honest criticism and common sense proved to be necessary, and yet perfectly consistent to a reasonable mind with the highest practical value assigned to the Bible as a whole. Here then were various tests and tokens for the designation of two parties among the Congregationalists. The one party was called Liberal. The other party remained rigid, and seemed to try to become more rigid, by clinging to the shadows of things whose substance had passed away, and by assuming the championship of a form of piety which belonged to another age, and to quite another class of characters. Now it was the assumption of this type of piety by those whom it did not become, simply because it was not theirs, which was very unattractive, not to say exceedingly repulsive, to Unitarians. It had lost all its living characteristics, its realities as embodied in the style of thought, demeanor, conviction, and life, and was driven to make its manifestation in words alone, — in what was said and written. To have their neighbors, who in real character and course of life showed no grace above others, who were just as devoted to thrift and prosperity, just as eager for good bargains, just as worldly and faulty, just as censorious and imperfect, yet professing to be "saints by calling," successors to stern old Puritans, heirs of the covenant, and sealed by God's spirit for a life of eternal bliss, because they held the five sharp points of an old creed of man's devising, and had passed through some mysterious inward change, in proof of which they could give nothing but their own assertions, — this experience, we say, was not of a sort to make the advocates of Orthodoxy very amiable in the eyes of Unitarians. When two parties who, as far as the eye of man can see or know, stand upon the same level of piety, intelligence, earnestness, and sincerity of purpose, are seeking to decide between them questions of Scripture truth, if the one party assume to itself the title of "the friends of Christ," it can hardly be supposed that the other party will accept very graciously the title which by construction is assigned to them of "the enemies of Christ." Nor did it tend to conciliate matters that the Orthodox freely wrote and spoke of the Unitarians as "the worldly party," the patrons of the theatre, the lovers of balls, festivities, dress, amusements, and other gayeties. Good sense, however, and "that common human nature," which has been found to attach to human beings independently of their creed, soon settled these not very dignified elements of the controversy. It has been made to appear that what is called "worldliness" of this sort is rather a token of one's social position, pecuniary means, and private tastes, than of his religious character. Certainly, in this community, at least, it would be difficult to establish a superiority in any Christian grace or excellence as having attached peculiarly to those who have *opposed* Unitarianism. Sensible persons of both parties have accorded in the conclusion, that the grave questions of Christian doctrine which are at issue between them are not to be settled by calling hard names.

Turning from this survey of the past, we attempt to sum up its results as in our own judgment they bear upon the present relations of parties. Endeavoring to exercise that degree of candor and impartiality of which we may be supposed to be capable while our sympathies favor one of these parties, we will venture to express plainly what we really think. Unitarianism has relatively failed in comparison with Orthodoxy at one point which should be paramount with a truly Christian denomination; and Unitarianism has met with eminent success, and has secured a triumph significant of further results, in a direction in which it has spent the strength of many earnest efforts.

Unitarianism has proved itself inferior to Orthodoxy as a working power, a method of presenting and applying the Gospel so as to engage the enthusiasm, the zeal, the hearty, devoted service of its disciples in devising eminently Christian schemes, and in carrying on great religious enterprises. The "coldness" with which the Orthodox have charged us we have felt, and instead of denying a plain, manifest truth, we prefer the grace of frankly acknowledging it. We cannot gather our strength and bring it to bear effectually in a great religious movement. Opportunities have slipped through our hands. Interests which we might have strengthened we have sacrificed. We have sustained many noble benevolent agencies, but the element which has been lacking to their cheerful, vigorous, and most Christian efficacy, is the very element which our views in their working processes have not yet developed. We do not connect the fountain-head of all evangelical power and motive and impulse with a hundred little ramifying conduits to bear it among the different classes of the community, as do our Orthodox brethren. We do not distinguish between the means necessary to foster piety in the home, the school, the literary and benevolent association, the church, and the congregation. The differences of opinion and the alienations of sympathy which exist among the Orthodox are smothered up when they make any public anniversary exhibition of their sectarian or Christian purposes; but with us, such differences and alienations form the very staple of debate at our conventions, and make up the report of our "doings" published to the world. If any two of us walking arm in arm on one side of a street should find that we perfectly accorded in opinion, we should feel bound to separate instantly, and the strife would be as to which should get the start in crossing; and this is true in spite of the fact that there is more real harmony, fraternal feeling, and mutual regard between our brethren, with all their amazing individualism, than among the ministers of any other sect in Christendom. Yet we cannot bring our forces to bear as do the Orthodox in combined zeal and earnestness of purpose. We have no pass-words, we have no connecting wires, no electricity to traverse them if we had them. It may be said that this confession only admits our failure in comparison with Orthodoxy at the very point in which Protestantism fails in comparison with Romanism, which leagues its forces and displays a working power in methods and ramifications of energy of a kind to amaze us all. This plea, however, will not cover more than about half of our relative lack, and will still leave a balance against us in reckoning for our comparative inefficiency, in the use of what we allege are more legitimate and more consistent Christian weapons, against worldliness and sin and impiety and coldness of heart. Unitarianism has certainly exhibited some marked deficiency, either of power, or of skill, or of ingenuity, or of enthusiasm. For ourselves, we should not admit this to be an absolute failure from a cause inherent in our system of doctrines, or our mode of interpreting the Gospel. We are at perfect liberty to improve on our methods, and the same main-spring which is the motive power to all Christian hearts may move us, though we have not yet learnt how most wisely to regulate and dispose the mechanism which connects it with the world around us. We are satisfied in our own minds that we have been at fault in the mode in which we have *dispensed* the Gospel, not in the mode in which we have received it.

The point at which Unitarianism has secured an eminent victory, in realizing the sure success and the prospective universal triumph of its foundation principle, is in its dethronement of dogmatism in religion, — that dogmatism which insists upon confining the power of the Gospel to a metaphysical system of doctrines set forth by man as the exponent of revealed truths. Unitarianism has inflicted a death-blow upon this dogmatism, which was the deadliest vice of Protestantism, because utterly inconsistent with its own charter of liberties, and fatal to its own dissent from authority. Unitarianism has had an immeasurable effect upon Orthodoxy in this one direction. Orthodox preaching is in some quarters so qualified in its general character, that if it sounds to the ear as its printed specimens utter themselves to our hearts and minds, we should be quite content to listen to it in several places. When we read in the controversial pamphlets of a half-century ago the positive assertions made by Orthodoxy, — that all which we retain of the Gospel is as nothing compared with the importance of what we reject, that all the sublime revelations, the spiritual truths, the divine precepts, and the heavenward promises of Scripture are lighter in the scale of faith than the dogmas of John Calvin, — and then turn to the pages of the eminent Orthodox writers of the present day, we stand amazed at the change. True, some lean and querulous and stingy souls still give forth their dreary or petulant utterances, but they are not the ones that win a large hearing, or speak for their party. The tone and matter of Dr. Edward Beecher's "Conflict of Ages," compared with the sulphurous preaching of his now venerable father, when he was the leader in revival meetings about this neighborhood, tells an interesting tale of the work that has been wrought here in the interval between the father's manhood and that of the son. True, the very problematical hypothesis by which the son has sought to relieve the Orthodox dogma of its dogmatism, is but a poor device. But he is not to blame for that, as he did the best he could; better indeed than could have been expected, for in assailing one dogma he has not substituted another. The two Orthodox men who now have the most influence over the higher class of minds to which Orthodoxy is to look for its advocacy in the next generation, are Professor Park and Dr. Bushnell, men of brilliant genius, of shining gifts, of eminent devotion, and of towering ability, and regarded by large circles of friends with profound regard and confidence. Those two noble expositors of truth as they receive it have added a century of vigorous life to many Orthodox churches around us, and have deferred the final dismay of that system for at least the same period of time. Professor Park's Convention Sermon is, in our judgment, one of the most remarkable and instructive pieces in all our religious literature. For subtlety, skill, power, richness of diction, pointedness of subject, and implications of deep things lying behind its utterances, it is a marvellous gem of beauties and of brilliants. Dr. Bushnell's writings, in some sentences unintelligible to our capacity, and in some points inexplicable as to their meaning, are rich in their revelations of a free and earnest spirit engaged upon themes which keep him struggling between the wings that lift him and the withes that bind him. Those two honored men have relieved Orthodoxy in some of its most offensive metaphysical enigmas. How have they blunted the five points of Calvinism! How have they reduced the subtile and perplexing philosophy of the Westminster

Catechism, by the rich rhetoric with which they have mitigated its physic into a gentle homœopathy! Unitarianism aimed thus to abate and soften religious dogmatism. It has succeeded; and the noblest element in its success is, that it must divide the honor with champions from the party of its opponents.

And now what is Unitarianism? It might seem as if this question presented to us the hardest element in the task which we have assumed. Unitarianism, as it has been popularly represented and received, and, indeed, as it has been set forth in any promiscuous collection of its voluminous literature, may seem to be a most undefined form of theology. Yet we insist that its essential principles are very few and very well determined, so that it is at least as definite a system as is that which goes by the name of Orthodoxy. There has been a wonderful variety in the range, the methods, and the results adopted by separate expounders and advocates of the essential principles of Unitarianism, simply because with their Unitarianism they have had a philosophy, or an idiosyncrasy, or a love of speculation, or a habit of mind or feeling, which they might have had in connection with any other form of religious opinion. Indeed, nothing would be easier to a skilful opponent than to gather from our literature a most astonishing array of inconsistent admissions, limitations, and definitions, and to infer from them that the sect is but a rope of sand, each individuality of which was composed only of angles, and sharp ones too. "What do Unitarians believe?" is a question which has perplexed many who felt bound to answer it when put to them, while it has been made to point ridicule or censure against our faith. How much of all this variety and inconsistency of belief and exposition is to be accounted to the reasonable necessities, the first principles, the essential terms, involved in the action of independent minds upon the subjects of faith, and upon the Scriptures which furnish its materials, only a very considerate judgment is competent to decide. How far these individual eccentricities reflect a prejudice on Unitarianism, is a matter for the confident to pronounce upon while the prudent are reserved.

In the antagonistic and apologetic position into which Unitarians were driven, they naturally dealt much with denials. In assailing dogmatism they had to assail doctrines; and in assailing doctrines they left many positive points of faith, common to them and to other Christians, to win something of their own assurance without a positive advocacy in their congregations. In the mean time the Orthodox party were fond of representing Unitarianism in its *minimum* of substance and of life. While we were saying, Such a verse of Scripture, or such a doctrine, means "only this," or "only that," — the Orthodox added, "Unitarians believe only this," or "only that." Saying nothing about the false view of our own position and aims which we may sometimes have been negligent in averting or correcting, if not instrumental in producing, the Orthodox, it must be asserted, have succeeded in fixing a reproach upon us in many quarters. Their polemical literature has had such a prevailing character of abuse and misrepresentation towards us, that many of their own communions have been greatly misled by it. Again, while we have suffered the utmost disadvantages of being a sect, we have never turned into sectarian channels the real strength of our fellowship. From the very first, a sectarian name, a sectarian organization, and a sectarian association were strenuously opposed by some of the most prominent Unitarians in this community. The "Association" has never engaged the hearty sympathy or the efficient aid of a quarter part of our real numbers. The formation of Unitarian societies in some of our towns and villages, where there seemed to be an opening for them, was discountenanced, on the ground that it was better for "liberal persons" to retain their connection with the Orthodox societies, with the expectation of gradually relaxing bigotry and modifying the creed. Some able men who have won distinction and place through the controversy, have not been emulous of repaying the favor by any show of sectarian zeal. In one sense, we seemed to begin to decline the moment we began to try to strengthen ourselves. The Unitarian sect has hindered the progress of Unitarianism. The softened aspects and manifestations of Orthodoxy, the bad name attached to us, and the dread of loosing from old moorings, with various local and family attachments, and the diminished prestige of mere preaching to many persons, who say "they will listen to, and believe what portion of it they please, and let the rest go," — these and other reasons which might be mentioned retain in other communions thousands and thousands of persons who are really Unitarians, unwittingly or consciously. In an early page of one of our journals, we find the words: "We cannot help believing, that, but for the existence of a Unitarian sect, there could be no obstacle, among a free, intelligent, and inquisitive people like ours, to the rapid and universal prevalence of Unitarianism itself." * The inference would seem to be, that Orthodoxy has been, in times past certainly, a more efficient agency in promoting Unitarian sentiment, than has a positive Unitarian sectarianism, with its imperfect methods, and the lack of sympathy on the part of its friends, and the resisting measures which it has provoked. And this we take to be about the truth, as nearly as it can be stated in a brief way. Unitarianism came in when nothing was done for it; but it is not as effective an agent in its own behalf as are circumstances, occasions, and emergencies working in the natural course of things, and

* Christian Examiner, September, 1830, p. 19.

after the methods of a complicated issue between truth and error. Wherever there is a propitious union of healthful religious feeling and of intelligence, in proportions and measurements that we will not attempt to define, there always has been, and there always will be, Unitarianism, in every age of the Christian Church, and in every spot of the earth.

These suggestions might seem only still more to embarrass an attempt to answer the question, "What is Unitarianism?" In one sense they do so; but in another sense they help us to answer the question, as all these suggestions must be kept in our minds as indicating the elements that enter into the Unitarian view of the substance and the significance of the Gospel of Jesus Christ. A proportion, we think a large proportion, of those who through force of one or another reason retain a nominal connection with the Orthodox Congregationalists, the Presbyterians, the Baptists, and the Episcopalians, in places where Unitarianism has uttered itself through books or pulpits, have degrees of sympathy with it which needs only to be better defined to become much stronger. We consider that it is of about equal importance to insist upon what we have in common with other Christian denominations, and upon the points which put us into opposition with them. Unitarianism stands in direct and positive opposition to Orthodoxy on three great doctrines, which Orthodoxy teaches, with emphasis, as vital to its system; namely, that the nature of human beings has been vitiated, corrupted, and disabled, in consequence of the sin of Adam, for which God has in judgment doomed our race to suffering and woe; that Jesus Christ is God, and therefore an object of religious homage and prayer; and that the death of Christ is made effectual to human salvation by reconciling God to man, and satisfying the claims of an insulted and outraged law. Unitarianism denies that these are doctrines of the Gospel, and offers very different doctrines, sustained by Scripture, in their place.

The rejection of these three Orthodox doctrines, and the belief of those which Unitarians substitute for them, constitutes Unitarianism. All the rest of Christianity is common ground between us and other denominations. On all other matters of Christian doctrine a Unitarian may be in entire accordance with the general views of the Orthodox, and yet be not one whit less a Unitarian. We do not say, that Unitarians, as a class, are in entire accordance with the Orthodox on all other doctrines, but that there is nothing in their Unitarianism to hinder that accordance. As regards the inspiration of the Scriptures; the special design and agency of the Gospel, as a Divine and miraculously attested scheme and a remedial provision for the redemption of men; the necessity of regeneration, or a change of heart, wrought and attested by the Spirit of God; justification by faith; the present mediatorial work of Jesus Christ in behalf of his Church and upon the soul and the life of a believer; revivals of religion, and the doctrine of future retribution; — as regards all these doctrines, there is nothing in the essential and characteristic substance of Unitarianism which puts a disciple of it into antagonism with Orthodoxy. There are Unitarians who hold the Orthodox views on all these doctrines, because they regard them as Christian doctrines. The issue between us and Orthodoxy does not, and never did, involve any necessary collision or variance on these points. At the opening of the controversy, it seemed as if the whole substance of the Gospel, and every ingredient of it, were under debate between us and the Orthodox, and many times and in many ways was it asserted, that the question between the two parties was that of a Gospel or no Gospel. Discussion has brought our differences within the range of three doctrines. As to the fundamental tenets of Orthodoxy already mentioned, Unitarianism in a strongly antagonistic position maintains the following: —

1. That human beings do not inherit from Adam a ruined nature; that there is no transfer from his guilt made to us, inflicting upon us a moral inability; that our relation to God has not been prejudiced by his fall; that life is not a foregone conclusion with any one of us when it begins; that we have not been condemned as a race, but shall be judged as individuals.

2. That, whatever be the rank of Jesus Christ in the scale of being, and whatever be his nature, he is not presented to us in the Scriptures as the Supreme God, or as a fractional part of the Godhead; therefore he is not the source, but is the channel, of Divine grace; he is not the object of our homage or our prayers, nor the ultimate object of our dependence and trust, but fulfils his highest work for us when he leads us on to the Father.

3. That the Scriptures do not lay the emphatic stress of Christ's redeeming work upon his death, above or apart from his life, character, and doctrine; and that his death as an element in his redeeming work is made effective for human salvation through its influence on the heart and the life of man, not through its vicarious value with God, nor through its removal of an abstract difficulty in the Divine government, which hinders the forgiveness of the penitent without further satisfaction.

Unitarianism defined a position in direct and complete antagonism to Orthodoxy on these three points, and on no others. On these three points Unitarianism has resolutely held its ground, and intends to hold it, firmly and without yielding a hair's breadth. Orthodoxy has been during the half-century reconsidering its position as regards one or another of these three points, modifying, qualifying, and abating its dogmatic statement of its three primary doctrines.

Now, if there has been any tendency to harmony and accordance of opinion and reconciliation of differences between the two parties, it is to be referred either to a recognition of sympathies, and a common belief in the other doctrines of the Gospel, in the realm of Christian truth and faith which was not appropriated exclusively by the Orthodox or by the Unitarians, or else to the fact that the Orthodox have a better appreciation of the strength of our position, and of the dubiousness of their own position, on the three points of doctrine just stated.

We propose in successive papers to deal with those three great doctrinal issues. And when we have disposed of those topics we shall have to discuss a very important question relating to the proper view of the Scriptures, and the mode of treating them and of criticising and expounding them, so far as that question has entered into the controversy. We hope thus to gather some of the best fruits of a half-century of sharp but not unprofitable strife between brethren.

5

UNITARIANISM AND ORTHODOXY

ON THE

NATURE AND THE STATE OF MAN.

UNITARIANISM AND ORTHODOXY

ON THE

NATURE AND THE STATE OF MAN.

We closed the summary review, in the preceding pages, of a Half-Century of the Unitarian Controversy in Massachusetts, with the statement of three great doctrinal issues around which a protracted and a thorough discussion between the two parties of the old Congregational Church had proved that all their differences now centre. Of course we are not unmindful of the possible suggestion that, as these three doctrinal issues concern the very fundamentals of Christian truth, and decide the opinions held by the respective parties on all other subordinate Christian doctrines, it can hardly be said that the controversy is perceptibly made more simple by being condensed into these terms. It is convenient, however, to avail ourselves of this condensation of terms, even if the simplification of them is only in the seeming. But we feel persuaded that there is a real as well as an apparent step taken towards a better conduct of the controversy when it is thus centred on its main issues. No one can read over the voluminous records of the strife without a conviction that, had the pains and the skill of both parties been spent upon a close and careful discussion of the preliminaries of the controversy, the incidental questions which it opened might have been made to aid in clearing much of its perplexity, instead of serving, as they did, to distract and confound, to irritate and to mislead, many readers on both sides. And after all it is found that the two parties still have bonds of union. They accord in their theories of church institution and organization, against Romanists, Prelatists, and Presbyterians. They cherish many sacred sympathies, memories, and historical associations, precious and venerable to both alike. Alike they cling to the revelation of God by Jesus Christ, to the Scriptures as a rule of faith, and to many common Christian convictions and experiences. They agree, too, upon a great many points of Christian doctrine which the Unitarians regard as, in fact, the fundamentals of Christian doctrine. As, however, these points, which to us are fundamental, though they are also admitted as such by the Orthodox, are by them connected with disputed doctrines, and are sometimes made subsidiary in vital importance to other doctrines, our real accordance in fundamentals with that party passes for but little. But as regards the three doctrines which we have already defined, the two parties are at variance; distinctly and positively opposed to each other. The controversy which commenced in the supposition of a great many other differences, as well as in the recognition of these three, while it has sunk or harmonized the others, has emphasized these. According to the side which any one may espouse on each or all of the three Christian doctrines relating to the Nature and the State of Man, the relation between Christ and God, and the Atonement, will he define his own position as to this controversy.

We now propose to gather up the results of a long discussion, as they bear upon the first of these doctrines.

The first point on which Unitarian sentiment is found to be in positive and entire antagonism with *the Stand-*

ards of Orthodoxy, is that which concerns the Nature and the State of Men as responsible creatures of God. Let us start with a frank understanding of our ground. Unitarians do not affirm that human beings are born *holy;* nor that the original elements of human nature are free from germs which grow and develop, if unrestrained, into sin; nor that no disadvantage has accrued to all the race of Adam from his disobedience, and from all the accumulations of wickedness that have gathered for ages in the world into which we are introduced. Unitarians do not deny that all men are actually sinners, needing the renewing grace and the forgiveness of God, dependent upon the Gospel of Christ as a remedial and redeeming religion, and having no other hope than that which Christ offers. Unitarians do not deny the great mystery which invests sin and evil, nor profess to have any marked advantage over Orthodoxy in looking back of that mystery or in dealing with it. But Unitarians do deny positively, and with all the earnestness of a sincere and solemn conviction, that the original Calvinistic doctrine (or any subsequent modification of that doctrine which has the authority of an accredited formula with the party) concerning the Nature and the State of Man, is either a Scriptural or a Christian doctrine.

Let it be remembered that we are dealing with a controversy whose present aspect refers us back to its early form and shape if we would judge intelligently of its character. It is essential, therefore, that we define very clearly one of the paramount conditions of the controversy when it opened, in order that we may appreciate its original elements. We have already said that the Unitarians understood and avowed that they were assailing, — not the undefined and modified semblance now called *Orthodoxy*, — but *Calvinism* which had expressed itself in *positive formulas*, and to which the Orthodox party professed an unqualified and unequivocal allegiance.

Since the controversy opened, Orthodoxy, being restless under each and all of the dogmatic statements in the creed of the three doctrines to which it committed itself, has exhibited its uneasiness in continual efforts to modify and qualify its formulas. Some of its disciples, feeling, precisely as our first Unitarians felt, a shrinking reluctance against the plain literal meaning of the creed, and knowing that they could not accept it as "the Fathers" held it, and yet fearing to commit themselves to our theology, have tried in various ways, with an amazing exercise of ingenuity, to soften and dilute the creed. Especially on this one doctrine of the complete original depravity of human nature have there been endless variations and shadings of opinion. Therefore we must keep in view what the doctrine was, — what it is now in *the creed*, — as defining the doctrine which the Unitarians assailed and denied. The original, substantial Calvinistic doctrine on this point we find, of course, in Calvin's works, — who received his views essentially from Augustine, — and in the formulas which professedly Calvinistic writers and authorities have advanced.

Professor Norton, in a tract entitled "Thoughts on True and False Religion," had represented Calvinism as a "religion which teaches that God has formed men so that they are by nature wholly inclined to all moral evil; that he has determined in consequence to inflict upon the greater part of our race the most terrible punishments, and that, unless he has seen fit to place us among the small number of those whom he has chosen out of the common ruin, he will be our eternal enemy and infinite tormentor; that having hated us from our birth, he will continue to exercise upon us for ever his unrelenting and omnipotent hatred." The writer referred any one who wished to examine this scheme to the Institutes of Calvin, and to the perfected development of it in the works of the Westminster Assembly. Here certainly there could be no question as to what form of *Orthodoxy* Mr. Norton was impugning: it was, distinctively, *Calvinism.*

The Christian Spectator, an Orthodox journal published at New Haven, in its number for May and June, 1822, quoted the above language of Mr. Norton, and reflected upon it with extreme severity of tone and epithet, accusing the writer of first *distorting*, and then stigmatizing as blasphemy, doctrines which had been received by a large proportion of intelligent and devout Christians. The reviewer in the Spectator added further, that the views portrayed by Mr. Norton had "never been taught or professed extensively, as fundamental doctrines of Christianity: that there never was a sect or body of men, denominated Christian, who would not reject this system as false and injurious, if presented to them as their creed: that there never was an individual author of any celebrity or influence, who ever taught or undertook to defend such doctrines; and that neither 'the Institutes of Calvin,' nor 'the works of the Westminster Assembly,' nor any of the Protestant Confessions of Faith, and, least of all, the Confessions of those to whom he intended it should be applied, contain doctrines which are fairly represented by any clause of the foregoing extract."

Mr. Norton, feeling his reputation as an honest man to be insulted by this direct assault upon his integrity, addressed a caustic letter to the editor of the Christian Spectator, the insertion of which in the pages of that journal he claimed as his right. In this letter he made a series of quotations from Calvin, from the works of the Westminster Assembly of Divines, and from President Edwards, fully and triumphantly proving all his points and disproving those of his reviewer, either by the positive assertions made in these quotations, or by the irresistible inferences to be drawn in perfect fairness from them. We admit that these extracts, when arranged and summed up in their doctrines, present a most shocking portraiture of Calvinism. We do not wonder that an Orthodox man should shrink from them with mingled feelings of horror and indignation, or that he should avail himself of all the skill of evasive dialectics and subtle metaphysics to find relief.

The editor of the Spectator declined to insert this letter, on the ground of its containing some "reproachful and menacing expressions," but promised to publish its substance if these were "purged" out of it. Still, though the editor refused to allow Mr. Norton to address his own reply to the readers of the Spectator, he proceeded to make a very imperfect and unfair representation of the contents of the letter, and, by garbled, partial, and perverted quotations from the authorities in the case, to endeavor to set aside the overwhelming evidence adduced by Mr. Norton in support of his positions. Mr. Norton therefore published his letter, with the remarks of the Spectator upon it, in the Christian Disciple for July and August, 1822, and added some further comments of his own. The utmost that his reviewer had effected was to show that Calvinistic authorities contained some contradictory and inconsistent passages. Of this fact Mr. Norton, of course, was well aware, but it was no concern of his to disprove it. He convicted his reviewer, however, of absolute misrepresentation in a professed quotation from Calvin; of a poor quibble in applying the words "*creation* of nature" to the divine endowment with which each of us enters upon existence, when Calvin had used them only of the nature created in *Adam;* and of confounding an issue of metaphysics concerning the doctrine of *necessity.* There Mr. Norton left the matter, as well he might.

It is only with pain and regret that at this distance of time a Christian of any denomination can review this episode in the controversy. Candor and justice, however, demand that we record our deep and unrelieved sense of the disingenuousness to which recourse was had on the Orthodox side in this issue. How can there be serious or useful discussion where there is such artifice, such evasion practised in asserting and denying, in shifting one's ground, in disputing the authority of the very *authorities* first appealed to, and in denying the fairest inferences from dogmatic statements? Mark the startling inconsistency between passages from the two attacks on Mr. Norton in the Spectator, as the second of them gives up the very point assumed in the first, and wholly abandons the original ground of the controversy. The Spectator first wrote thus: "We are often compelled to complain, that the opponents of Calvinism never fairly attack its doctrines, as they are stated by Calvin himself, or exhibited in the creeds of the churches, or the writings of the authors who bear his name." But after Mr. Norton had given a most scholarly and thorough answer to this plea, the same editorial pen, or authority, which had so recently sanctioned the above statement, was compelled — it is a sad revelation to make — to write or to sanction the following: "What Calvin believed and taught, and what any modern Calvinistic authors have taught, are questions of no real importance in the present discussion, any further than their opinions are proved to be prevalent in our own country." What an astounding inconsistency!

But why, — it may be asked, — why should we hold the Orthodox to the very form of words which was chosen centuries ago to express a doctrine the terms of which have since been modified? We answer, that we do this in order to meet the claims of historical truth and justice, and in order that we may clearly understand that of which we are speaking. The question does not, at this stage of it, concern the qualifications and abatements which in recent years may have been made of this doctrine of Orthodoxy. Unitarianism may or may not oppose these deviations and reductions. But at the opening of the controversy it was the real Calvinistic doctrine which was assailed, — the doctrine of the Westminster Assembly's Catechism which our fathers had accepted, — the doctrine of the New England Confession of Faith, which our churches sent forth in 1680. Fifty years ago the Orthodox began to complain, and they have ever since complained, that Unitarians misrepresented them in charging upon them "in this neighborhood" a shape of Orthodoxy which had been held by Calvinists of a former age, and which survived only in other parts of this country. And here we must be pardoned for giving frank expression to a disagreeable truth. There seems to Unitarians to be something evasive and very unworthy in the pleas with which the Orthodox have met our exposures of what we regard as the errors of their system. They censure us and deny us the Christian name because we reject their creed; and when, with the best faculties which we possess for analyzing that creed, we attempt to state the reasons why we reject it, they proceed to tell us that they themselves do not hold the creed in what is to us its plain signification. We have endeavored to state fairly its essential doctrines, and the honest, unexaggerated inferences which logically flow from them. But no statement which we can make of the system is ever allowed by the Orthodox to be fair; some private qualifications which they attach to it in their own minds, and of which we have no means of knowing or judging, justify them, as they think, in charging us with misrepresentation. Now some Unitarians, no doubt, have made caricatures of Orthodoxy, and have aimed to load it with offensive, shocking, and blasphemous conditions. These exaggerators of the hideousness of Orthodoxy on our side correspond in temper and spirit, if not in tone, with those among our opponents whose delight is in stating Unitarianism at its *minimum* of every substance and effect, save those of pride and chilliness. But there have been candid and truth-loving men among us, and when such had tried their best to set forth their conceptions of Calvinism at one or more points, indorsing their statements with the testimony as to what had once been taught them and believed by them, the remonstrance was raised, "You are bearing false witness; you are ridiculing us."

Let it therefore be again repeated, Unitarianism opposed and still opposes the Calvinistic doctrine of the entailed corruption of human nature in all our race as the punishment of Adam's guilt. Nor did the Unitarians err in addressing their arguments against that authoritative statement of Calvinism which is given in the Orthodox creeds. The Orthodox wished to have the praise, they claimed the honorable and grateful repute, of "adhering to the faith of the fathers of New England." They claimed also the exclusive inheritance of the old piety, on the score of holding its doctrinal standards. Was not the assertion repeated by them even to weariness, — too often certainly to be regarded as a mere empty boast, — "We hold the doctrines of the Reformation, the doctrines of the fathers of New England"? Now the Calvinistic doctrines were held heartily and firmly, and without subterfuges of metaphysics, by the fathers of New England. Their professed successors cannot enjoy at the same time the honor of holding their opinions and the privilege of changing them. We are ready to grant to the Orthodox the fullest benefit of all the modifications of this doctrine which the most ingenious man among them is able to devise. But we must urge that these modifications all accrue to our side, as they relax and soften and qualify the sternness of our old foe, and are yielded or availed of for the sake of mitigating the repulsiveness of the original doctrine. When Orthodoxy identifies itself with Calvinism, we, of course, must confront and oppose Calvinism. When Calvinism, with its teeth drawn, and its claws filed, and its horns lowered, and its hoofs covered, has tamed itself down into something called Orthodoxy, we shall first look at the thing from a safe distance, to judge how near it is best to come to it, and with what weapons we must be provided. How long actually it will take Calvinism really to transform itself into an angel of light, it is impossible to say. Time and truth have had a wonderful effect upon its visage, but its old trust-deeds, proclamations, and formulas are unalterable.

Here then is the doctrine which Unitarians understood that they were opposing. We quote from the sixth chapter of the Confession of Faith of the New England Churches.

"God having made a covenant of works and life thereupon, with our first parents, and all their posterity in them, they being seduced by the subtlety and temptation of Satan, did wilfully transgress the law of their creation, and break the covenant in eating the forbidden fruit. By this sin they, and we in them, fell from original righteousness and communion with God, and so became dead in sin, and wholly defiled in all the faculties and parts of soul and body. They being the root, and by God's appointment standing in the room and stead of all mankind, the guilt of this sin was imputed, and corrupted nature conveyed to all their posterity descending from them by ordinary generation. From this original corruption, whereby we are utterly indisposed, disabled, and made opposite to all good, and wholly inclined to all evil, do proceed all actual transgressions. This corruption of nature during this life doth remain in those that are regenerated; and although it be through Christ pardoned and mortified, yet both itself and all the motions thereof are truly and properly sin. Every sin, both original and actual, being a transgression of the righteous law of God, and contrary thereunto, doth in its own nature bring guilt upon the sinner, whereby he is bound over to the wrath of God and curse of the law, and so made subject to death, with all miseries, spiritual, temporal, and eternal."

The Shorter Catechism of the Assembly, which also had been formally recognized by our churches, and was taught to all our children, advances the same doctrine on the same grounds, and tells us that "All mankind, by the fall [of Adam], lost communion with God, are under his wrath and curse, and so made liable to all the miseries of this life, to death itself, and to the pains of hell for ever."

We purposely abstain from adding to these authoritative statements of doctrine any quotations from approved Calvinistic writers, which follow it out into its revolting and blasphemous details. We think that the hideous and yet perfectly consistent speculations and representations made by Edwards, to set forth the horrors of hell-torments, the anguish of the reprobate who suffer them, and the exquisite happiness which the "righteous" derive from contemplating them, have done their service in controversy. It only aggravates our opponents if we renew those fearful delineations. We are content to follow the doctrine as nakedly presented in the formula. This is the doctrine which by profession one hundred years ago, and in sober sincerity two hundred years ago, underlaid the theology — the Calvinistic, the Orthodox theology — of New England. It was made the starting-point of the Christian system. It decided the terms of relation and duty, of accountability, judgment, and doom, in which men stood to God. It was made to establish the necessity and the method of redemption by an infinite sacrifice to God, designed to serve as a substitute with God for the sufferings of men. When Unitarians brought this doctrine into prominence, and made its positive, literal assertions, and the legitimate logical inferences from them, a ground for repudiating such theology, an alternative was presented to the Orthodox party. It offered them a choice between two honest and manly methods of pursuing the controversy in allegiance to simple truth, and with an entire security against those odious passions and recriminations which entered into it. The one method would have held them to a candid allowance that they were pledged to that doctrine, with all the legitimate logical inferences which of course must be admitted to result from it as the basis of a system; and to a resolute, unswerving, and unabashed support of it against all opposition. The other method would have dictated to them to state frankly any abatement or qualification under which they might wish to accept the doctrine, and to insist upon their right so to modify it, and to be made answerable for only a mitigated form of the doctrine. But instead of following either of these methods, the disputants on the Orthodox side endeavored to devise a third method, fashioned from some of the proper elements of the other two, yet lacking, in our judgment, the candor and truthfulness of both of them. A *profession* was made of holding in all loyalty and confidence the faith of the Fathers; a *confession* was very reluctantly drawn out, that that faith was accepted only through certain undefined abatements made of it by a new philosophy of doctrine. We have read much of the controversial literature of the half-century, but we have not met with one single page which boldly meets the real issue opened by such a plea for Calvinism as would have been offered two hundred years ago. The very best proof possible that Orthodoxy did not at least understand the ground it had undertaken to occupy, and was consequently in danger of putting at risk and yielding something of what it was trying to defend, is offered us in the following curious fact, — that, in conducting the controversy with us, Orthodoxy opened controversies in its own ranks that have never yet been decided or pacified. "The Spirit of the Pilgrims" was established to do battle with Unitarians. But just midway in its series of volumes, the reader will find that it allowed us a breathing spell, while it occupied its pages with the doctrinal contentions in its own household, which at once arose when Orthodoxy undertook its own defence. Drs. Taylor, Tyler, Beecher, and Woods address each other, as well as ourselves, in those pages.

Dr. Woods, who aimed for candor and courtesy in his argument, realized the necessity of making a distinct avowal on this point; and he was the first writer of ability on his side who yielded to the pressure of the Unitarian exposition of Calvinism by itself. He therefore wrote as follows: "If there is any principle respecting the moral government of God which the Orthodox clergy in New England earnestly labor to inculcate, it is this: that, as accountable beings, *we have a conscience and a power of knowing and performing our duty.* Our zeal in defence of this principle has been such as to occasion no small umbrage to some, who are attached to every feature and every phraseology of Calvinism. On this subject there is, in fact, a well-known difference between our views, and those of some modern, as well as more ancient divines, who rank high on the side of Orthodoxy." * How those who, according to the creed just quoted, are "wholly defiled in all the faculties and parts of soul and body," and "disabled, and made opposite to all good," have still "a power of knowing and performing their duty," Dr. Woods does not attempt to show. The difference, therefore, by his own statement, between those who held his views, and the true Calvinists, is, that he tried to hold to Calvinism and to something utterly inconsistent with Calvinism. No wonder that "zeal in defence of this principle" occasioned "no small umbrage."

Thus it was that, the moment a decided opposition was raised by Unitarians to this Calvinistic doctrine, those who came forward to vindicate it began to evade

* Letters to Unitarians, p. 130.

its full force. They shrank from facing it; they shrink from it now: they try to soften it. A hair's breadth of relief from the pressure of the doctrine has been held as a blessing by those who have argued in its defence. We might try to present here a series of the ingenious or futile, the actual or only apparent modifications, and attempted modifications, of this Calvinistic doctrine. But some of them are unintelligible to ourselves, and others of them which we think we understand we know we could not make intelligible to our readers. By and by we must refer to some of them. We must not, however, leave an impression that, singly or together, they give much relief. They are of service to us, as showing a constant uneasiness under any form in which the old doctrine has as yet been presented, and as indicating how trifling a relaxation of its old terms will be welcomed as a comfort.

The doctrine still stands, however, unchanged in word, unrelaxed in authority, in the formulas of Orthodox churches. Still is the repute of holding the faith of the Fathers claimed by those who are called Orthodox. The Westminster Catechism and Confession are the standards of the American Presbyterian Church. The New England Confession is the doctrinal foundation of the Saybrook Platform, which was re-adopted by the General Association of Connecticut in 1810. The Reformed Dutch Church uses the Confession of Faith of the Synod of Dort, which certainly does not soften this one Calvinistic doctrine. We know, too, that those who formed and phrased these standards held this doctrine with an unflinching steadfastness, in the boldness and fearlessness of which they seem even to have found a trifle of merit on their own part, while they never shrank from the most unrelieved statement of the doctrine. And this is the doctrine which Unitarianism rejected, positively, and without qualification, concession, or tolerance; asserting that it is not taught in the Bible, but is utterly inconsistent with the teachings of that book; that it dishonors God by ascribing to him a method arbitrary, unjust, and wholly subversive of all righteous law; that it wrongs human nature, destroys moral responsibility, corrupts the Christian system, unsettles morality, and leads to infidelity and irreligion. This is the ground of opposition, and these are the terms of it which Unitarianism recognized at the opening of the controversy. Unitarianism has held its ground without misgiving or compromise. Unitarianism means to hold its ground, — no more and no less than its ground, — on this matter of doctrine. Its courage and assurance and confidence have steadily increased, as it has realized its own strength and the weakness of its antagonist on this doctrine of the entail on all the human race, on account of the sin of one man, of a corrupted nature, which must work corruption in this life, and which is sentenced to the torments of hell for ever.

When the human mind calmly and deliberately, without bias, but with all the seriousness of which it is capable, brings itself to confront that doctrine, two great tests will present themselves for trying its truth. How does it consist with faith in a God of adorable attributes, a Being of infinite wisdom, power, and benevolence? How has the preaching of it affected the great mass of those to whom it has been taught, in persuading them to believe it, and in impressing them with any sense of its appalling significance corresponding to its terrific threatenings? It is impossible for any active mind to repress its own instinctive impulse to apply these two great tests to the doctrine. Indeed, the irresistible evidence furnished by any fair inquiry through the second test, as it presents us with matters of practical experience, is so conclusive against this doctrine, that we are content with simply asserting, without any argument, that the doctrine cannot abide the first test. The utter unconcern, the blank sense of unreality, with which the vast mass of human beings have heard that doctrine preached and taught, has proved it to be in fact but little better than a bugbear. It is to be remembered that our churches here were constituted at first of men and women who had been *picked out* as already believers of the doctrine; but as soon as they had descendants, and the increase of population had brought society into that state of mixed and various elements which is natural under ordinary circumstances, the doctrine became a fable to a larger number of persons than those to whom it was a truth. Indeed, the preaching of the doctrine never excited the dread in any one of our communities which attended merely the apprehension of a visitation of the small-pox. But, in the mean while, what was the influence of the theoretical truth and authority of this doctrine upon all the best interests of religion among us? It caused an untold amount of unbelief and indifference and irreligion.

Consider, now, how appalling and crushing is this old Calvinistic dogma. God fashioned this globe as the habitation of a race of his own intelligent creatures, of beings made in his likeness and gifted with his inspiration. God then staked the issue as to the nature, the character, the experience, and the doom of all the uncounted millions to be born here "by ordinary generation," through all ages, upon a single act of the first pair who represented humanity on this fresh earth. God was thwarted in his purpose at the very start. His first two children acted for all his children, and by the deed of a moment, instigated not by any evil inclination of their own, — for by the theory they were created *holy*, — but by the subtlety of a wicked spirit, consigned themselves and all their posterity to the dread pit of torments. Human reason instantly suggests, if God was so early thwarted in his plan because the constitution of those two beings, with their state of exposure to Satan, brought them so instantaneously to ruin, why did he not at once cut short the growth from a corrupted stock, forbid the mischief to extend even into one more generation, and create a second pair? If the doctrine be true, we enter upon life at a dreadful disadvantage. As the famous Dr. Bellamy frankly affirmed, in full consistency with his creed, "Mankind were by their fall [meaning by *their*, Adam's] brought into a state of being *infinitely worse than not to be.*"* We as frankly own, that Unitarians can say nothing worse of this doctrine than one of its own defenders said of it in that sentence. And yet we should even now be met with the old charge of misrepresentation, if by way of construction and inference from that assertion we should say, that Dr. Bellamy admitted that all the power which God has exerted in the creation of all human beings since the first two, has resulted in something infinitely worse than would have been a perfect blank of non-existence. Our patrimony is all spent. The portion of our father's goods which would have fallen to us was all squandered by our eldest brother. Scripture tells us that there is a curse upon the fields of our labor; but Calvin has gone beyond the Scripture, which cursed neither Adam nor Eve, and has taught us that there is a curse upon the soul of every infant, even while it is in the womb. The prospect, the hope, the elating, spurring motive of a possible charm and blessing in existence, is destroyed for us by a foregone conclusion at our birth. Tell a young man, in the prime of his manhood, that, as his father died leaving unpaid debts, he must give up all the fruits of his own toil till those debts are discharged, and the buoyancy of youth and a filial sentiment may perhaps bear him cheerfully through the sacrifice. Tell a young man, that his father was bound

---

* Works, Vol. I. p. 333.

at his death by an unfulfilled contract, and manly honor may induce the son to complete it. Or tell that young man, that his deceased parent died in a penitentiary where he had spent but half of the years for which he was sentenced, and that he, the son, must go in and serve out the sentence. Possibly, even then, a loyalty to the laws of a community, which, as they secure to a son his father's property, might also impose a father's obligations, might induce the son to acquiesce uncomplainingly in the hard exaction. But tell us, all who live, or ever have lived, or ever shall live, of the race of Adam, that we accede to the obligations of one of his debts which there is no paying by all our labors, — that we are held to a contract which we never have made, and which God, one of the parties to it, has discharged himself from keeping according to its original terms with us, whom he has nevertheless compelled to be the other party to it, — and that while we are yet in the womb a transfer is made to us of an endless sentence in the pit of hell; — tell us all this, and what heart of man, what hope, what faith, can face it, as the appointment of a just God? A child has to be taught that doctrine. And what a lesson it is for a father or a mother to teach to a child, — to teach, too, as a doctrine of the Bible, the will of God!

We read in that Bible of Jehovah and of Baal. The book leaves us at perfect liberty, — indeed, it asks us *to choose* either of those beings as our God. By what ground of choice do we take Jehovah, and not Baal, for our Deity, to believe in, to worship, to love? Our choice is not decided by the words, the names, applied to the one or the other of those deities, but by the character, the dealings, the purposes, ascribed to each of them. We choose the ONE who is to be loved, to be revered, because of his holiness, his justice, his righteousness, his benignity. And so reason enters its protest against that doctrine. For there is a certain test principle within us, call it reason, judgment, or by whatever name we will, which we must apply at least in first accepting the Bible on the score of what it contains. There is no denying that reason, the highest gift of God to us, is shocked by that doctrine. Even the defenders of the doctrine allow this. Dr. Dwight says, "Perhaps no doctrine is more reluctantly received by the human mind." * Even if the doctrine were plainly and positively taught in *a* Bible, the issue would then be, Does that Bible authenticate the doctrine? or, Does that doctrine disprove and nullify the claims of the Bible? We feel no hesitation in affirming, that a Bible which advanced that doctrine would divest itself of the first and all-essential proof from its contents that it came from inspiration of God, and would throw upon all the other elements of such proof a burden which it is almost inconceivable that they could bear.

Below this and all similar discussions as to Scripture doctrine, lies a question, which, although it may be uncandidly and unfairly presented or arrayed, must be honorably allowed its full pertinence and propriety; namely, Does the system of doctrine taught in the Bible conform itself to, or outrage, the highest and purest exercise of the natural abilities which God has given to his creatures for interpreting a revelation from him? Are we driven to the alternative of living wholly without God, without faith, or of conforming our faith to a shocking and unreasonable representation of God and his ways? Does the Bible teach such a scheme as those who wish to have its help in a right and holy life can accept? If it does not, it will be classed with the Shasters, the Vedas, and the Koran. Theologians of all parties and sects may assure themselves that this is henceforward the real issue on trial before the world. And the parties for trying that issue are not a few classes of theological stu-

* Sermon XXIX.

dents, trained under professional influences, made to cramp the natural processes of their minds by subtle metaphysical speculations, and taught to infuse the pure zeal of earnest hearts for evangelizing the world into a strained allegiance to a creed which the heart repudiates. No! Not one in a score of those whom Orthodoxy addresses with this dogma accepts it, believes it, or does otherwise than loathe it. Let Orthodoxy regard, before it is too late, that trial of its dogmas which the other nineteen out of every twenty of those who listen to it are making. Dr. Woods says: "Without supposing that Unitarians have a preconceived opinion which they wish to support, I am not able to account for it, that they should interpret the word of God as they do."* It is even so. Unitarians, we are free to confess, have a *preconceived opinion*, though it is by no means confined to avowed Unitarians. It is only by and through the help of that *preconceived opinion* that we are able or disposed to take the first step towards receiving the Bible as in any sense "the word of God," and not the word of Baal. The *preconceived opinion* which we possess and exercise is just as much a revelation from God as anything that Prophet or Apostle ever wrote; and revelation was given to add something more to it, not to mock and outrage and deny it. The same Andover theologian, in addressing Unitarians previously (Letter IV.) had written: "We have nothing to do with the question, how the common doctrine of depravity can consist with the moral perfection of God." But, it may be asked, in what way, through what means and processes, are we persuaded of "the moral perfection of God"? Certainly not through a doctrine which is utterly inconsistent with all the instincts and perceptions which God has given us. Would Dr. Woods maintain, that we have the means of assuring

* Works, Vol. IV. p. 271.

to ourselves the perfection of the Deity, wholly apart from the study of his methods in nature and revelation? Would he maintain, that by these supposed means we can so convince ourselves of that sublime truth, that no amount of injustice or cruelty attributed to God would either shake our faith in him, or bring into doubt the record of an alleged revelation which so impugned his equity? The *methods* of the Divine government cannot be distinguished so positively from the *attributes* of the Deity, as to leave our confidence in his moral perfection unimpaired by the slightest deviation from absolute equity in his dealings with us.

The question will naturally present itself to many minds, How have men ever been made able or willing to accept this doctrine? How have they overcome the shrinking reluctance of their own reason at a doctrine which they supposed was taught in the Bible? Why did they not rather discredit the Bible, than accept the doctrine? Much might be said in reply to this question. If we had space and motive for its thorough discussion, we should raise a doubt whether the doctrine ever had been really and intensely believed by any large number of intelligent persons. We are aware that this assertion will provoke one of those positive, protesting affirmations, that millions of pious Christians have heartily believed the doctrine. We are willing to admit that they thought they believed it. But this is very far from satisfying us that all, or even the larger part, of those who have nominally professed to hold this doctrine, have ever grasped and wrestled with its appalling horrors, and, after stoutly and intelligently pursuing it by the logic of its antecedents and its consequences, have yielded to an entire persuasion that it is the truth of God. If it be said that millions of the believers in the Molochs and Juggernauts of heathenism have held, without misgiving, doctrines of a similar character concerning their gods, we reply that there is an unspeakable difference between the two classes of believers, — the Christian and the heathen, — as indicated by *the whole* of their respective religions. Heathenism is self-consistent. Its doctrines harmonize with each other, and one who accepts a portion of them can accept the rest. But a Christian who professes to believe this doctrine, that a corrupted nature, which dooms us all to unending torments, has been entailed upon us by ordinary generation on account of the sin of Adam, is compelled to receive it in connection with Scripture doctrines of the Divine justice and benignity, and of human individuality in duty and responsibility, which are totally and irreconcilably inconsistent with it. So we infer that his *belief* must necessarily be mistrustful, wavering, and not fully assured. Whether it be a fact that most, if not all, of the men and women who have professed to believe this doctrine have had the effort of belief facilitated to them by the assurance that, through some remedial process of free grace, they had been delivered personally from the terrific sweep of the doctrine, is a suggestion which we do not care to follow out. Any one who could believe this doctrine concerning all his race the more readily, because, without any merit of his own, he was rescued from its eternal sentence, would be a monster of selfishness.

Those who have professed and have tried, successfully or otherwise, to believe this doctrine, have held it on the ground of the "sovereignty of God." They have referred it to the dread and irresistible prerogative of that Being who has a right to fashion clay to honor or to dishonor, to do what he will and as he will with his creatures, and who doubtless will be able to vindicate *his justice*, even to those who call it *injustice*. In stern loyalty to that view of the sovereignty of God, sincere and pious men and women have choked down the risings of a spirit rebelling against this doctrine.

It is plain that only the most positive authority and

the most explicit testimony could lead us even to entertain such a doctrine as having a claim on our thoughts. It is but little to say that the authority, the testimony adduced for the doctrine, are totally inadequate to sustain it. The evidence adduced for it from the Scriptures is essentially drawn from a single passage in the Old Testament, and a single passage in the New Testament. There are indeed many sentences scattered over the Bible which are alleged as incidentally confirming and illustrating the doctrine. But its intelligent believers will not deny that, were it not for the two passages which are supposed explicitly to assert it, the doctrine would not be claimed as a Bible doctrine.

The first of these two passages is the narrative in the Book of Genesis, of the creation, the sin, and the punishment of Adam. Even if we interpret that narrative in the most rigidly literal manner, we cannot find in it the faintest intimation of the doctrine of the Westminster Catechism. Not one word is said in the narrative to imply that the sin of Adam passed over to his own children even, much less to all his posterity. It is not asserted that his act of sin corrupted his own *nature* even, much less the nature with which God, for all time to come, would endow his posterity. What a stupendous interpolation does the creed force into the record, in its positive, but most false assertion, that Adam was acting for all his posterity, and that he "stood in the room and stead of all mankind," and that *death for him* means *eternal torments for all his race!* There is not a word of it in the record. Adam is addressed as an individual, acting by himself and for himself alone, and for no one except or beyond himself. "Thou shalt," and "Thou shalt not," is the emphatic announcement of his own unshared obligation and responsibility. The most literal interpretation of the record confutes the creed. But no one — no, not a single intelligent reader — confines himself to a strictly literal interpretation of that narrative. Whatever be the religious opinions of such a reader, he sees at once that some allowance, more or less, must be made for the Oriental imagery, the figures of speech, the rhetoric and the drapery, of that concise record of a far-off age. All interpreters make such allowances, — not the same allowances, indeed, in matter and degree, but some allowances; they all depart from the letter of the narrative, and explain it constructively and inferentially, the question between interpreters being, Which explanation is the right one?

Every just and consistent claim of that narrative is met when we regard it as giving a sketch of the workings and the experiences of humanity on this earth, in an allegorical representation, by which an individual is made to stand as a type of us all. *Adam* is and means *Man*, and Adam's experience is representative of the experience of all human beings. We are all created as he was. Human nature works in us as it worked in him. We sin as he sinned; we suffer as he suffered; we die as he died. We do not sin *because* he sinned, but *as* he sinned; *in like manner*, since we have a like nature. *We* do not *suffer* because *he sinned*, but because we ourselves sin. The narrative teaches us that a being constituted as we are, — a type of humanity on the earth, — with our endowments and limitations of nature, our balanced powers and infirmities, subjected to the tenure and the exposures of life here, would be capable of sinning and liable to sin, — that he would sin, and that his sin would subject him to labor and sorrow and death. This is the solemn, yet not unreasonable, doctrine of the narrative. It is sufficiently serious and overshadowing in the dismay and awe which it casts over us. Yet we accept the lesson in all its solemnity, and would not trifle with a letter which is used in conveying it to us. It would be invested with an unrelieved gloom to us, did not the narrative immediately connect with this typical representation of the workings of the experiment of humanity, the promise of continued aid, and of mercy and blessing and redemption from God. So far is the narrative from asserting that the personal sin of Adam entailed a vitiated nature on his posterity, that it expressly tells us that one of the two sons of Adam was righteous and approved of God. But supposing even that the original human stock had been corrupted in Adam, the flood was designed to secure a new and purified stock, and the progenitor in that hope, in whom it is written that the world had a new start, was "righteous Noah," while all human beings, save himself and his family, were cut off. It is written, "Noah was a just man, and perfect in his generations; and Noah walked with God." (Genesis vi. 9.) His family started afresh, with a new blessing from God: "And God blessed Noah and his sons." Why then, if *character* is propagated from a parent, — why did not Noah propagate a pure stock?

That one narrative of Adam in and out of Paradise is the only passage in the Old Testament which can be alleged as recognizing in any way our connection with his personal sin or *Fall.* Not another sentence, not another line in all the elder Scriptures, ever makes the slightest reference to the subject. No oracle, vision, chronicle, proverb, or psalm recognizes the doctrine. Not a single one of the inspired prophets of the Almighty to the Jews ever uttered, so far as we know, one word implying that Adam acted for all his posterity, ruined us all in his fall, and so foreclosed the trial of existence for all who should ever live. Is not this an amazing fact, — that those sacred oracles should be so dumbly silent about a matter which is said to underlie the whole doctrinal teaching of revelation!

One passage in the New Testament furnishes all the substantial authority which the Gospel is supposed to give to this doctrine. Not a word, however, can be quoted from the Saviour's lips in recognition, still less as an assertion, of the doctrine. The passage referred to is not from the teaching of Christ, but from an argumentative letter of St. Paul. In the fifth chapter of the Epistle to the Romans, we read an illustrative comment on the narrative in Genesis, — not a new revelation of doctrine. We find nothing in the Apostle's statement which conflicts with, but, on the contrary, everything to favor, the view we have already derived from the earlier record. If in the peculiar style or method of the Apostle's reasoning he may seem to imply more than the record conveys from which he quotes, that is a trace of a habit of his which the intelligent interpreter of his writings meets with in other places in his Epistles. His words are: "As by one man sin entered into the world, and death by sin, so death passed upon all men, for that all have sinned." And this is saying, *not* that we all sin because our progenitor sinned, *nor* that we all die because he sinned, but that, as the first man was a sinner and a mortal, so we are all sinners and all mortal; not because of a corrupt nature, but because of a human nature.

Yet it is said that this doctrine of a disabled nature entailed upon us by ordinary generation finds support in the whole system of revealed truth. We affirm that it is wholly and at every point inconsistent with that system, and with each of the doctrinal elements that enter into it. It is not consistent with the attributes of God, as Wise, and Good, and Righteous. To say that his whole scheme was thwarted, and that one lapse of one individual ruined a race of beings, and visited upon the unborn in endless succession the guilt of a sin to which they were not parties, — to say this, will not harmonize with the character of God. Some Orthodox writers have presumed that they involved Unitarians in a dilemma, by reminding us, that, though we assert that this doctrine of *native depravity* is not consistent with justice in our Creator, we still have to admit that the existence of Evil *is* consistent with the attributes of that Being. But we do not recognize the dilemma. The allowance of evil may be a means of good for all men, but native depravity must insure the ruin of untold millions. Dr. Woods* speaks of "that vulgar charge, which contains too much apparent truth to be directly denied, and yet too much falsehood to be admitted, that we [the Orthodox] represent men to be as God made them, incapable of any good till renewed by *irresistible* influence, irreversibly appointed to destruction without any regard to their sins." We will not use the word *quibble* in connection with anything that *seemed* like an argument to Dr. Woods. We must say, however, that the Westminster creed asserts literally, positively, and fully of God, all that Dr. Woods here repudiates. The loophole for escape, however, lies in this plea, — that when we are born into this world we are not what *God* made us, but what *Adam* made us.

Again, this doctrine is inconsistent with what revelation teaches of the nature of man, as a free, moral, and accountable being, capable of good and evil, living in individual responsibility, never bearing the iniquity even of his nearest in kin, nor having his teeth set on edge because his father had eaten sour grapes. It is inconsistent, too, with the purpose of life, as an opportunity, a gift, a fair trial, an unprejudiced experiment, and not a foregone conclusion to each and every human being. The doctrine is inconsistent at every point with the Christian scheme. The Calvinistic system, which teaches this doctrine, expressly affirms that the Gospel of Christ does not save all men. So, according to this doctrine, the Christian remedy is not equal to meeting the disease entailed

* Works, Vol. IV. pp. 335, 336.

upon our race. Adam did more of harm to our race than Christ can do of benefit. God — for in the Calvinistic scheme Christ is God — cannot wholly undo for the innocent the mischief wrought upon them by one of his own creatures! Well may the modern Calvinist object to *inferences* from his doctrine, however rigidly fair the logic by which they are drawn. Now St. Paul says that the free gift of Redemption from God by Christ is *more*, instead of *less*, than the offence of sin by Adam; that grace *exceeds*, rather than *falls short of* the occasion for it. "Where sin abounded, grace did much more abound," is the Apostle's emphatic statement. But it cannot be true in an economy under which a human being entails sin and ruin upon his whole race, while a Divine Being — the Redeemer — rescues only a portion of that race. "Not as the offence," says St. Paul, "so also is the free gift. For if through the offence of one many be dead, much more the grace of God, and the gift by grace, by one man, Jesus Christ, hath abounded unto many." (Romans v. 15.) But is it so by the Calvinistic scheme? Look at it and see. Adam brought ruin upon every one of his posterity. "The guilt of his sin is imputed, and corrupted nature conveyed to all by ordinary generation," says the creed. Adam, then, made shipwreck of the race. Christ saves individuals here and there. The first pair could communicate their corrupted nature to unborn millions; but Christian parents, regenerated, purified, and sanctified by Christ, cannot communicate their renewed nature to a single one in a large family of their own children. It would be difficult, with such a theology as this, to calculate by how much the free gift is *less* than the offence. But our Orthodox brethren must devise a more subtile philosophy than they have yet invented, to rectify the loss on their side of the balance by the excess on the Apostle's side. We cannot but conclude that this doctrine, instead of being conformed to the Christian system, is in utter discordance with it. Sin has come in like an ocean tide, bearing all before it; the Orthodox Gospel saves only here and there a wreck from the dreary wastes of woe.

We must now fix our attention for a moment upon one of the most odious features of this doctrine, because it was there that the struggle against it was concentrated by its opponents, and its professed believers began their attempts at modifying it. Observe in the creed the assertion, made as positively and literally as language will allow, that a corrupted nature is conveyed, by ordinary generation, to all of Adam's posterity, in consequence of his personal sin. To an ingenuous mind this assertion can convey but one idea. The lamentable shifts and evasions and subtilties to which Orthodox theologians have had recourse during the last half-century, in trying to evade the plain meaning of this article of their creed, are a scandal upon our whole profession. That we ought to expect a long and sad reckoning to be visited upon us, in a widely diffused unbelief, a distrust of religious teaching, and a general and dismal sense of unreality about theological dogmas, is but a looking for a retribution the tokens of which are too evident to be disputed. If this Orthodox doctrine is not a most shameful trifling with solemnities, as well as with language, it asserts that, by the constitution and appointment of God, the one man Adam had the power to communicate a vitiated nature, like an hereditary disease, not merely to the bodies, but to the souls, of all human beings, and that the possession of that vitiated nature disables us for anything good, and inclines us to all evil, involving us all in guilt, and dooming us all to woe. This doctrine either contradicts truth and reason, in affirming that any one can be a partaker in sin committed before his birth, or it contradicts justice and righteousness, by subjecting us to punishment for the offence of another. Now the doctrine of *a sinful nature* being propagated by bodily descent, like an hereditary disease, is the most outrageous and malignant form of materialism ever devised. It makes *man*, instead of *God*, to be "the *Father of Spirits*." And what is the meaning of the phrase, *a sinful nature?* Does not this assign to nature what can be assigned only to *character?* Would Orthodoxy persuade us that we create our own *nature?* Would Orthodoxy transfer from God to Adam the office of endowing human souls? Character exhibits moral qualities, and within the range of its freedom involves responsibility; but *nature* is an original limitation and confine within which there is no responsibility. A sinful action is a possibility, a sinful nature is an impossibility.

An episode in the controversy upon the Scripture doctrine concerning the nature and the state of man, related to the doom of those who died in infancy. We must make some reference to this episode, though it must needs be brief.

The Christian Disciple for May and June, 1823, had quoted the following sentences from Dr. Twiss, Prolocutor of the Westminster Assembly: "In regard to those who are condemned to eternal death solely on account of original sin, their condemnation to eternal death is the consequence of Adam's transgression alone. But many infants depart this life in original sin, and consequently are condemned to eternal death on account of original sin alone; therefore the *condemnation of many* INFANTS *to* ETERNAL DEATH is the consequence of Adam's transgression *solely*." "Adam's sin is made ours by the imputation of God; *so that it has exposed* INNUMERABLE INFANTS *to* DIVINE WRATH, *who were guilty of this sin*, AND OF NO OTHER." "There,"—adds the Disciple,—"we ask whether any Unitarian ever attempted to color or exaggerate a doctrine like this,—a doctrine taught in so many words by the Prolocutor of the Assembly of Divines at Westminster, and by a thousand others, — a doctrine, moreover, which follows necessarily from the Calvinistic system, and which would now be insisted on by all real and consistent Calvinists, if they thought their people would bear it?" (p. 220.) In an earlier volume of the same periodical had occurred this sentence: "We suspect that Orthodox congregations are less accustomed than formerly, to hear of infants being justly liable to the eternal pains of hell." * Dr. Lyman Beecher, in a note to the seventh edition, published in 1827, of a sermon originally preached and printed in 1808, repelled as a calumny the charge that Calvinists believe and teach "the monstrous doctrine that infants are damned." He asserted among other things, that, having lived fifty years, "and been conversant for thirty years with the most approved Calvinistic writers, he had never seen nor heard of any book which contained such a sentiment." He added: "And I would earnestly and affectionately recommend to all persons who have been accustomed to propagate this slander, that they commit to memory without delay the ninth commandment, which is, 'Thou shalt not bear false witness against thy neighbor.'" The Christian Examiner (Vol. IV. p. 431, for 1827) boldly took up the implied challenge of Dr. Beecher, and positively affirmed that "the doctrine of infant damnation has been expressly maintained by leading Calvinists, and is connected with essential, vital principles of the Calvinistic system." Then followed a series of articles in the Examiner, and a series of letters by Dr. Beecher in the Spirit of the Pilgrims, in exchange, not exactly of *courtesies*, but of arguments and testimonies, and of what were designed for arguments and testimonies, on either side of the issue thus opened. To say, as in the spirit of perfect candor and full sincerity we are compelled to say, that

* Christian Disciple for 1819, p. 279.

Dr. Beecher was utterly and most ingloriously vanquished, and that his opponent gained a complete and unquestionable victory, — to say this, while it affords us no pleasure whatever, may be accounted as only a partisan boast on our part. If any one is inclined to judge, not us, but our decision or opinion on this matter, we will be content with receiving his promise that he will read the articles referred to in the fourth and fifth volumes of the Christian Examiner. Never, in our judgment, was there a more fair, or thorough, or exhaustive, or decisive course of argument, authenticated at every point, brought to sustain an assumed position in a matter of controversy, than may be found in those papers. The utmost that Dr. Beecher could be induced to admit sustained only the assertion already quoted by us from the Christian Disciple, that Calvinism taught "that infants are justly liable to the pains of hell." He acknowledged that, according to his creed, "infants, by the imputation of Adam's sin, are depraved and guilty, and on this account children of wrath, and exposed justly to future punishment." * He admitted it also to be a doctrine of Calvinism, according to Turretin, "that infants *deserve* damnation, because, though not subjects of law as regards *action*, they are as regards *disposition*." We should have been fully content to have accepted these admissions as a complete warrant for the assertion that the doctrine of infant damnation "is connected with vital, essential principles of the Calvinistic system." The essence of the horrifying imputation which Calvinism casts upon the Creator consists rather in ascribing to him the making of dying infants *liable* to the doom of hell, than in positively affirming that any infants suffer that doom. The Westminster Catechism and the New England Confession tell us that "*Elect* infants dying in infancy are saved by Christ." But all the reserved and

* Spirit of the Pilgrims, Vol. I. p. 46.

implied difference which there is between *infants* and *elect* infants is certainly suggestive of a class of *non-elect* infants, and if the distinction in the terms secures salvation to the *elect*, it intimates perdition for the *non-elect*, "dying in infancy."

If, besides drawing out these Orthodox allowances and implications, Unitarianism had wished to repel the charge of having invented this calumny against Orthodoxy or Calvinism, a very few quotations like the following from writers not on the Unitarian side would have sufficed.

Bishop Jeremy Taylor writes thus: "Gregorius Ariminensis, Driedo, Luther, Melancthon, and Tilmanus Heshusius, are fallen into the worst of St. Austin's [Augustine's] opinion, and sentence poor infants to the flames of hell for original sin, if they die before baptism." *

Rev. Thomas Stackhouse writes thus: "The Calvinists carry the matter much farther [than the Schoolmen], asserting that original sin (besides an exclusion from heaven) deserves the punishment of *damnation;* and therefore they conclude that such infants as die unbaptized, and are not of the number of the *elect* (which have always a particular exemption), are, for the transgression of our first parents, condemned to the eternal torments of hell-fire. It must be confessed that the doctrine of the Church of England makes too near approaches to this opinion, when it tells us that, 'in every person born into the world, original sin deserves God's wrath and damnation,' — for the words seem to be too strong and express, to admit of those mollifying constructions which some, by way of apology, have thought proper to put upon them." †

While it would be the most hopeless of all tasks for a Calvinist to attempt to set aside the assertions quoted from "leading Calvinists," beginning with Calvin him-

* Heber's Taylor, Vol. IX. p. 91.

† Body of Divinity, 1760, pp. 292, 293.

self, in proof that the damnation of some infants has been expressly taught by them, it would be equally vain for such an advocate to dispute the logical inference of the doctrine from the Calvinistic system. How can the doctrine be kept out, as a consequence of that view of the nature and the state of man which we have been examining as a matter of controversy?

We must now attempt to state, in terms as brief and plain as is possible, the doctrinal position which Unitarianism has taken in rejecting this Calvinistic dogma of the ruin of the human race by the sin of the first man, and the consequent entail upon every human being of a depraved nature, the burden of which is guilt, the fruit of which is sin, and the doom of which is eternal woe. It can hardly be said that Unitarianism has fashioned any dogma of its own upon this point. Like all other classes of Christians, like all other serious thinkers, we are baffled by the original moral mystery involved in the existence or allowance of evil in the universe of God. The solution of that mystery would be an essential condition of any full and complete doctrinal formula as to the source of sin in man's heart and life; but before that mystery we bow in a bewildered amazement, and with an oppressed spirit which cannot look for relief in this stage and scene of our being. The great and leading position which Unitarianism takes in antagonism with the Calvinistic doctrine on this point is, that there must be some other construction put upon the facts and the arguments which are the materials for a theory, a construction radically opposed to that which Orthodoxy gives them. Unitarianism lives upon the conviction, that earth or heaven must afford some other explanation of our frailty and sinfulness than the assertion that the fruits of one man's disobedience are entailed upon all his posterity. Unitarianism lives upon the assurance that there must be some other mode of representing the essential terms of the Divine government over us, than by including among them this of the propagation through ordinary physical generation of a corrupted moral nature, the possession and the exercise of which makes us guilty before God. If God be the righteous legislator and judge of every human soul, he cannot hold us amenable to a higher standard than our natures will admit, nor visit upon us a sentence for another's sin, nor extend our responsibility beyond the range of our individual ability. By no effort of reasoning, and by no humbling restraint placed upon our impulse to reason, — by no straining of the mind to reach after truth above its grasp, and by no violent crushing down of our rebellious remonstrances, — can we reconcile the Calvinistic doctrine with our instinctive or our educated conceptions of God, the Wise, the Omnipotent, the Righteous. If this mortal life of ours puts us on trial for an eternity of conscious existence, no retributive results there can have in them the first element of justice, unless we have had an unprejudiced start here. Any disability of nature, any taint or bias or proclivity which precedes the conscious exercise of our powers, becomes an infinite injustice to us when its consequences are projected into a future state.

Yet Unitarianism recognizes the deep and the unsounded perplexities of this subject. No serious person can ever think or speak otherwise than with a profound and oppressive solemnity and dread about sin, the perversion and debasement of moral powers, the source of unmeasured woe, the defying attitude of human beings toward God. It is a relief to us to know that even the Orthodox theory of it is compelled to recognize for sin an origin or agency apart from the sphere of humanity, in attributing the instigation of it to a Spirit of Evil. Still Orthodoxy leaves wholly unexplained the alleged fact, that the Good Spirit subjected the first pair, on whose conduct the fate of uncounted millions of intelligent beings was staked, to the machinations of that Evil Spirit. Unitarianism admits all the perplexing mysteries of fact and experience about sin, but does not feel disposed to deepen or increase them by involving them with satanic agencies, or with dates or incidents prior to or outside of human life on this globe. Unitarianism does not deny the sinfulness of man, nor does it discharge that sinfulness of positive guilt, nor does it trifle with the consequences of sin here or hereafter. Some of the most appalling admissions, and some of the most startling assertions as to the guilt and the devastations of sin, are to be found in the writings of Unitarians. We think our general views of it are all the more serious, because we ascribe it to character, not to nature, and regard it as a wilful wrong-doing, not as an inherited disease. Unitarians ask the Orthodox to help them, and they offer their aid to the Orthodox, that together we may try to cast some rays of reason, light, and truth upon this mystery of sin. But Unitarians insist, firmly and positively, without yielding on this point a hair's breadth, that the explanation proposed shall not involve the dogma that we are born with a depraved heart, that life is a foregone conclusion when it begins, that the nature which is God's endowment of us is corrupt, and that the character which is the development of that nature and the element of our accountability is from the first committed to a diseased and wicked growth. Calvin tells us (Comment. on Ephesians ii. 3): "We are not born such beings as Adam was created in the beginning, but are the corrupt descendants of a degenerate and adulterate parent." Dr. Woods, even in a note designed to relieve this dreary doctrine (Letter XI.), says: "There is nothing which hinders man from obedience but his depraved disposition, his wicked heart." What a dismal way of intimating that an impossibility might be a possibility, if it were not an impossibility! Suppose Dr. Woods, travelling with a companion on a dreary wilderness way, and coming to a well which he knew to be poisoned, should say: "There is nothing to hinder our being saved from a terrific death, and helped on to our happy homes, by the waters of this well, *except* that they are mixed with a deadly poison." His companion, if not an Orthodox casuist, would be apt to reply, that the exception was fatal to any desired good from the waters. It is but little to say of the Calvinistic doctrine, that it relieves us of all responsibility. It substitutes a Pharaoh for our God, ever demanding his tale of brick while he withholds the material of them. Unitarians, therefore, insist that as to that weakness or liability in human nature which shows itself as we grow up as sinfulness, some other explanation of its origin shall be found than to call it an entailed curse, and some other reason shall be assigned for its existence in us than the sin of a progenitor, and some other title be given to it than guilt, and some other retribution be announced for our helpless disability than that of a hopeless hell.

Unitarians have been seeking, and are still seeking, for relief and for such satisfaction as may be within the reach of human faculties, concerning the problem of evil. They have received some most valuable aid in their speculations from Orthodox writers, who have worked, to some extent, with us and for us, while appearing to work against us. All the modifications, abatements, and palliatives of which professedly Orthodox writers have felt compelled to avail themselves in dealing with their doctrine, have been of great service to us. In the mean while Unitarianism, taking Scripture for its guide, develops its own peculiar views somewhat after the manner following. After God had fashioned and furnished this earth, he left it for long ages without a human inhabitant, while vegetables and animals lived and died upon it. The remains of these primeval plants and creatures, imbedded in some of the lower strata of the earth, bear witness for themselves. In his own good time, God was pleased to create a race of human beings to inhabit this earth in a series of generations. Some of the conditions and limitations to which the life and the range of existence of these beings would necessarily be subjected, were fixed in the elementary constitution and arrangements of the scene of their abode. They are human beings, a race lower than the angels. They are spirits in bodies of clay, formed from the dust of the earth, breathed into by the breath of God. By the universal law of all elemental organizations, human bodies need renewal, are exposed to disease and accident, and subject to waste, decay, and death. These human beings are moral beings. So far as they are accountable beings they are free, and so far as they are free beings they are accountable. That they may be free to do right, they must also be free to do wrong. Adam, the representative man, was capable of sinning, and as the extremest Calvinist never pretended that Adam was created with a depraved nature, the conclusion is irresistible that a human being may be capable of sinning, and may actually sin, without having any original taint of corruption or depravity. This inevitable inference visits an utter discomfiture on the Calvinistic dogma, that *our* sin can have no other origin or source than a vitiated nature. If Adam could commit actual sin, though he was not born in original sin, so may each one of his posterity err as he did without inheriting iniquity from him. The only idea which we can form of the purpose for which human beings exist, is that they may serve the ends of their Creator by the best use of the faculties he has given them. In connection with all the physical powers and relations of these beings, relations which concern the body and its wants, we think we discern an inner life, a nobler range of existence, in the elements of thought, of affection, of conscience, a life of the mind and the spirit, amid cares and conflicts, failures and attainments, lapses and recoveries. That this higher life may be served, good and evil must be placed before these human beings, while the command is addressed to them to "overcome evil with good." However far we may carry the assertion or the allowance of an unexceptionable and a universal human sinfulness, we must stop short of the admission that man is necessarily a sinner, for this admission at once severs the connection between sin and responsibility. This necessary sinfulness is admitted, if it be affirmed that man has a corrupted nature. An evil tree can bring forth only evil fruit. The decision as regards our moral character cannot be supposed to have been made at our birth, but the means, the materials for making it, must lie latent in the germ of humanity, and life will afford the opportunity and the scene of their development. We are not born holy, for then we should be what the angels now are, who are denizens of heaven while we are creatures of the earth. We are not born fiends, for we are made after the similitude of God. As these beings must be capable of doing wrong in order that they may be able to do right, they should not be restrained physically or morally from feeling impulses to do wrong. They should be addressed by the power of outward temptations, and there should be internal weaknesses, spots on their breasts, not defended by heavenly mail, — spots and weaknesses which temptation should assail. Righteousness, holiness, conformity to the will of God, is the highest possible result which we could look for to be attained by such beings, and we should never dream of realizing it as a birthright, nor as an instinct, nor as secured by an inward impulse, nor by outward help. It should be the result of life-long struggles and strivings, of falling and of rising often, of groanings and weepings, of aching and praying, of sinning and repenting. It is enough for man if he can die a reconciled penitent. It is enough for him if he can reach at the end of his course, after a life of blind and troubled wanderings, that same Father's house from which he went out as an infant and an embryo spirit.

Should any one object that it is not worthy of God to be charged with the creation of such a race of beings, we reply, that this is just the race of beings that inhabits this earth, and that the fact speaks for itself. Here they are, and they have never been anything different from what they are. At any rate, the sort of beings which we have aimed to portray from the reality of life are, in our judgment, infinitely more worthy of God than are those which Calvinism ascribes to him. Imperfect then we are; imperfect, frail, and mortal. Adam proved in his own case the result of the experiment made by God with the elements and conditions involved in the constitution of a human being. The result of the experiment in one case of course signified what would be its result in all cases. As Adam was a sinner and a mortal, so all human beings are sinners and all are mortal; *not because he was a sinner, but because they are all like him in their humanity.* But is this nature of ours *corrupt* and *depraved* because it is *imperfect?* Does the fact that we must all learn righteousness prove that we have previously graduated in iniquity? Does our imperfection prove that we are cursed, and does our being under that curse prove our guilt? Let us see.

There are four elements needed, as we say, to make up a human being, — a body, a heart, a mind, and a spirit. These are all undeveloped, untrained at our birth. How do we regard the infirmities, the imperfections, the need of discipline, help, and reinforcement to which they are respectively subject?

If a child is born with an inherited bodily defect, crippled, deformed, maimed, or blind, he is an object of our tender commiseration. Who ever blames him for his defect? Who would address to him a word of reproof, or inflict upon him a blow, as for sin? Even if his defect is entailed upon him for the sin of his parents, this is not his personal guilt, and though it subjects him to suffering, his suffering is not punishment. His visitation is directly from the hand of God.

If a child is born with a feeble intellectual faculty, and it is very hard to teach him, and teaching utterly fails through his dulness of mind, still there is no guilt in this, but simply an original natural deficiency.

If a child is lacking in affectionate sensibilities of heart, and shows from infancy an ungovernable temper, the parents will try patient culture to subdue and train the child's heart, and up to its mature years its faults are for the most part spoken of as constitutional infirmities, rarely as guilt, while its moderate success in self-restraint is estimated as a heroism in self-discipline.

Thus it is that we disconnect all natural defects of body, mind, and heart from the imputation of guilt. We do not expect a child to walk till it has *learned* to walk; nor to read till it has *learned* to read. We are satisfied always if a child learns anything after it has been taught, and the more valuable the art or science or knowledge which is communicated, the more content are we to multiply efforts, to extend patience, and to prolong time in imparting it, and in looking for the fruits of the instruction. But now mark the inconsistency of Orthodoxy as it deals with the fourth element in a human being, — the spirit. While the whole of life is allowed to be education and preparation in the training and use of all our lower faculties, the very dawn of life is expected to show a full-formed perfection in the exercise and manifestation of our highest faculty. Orthodoxy tolerates infants that cannot walk, or read, or love their parents beyond others; but it will not tolerate an infant that does not love and obey God in perfect holiness of spirit. If the spirit of this little helpless being does not instinctively discern and follow the supreme good, and without any struggle, training, or conflict, any guidance or experience, yield itself to the love of piety, then Orthodoxy cries out, A *Fall*, a *Corruption*, an *Alienation* from God! Over the waste of dreary ages, and through the ashes of mortal generations, Orthodoxy tries to trace back the venom in that infant's constitution to the slime which the old serpent dropped from its mouth when it spake its deceiving word to Eve.

Dr. Woods puts to Dr. Ware this question: "Do children show a heart to love God supremely, when they are two or three years old?" * We may answer the question by asking another: Why should they? When it takes the highest spiritual exercises of an eminent saint to fashion forth an adequate conception of God, how can we expect a child two or three years old to love that God supremely?

It seems to us as if Orthodoxy involved not only the notion that Adam, not God, is the father of all human spirits, but likewise the implication that God has nothing to do in his usual providence with the training of any human spirits except those of the elect. Does not Orthodoxy convey the implication, that when human spirits are launched upon this earth, God, as a usual thing, has done with them? Now we regard the beings we have described from the realities of life as constantly dependent on the Divine guardianship and grace; as constantly needing new replenishments of spiritual power and aid; and as constantly receiving, or at liberty to avail themselves of, such help in their earthly training. We do not believe that we are all orphaned of heavenly affection and care the day after we are born, — left as infants in a wilderness cast to the wolves. It is not our doctrine,

* Reply, Chap. II.

that the influences of God's Spirit are granted to some and withheld from others. We believe that his Spirit is ever prompting and helping all spirits, and is rejected when not yielded to and accepted. That aid of the Spirit is not a specialty even, still less a partiality, any more than is a parent's needful advice and oversight in the training of all his children. That spiritual influence is the needful and the natural complement to the elements of our nature, and to the other influences which develop it.

We should need space exceeding that which we have already occupied, if we attempted to do anything like justice in stating the various modifications which have been introduced during the last century into the old Calvinistic doctrine of the corrupted and disabled nature and the doomed state of man. These modifications are designed to relieve and soften the doctrine, to make it less revolting, and, if possible, more reasonable. It is to be understood that these palliating devices are invented by men who still profess to hold substantially the doctrine of the Catechism and the Confession, and who claim a right to avail themselves of the utmost liberty of explanation and abatement. When we contemplate as a whole the subtilties, the worse than dubious ingenuities, and the self-convicted duplicity in evasion, which have been spent upon this Calvinistic doctrine by some of its nominal disciples, a rising disgust for everything associated with this department of our theological literature nearly overwhelms us. There is but one suggestion that relieves our feelings; it is, that all these efforts are made out of a tender desire to reconcile the God of the creed with the God of the heart. It is not strange, however, that Unitarians should watch with a very lively interest, and occasionally with a sort of subdued and mischievous satisfaction, the processes and the results of these modifications of Calvinism. The disciples of that system must have become fully aware that it is a venturous and a hazardous work to attempt to bring its dogmas into reconciliation with right reason.

There are three elements entering into the doctrine of the entail from Adam upon all his posterity of a disabled nature, and they suggest three questions: First, is this disability of nature a fact? Second, is it to be regarded as constituting, in the eye of God, personal guilt? Third, does it involve an everlasting and inexpressible penalty? Of course a very large range is opened for pleading and for modifying opinions in the discussion of these three elements of the old doctrine. Doctor Chauncy, who held the Calvinistic views in the most moderate form, if he held them at all, took refuge in Universalism, as did the late amiable and earnest John Foster, of whose orthodoxy there is no question.

Down almost to the time of the commencement of our great controversy, the general teaching of Orthodoxy conformed to the doctrine of the Confession, that a corrupted nature, a vitiated and depraved constitution, was transmitted from Adam to all his posterity, by natural descent, exactly as a bodily disease, a gout or a consumption, would be transmitted. This certainly implies a physical inheritance of depravity, a depravity running in the blood; and this legitimate inference from the doctrine was prevailingly drawn from it, and prevailingly accepted. It was at this point that the shock of the doctrine was first and most strongly felt, and here an issue had been opened between Orthodox theologians before Unitarians were a recognized party in the case. Dr. Lyman Beecher has given us a very concise summary of the matter in hand, in substance as follows.* He reminds us that Pelagius maintained that infants were born pure, and became depraved by a corrupted

* Spirit of the Pilgrims, Vol. I. p. 158.

moral atmosphere and by bad example, while he denied that there is any certain connection between the sin of Adam and that of his posterity. Augustine, on the other hand, asserted an innate, hereditary depravity, by the imputation of Adam's sin. Dr. Beecher adds, that the Reformers agreed with Augustine in the belief that sin was propagated with flesh and blood. Certainly one would think that, after this admission, it was no Unitarian slander to charge this doctrine upon those whose boast it was that they held to "the doctrines of the Reformation." This doctrine was first openly assailed after the Reformation, says Dr. Beecher, by the Arminians and the Remonstrants, and was one of the Five Points under sharp debate in the Synod of Dort. The Pelagian doctrine, having been revived at the Synod, has found acceptance and prevalence in the Established Church of England, while "our fathers," down to the time of Edwards, and including him, held close to the views of the Reformers. After the time of Edwards, Dr. Beecher proceeds to tell us, the way of stating the doctrine was changed. "Now, the New or Hopkinsian divinity holds that men are not guilty of Adam's sin, and that depravity is not of the substance of the soul, nor an inherent or physical quality, but is wholly voluntary, and consists in the transgression of law, in such circumstances as constitutes accountability and desert of punishment." Our readers will observe that, while the old doctrine has a meaning perfectly lucid, which explains itself to us at a glance, the modifications of it are for the most part stated in a cloudy, obscure, unintelligible way, as if their vagueness and indefiniteness of terms would afford a sensible relief. Dr. Beecher, if hard pressed in close conversation by a clear-headed questioner, would have to admit that "the transgression of law," and the "circumstances," of which he speaks, involve the original elements of the nature which an infant receives from the Creator on being born into this world.

In the first number of the periodical just quoted, we find the Orthodox belief on this doctrine stated thus: "That since the Fall of Adam, men are, in their natural state, altogether destitute of true holiness, and entirely depraved. That men, though thus depraved, are justly required to love God with all the heart, and justly punishable for disobedience; or, in other words, they are complete moral agents, proper subjects of moral government, and truly accountable to God for their actions." * One year passed, and then the same periodical announced the following: "We do not believe that the posterity of Adam are personally chargeable with eating the forbidden fruit [that is, they did not bite the same apple]; or that their constitution is so depraved as to leave them no natural ability to love and serve God, or as to render it improper for him to require obedience." † Again is the scale of modifications a scale of unintelligibilities. How plain, as well as strong in contrast, is the language of President Edwards, when he tells us: "All natural men's affections are governed by malice against God, and they hate him worse than they do the Devil." Considering that these natural affections have their source in the heart, and that the heart is the endowment which we receive from God, the inference from the assertion is unavoidable, unless we again have recourse to the notion that Adam, and not God, is our Creator.

Yet, strange to say, there has been a dispute among the Orthodox as to whether Edwards did or did not teach the doctrine of the physical entail of depravity! Strange to say, he has been claimed as an authority, both by those who believe the old doctrine in this form, and by those who deny it. Any unprofessional reader

* Spirit of the Pilgrims, Vol. I. p. 11. † Ibid., Vol. II. p. 4.

who should attempt to peruse the discussion of this question, Did Edwards, or did he not, teach that human nature was constitutionally depraved by physical entail? would be apt to give over the task with a rather hopeless idea of the lucidness of some doctors of divinity.

The Orthodox Congregationalists around us have agreed upon some terms of amity touching their differences of Old School and New School, as to the matter of Original Sin, and the essential quality of our depravity. But the Presbyterians, who build upon the Westminster Catechism, and mean to stand or to fall with that, are by no means inclined to pacification on this issue. There has been a fierce strife carried on under the blinding cloud of dust raised by the fraternal quarrel of the Old and the New Schools, as to whether man's *Inability* to meet the requirements of God's law is a *Natural* Inability, or a *Moral* Inability. The Rev. Ezra Stiles Ely, in his "Contrast between Calvinism and Hopkinsianism," (published in 1811,) has given us a sharp rehearsal of the controversy, as between the real Orthodoxy of our Middle States and the diluted Orthodoxy of New England. But to us this question between the two Schools is not even a war of words; for the word *Inability*, the only emphatic and decisive word involved in their doctrine, is a word accepted and used on both sides. All in vain does Dr. Woods tell us that *Moral Inability*, in which he believes, means only "a strong disinclination" to do the will of God, and that "it *constitutes* blameworthiness," — "while *Natural Inability*," in which he does not believe, "*frees* from blameworthiness."* For he also tells us, in his Fifth Letter to us, "that men are subjects of an innate moral depravity, in other words, that they are from the first inclined to evil." *From the first!* — the whole doctrine goes with those words. The

* Works, Vol. IV. p. 285.

force, the stress, the strain of the doctrine, lies in the word *Inability*, — that noun substantive which tells the effect of a death-blow struck at the very core of our being. It makes very little difference whether we connect with that substantive the epithet *Natural* or *Moral*, for the adjective seems in this instance almost to lose the office assigned to it in the grammar, of *qualifying* a noun. Yet the two epithets make two Schools. How significant is the token that a hair's breadth of relief, or of supposed relief, by vagueness of words, under the old doctrine, is welcomed as a blessing. One School tells us man's depravity consists in this: "He *cannot* do right if he wishes to do so." "No," says the other School; "it consists in this: He *will not* do right if he can." *He can't if he will! — He won't if he can!* A precious difference! It is well for the two Schools that they have both retained the word Inability. Their Orthodoxy is safe so long as they hold to that, but their *loyalty* to Orthodoxy is doubtful if they are bent on neutralizing the substantive by any adjective. There certainly is a real difference between a lack of *power*, and a lack of the *will* to do one's duty; but if the lack of *will* springs from a lack of *power to will*, or of a capacity of being influenced by the will otherwise than to disobedience, a moral want of will becomes essentially a natural want of power.

Then there is what may be called "the Privative Theory" of our depravity. Some Orthodox men have found an appreciable degree of comfort in this theory. It suggests, that, besides having all the faculties and opportunities which we have for meeting our responsibility to God, Adam was favored with a peculiar spiritual guardianship, an additional inducement and protection from a closer intercourse with the grace of God, which additional security has been withdrawn from all his posterity; leaving them, under the *privation* of divine grace, to the common influences and circumstances of our appointed state of being. Well may we ask: If Adam, with such an additional security, could not retain his innocence, is our condition fairly allotted to us, when it visits upon us the inheritance of his depravity, and *deprives* us of his original aid from the Divine Father?

Still another modification of the old doctrine is proposed in the theory, that we are not at our birth positively and actually sinful, but are simply *destitute of holiness.* An infant is destitute of holiness! Very true. So he is. And so he is destitute of arithmetic and spelling. But this does not prove that he is ruined, nor that he will go to the pit. It certainly does not prove that he deserves to go to the pit, for a natural lack of the knowledge or the attainments for the purpose of acquiring which he is brought into this world as a school. As well might we complain of an oak for not bearing full-grown trees instead of little acorns.

The most recent and every way the most astonishing device that has been suggested by one professing to hold the old Orthodox doctrine, for the sake of abating its manifest inconsistency with the righteous method of government established by God, is that proposed by Dr. Edward Beecher, in his marvellously significant book entitled " The Conflict of Ages." He admits, he asserts, he strenuously and emphatically protests against, the conflicting relation which Orthodoxy presents to us between what God requires of us and the nature and opportunity which we have for meeting his demands. God calls us into being with a depraved nature, exposes us to the corrupting influences of a fallen world, and subjects us to the assaults of evil spirits, and then holds over us a law of holiness which we are incapacitated from obeying, while any falling short of it condemns us to an unending woe. No Unitarian pen has ever made a more painful or a more appalling statement of the irreconcilable conflict between Orthodox doctrine and the laws of honor and justice ascribed to the Divine government, than the pen of Dr. Beecher has written out with a most heroic sturdiness of candor. His conclusion is, that, according to the Orthodox doctrine, God has not dealt fairly with us, but is practising toward us a tyranny of the most ruthless sort. God has not given us a fair start, an unprejudiced, free, and hopeful trial for an immortal issue. If God has appointed our earthly existence as a probation for eternal life, he should have created us with an integrity of nature and a healthfulness of soul which would have excluded every sinful proclivity or bias; indeed, we might even claim that we should have been biassed in the direction of holiness. Orthodoxy says we are not born in this state of innocence. Dr. Beecher says the same, and he says it with an unquestioned loyalty to the creed in conformity with which he discharges his office of a Christian minister. How then does he reconcile the "Conflict" which he has so nobly and so faithfully delineated? Why thus. He says that we *once* had a fair and unprejudiced start in the unending career of existence; — not indeed here, in this world, but elsewhere. We were not *created* when we were born into this world. We had been created and had existed in another place, and in another state, as spirits, and had sinned, and fallen, and been condemned. God is giving us here a new trial under the light of the Gospel. Reserved in some of the gloomy caverns of sentenced guilt and hopeless despair in this universe, are imprisoned the rebel crew of angels who sided with Satan in the great rebellion in heaven. When an infant body is born into this world, God looses from the chains of that prison-house one of these condemned spirits, with the chance of being numbered among the elect as one whom the Gospel of Christ may redeem. Behold how wonderfully this solution of the problem converts the darkest imputation ever cast upon the righteous government of God into a most winning display of his grace, in offering a new opportunity to beings already condemned! Calvinism requires of beings created as sinners that they should live as angels. Dr. Beecher sees the countenance of an old fiend under the sweet features of infancy, and takes the fair mask as the symbol of a redemption which, by the grace of God through Jesus Christ, shall recall that victim of the pit to the communion of the saints above. Such is the latest modification of Calvinism.

We have thus given — at a tedious, though a necessary length — a statement of the controversy opened fifty years ago, and ever since kept open, between Unitarianism and Orthodoxy, on the Scripture doctrine of the Nature and the State of Man. We have stated the Calvinistic doctrine in the words of the old formula, which is even to this day nominally held in Orthodox churches and schools of theology. We have avowed the positive denial of that doctrine, and of every accepted modification of it, by Unitarianism, and have presented the general views which Unitarians in the lack of a dogma adopt as a substitute for that doctrine. There is a vast difference between falling *from* and falling *short of* holiness. We deny that there has ever been on this earth a *fall* of a single human being *from holiness*, and assert the fact that all human beings *fall short of holiness*. Finally, we have made a brief reference to some of the modifying and qualifying theories which Orthodox writers have invented to relieve the strain of their own doctrine.

And now comes a question which embraces two terms, as it concerns the present bearings and aspect of this controversy to the original parties to it: Is Unitarianism yielding its opinion, reconciling its difference, abating its opposition, and going over to Orthodoxy, on the ground covered by this doctrine? We answer positively, No! Unitarianism does not yield an inch. It holds its ground firmly and resolutely, and means to hold it. It was never better assured of its position than now.

Is Orthodoxy yielding its ground on this doctrine? Our readers shall answer that question for themselves.

In the mean while, how shall the two parties to an old strife regard their present relations to each other, in view of their fundamental variance concerning this one doctrine involved in the dark mystery of sin? Let us cease from all acrimony and strife, and try together to throw what light we can upon the problem. A truer philosophy of life and of man may help us. A better understanding of the Scriptures may aid us. But after all, Unitarians and Orthodox will be most likely to throw light on this sad mystery of sin, when with Christian hearts and hands they strive faithfully, in their own way, to rid themselves and the world of its malignant power.

UNITARIANISM AND ORTHODOXY

ON

GOD AND CHRIST.

UNITARIANISM AND ORTHODOXY

ON

GOD AND CHRIST.

The second of the three great, comprehensive doctrinal issues to which, as we have inferred, the controversy between the Unitarians and the Orthodox has been reduced, after an half-century of earnest and various discussion, now invites our attention. Our aim is to sum up its prominent points, to concentrate its scattered disputes, and to seek the results to which either party may have been brought, so far as they involve concession, or qualification, or a reassertion of the original grounds of the controversy.

The controversy centres upon this question, — Is Jesus Christ presented to us in the New Testament as possessing the underived honors of the Godhead, as claiming by himself and by his Apostles the supreme prerogative of Deity, and therefore as an object of worship and prayer, and of our ultimate religious dependence? Orthodoxy answers this question in the affirmative, Unitarianism answers it in the negative.

In strictness of construction, this one point of doctrinal difference might be regarded as constituting the sole issue which divides the two parties. For controversial discussion has made it evident that the doctrine of the Deity of Christ has been maintained chiefly on account of the relations which are presumed by Orthodoxy to exist between this and its two other fundamental doctrines,—the depravity of human nature, and a vicarious sacrifice made to God for the redemption of men. Orthodoxy affirms, that nothing short of an infinite expiation could suffice to redeem our race from the consequences of Adam's fall; therefore Christ, the Redeemer, must be God. Orthodoxy affirms, that only the Being against whom the offence of sin is committed could provide an adequate penalty for it, as it required an infinite penalty, and therefore the sacrifice made for it was the sacrifice of God. It is thus that the doctrine of the Deity of Christ has been supposed to be vital to the Christian system, as alone consistent with its other doctrines concerning God and man, and the relations of enmity and the proffered terms of reconciliation between them. The doctrine having been thus pronounced essential to the theological exposition of the Christian faith, it is made to carry with it, not only such weight of authority as it is claimed to derive from its positive announcement in the Scriptures, but also such strong incidental support and warrant as attach to it from its inter-relations with other so-called fundamental doctrines. The bias of error on any single point touching this matter may thus prejudice a fair view of either one or of all the great elements of the Christian scheme. It is the very decided, and, we must believe, the very fairly reached and the very intelligent conviction of Unitarians, that the supposed exigencies of the Orthodox system are to the full as constraining a reason with its disciples for holding to the doctrine of the Deity of Christ, as is the force of direct argument for it from the text of Scripture. If this bias be real, it must needs be very strong. Orthodoxy, therefore, proclaims that the Deity of Christ enters into the very substance of the Gospel, and Orthodoxy commits itself to that doctrine.

The doctrine of the Deity of Christ enters into the more general doctrine of the Trinity of persons in the Godhead, and is, indeed, the chief element in this doctrine, as the process necessary for developing the Deity of Christ requires a previous recognition of a possible complexity in the Godhead. The doctrine of the Trinity is, that in the one God are united three distinct, co-equal, and co-eternal persons, revealed to us by the titles of the Father, the Son, and the Holy Spirit. What an untold amount of thinking, reasoning, arguing, asserting, and denying has been spent upon this theme! When we regard it as a matter of mere speculation, in dealing with which words must for the most part stand in place of ideas, we may be impatient that in this short life of man, where his zeal and strength are all needed for great Christian duties, he should have bestowed so much of thought and interest upon a metaphysical abstraction. But when we regard the issue as one that has been raised to be decided by a most careful, thorough, intelligent, and reverential interpretation of the New Testament, we are the more reconciled to the spending of so much study upon it, because of the possible incidental benefits resulting to our Scriptural knowledge and culture. And yet once more, rising to a still higher view, when we look at the issue here raised as it bears directly or indirectly upon the whole doctrinal substance of revelation, our impatience yields, — we become more than reconciled to the discussion as it offers to guide us to its various and momentous relations to all Christian truth. We accept the subject, as one alike of speculative, Scriptural, and practical interest.

As we enter anew upon this ancient topic of acrimonious strife, of ardent controversy, and of perplexed debate, let it be with due preparation of thought and feeling. High abstractions, profound speculations, and themes of mystery are comprehended in this discussion, as well as the simple verities which have a solemn interest for the unlearned, who wish to believe as Christians. It is no subject for our presumption to deal with, nor for our dogmatism to decide. If we choose to concern ourselves with a question as to the mode of the Divine existence, or if we feel that an inquiry on this point seriously involves the clearness and the correctness of our doctrinal belief, we must remember that the subject is wholly unlike those which relate to our own characters and experience; so that our familiar methods and processes, and certainly our bold and impatient spirit of curious investigation, will no longer serve us. Men will interest themselves with questions about the origin of this globe, the date when human life began upon it, and the time appointed for its dissolution. Men will even discuss and argue the probabilities as to whether the other orbs of heaven, within our view, are occupied by beings in any respect like ourselves. Very slender are our grounds for the adoption of theories, and very meagre are our results after debating such questions. And yet, as these relate to matters of sense, to physical operations, to mathematical calculations, and fall within the province of exact science, we have certain resources for dealing with them with considerable satisfaction. We can hammer out from the earth's rocky breast some of her secrets; we can put to the test the question whether the fires of the sun are wasting; we can push forth the telescopic tube and dilate with our lenses the compass of the planetary orbs, and put the heavens well-nigh out of countenance by the boldness of our own gaze, as we pronounce upon what nutriment of fog, or flame, or stone, or ice, the inhabitants of those orbs must respectively subsist. But a question concerning the mode of the Divine existence is remote from all these, and all other similarly profound and vast questions. By searching we cannot find out God. We cannot hope that any of the incomprehensibilities which invest him will yield to our reasoning. We have never seen it affirmed, we are confident it never can be proved, that the effort of faith which is essential to a conception of God will be one whit relieved or facilitated by conceiving of him under the form of a Trinity. The vast and awful solemnity remains still to confound or to dazzle us. We find a warrant for intermeddling with this loftiest of all themes, —the existence of God,—in the fact that revelation addresses it to our faith through our reverent and intelligent thought. But all questions as to *the mode* of the Divine existence are voluntarily opened by us. These are not forbidden, and certainly, if one of the great purposes of revelation was to disclose to us the doctrine of the Trinity, and if the whole scheme of Christian truth centres upon that doctrine, it becomes as legitimate, indeed as importunate, a theme of thought and interest, and, under proper conditions, of controversy, as any that can engage our minds.

Let us understand, too, how the subject before us has come to enter into controversy. The most superficial reader of church history is made aware that the controversy, instead of being one of recent origin, has followed down the fortunes of our faith from a very early age. He learns, also, that the party differences and strifes which the controversy from its beginning excited, called together numerous general and local councils of Christian ministers, were brought before imperial tribunals, and disposed of, or at least taken cognizance of, by civil edicts. He discovers that the disputed terms of the controversy have been blazoned on the banners of contending armies, and have been authenticated, not only by the legitimate processes of Scripture criticism and fair argument, but by the ruder methods of fines, prisons, banishments, excommunications, and executions. The popular notion among the uninformed members of orthodox sects, favored often by the uncandid authorities on which the ignorant and prejudiced rely, is, that the plain doctrine of Scripture is Trinitarianism; that the Saviour and his Apostles taught this doctrine and founded their churches upon it; that the early Fathers and all other Christians unanimously believed it; that no question for long ages attached to it; that the whole Church down to quite a recent time agreed upon it; and that only a daring heretic here and there has ever doubted or assailed the doctrine. The Unitarian, on the other hand, is perfectly satisfied that the teaching of Scripture is in complete opposition to Trinitarianism; that violence must be done to the text in order to support it; that the Apostles never recognized, never even heard of it; that such of the Fathers as in their confused and inconsistent teachings give it more or less of their countenance, derived it from unscriptural sources, from previous philosophical fancies; that the doctrine from its first announcement was controverted, and that it is itself a heresy whose origin and whole way of strife are thoroughly known to us.

We select, out of a multitude of statements of the doctrine of the Trinity lying at our hand, that which is given in the Confession of Faith adopted by the New England churches in 1680, as follows: —

"There is but One only living and true God. In the Unity of the Godhead there be Three Persons, of one substance, power, and eternity: God the Father, God the Son, and God the Holy Ghost. Which doctrine of the Trinity is the foundation of all our communion with God, and comfortable dependence upon him."

We might exhaust all our space in giving a series of statements and definitions of this doctrine; and then we might occupy twice the number of pages in simply arranging the various modifications of conception and belief which have marked the chronological history, or the symbolical adoption, or the heretical aberrations from any one of the several orthodox formulas of this doctrine. A volume which should faithfully present the abundant materials of that nature for filling it, might well pass among us for a relic rescued from Babel. The doctrine of the Trinity is confessedly incomprehensible, and many readers of the controversies about it must feel a profound regret that it was not allowed from the first to be inexpressible likewise. Indeed, the question is a fair one, Has not the doctrine really proved itself to be inexpressible? It is this great variety of terms and forms of speech used for announcing the doctrine, and the failure of all of them to leave an intelligible idea in the mind, that first excites the anxious distrust of many persons to whom this doctrine is presented as "the foundation of all our communion with God." We find even Calvin objecting to the use of the word *persons* for defining the distinctions in the Godhead. He called the word *barbarous;* he regretted its use; he wished that some other phraseology might be substituted for announcing the doctrinal formula. The excellent Dr. Watts called the doctrine of "*three persons*" a "strange and perplexing notion." A great deal of ingenuity has been exercised by intelligent but bewildered theologians for devising a simpler, a more intelligible, a less self-contradictory, and a "more Scriptural" method for stating the doctrine. Evidently some of the best minds have been exercised upon it in vain. The unanimous decision of all competent teachers who hold and try to communicate the doctrine now is, that when the word *person* is used to express each of the Three in the One God, it does not have the same sense that is attached to it in any one or in all of the other uses of the word. A very worthy volunteer in the work of teaching a doctrine of which he could make no intelligible expression, after confounding his own thought, fairly gave over the more dignified and professional speech of his calling, and avowed that it was "necessary to believe in *Three Somewhats* as equally divine."

This is an amazing perplexity to be put at the very threshold of an entrance to the Christian doctrines. We cannot but feel a strong persuasion that, if all the bewildering and confounding speculations which have attached to this doctrine—and which, while they have embarrassed the reception of it in any intelligible form, have also established the supposed necessity of accepting it in some form — could be wholly set aside, Christians would come to the discussion of such a theory in a far more candid state of mind. They are now prepossessed and prejudiced on this subject. We cannot believe for one moment, that, if it were left to this age and the present resources of speculative conception in religious philosophy to fashion forth a dogmatic statement concerning the Divine nature, any such notion as Trinitarianism includes would find acceptance, even if it should find a suggestion or an advocate. All the attempts which are made to state the doctrine more intelligibly or more simply have resulted in such refined or sublimated metaphysics, that we almost forget the mathematical puzzle of the original formula, while we turn back to it as for a sort of relief.

There has been, however, one essential step of real progress secured in the discussion of this subject. Those who will turn over the voluminous records of the Trinitarian controversy, as conducted by English divines in the last century, will find it doubly and trebly perplexed beyond its own intrinsic difficulties, if that be possible, by a complicated and intricate network of definitions, schemes, and secondary issues. If any one should feel compelled to trace the course of opinion in all its windings and relations between the starting-point of doctrine as an accepted creed defined it, and the attempts of religious teachers to give it an exposition conformed to the utterances of their own individual views, he would have need to bury himself in heaps of antiquated books. As, for instance, after mastering Dr. Samuel Clarke's modification of the doctrinal Trinity, he would have to master Dr. Waterland's refutation of that modification, and this would be a specimen task of a work which would occupy a long life. But as this sort of rubbish has accumulated in masses in sight of which heart and flesh absolutely quail, it has come to be understood that henceforward no one is expected to meddle with it. He would be a high offender who should venture to open anew the specific issues of the modes and schemes which our fathers felt compelled to entertain. Our recent discussions have on this account been greatly simplified, and will become even yet more simple as they become wholly Scriptural.

The doctrine of the Trinity has indeed been so sublimated and refined, and so reduced in the rigidity of its old technical terms, that it may now be said to offer itself in some quite inoffensive and unobjectionable shapes to that large number of persons who feel bound to accept it in some shape, and yet are aware that in full mental honesty they can accept it only in the least dogmatic and most accommodated shape. Though for our own part we can connect no intelligible idea with such an assertion as Dr. Bushnell makes, for example, when he says that God has been "eternally *threeing* himself," we can recognize the fact that genius and fancy and irrepressible restlessness of mind are determined to festoon and array a dogma whose angular sharpness and whose barrenness of look would offend. If we could only find any occasion for believing a Trinity in the Godhead, in any form of the dogma, Archbishop Whately might largely help us to make the very little effort which is all that is left as essential. In some of the modern shapings of the doctrine, we confess that there is no reason for rejecting it which will weigh against the slightest good reason for receiving it. But that slightest reason for receiving it is the very thing which fails us: it is wholly lacking.

We have said that the chief reason for asserting the doctrine of the Trinity is that it may include or cover the doctrine of the Deity of Christ. Frankly, and with general consent, is this admission yielded by Orthodox writers. Professor Stuart says: "All difficulties in respect to the doctrine of the Trinity are essentially connected with proving or disproving the divinity [he means *the Deity*] of Christ." * "When this [the Deity of Christ] is admitted or rejected, no possible objection can be felt to admitting or rejecting the doctrine of the Trinity." † The plain inference from such statements evidently is, that the Deity of a *third* personality in the Godhead (the Holy Spirit) is affirmed and insisted upon, in order to secure and make good the Deity of a *second* personality in the Godhead. The Holy Spirit is admitted to the prerogative of a distinct *personality* in order to facilitate that distribution of the essence of the Godhead which will assign to Jesus Christ the rank of the Supreme. And this device is adopted, because into some of the texts which are needed inferentially to confirm the assumption that Christ is God, the Holy Spirit enters by equally distinct mention.

It is even so. There is no other reason for asserting the separate personality of the Holy Spirit, except as that will bear upon the claim for Christ of the underived and self-subsisting prerogative of Deity. The weakest point in all the arguments in support or defence of Trinitarianism, is that which attempts to prove from Scripture

---

* Letters to Dr. Channing, 3d edition, p. 45. † Ibid., p. 59.

the separate personality of the Holy Spirit. Yet weak as this point in such arguments always is, laboring at the very start, made essential by an indirect instead of a direct and independent necessity, and requiring a most tortuous and unsatisfactory dealing with the phraseology of Scripture, it is the very point on which Orthodox divines spend the least of their strength, as if conscious of their weakness. The personality of the Spirit is expected to come in by indulgent construction after the divisibility of the Godhead has been affirmed for the sake of sharing its attributes between Christ and the Father. So obvious is it to all minds not prejudiced by a dogma, that the term Holy Spirit, wherever it is used in the Bible, may always have its whole meaning recognized when it is regarded as expressing the agency or influence of God's spiritual operations. We might as well attempt to claim a distinct personality for the Wisdom of God, or the Power of God, or the Fear of God, or the Love of God, as to claim it for the Spirit of God. God is himself a SPIRIT; that is the very loftiest and fullest title by which the Saviour made him an object of our faith. All the agency of God is spiritual, though for convenience of distinction we generally withdraw that epithet from uses relating to God's agency in the physical world, and confine it to the methods of his operation on his intelligent creation. The advocate of Trinitarianism thinks that he visits upon us a perfectly overwhelming argument, when he gathers texts from the Bible to prove that Divine attributes of Creation, Omnipresence, Wisdom, Might, and operative energy are assigned to the Spirit. It would be strange if they were not so assigned. We are amazed that any one should offer these manifest inferences of simple truth, the conditions which constitute the great truth that "God is a Spirit," in proof of the astounding dogma that one third part of the Godhead is Spirit. God is himself a Spirit. Now if we distinguish the Spirit as a divided personality in the Godhead, what crowning attribute have we left for the Father? The device would seem to us puerile, if it did not appear monstrous, which would distinguish, not the agency, but the *nature* of God by a division, or a duplication, of his essence into God the Father as one person, and God the Spirit as another person. How can a reader of Scripture fail to recognize the fact that the Spirit of God is itself but one of many terms used for expressing the operating, penetrating, and sanctifying energy and influence of the Supreme Being? If Scripture, in deference to the straits of our limited power of intellectual conception, gives us several terms for defining the methods and the attributes of the One Supreme, shall we seize upon them, and, instead of using them for the purpose for which they are given, turn them back upon the Unity of the Godhead, to confound it with a plurality?

It is at this point, of course, that one who has been educated under this Trinitarian dogma, and is seeking to test its truth, or one who is brought into debate with a professed believer in it, will begin to raise the question whether the Scriptures teach, or the Christian scheme includes, any doctrine of a Trinity of co-equal and co-eternal Persons in the One God. Though the doctrine is advanced chiefly as a help towards the proof of another doctrine of the Deity of Christ, we object to the doctrine, in the first place, on grounds wholly distinct from its relation to that article of the Trinitarian faith. We object, in general, to the doctrine of the Trinity, that it is an invention of the human mind, for which the Scriptures afford no warrant; and that its prominent effect is to introduce into the system of truths taught in the Scriptures an extraneous, artificial, and perplexing dogma, wholly inconsistent with, utterly unlike to, the acknowledged and accepted doctrines of Scripture. We do not object, as is often charged upon us, that the doctrine involves a mystery. On the contrary, we object that the doctrine when urged upon us as a mystery misuses and perverts the word *mystery*, and avails itself of the acknowledged and allowed credibility of what the word *mystery* properly signifies, to propose to us something quite unlike a mystery; namely, a statement that is absurd, so far as it is intelligible, and that is inconsistent in the very terms which it brings together for making its proposition. We accept all such religious truths as can fairly be covered by the word *mystery*. We live religiously upon such truths; they are the nutriment of our spirits,—of infinitely larger account to us than anything we can learn or understand. We are made familiar, by every moment's exercise of close thought, with the necessity of accepting mysteries, and we know very well what a sensation and sentiment they send down into the innermost chambers of our being. But we are conscious of feeling quite a different sensation and sentiment when this doctrine of the Trinity is proposed to us under the covert of a mystery. Quite another quality in it than that of its mysterious character at once suggests itself to us. Its utter absurdity, its attempt to say something which it fails to say *intelligibly*, simply because it cannot say it *truly*, is the first painful consciousness attaching to the doctrine. If the doctrine be true, then it is the only doctrine of the Gospel which causes the same sort of puzzling, confounding, bewildering effect on the mind that seeks to entertain it. It sets us into the frame into which we fall when any one proposes to us an enigma, or a conundrum. It lays at the very threshold of the Christian faith an obstacle at which we stumble. It requires of us a summoning of resources, or a concession, a yielding up, of our natural desire for intelligent apprehension, as if to be addressed by some profound truth, when in fact we are only bewildered. The state of mind into which we should be driven by an attempt to accept the doctrine of the Trinity as fundamental to the Gospel, would be of no service to us in dealing with the real doctrines of the Gospel. The doctrine is not homogeneous with the contents of revelation; it is unevangelical and anti-evangelical in all its characteristic elements. Just where we need the clearest exercise of our thoughts, and wish to accommodate our ideas to our theme, and to engage the orderly action of all our faculties, we are beclouded and staggered, and thrown into a maze. Has not our whole theology been made to suffer, by thus taking its start from a metaphysical subtilty which confuses the mind, instead of from one august truth which lifts and solemnizes the spirit?

How much of sublime and penetrating power did the Hebrew faith carry with it in the announcement, "Hear, O Israel, the Lord thy God is One Lord!" Would we as Christians sacrifice anything of this majestic utterance by substituting for it, "Hear, O Christian, the Lord thy God is one God in a Trinity of Persons"? The Trinitarian, however, assures us that his belief of a triplicate personality in the Godhead does not impair his belief in the Divine Unity. How inoperative then must be his Trinitarian belief, unless, as is probably the case, the idea which he has in his mind fails to find expression in any phraseology that can give a verbal announcement of the doctrine of the Trinity. The purest attraction, the most spiritual warrant of revealed religion, is the oneness of God. It is by that distinction that revealed religion stands loftily and simply elevated above all earth-born religions. Yet this high distinction is at once impaired, and in some measure neutralized, by a doctrine of tri-personality in unity. Long use has accustomed us to the assertion of this doctrine in words, but none the less is it chargeable with an influence prejudicial to the best exercise of our faculties upon the great truths of Gospel revelation. A question for which this age is fully ready, instructed as it has been by so much experience in the past, is this, and it is a question which earnestly addresses itself to earnest persons in all communions: — Cannot full justice be done to the Christian scheme, and to the orderly connection of every one of its dependent truths, without any use of this doctrine of the Trinity? Do we need it? Can we not dispense with it, and yet be Christian believers?

Having thus begun the statement of our objections to this scholastic doctrine of the Trinity, by impugning it as unintelligible and confounding, not enlightening or solemnizing, we are led on through a series of valid and strengthening reasons, which amount, in our own mind, to an unanswerable refutation of it.

Though Christians have insisted upon the fundamental character of this doctrine, they find it utterly impossible to state it in the language of Scripture. A human formula is necessarily the vehicle for its expression. Though the Scriptures, as we often affirm, have a peculiar directness and simplicity of phrase, and excel all other forms of literature in the conciseness and vigor with which they express truths and precepts, they nevertheless fail to furnish one single sentence which can be used in a creed to announce the Trinity. Yes, this so-called primary and all-essential article of the Christian faith, — "the foundation of all our communion with God," — cannot be uttered in any Divine oracle, but must look to uninspired men for an expression. No announcement of it can be quoted from the lips of prophet or apostle, or from Him who spake as never man spake. A piecemeal selection of the elements which are to be wrought up into the doctrine must be gathered from isolated sentences and phrases of the Bible, and even then one of the most familiar and well-defined words of our language — the word *person*, which is already appropriated past changing to mark the separate individuality of one complete being — must be perverted to a wholly new use, while they who thus pervert it profess to dislike it, and aver that it wholly fails to convey the idea that is in their minds. Are they sure that there is any real, well-developed idea in their minds, seeing that they cannot express it without perverting language, and even then are forced to confess that they fail to express it. Are they sure, too, that the idea which they wish to express is one received from the Scriptures? Does Scripture bid us believe, as a fundamental, a doctrine which Scripture itself does not announce in its own "form of sound words"?

Again, a fundamental doctrine ought to be emphatically announced and constantly reiterated. Now all candid persons must admit that no stress, no prominence, no directness or earnestness of statement, is made of this doctrine in the Scriptures corresponding to the emphatic and pre-eminent place assigned to it in all Orthodox creeds. Considering too with what strenuous positiveness and reiteration the Unity of God is there asserted, ought there not to have been a balancing of this assertion by as emphatic a proclamation of the Trinity? This triplicity of constitution of the Godhead was certainly a new doctrine to the world. It was new to the Jews. It demanded, therefore, at least one announcement from each Apostle, and each Evangelist, in terms as clear and strong as the resources and capacities of human language will admit. What is most remarkable under this head of objection is the fact, that, on the occasions upon which we should have looked for the most distinct statement of the doctrine, it was held back. The baptismal formula, which, unlike as it is to the formula of the creed, does gather together the three component elements of the Trinity, stops far short of the assertion that three personalities are mentioned, — and that such three make up the one God of the Gospel. The most natural and unprejudiced construction of that baptismal formula views it as announcing a Gospel message from God the Father, through Christ his beloved Son, attested by spiritual evidences from God's Holy Spirit. What an opportunity was there here for the statement — what an imperative demand was there for the statement, if fundamentally true, and of paramount importance — of the full doctrine of the Trinity! But it is not here! After the crucifixion, the resurrection, and the ascension of Jesus, after the miraculous illumination of the Apostles on the Feast of Pentecost, one signal event occurred. The religion which, with its author, the Jewish rulers supposed had been committed to a hopeless tomb, was resuscitated. Instead of having heard the last of it, the world was now to begin to listen to a new and unceasing proclamation of it. The opportunity for making its first re-announcement came to Peter after an astounding manifestation of Divine power. And what an opportunity there was, what a pressing and emergent necessity and demand there was, for proclaiming the doctrine which Christians now make fundamental in their creed! We should look and listen to hear Peter announcing to the Jewish rulers that in the person of Jesus Christ they had rejected and condemned one who shared the underived attributes of their own Jehovah. But no! What says he? This: — "Ye men of Israel, hear these words: Jesus of Nazareth, a man approved of God among you by miracles and wonders and signs, which God did by him in the midst of you, as ye yourselves also know; him, being delivered by the determinate counsel and foreknowledge of God, ye have taken, and by wicked hands have crucified and slain: whom God hath raised up." (Acts ii. 22 – 24.) And on how many other occasions through Judæa, Asia Minor, and at Rome, on the first promulgation of our faith, was it incumbent on its preachers to have put foremost its foundation doctrine! But if the Trinity be such a doctrine, they did not make one single statement of it which will serve the use of the creed. And now what can be offered in frankness, and in the thorough simplicity and ingenuousness of true candor, to meet the force of this objection?

Another fact most significant of the unscriptural character of the doctrine of the Trinity is, that the texts which are quoted to support it are peculiarly embarrassed with doubts and questions as to authenticity, exactness of rendering, and signification. The three prominent proof-texts most likely to be first adduced, and which promise at first sight to be most available, are the least reliable. Of these three favorite passages with Trinitarians, on which so much scholarship and ingenious reasoning and pleading have been expended, the foremost one is that in 1 John v. 7. This text comes nearest of any in the Bible to a statement of the Trinitarian formula, though still falling short of the statement by all the distance of the difference between Three *agreeing in* One, and Three *being* One. Yet this text is now discredited as wholly without authority, as a corruption, an interpolation, foisted into the record. Every Christian scholar, of whatever denomination, competent to pass an instructed opinion on the matter, admits that St. John did not write that sentence, and that the words were most unwarrantably introduced into a manuscript written some centuries after the Apostolic age, the crowning proof of the fact being that no one of the Fathers quotes the text. Now let us at least have the benefit of this allowance, — *that the only sentence which is acknowledged to be spurious in the New Testament as we read it, was introduced and is retained for the sake of its supposed announcement and support of the doctrine of the Trinity.* That text is to us a type of the unscriptural origin and the unscriptural character of the doctrine.

The second of these favorite Trinitarian proof-texts is 1 Timothy iii. 16: "Great is the mystery of godliness: God was manifest in the flesh," &c. As the passage stands, it neither presents the slightest embarrassment to the Unitarian, nor affords the slightest support to Trinitarianism. But with the gloss and the forced construction put upon the passage, the word *mystery* is interpreted as signifying, not a disclosure of something before concealed or unknown, but as implying an announcement of an occult and impenetrable secret; and the word *godliness*, which means simply *piety*, is regarded as designating the *Godhead*, or the mode of the Divine Existence. Our readers are probably for the most part well informed as to the question of scholarly criticism opened on the text, whether a very ancient Greek manuscript has the character *O* or *Θ*, and whether, as a consequence, we should read in the English, "*Which* was manifest in the flesh," or "*God* was manifest in the flesh." As the Unitarian may claim, on grounds of criticism, that the passage should read, "Great is that marvel of piety which was manifested in the flesh," so also the Unitarian may consent to withdraw all such criticism from the text, and read it as others read it, while he asks, with some considerable earnestness, what shadow of argument can be drawn from it in support of the Trinity. Are Unitarians to be forbidden to believe that "God was manifested in the flesh," or that Christ was a marvellous exhibition of piety?*

* Professor Stuart, in the Biblical Repository, 1832, p. 79, says: "I cannot feel that the contest on the subject of the reading can profit one side so much, or harm the other so much, as disputants respecting the doctrine of the Trinity have supposed. Whoever attentively studies John xvii. 20-26, 1 John i. 3, ii. 5, iv. 15, 16, and other passages of the like tenor, will see that 'God might be manifest' in the person of Christ, without the necessary implication of the proper divinity [Deity] of the Saviour; at least, that the phraseology

11 *

The third of these favorite Trinitarian proof-texts is Acts xx. 28: "Feed the Church of God, which he hath purchased with his own blood." The question raised by variations in manuscripts, and other sources of critical information, is whether we should read "the Church of God" or "the Church of the Lord." Our aim here is not to present the merits on either side of the results which criticism reaches on these texts, but simply to show that the passages which Trinitarians would be most likely to quote are the very ones which are most embarrassed or dubious in their authority or their signification. Professor Samuel Davidson, an Orthodox critic whose conclusions are among the most recent ones which have been offered to scholars, after a most candid arbitration between the disputed words in the Greek which give the two renderings, decides strongly in favor of "the Church of the Lord."*

But what a dreary and repelling task it is to go over the New Testament, or the whole Bible, to hunt out words, phrases, and sentences that may constructively or inferentially be turned to the support of a doctrine which ought to lie patent on the page. It would seem as if Trinitarians had reconciled themselves to the condition, that the only consistent way in which Scripture could convey to us such an enigmatical and puzzling doctrine, was by a method which should engage the most tortuous, adroit, and mazy ingenuity of the human faculties in seeking for results that must partake of the character of the process for reaching them. Roman Catholic critics acknowledge manfully, as did Dr. New-

---

of Scripture does admit of other constructions besides this; and other ones, moreover, which are not forced."

* Treatise on Biblical Criticism, Vol. II. pp. 441-448. We may add, that Dr. Davidson, though a Trinitarian, is as decided in his rejection of 1 John v. 7, as "spurious," and in his accordance with the critical judgment which reads 1 Tim. iii. 16, "Great is that mystery of godliness *which* was manifested in the flesh," &c.

man while he was yet an Oxford divine, that the Trinity is not a Bible doctrine, but a Church doctrine, and that our knowledge and recognition of it and its authority rest for us on the same basis as does the substitution of the Christian Sunday for the Jewish Sabbath. And if the method by which Trinitarians hunt through the Bible for intimations and implications of the doctrine of the Trinity be a repulsive one, not the less uninviting is the task of answering all such arguments by a similar process. Since the doctrine gained currency in the world, and found a positive statement in many creeds, the Scriptures have been translated into the vernacular languages of Christendom under the bias of a Trinitarian belief. The present Archbishop of Canterbury, who ought to be the highest of human authorities, speaks, in his discourse on Apostolic Preaching, of "the many passages of Scripture which have suffered by the general bias of the age in which our translation was made," — the bias of Calvinism. Those who have argued for the Trinity, having started with a bias, helped by their ingenuity and guided by their fancy, have, with a vast deal of pains, gone through the whole Bible, trying to see how many intimations of this doctrine they could cull out. There has been an amazing amount of trifling exercised in this direction. Some who have ridiculed or censured the follies of Rabbinical and allegorical interpretation, or the puerilities of the Cabala, have rivalled these follies in their attempts to find hints of the Trinity in sentences whose writers evidently never dreamed of the doctrine. Thus the use of the Hebrew plural in the word (Elohim) for God, and the use of the plural pronoun when "God said, Let *us* make man in our own image," modes of speech used to denote majesty or sovereignty, are urged in proof of a companionship in the Deity. Sentences are quoted asserting that no man hath seen or can see God, and are compared with other sentences which speak of manifestations of God to the patriarchs and others; and the conclusion is drawn, that the Jehovah of the Old Testament was the revealing Son, not the Father. Yet even then the chain of intended proofs breaks at one link, while another link is in the welding; for if a manifestation of one person in the Trinity was impossible, how could there be a manifestation of another person in it? Again, the assertion is quoted as from God, that he "will not give his glory to another," and then an argument is raised to show that the honors of God are assigned to Christ; while the inference follows that Christ is God.

We have no heart for going through this unnatural, this offensive task of tracing the windings of this textual ingenuity, or of answering its characteristic results. The process has no natural limitations or rules, because it has no reasonable basis, no first grounds. It is all a forced work, and fancy will make more or less of it according as it is pursued by those who have more or less of fancy,—fancy, however, of a very inferior sort.

For we have to object once more, that the Scriptures bear a positive testimony against this doctrine of the Trinity, by insisting upon the absolute Unity of God. Trinitarians think that they recognize the force of these reiterated and emphatic assertions of Scripture by afterwards gathering up into one God those whom they have made three divine persons. But as the analysis was forced, the synthesis must be strained. As the ingenuity of the human mind could alone devise the triplicate distinction, the same ingenuity has to nullify its own work to construct the Unity. Trinitarians do indeed assure us that there is no incongruity, nothing inconceivable, in the essential substance of their doctrinal statement. But we must be judges as to that matter, certainly so far as our own minds are concerned. Our minds assure us that violence must be done to the most explicit statements of every page of Scripture, before it can be made to yield to us the doctrine of the Trinity.

We object, finally, to this doctrine, that we know its origin to have been, not in the Scriptures, but outside of them. It was the Greek Philosophy of Alexandria, and not the Hebrew or Christian Theology of Jerusalem, that gave birth to this doctrine. We can trace its fount, its spring, its incomings. There is no historical fact more fully supported than that of the addiction of the Church Fathers to the study of the Greek Philosophy; they loved it, they fondly pursued it, they were infected by it, their speculations were influenced by it, their Christian faith received intermixture from it. Dr. Cæsar Morgan acknowledges this fact most candidly, though he pursues a critical examination of all the passages in Plato which are thought to contain references to an ante-Christian Trinity, for the sake of proving that the Fathers did not get the doctrine from the philosopher. But the argument which he assails does not yield to his assault upon it. We might as well dispute whether an ancient tragedy, whose catastrophe turns on Fate, were of Grecian or Jewish origin, as debate the issue whether a theosophical fiction concerning the Godhead, which involves the most acute subtilty of philosophy, sprang from the Abrahamic faith or from Hellenic Gnosticism. The history of the doctrine of the Trinity makes to us an evident display of a development, an amplification and steady augmentation, from a germ which was forced into an artificial growth. It was an evolved doctrine which was constantly seeking to define itself, which was never at rest, and which never has been at rest under any of the definitions which it has found for itself. A comparison of the three old creeds, the so-called Apostles', the Nicene, and the Athanasian, with a reference to their dates, will unmistakably reveal of what processes and elements the doctrine of the Trinity is the product.

We return now to that great doctrine of controverted theology, the Deity of Christ, to maintain which, as we have said, the doctrine of a Trinity of Persons in the Unity of the Godhead is so strenuously asserted in Orthodox creeds. Very many Trinitarians have candidly acknowledged the force of one or all of the objections which have just been hinted at. They allow that the Trinitarian scheme is burdened with the most serious perplexities to the understanding, that it is not simply a mystery, like some of the other tenets of their faith, but a confounding and puzzling enigma, teasing their minds, rather than yielding them an instructive idea,—straining their comprehension instead of enlightening it. And yet those who most candidly make this allowance insist, with their fellow-believers, upon the vital truth and importance of the doctrine of the Trinity, as involving the essential doctrine of the Deity of Christ. This latter doctrine then presents itself to us as really the primary rudiment of a scheme of which, in other aspects, it claims to be only one of the conditions and consequences. A Trinity is insisted upon in order that it may include the Deity of Christ, and then the Deity of Christ is affirmed as an element of the Trinity. We do not err in saying that the doctrine now before us is charged with the double obligation of sustaining its own truth, and also that of the doctrine of the Trinity, by the positive authority of the Scriptures. Orthodoxy has a dogma on this point, but Unitarianism has no dogma, except in the quality of denying a dogma. Let the issue be fairly understood. The question is not whether the Scriptures do or do not assign to Jesus Christ an exalted and mysterious nature and range of being, which lift him above the sphere of humanity. The question is not whether from what is revealed of the Saviour we can fashion a full and satisfactory theory, which will make him to us a perfectly intelligible and well-defined being, holding a fixed place on the scale between man and God. But the question is this: Do all the offices and functions and honors assigned to Jesus Christ exhibit him as undistinguishable from God in time and essence and underived existence, and in self-centred, inherent qualities? Is he, or is he not, presented to us as a fractional part of the Godhead, — the object, not the medium, of prayer, — the source, not the agent, of redemption, — the substitute, not the representative, of Jehovah, — as the occupant of heaven's high throne, not as seated "by the right hand" of the Supreme? We are not to be driven, as to a sole alternative, to the affirming that Christ was a man, because he was not God, nor to the holding ourselves bound to show what he was less than God, nor yet to the assigning him a sphere of his own distinct at every point from that of Deity, because we say that the New Testament presents him as receiving everything from the Father. What that everything *includes*, it would be presumptuous in us to define; but it is not presumptuous in us to say that it *excludes* underived prerogatives. There is indeed large room for choice amid the range of speculative opinions which Unitarianism has covered on this point, in seeking to find a substitute for the Trinitarian opinion. The office which we have assigned to ourselves in this review of the substantial issues of a protracted controversy, does not require an elaborate and exhaustive statement of Unitarian views on this point. We have but to present the antagonistic positions of the parties in this controversy.

If there are two connected truths taught with emphatic and reiterated distinctness in the New Testament, — or rather we should say, if there are two such truths taken for granted there, — they are that of the sole and simple unity of God the Father, and that of the derived and dependent relation to him of Jesus Christ. In order to secure distinctness and clearness of thought upon Scripture doctrine, we must subordinate the Son to the Father, and having done this to take our first step in Christian faith, we cannot complete our progress in that faith by confounding the Son with the Father. We must distinguish between that being who appeared in Judæa as a messenger from God, and the God whose messenger he was. The office of Christ in warming and clothing and making welcome to us what otherwise would have been a cold and naked and distant doctrine of Deism, appears to us exceedingly unlike what it is represented to have been by the excellent Dr. Arnold. Often, and most approvingly, triumphantly indeed, has the following remark of his been quoted: —

> "While I am most ready to allow the provoking and most ill-judged language in which the truth as I hold it to be respecting God has been expressed by Trinitarians, so, on the other hand, I am inclined to think that Unitarians have deceived themselves by fancying that they could understand the notion of one God any better than that of God in Christ; whereas it seems to me, that it is only of God in Christ that I can in my present state of being conceive anything at all. To know God the Father, that is, God as he is in himself, in his to us incomprehensible essence, seems the great and most blessed promise reserved for us when this mortal shall have put on immortality." *

There is a singular confusion of thought and inconsistency of sentiment in these sentences, which glance off from a beautiful truth into a foggy fancy. Christ comes to facilitate our conceptions of God, to be the medium for our vision, our confidence, and our knowledge of God, to make clearer and stronger to us the sublime truth of Deity; and Christ effects this, Dr. Arnold implies, by substituting himself for the Being whom he represents, reveals, and brings nearer to us! If from our own point of view we can discern any change which

* Letter to William Smith, Esq., March 9, 1833, in Life by Stanley.

in process of years will be sure to manifest itself in the technics of theology, it is this, — that theologians who have been so long trying to accommodate this doctrine of some sort of a Trinity to their belief, will surrender it altogether at the very point at which they have felt bound to accept it; namely, that point at which a recognition of the doctrine of the Trinity has been thought essential to the defence of the Deity of Christ.

Unitarianism is committed to this fundamental position, that, however exalted, however mysterious, however undefined by limitations in a divine or a human direction, may be the nature and the rank of Jesus Christ, he is not presented to us in the Gospel as claiming the underived prerogatives of Deity; nor, consequently, as an object of our homage or prayer. All those reiterated commonplaces of reproach cast upon us, — of denying the Lord that bought us, — of defrauding him of his due honor, — of relying for salvation on a created being, — are based upon assumptions which suppose us to yield in one form what we object to under another form of doctrine. It is a gross perversion of the Apostle's language to say that he meant, by a denial of the Lord, a denial of him as our God: we do not defraud Jesus of his due honor, when we honor him for what he is, precisely as we honor God for what He is; and if we rely on the being "whom God has set forth to be our Prince and Saviour," we feel that the reliance is worthy of our trust. We certainly cannot be said to withhold the honor due to Christ, if, persuaded as we are that he always, and in the strongest terms of definite precept, claims our supreme homage for his Father and our Father, we restrict the tribute paid to himself within the limitations of religious awe. We do not understand the object of the Gospel to be to give us an idea of a complexity of personality in the Godhead, but to exalt, refine, and render practically effective the old reverence associated with the unchangeable Jehovah. Christ, we think, came into the world to show us the Father, not to divide our homage with the Father. He came to lead us to God, not to draw us to himself as our God. He continually, and with much variety of language, refers us to One above himself, without whom he could do nothing, the Source of all his powers and gifts, the Being before whom he was himself to bring and lay down the tokens of his fulfilled commission. He forbids all homage or supplication addressed to himself, and enjoins that such exercises be offered to God.

Unitarians, therefore, are concerned to hold and to vindicate the sole unity, the undivided sovereignty, of God. If any spiritual penalty is to be visited upon us here or hereafter for our opinion or our teaching on this point, we must submit to bear it. We do and shall plead, however, that some one emphatic sentence — one at least — ought to have been recorded from the Saviour in assertion of his underived Deity, equal in the positiveness of its statement to that of a hundred sentences in which he affirms his subordination to God.

If the proportions and the completeness of a view, however summary, did not require it, we would most gladly omit all reference to that very unwelcome work of following the argument for the Deity of Christ into those ambushes of sentences, half-sentences, and phrases called texts, — proof-texts, — in which it is thought to hide. We can urge ourselves only to the very briefest recognition of this element in the controversy. The processes for constructing and for answering what is called argument on this point, are precisely like those already referred to in connection with a plea for or against the doctrine of the Trinity. A conception which has originated outside of the Scriptures, from the exigencies of speculation and theorizing, is ingeniously carried into a textual examination of the Scriptures, and is made to claim support from them by pleas which would not be considered valid in the interpretation of any other documents. Happily, however, long and free discussion has simplified the terms of this questionable method. The marvellous discovery has been made by a most careful and candid student of the works of Christian divines, that each single text and each single process of reasoning by which Trinitarianism has sought to prove its Scriptural authority, has been surrendered as wholly unavailable for that purpose by a series of writers of highest eminence and scholarship in various Trinitarian communions.* Yet more remarkable, too, is the fact, that in the very closest proximity to the sentences or the half-sentences which are claimed as intimating, darkly or clearly, the Deity of Christ, are found other sentences of a most explicit character which are in direct opposition to such an inference.

The first sentences of John's Gospel are quoted triumphantly by Trinitarians, with this brief comment: Christ is the Word; the Word is said to be God; therefore Christ is God. Now suppose in those sentences we substitute, not only *Christ* in place of the *Word*, but also a Trinitarian equivalent for God. That equivalent must be either the term *Father*, or the term *Trinity*. We will try both of them, thus: "In the beginning was Christ, and Christ was with the Father, and Christ was the Father." That will not do. "In the beginning was Christ, and Christ was with the Trinity, and Christ was the Trinity." Neither will that do.

We are reminded that Jesus enjoined "that all men should honor the Son, even as they honor the Father." (John v. 23.) But do the words "*even as*," when so used, imply identity of being in two who are to be honored, or that an identical regard is required for each?

---

* See "Concessions of Trinitarians," &c., by John Wilson.

Can we not honor the Son for what he is, even as we honor the Father for what He is? Is it an unusual thing for a principal in sending a deputy on an embassy to ask for his representative a regard conformed to what would be paid to himself? For Jesus himself adds, "He that honoreth not the Son, honoreth not the Father which hath sent him," — certainly recognizing his own dependence.

We are reminded that Thomas, on recognizing his Master by his wounds, exclaims, "My Lord, and my God!" (John xx. 28,) and the Trinitarian insists that he applied both terms to the Saviour. But must Thomas be precluded from the possibility of having both Christ and God in his mind in that moment of surprise and earnest outbursting of emotion? Could he not apostrophize the Deity as we ourselves do under excitement on far lesser occasions?

We are reminded that the martyr Stephen, rapt in a vision of glory at his death, "saw Jesus standing on the right hand of God." (Acts vii. 55.) He saw *two* beings then. But our translators have introduced into a subsequent verse the word *God*, which is not in the original, thus: "And they stoned Stephen, calling upon *God*, and saying, Lord Jesus," instead of "calling out and saying, Lord Jesus," &c. (verse 59.)

We are reminded that Jesus says, "I and my Father are one." (John x. 30.) But does he not twice pray that his disciples may be in the same unity which exists between him and his Father? "That they may be one, as we are." (John xvii. 11.) "That they all may be one: as thou, Father, art in me, and I in thee, that they also may be one in us." (verse 21.)

We are reminded of Paul's assertion, that "all things are put under Christ." (1 Cor. xv. 27.) But does not the Apostle add, as if to guard against all possibility of misconception, — "It is manifest that He is excepted who did put all things under him; and when all things shall be subdued unto him, then shall the Son also himself be subject unto Him that put all things under him, that God may be all in all"?

We are reminded that the same Apostle says of Christ (Coloss. i. 16), whom he has just called "the first-born of every creature": "For by him were all things created that are in heaven, and that are in earth," &c. But when the Apostle proceeds to add, "For it pleased the Father that in him should all fulness dwell," (verse 19,) he leaves us to infer that all things were created and disposed *with reference* to Christ: "All things were created by him and for him."

We are reminded that the writer of the Epistle to the Hebrews quotes a Psalm as addressing the Son, thus: "Thy throne, O God, is for ever and ever!" (i. 8.) But saying nothing of the sufficient reasons for reading the passage, "God is thy throne for ever and ever," what are we to do with the next verse, which says: "Thou hast loved righteousness, and hated iniquity; therefore God, even thy God, hath anointed thee with the oil of gladness above thy fellows"?

But even this hopeless method of attempting to deduce from scattered sentences or half-sentences the proof of a doctrine which is positively precluded by contiguous sentences of the plainest import, — even this task must be pursued under the pressure of a necessity for proving that Christ, himself one in the Trinity of the Godhead, united in his own person a divine nature and a human nature. If that dogma did not take its start in a complete renunciation of the natural demand that an intelligible idea should be connected with every positive assertion, the dogma would have to yield itself at a very early stage of the process for pursuing it through the New Testament. Now an Apostle tells us, that we ourselves are "partakers of the divine nature"; but we interpret the words as teaching us that this gift of God in us distinguishes us from brutes and makes us *men,*— not men *and God;* still less does it make us partakers in the *underived prerogative of Deity,*—divine in our own right. We institute no comparison between the measurements of the divine gift in us, and that in Christ, for we believe there is no room for such a comparison, as Christ had the spirit of God without measure. But a gift, however unlimited in its measurement, does not change the receiver into the giver, nor transfer the original prerogative of self-centring fulness of essence. The more such a gift imparts, the more does it strengthen the difference between its source and its receiver as such, and the closer does it make the dependence of its object upon its original. This fiction of a double nature in Christ does not cover the phenomena for the explanation of which theologians have recourse to it. Jesus says of his highest gifts and powers, those which in him are most exalting and most divine, that he received them from the Being who also gave him a body for the manifestation of them. We might possibly conceive of Deity under a form of flesh, and listen to the speech of the tongue which should refer its wisdom to the indwelling God. But what if the indwelling Spirit refers us to the Source of which it is a ray? The qualities in Christ which lift him nearest to the Supreme are the very ones to which he most emphatically assigns the proof of his dependence upon God. All power in heaven and on earth is his; but not self-possessed,—for he says it was *given* to him. He had power to lay down his life, and he had power to take it again, and that, too, he had "*received* from the Father." When a believer in the double nature of Christ—that is, as defined by the popular theology—undertakes to go through the New Testament, and assign his words and deeds respectively to his Deity or his humanity, he will find that he gathers a reserved list of qualities and elements of a doubtful reference. As these present themselves, the inquirer is forced to ask, Did Christ say this as God or as man? Often will such a process make it appear that what Christ is represented as saying or doing in his human nature is above the sphere of humanity, and that what is affirmed of him in his divine nature is below the sphere of Deity.

And what becomes of the individuality, the personality of Christ, the consistency of his character, and the identity of his consciousness, when in the sacred drama of his Gospel manifestation he is represented as performing in two parts, and without change of fleshly garb or tone or speech lays aside now his Deity and now his humanity in alternate moments and in successive sentences of his discourse? His prayers must be construed as soliloquies: his deeds of power must be referred to himself, and his professions of dependence to one element of that self, speaking of another element in the same self. The incongruity, the incoherence, which the Orthodox doctrine of two natures in Christ either puts into or draws from the Scriptures, is not the least of the confounding conditions of the theory. When an individual speaks of himself to others, they understand him as speaking of all that is embraced under his seeming and his real individuality. Unless he has announced himself as representing two characters, and as free to pass from the one impersonation into the other without giving warning of the transition, his two characters will be regarded as making up one character, and some deeds and utterances which would have been intelligible if assigned to either of his impersonations, become inexplicable if referred to his composite character. Only through the help of an illustration — for which, however, we need not apologize, as the candid will recognize the simple intent of a parallelism at only one point — can we express the real embarrassment which we meet in attempting to deal with the theory of a double nature in Christ. Let it be allowed us, then, to conceive of a man who is concerned in business under two relations,—first as an individual, and second as a member of a firm of three partners. Under each of these relations he receives and writes letters, meets at his two offices those with whom he has dealings, and speaks and acts under the exigencies of his double mercantile connections. As a member of the firm he has visited its place of business, consulted its books, and read letters which have made known to him certain facts of a very serious import and interest to others. He goes to his place for transacting the business which he does on his private account. While there, a friend, who is deeply concerned in the very matters of which he has just come to the knowledge, enters and asks for information about them, addressing him as an individual possessing one mind, one consciousness. He replies that he knows nothing about the matter, keeping in reserve, however, the explanation which he makes to himself, that he means that his private letters are silent on the subject. Does he deal fairly with his questioner, especially if that questioner has appealed to him on the very ground of his well-known extended and various relations to the business affairs of the world, and perhaps on the day previous has heard him speak in that character? Precisely this question would be continually presenting itself to us in embarrassing and painful shapes if we accepted the theory of a double nature in Christ, under which, when questioned as an individual on the ground of all he ever claimed to know and to be, he replied according to his choice of characters for the moment, by a claim founded on his Deity, or a profession of limited knowledge or ignorance justified by his humanity. The Jews understood that the same individuality of being addressed them in the words, "I can of mine own self do nothing," as in the words, "I will raise him up at the last day." Not the least intimation does the Saviour appear to have given to his disciples in their privacy, that the mystery which invested him was to be solved by distributing his words and deeds, his claims of unlimited power, and his acknowledgments of dependence upon one above him, to two natures united in him. If he had two natures he must have borne two characters, and his discourses and actions must be referred respectively to the one or the other, so far as is possible. But when ingenuity has exhausted itself in this task, it will still have to account for phenomena attendant upon the Saviour which are referable neither to a Self-Existent and Infinite God, nor to any manifestation ever yet made of human nature. We reject this theological figment of a double nature, as a pure invention of human brains, a Gnostic conceit, unwarranted by the record, and unavailable for the solution of the mystery which invests the Messiah. The Gospel is not chargeable with it.

But after Unitarians have formed and avowed a most positive and unqualified conviction, as the characteristic distinction of their creed, that Jesus Christ is not presented to us in the Scriptures as claiming the underived prerogatives of Deity, nor as the object of our worship or our ultimate trust, Unitarians have to answer to themselves and to others the question which the Saviour puts to all his disciples, "What think ye of Christ?" It is indeed a matter for thought, for serious and perplexing thought. The field over which that thought will range is so wide, and men will bring to it such various capacities, methods, and biases, that they will find themselves led to speculate towards different conclusions. Obvious it is to every candid mind, of whatever sect, that there is nothing in the fixed fundamental tenet of Unitarianism on this point, which prevents our rising to the highest possible conception of the nature, the offices, and the agency of Christ. Trinitarians sometimes speak of us as if, in denying an underived divinity to Christ, we actually deprived ourselves of a God in whom we might trust, and left the central throne of heaven empty because we do not seat upon it the vicegerent of the Most High. We can tell them that our doctrine gives to us the same God whom they worship, and another being, — yes, a Divine Being besides. We know of nothing that hinders but that God may impart, may delegate, any measurement of his own properties, save simply that of self-existence. And as the properties of God are infinite, the One who partakes of them in the highest measurement must be exalted above human powers of conception for defining the compass of his *nature*, leaving, however, one single limiting distinction, — that, as there can be but One Infinite, Self-Existent, Supreme, the Son must be subordinated to the Father. And this is the truth which is in part declared and in part intimated in the Saviour's own affirmation, "My Father is greater than I." The declaration subordinates Christ to God, the intimation exalts Christ all but infinitely above humanity. It would be preposterous, for a being standing in human form among men, to utter the blank and stolid conceit of owning his inferiority to God. A distinctive exaltation above the sphere of humanity is the essence of the meaning of that utterance. The pointing upwards to the one who is *Highest* as the only one who is *higher*, distinguishes Christ alike from Deity and from humanity. The universe of being is to us enriched by an additional being, through the view which we entertain of Christ. The awful vacuum between the loftiest partakers of angelic natures and the Supreme has now a radiant occupant, who fills the whole of it. That Unitarians are disposed to conceive of Christ under the highest exposition which the strongest phrase or sentence of Scripture makes of him, is an admission which they will not ask of the charity, for they demand it of the justice, of their opponents. How absurd it is to charge us with derogating from the claims or the honor of Jesus! Such censorious words imply a motive which we know is not in our hearts. What possible inducement could we have to entertain it? Between us and other Christians, what different influences in purpose or inclination can be traced, which would warrant such an impugning of our sincerity as is implied in these odious charges? To derogate from the just claims or honor of another, to reduce his dignity, or to withhold his rightful tribute, implies always a mean or a malignant feeling; and if Unitarians deserve such a charge, let it be spoken boldly, in manly candor, and not intimated by covert insinuations. During the progress of this controversy many an Orthodox preacher in city and country pulpits, relying upon his own conceit, or trusting to the oracular authority which he may have with those who are willing to listen to him as a teacher of Christian truth, has ventured to tell them in unqualified terms, "Unitarians degrade and deny the Saviour." It is difficult to suppose that any one can so speak *of professed Christians*, without communicating to himself at least a glow of unchristian passion, even if the language were not suggested by such a feeling. But imagine these preachers to have substituted some such language as this: "Unitarians, with all the means of knowing the truth which I myself have, and in the exercise of a desire, which I have no right to think is not as thoroughly sincere and pure as my own desire, to discover what the truth is, believe that Christ, however exalted he may be, is not identical with God." We venture to say that this latter style of address, if it had prevailed, would have given us a better opinion of the candor of Orthodox preachers in seeking to instruct large classes of those who are disposed to listen to them most confidingly, than we have now.

Our sole aim and wish are to gather from the New

Testament as intelligible and adequate a conception as is possible of Jesus Christ. We are concerned to do this through the force of two equally serious and sincere motives, — the one having in view the strength and clearness of our own mental and spiritual apprehension of him as the Messiah, the other looking to a reverent gratitude to Christ himself in assigning him his place in our hearts. We wish to think rightly of Christ, in order that we may believe in him, may rest our confidence in his authority and his sufficiency; and in order that we may love him, as he made our affection the highest condition for putting us into such a relation to him as will constitute him our Saviour. It is simply and wholly through force of convictions wrought by a serious study of the Scriptures, that Unitarians, who agree in a denial of the Deity of Christ, are led to differ in their metaphysical views of him. Their differences range over the whole field of conception between an idea of Christ as a man miraculously endowed, and an idea of him as the sharer of God's throne, his counsellor and companion, holding rank above all other orders of being, and touching upon the prerogatives of Deity. To some, the Arian hypothesis of Christ as pre-existent, ranking above all angels, and dwelling before all worlds were made in the bosom of God, has been a favorite conviction. To others, this hypothesis is barren of all that gives to a high theme of faith its glow and grandeur, as it vainly attempts to exalt Christ chiefly by extending his existence through a longer space of time. Others still insist that the very last question suggested by the New Testament, as a matter of concern to us, is that of Christ's nature, inasmuch as we are interested only in his office, and have to do with him only as a visitor to this earth for the especial purposes of revelation which he has now fulfilled. And yet again, we have met on Unitarian pages an accepted use of the phrase "the eternal generation of the Son." We know that those who use this phrase neither intend to utter an absurdity, nor to signify that they are saying something while yet they say nothing. Still we are sure that we do not get their idea, for we get no idea at all from their words. The generation of a son, or the birth of a son, indicates an event, an incident that transpires at some point in time. Now if the epithet *mysterious*, or *original*, or *undated*, or a like epithet, was connected with the word, we should acknowledge the presence of an idea; but to connect *eternal* with the *generation* of anything, if it effects any purpose, takes back in one of the words what is asserted in the other. Happily, however, it is an understood canon of language that every idea, if it is an idea which requires two words to express it, may be stated in at least two ways,—generally in several ways, but always in two. Now if those who use the phrase "the eternal generation of the Son," as expressing a point in their belief, will put their idea into another form of expression, we may perhaps be helped to understand their meaning.

Those Unitarians who regard Jesus as presented to us under a simply human aspect, hold this opinion not necessarily through the force of any prejudice, but as the transcript and substance of what they think the plain New Testament teaching upon it. They believe that miraculous endowments from God on a basis of pure humanity — complemented, perfected, and inspired manhood — fill out every representation there made of Christ, account for all he was and did, ratify all that he taught or promised, adapt him to all our necessities as a "high-priest touched with the feelings of our infirmities," as "the faithful and true witness" of God, and as "able to save unto the uttermost those who come unto God by him." And when those who thus believe are taunted or challenged for relying, — as the rebuke is worded, — for "relying for salvation on a created being," they have but to answer, that they no more rely for their salvation than they did for their existence upon *a created being*, as their reliance is simply and ultimately upon God, though it may be mediately upon any agency or method which God may have chosen. For if God chose a created being to be the medium of our salvation, as he made created beings to be the mediums of our existence, his power and wisdom in the choice of such an agency or method are not to be questioned, while "the grace is still the same." If any one should refuse to accept the proffer of salvation through such an agency, as too humble or inadequate, he might be reminded of the rebuke conveyed to the Syrian leper by his servant, when he compared the river of Israel so contemptuously with Abana and Pharpar. This taunt of relying for salvation on a created being is meant, of course, to convey the idea that the Scriptures teach that not only the Source, but the *Mediator*, of our salvation is an uncreated being. But this, however, opens again the whole question as to what the teaching of Scripture on this point is. Let that sole, simple issue stand clear of all such taunts upon those who, as sincerely and as intelligently as others who come to different conclusions, are brought to the belief that Christ is presented to us in Scripture as the perfection of humanity, or, in the words of Peter, as, "a man approved of God by miracles, and wonders, and signs which God did by him."

Yet others among the Unitarians have been as strenuous as have been any of the believers in the Trinity in rejecting this humanitarian view of Christ. Earnest have been the protests of many among us against that view. Some have firmly believed that the truth lay wholly in an opposite direction, and so have embraced the theory of the pre-existence, the super-angelic glory of Christ, as being the first-born of the creation of God, constituting a sacred companionship in the otherwise lonely majesty of heaven, the sharer and almost the equal in essence with the Supreme, waiting that fulness of time which should bring him in human form to this earth. One may hold this belief as millions have held it, and still be in all strictness a Unitarian; for Unitarianism is committed simply to a distinction between God and Christ, — a distinction which subordinates Christ to God. Certainly here is a wide range for faith, — wide enough for every phase of mental conception, wide enough to fill out every form of language, every shaping of thought, which we find in the Scriptures. We must distinguish between God and Christ, and the attempt to confound them would to us require a yielding up of the most explicit statements of the New Testament, which give added distinctness to our conceptions of both those beings by assigning to each a work that individualizes their relation to us. Even though, in the work of redemption, and in the manifestation made to us of the Father in the Son, there is a blending of their glory, and we find it hard to separate their office and agency, they are still seen to part at the very point in which they are in closest union; just as when a powerful telescope is turned towards one of those sparkling orbs which glitter in the midnight sky, it seems to the eye to be single, but the keenest gaze resolves it into a double star, one of which is of the first magnitude, and the other of which is not. Dr. Woods (in his Ninth Letter to Unitarians) says that the distinction between the Father and the Son "is of such a nature that they are *two*, and are in Scripture represented to be two as *really* as Moses and Aaron, though not in a sense inconsistent with their essential unity." The obvious meaning of the last clause of this sentence is, evidently, not the meaning which the writer intended to convey; but conveniently for himself, though disappointingly to us, he stops short of conveying what meaning he must have thought he had in his own mind.

It seems to us that some of the highest and most precious uses for which God was manifested in the person of Christ, are wholly sacrificed when Christ is merged back into Deity. Some of our own writers, in the sedate calmness of written discourse, as well as in the loftiest strains of their devotional rhetoric, have expressed their earnest belief in "the Incarnation of God," and have spoken of Christ, not simply as the Incarnate Word of God, but as the Incarnate God. It is evident that the use of this phrase must involve some of those indeterminate and undefined significations attaching to phraseology, the materials of which are metaphysical, while its purpose is to convey a most literal and direct meaning. The phrase is burdened not only with all the wealth and majesty of Christian conceptions, but also with all the poverty and meanness of Hindoo doctrines. In fact, it is one of those phrases which indicates either a doubtful fancy, or an adequate and intelligible and satisfactory interpretation of one of the highest conceptions of the spirit, — according to the companionship which it may find in the other religious ideas of each human mind. But our point is this: that Jesus Christ is presented to us as a real and distinct being, — as a real individuality, not merely as the medium of a manifestation. To resolve him back into Deity, while it makes no addition to the Godhead, deprives us of a being nearer to our conceptions, and more available to some of our highest needs of guidance, knowledge, and confidence. The moon we know receives all its light from the sun, imparting only to us the brightness and blessing which it has received. But having received those rays from its source, it has a power of concentrating and reflecting them, and that power in the moon of concentrating and reflecting the rays of the sun is the subsidiary condition which makes the moon a helpful orb to us. The sun would have no perceptible increase of light if it called in the beams which it lends to our beautiful satellite, but then we should lose one of heaven's fairest objects. If it were to be proved that there really is no organized body answering to what we call the moon, but that the sun's rays not only gild, but also by some wondrous process create, the appearance of such an orb, by casting a blazing focus like a spectrum into one spot amid the mists of heaven, the realms of space would be deprived of a solid body, and in place of it we should have a phantasm. Similar would be the loss among the objects of our religious faith and devotional reliance, if Christ, as a distinct reality, is resolved into a radiation of God. We believe, indeed, that his light is not his own, yet we also believe that that light does not create a phantom form, but is concentrated and reflected by the Son, who "has life" and being "in himself."

Nor is it only in the earthly offices and ministry of Christ that we find reason to distinguish him from God. The straits of devotion, trust, aspiration, and religious experience are relieved by a firm belief in him who is seated at the right hand of the Supreme, still intrusted with the mission which thirty years of an earthly ministry did not complete. We believe in the present existence of Christ, not as God, but as Christ. We believe in his present agency for his Church. The Scriptures positively affirm that he is now watching over his own work, advancing his own cause. He is called our Advocate and Intercessor with the Father. Christian trust and love, and the conscious want and dependence of the heart, can fill out the meaning of those terms if — and only if — Christ is still existing, not as God, but as *Christ.* It is utterly impossible to give any natural or intelligible meaning to those terms, if we call Christ God; for then we have God interceding with God, and we lose our Mediator. Trinitarianism teaches that Christ parted with all that in him and about him was not God when he left the earth, and in dropping the flesh, which alone brought him into sympathy of nature with us, returned to the sky in the simple exaltation of Deity. If so, his separate ministry for us has ceased. But we need it still, and never more than since he has passed into the heavens. We need him still, as a being distinguishable by our thought and faith from God, that he may lead us up to God, and reconcile us to God. The Trinitarian view of him now is but a barren theory of metaphysics to us. Reliance upon his written teachings is but a cold, didactic exercise, unless quickened by faith in an ever-living Christ.

The candor with which we have aimed to pursue this discussion requires of us one frank confession at its close. We are concerned to state with emphasis the fact that, as one result of the controversy on this point, there has been a marked and most edifying change in the prevailing tone of Unitarian discourse upon the offices and the agency of Christ. We are willing, too, to admit our indebtedness to some cautions and remonstrances from our doctrinal opponents, while we also affirm that our experiences within our own fold and within our own breasts have ratified these remonstrances as not wholly uncalled for and as highly salutary to us. Not forgetting the many tracts and essays and sermons by early Unitarians, whose fervor of faith and exalted trust in the mediatorial and superhuman offices of Christ fed the piety of multitudes of our cherished and sainted dead, we admit that some of high repute among us have favored what are called low, and chilling, and inadequate views of the Author and Finisher of our faith. One of the least available uses which Christ serves to us is that of an "Example," simply because the availableness of an example consists in exciting and aiding us to imitate it, and our imitation of Christ must necessarily be at so fearfully long and hopeless a distance, that even to lay much stress on his being an example to us would be more apt to mislead us into an over-confidence in ourselves as imitators, than to an adequate conception of that perfect being. We may imitate some actions of the Saviour, — but to imitate *him* is a task which means more than the words convey. If we were to spend a lifetime on the study of Newton's Principia, and were to undertake to verify every process in his deductions, we should be disposed to take the name of a disciple, rather than that of an imitator of Newton. Have not Unitarians overlooked some of the proportions of truth in speaking of Christ as an example? There may have been no speculative error in this, seeing that Christ set before us God himself as our example. But if that has been to any a paramount view of Christ, it may have practically obscured some of his other offices.

Nor does the epithet "Teacher" suit any high devotional conception of Christ. When curious dividers of the word of truth have proclaimed that every didactic lesson, every precept, every moral truth, taught by Christ, may be paralleled by a quotation from Hebrew or classic pages, what is there left to signalize him as a teacher? True, we may sublimate the word Teacher, and make it embrace the authority, the evidences, and the attractions of the lessons conveyed by the only perfect and heaven-attested Teacher; but that is connecting the epithet with Christ rather for the sake of exalting the word than for the purpose of giving him his highest title. The distinction of a teacher is his doctrine, and when that doctrine so far transcends any other teaching as to embrace not only the loftiest lessons, but also the influences, the appeals, and the aid which give them their power over the soul, the functions of a Teacher are absorbed in the offices of a Saviour. A didactic view of the Gospel has found perhaps an excess and disproportion of favor among Unitarians.

"You do not make enough of Christ," has been the remonstrance addressed to us. We have listened to it. If it ever offended us, it shall henceforward be of service to us. We believe that it has been of service to us, for the reason that some in our own communion have made it a self-reproaching accusation, which has warmed their hearts and deepened their Christian love. We have not made enough of Christ. No denomination of Christians makes enough of Christ. Unitarians, having been compelled to treat of Christ by methods which metaphysically subordinate him, have been in danger of losing sight of the best influence from him and of the conditions for securing it. We should be glad to feel that we have done with the metaphysical discussion, and may henceforward forego it, that we may give all our thought to the devotional, the spiritual apprehension of Christ. This is to us the great, the best result of the controversy.

Henceforth it shall be with less and less of reason furnished by us, that our opponents shall say, "You do not make enough of Christ." Having distinguished him from God, we feel all the more our need of him to guide us to God, to manifest God to us. We recognize in our own deepest wants the craving to which he ministers. We know and own that, in a Gospel which comes by Christ, Christ must be the foremost object, and that every sentiment engaged by that Gospel must yield some tribute of heart and soul to him. If in the ardor of controversy we have seemed to depreciate any office of Christ, or, in our jealousy for the prerogative of the Supreme, to forget any of our obligations of love and reverence to his Messiah, we can say that it has been so only in the seeming, and not in reality. If in the spirit of charity our opponents have charged us with our seeming error on this point, we thank them for it. We would, however, remind them, that we are not driven to such a mistake by any exigencies of our doctrinal position, as denying the Trinity and the underived Deity of Christ. "To us there is one God, the Father, of whom are all things, and we in him; and one Lord Jesus Christ, by whom are all things, and we by him." (1 Cor. viii. 6.) Our negations may be the most striking characteristic of our creed to its opponents; but our positive faith is the condition of its power and truth and value to ourselves.

UNITARIANISM AND ORTHODOXY

ON

THE ATONEMENT.

UNITARIANISM AND ORTHODOXY

ON

THE ATONEMENT.

PURSUING our general review of a half-century of the controversy still in agitation between the divided representatives of the old Congregational body of New England, we have summed up the views of the two parties on two of their great doctrinal issues. It remains for us to follow the same method in dealing with what we have already defined as the third of the chief topics of discussion and division. This concerns the Scripture doctrine of the Atonement: the agency of Jesus Christ in securing the reconciliation between God and men; the need of such an agency, the mode of its operation and of its efficacy.

"Unitarians deny the doctrine of the Atonement," is the judgment pronounced against us by the Orthodox. "Unitarians believe the doctrine of the Atonement," is our earnest, self-convinced, and solemn assertion, made in answer to that judgment. What then? Is it a question of veracity between us, involving a slander or falsehood on the one side, and a plea of self-defence on the other? No! There may be misunderstanding, there may be misrepresentation, but we make no charge of intentional falsifying. Is it then a question as to the meaning of a word, so that, while the parties respectively affirm or deny, they do not affirm and deny the same thing, because they attach quite different significations to the same word on which the whole issue hangs? There certainly is involved in the controversy much difference of opinion and much debate as to the meaning of a few very important words, especially of the word *atonement.* The controversy some years ago turned far more than it does now upon the meaning of that one word. Unitarians insisted, that the word *atonement*, according to its etymology and its actual use at the time when our English version of the Bible adopted it, signified *reconciliation.* Unitarians also urged, that a false view of the Scripture doctrine had connected an erroneous association with the word *atonement*, had in fact changed its popular signification; and that the word *reconciliation* ought to be substituted for it in the only place where it occurs in the New Testament. Orthodox controversialists stoutly and obstinately denied these assertions. Happily, however, that point may now be regarded as yielded by them. So far, the controversy as a strife about words has abated. But while the embarrassment of one merely verbal dispute is set aside, the controversy is still largely and almost hopelessly complicated with questions as to the signification and the interpretation of terms of language. Charity, therefore, requires of us to explain that, when the Orthodox so flatly and positively affirm that Unitarians *do not* believe the doctrine of the Atonement, in spite of the assertion of the Unitarians that they do believe it, the Orthodox mean simply that Unitarians do not accept *their interpretation* of the Scripture doctrine. The Orthodox, taking for granted the infallibility of their decision in scholarship, criticism, and matters of open debate in the articles of Christian faith, identify their conclusions with Scripture doctrine. They hold Unitarians not only to a belief of the Scripture doctrine of Atonement, but also to a reception of their construction and interpretation of that doctrine. It is thus that an issue is opened between the two parties, and fairly opened. The controversy has so far warranted its own just grounds and occasion, as to prove that the assurance heretofore exhibited, in quietly taking for granted the identity of Orthodoxy and of Scripture doctrine, had better give way to the more becoming and deliberate processes of patient, serious, and humble examination. Disciples of Christ, as sincere and faithful as any of those whose names shine on the records of the Church Universal: scholars as profoundly versed in the mysteries of tongues and interpretation as any of those whom Orthodoxy has accepted for oracles: and humble, obedient, and hopeful disciples of the faith in every condition of human life, have found a glorious and merciful doctrine of Atonement in the Scriptures, quite different from that which Orthodoxy teaches. The issue, then, is not whether the Orthodox speak truth or untruth when they affirm that Unitarians do not believe the atonement; but the issue is simply and solely this, — What is the Scripture doctrine of the atoning work of Christ? If the Orthodox have any advantage over the Unitarians, as respects sincerity of purpose, or docility of mind, or humility of spirit, they have but to claim it, and to prove their claim. They will find us quite easy of conviction on proper proof. Failing any such inequality of position or advantage, the issue between the parties seems to be, as in fact it always has been, one depending entirely upon an honest and intelligent interpretation of the Scriptures. The candid Bishop Butler has frankly remarked, "There is not, I think, anything relating to Christianity which has been more objected against, than the mediation of Christ in some or other of its parts." * The admission affords

* Analogy, Part II. Chap. V.

an admirable introduction to every attempt at a fair inquiry, for the sake of discovering where the strength of the objection to the Orthodox doctrine really lies.

Would that the time had fully come for the treatment of this theme solely under a positive form of statement, simply to present accepted truth in all its manifold relations of tenderness and power for the heart of man; because the Christian doctrine of Atonement is a doctrine which, by the consent of all parties, addresses the heart. There are two emphatic reasons which make it above all things desirable that this doctrine, instead of being a ground of division and alienation between Christian believers, should be the very point of their warmest sympathy and union. For, first, the doctrine which opens the way for our reconciliation to God, ought to reconcile us to each other, to engage our common love, to harmonize all our alienations, and to be the bond of peace between believers. And second, as this is one of the fundamental doctrines of Christian theology, it must constitute one of the chief tests of the truth and value of that great remedial scheme of the Gospel. The doctrine truly stated must furnish the strongest testimony for the truth and the adequacy of the alleged Divine intervention for the deliverance of men; while any false view or perversion of the doctrine will at once constitute the most offensive obstacle in the way of a confiding belief, and will make the Gospel most impotent where it ought to be most effective in its power. Indeed, our consciousness of moral and spiritual disease, our sense of exposure under sin and of our need of redemption, the measure of our love and gratitude to Christ as the medium of relief, and our views of the character, attributes, and government of God, will all be affected by our view of the nature and method of that remedy which the Gospel has provided.

We think we express the prevailing sentiment among

Unitarians when we say that this is the theme upon which they love the least to dispute, are the most reluctant to engage in controversy, and are the most anxious to have a clear understanding with their opponents as to the grounds of division and the prospects of harmonizing our differences. We feel that the subject is alien from all strife, a subject eminently engaging, pacifying, and constraining of sympathy and harmony. That Christ died for us in any sense, ought to exclude his death from angry or passionate controversy among those who claim to share the benefits of his sacrifice. It is a grievous thing to us to be told that we deny his Atonement, and then to have so severe a charge vindicated by forcing upon the Scriptures a doctrine which we are persuaded is not taught there, but is an inference or invention of the mind of man. And especially is it grievous to us to be charged, as even now we are charged,—when we affirm that we believe the doctrine,—with using words deceptively, and with trying to claim Orthodox sympathy of belief under double meanings of language and the perversion of terms from their ordinary significations. It is only from the sense and the smart of the wrong thus inflicted upon us, that we still engage in controversy upon this doctrine. We say that we do find a doctrine of Atonement in the Scriptures, and that we heartily and gratefully believe it: that the doctrine exalts Christ as the Saviour, wins to him our highest trust and love, and brings us adoringly to praise that once alienated Father in heaven, whose love has provided a means for the redemption and salvation of men. Our opponents, venturing at once to assume their own infallibility in the dogmatic view which they have formed of the method and efficacy of the Atonement, and to pronounce upon the inadequacy of the faith which we hold and love, charge us with a denial of the Scripture doctrine of Atonement. Hence arises the issue between us. We are perfectly ready to meet it.

On no other of the larger or the lesser topics that have entered into this controversy has there been so wide a variation, and so marked a modification in the specific terms of the Orthodox doctrine, as on this of the Atonement. Without claiming that Orthodoxy has made any distinct approximation to our views, or has essentially relieved what is and has always been to Unitarians the most unscriptural and offensive quality of its doctrine of the Atonement, we may safely affirm that it has essentially changed its own dogmatic position. The definition of the Atonement made by the leading Orthodox divines of the present day is quite different from that given two centuries ago by those whom they claim to represent. Notwithstanding the very bold assertions made in the religious newspapers issued from week to week this current year, that Orthodoxy has not departed from its standards, and that it still holds to "the substance" of the Calvinistic formulas, it is impossible for us to assent to the assertions, when we compare pages of the old divinity on our shelves with the recent productions of some of the most eminent men of the Orthodox communions. Would Cotton, Hooker, Shepherd, Edwards, or Hopkins have admitted, with Dr. E. Beecher, that the system of Orthodoxy is utterly inconsistent with the principles of honor and justice in the Divine government? Or with Professor Park, that the rhetoric of Orthodoxy needs to be toned down, if one would harmonize it with logical truth? Or with Dr. Bushnell, that the death of Christ is a dramatic scene, in which we must discriminate between the subjective and the objective meaning? Ask the aged persons among us who used to listen to Orthodox preaching, if its tone, and even its substance, are not changed.

Therefore, the issue between us now is not exactly

what it was even fifty years ago. Those terrific and harrowing representations of some of the Divine attributes which were current in the old divinity, do not enter into modern preaching. Those dramatic representations of the covenant work between God and Christ, involving stipulations as to what the Father should require to soothe his wrath and accept as the ransom of human souls, and as to how much the Son should suffer, are now withdrawn, either in deference to the exactions of good taste, or as a consequence of an actual change of opinion. Some of the many sharp points of the Orthodox doctrine are worn smooth. Vague terms which may be unobjectionable are substituted for very shocking terms once in common use. It is getting to be difficult now to discuss the real issue between the parties, without a vast deal of definition and interpretation, and clearing up of the outworks of language and ideas. We take in our hands some of the modern essays on the doctrine of the Atonement, and as we begin the perusal it would seem as if some of the views most antagonistic to our own convictions were about to receive a most offensive statement, leading farther and farther as the argument progressed to a perfectly heathen conclusion. But no! They melt and soften and become very yielding, till, what with dramatic uses of language and shapings of thought and governmental theories, the sternness of the reader's brow is relaxed, his dissent is soothed, a degree of sympathy, a stage of conviction, is wrought within him, and he asks, Is the old doctrine reduced down to this?

But what is the doctrine? and where does the controversy upon it between Unitarianism and Orthodoxy commence? and in what directions do the parties diverge? and what is the substance of their difference? We shall soon have to ask here, as we have asked concerning the two previous topics which we have discussed, What was the doctrine when the controversy opened, and before it had been reduced to simpler and more vague and elusive terms as the result of controversy?

The English word, the noun *atonement*, occurs but once in our version of the New Testament (Romans v. 11). No respectable scholar or writer would now affirm or argue, — as was once affirmed and argued, — that the original word in the Greek should here be rendered by an English word conveying the sense of compensation, commutation, or expiation.* The verb to which the noun is related means, and is translated, *to reconcile*, and atonement, or at-onement, is reconciliation, as in other instances it is rendered. An explicit avowal to this effect has recently been made by Professor Pond of the Bangor Theological Seminary: † "An atonement, therefore, in the sense of our translators, is a reconciliation. But the word has undergone a slight change of meaning within the last two hundred years. As now used, it denotes not so much a reconciliation, as that which is done *to open and prepare the way for* a reconciliation. As used by Evangelical Christians, it refers to what has been done by our Lord Jesus Christ, to *open a way* for the recovery and salvation of sinful men, that so a reconciliation may be effected between them and their Maker." It is something to have the fact clearly and fully admitted that the Apostle's word does not imply the sense which has long been associated in controversy with the word *atonement*, a sense which Dr. Webster has very unwarrantably introduced into his English Dictionary. Our literature in the age of Shakespeare will show the signification of the word then to have been *reconciliation*. The perversion of the Scripture

* Dr. Woods says: "The word *atonement* has become ambiguous, its common use being somewhat different from its use in Scripture." (Works, Vol. II. p. 493.)

† See his Article in Bibliotheca Sacra for January, 1856, p. 130.

doctrine gave to the word *atonement* the new use which it begins to have in the literature of the age of Queen Ann.* We might, indeed, raise a question as to the perfect accuracy of the signification which Dr. Pond says that Orthodoxy now assigns to the word. We certainly should wish to include under "what has been *done* by Jesus Christ," what was *said* by him, with the same design of opening a way for reconciliation.

The doctrine of Atonement or reconciliation is one of a large sweep and compass, and the first condition for any fair and satisfactory treatment of it is to secure the discussion of it, at the very start, against all such influence from definitions or limitations, as will surely give us a part instead of the whole doctrine. The question is, not what theory about it will the thought or the reason of man adopt or approve, but what do the Scriptures teach us concerning the doctrine, as it is exclusively a doctrine of revelation? The sweep of the doctrine embraces a great many contingencies dependent upon a duplication or an alternative connected with all of the large elements which enter into it. Thus Christ may be regarded either as a medium for announcing terms of reconciliation from God, or as an agent for facilitating and accomplishing such a reconciliation; or he may be both the announcer and the agent of the process of reconciliation. The Orthodox doctrine assumes that sin is

---

* "*Lod.* Is there division 'twixt thy lord and Cassio?
"*Des.* A most unhappy one; I would do much
T' atone them, for the love I bear to Cassio."
Shaksp. *Othello,* Act. IV. Sc. 1.

"Or each atone his guilty love with life." — Pope.

The transition between the two meanings is well marked in Milton:

"Man, ...
. . . . . once dead in sins and lost,
Atonement for himself or offering meet,
Indebted and undone, hath none to bring."
Par. Lost, Book III. l. 234.

an infinite wrong, and deserves an infinite punishment or requires an infinite expiation, because it is committed against an Infinite Being. This is looking at facts from one point of view, namely, the Divine. But the alternative point of view would suggest the question, How can sin be of such infinite demerit, seeing that it is committed by a finite and limited being? Another duplication of issues presents itself in the rivalry of claims on our fullest affections raised by the confusion in the Orthodox theology which refers the prime movement for our redemption to the *love of God*, or to the *interposition of Christ.* This confusion is not removed by the interchange of such references, or by the attempt to prove them identical. When Calvinism tells us that the Father *chose* and *appointed* and *qualified* the Son to be our Redeemer, and also that the Son *offered* himself to be our sacrifice, one who would have clear thoughts, so far as he has any, must ask, Which of these two statements would Orthodoxy have us accept? Again, Was Christ's death an actual expiation, equivalent in anguish to all the sufferings that sinners would have endured, or was it a demonstrative exhibition of a legal penalty? Once more, Did or did not the Divine nature of Christ share in his sufferings? Still other alternatives of doctrine present themselves in the divergencies of Orthodox teaching as to the relations between the Divine Justice and the Divine Mercy, by which God might or might not freely forgive, while his law might or might not freely remit; and in the discordant opinions as to whether a knowledge of the sacrifice to be made, and now made by Christ, was and is necessary or not necessary to all who share in its benefits. And finally, Is the Atonement limited or unlimited in its efficacy? These are all complications of the controversy for us, and the grounds of minor controversies among the Orthodox themselves.

There is no chapter in the old Confession of Faith

of the New England churches, which is still the standard for the Orthodox Congregationalists, devoted specifically to the doctrine of the Atonement. The word itself does not occur in that formula, nor even in the Westminster Catechism. The substantial Orthodox doctrine under which our fathers were educated, and which was had in view at the opening of the Unitarian controversy, is found in Chapter VIII. of the Confession, under the title "Of Christ the Mediator," as follows: —

"It pleased God in his eternal purpose to choose and ordain the Lord Jesus, his only begotten Son, according to a covenant made between them both, to be the mediator between God and man: the prophet, priest, and king, the head and Saviour of his Church, the heir of all things, and judge of the world: unto whom he did from all eternity give a people to be his seed, and to be by him in time redeemed, called, justified, sanctified, and glorified. The Son of God, the second person in the Trinity, being very and eternal God of one substance, and equal with the Father, did, when the fulness of time was come, take upon him man's nature, with all the essential properties and common infirmities thereof, yet without sin; being conceived by the power of the Holy Ghost in the womb of the Virgin Mary, of her substance, — which person is very God and very man, yet one Christ, the only mediator between God and man; — was sanctified and anointed with the Holy Spirit above measure, — that he might be thoroughly furnished to execute the office of a mediator and surety: which office he took not unto himself, but was thereunto called by his Father, — and did most willingly undertake; which that he might discharge, he was made under the law, and did perfectly fulfil it, and underwent the punishment due to us, which we should have borne and suffered, being made sin and a curse for us, enduring most grievous torments immediately from God in his soul, and most painful sufferings in his body, was crucified and died, was buried and remained under the power of death: — by his perfect obedience and sacrifice of himself, which he through the Eternal Spirit once offered up unto God, he hath fully satisfied the justice of God, and purchased not only reconciliation, but an everlasting inheritance in the kingdom of heaven for all those whom the Father hath given unto him. Although the work of redemption was not actually wrought by Christ till after his incarnation, yet the virtue, efficacy, and benefits thereof were communicated to the elect in all ages successively from the beginning of the world," &c.

We must bear as well as we can the confusion of terms and the irreconcilable statements in this formula; they are some of the dreary conditions to which any one must submit in reading even, and still more in attempting to digest, the schemes of divinity wrought out from the fancies of theologians. Here we are told of a covenant between two persons, when in fact there was but *One;* of a Mediator between two parties, who was himself one of those parties; of an office "willingly undertaken" by the Son, which, however, "he did not take upon himself," because "he was called to it by the Father"; of a being who was essentially the Supreme God, who yet "was sanctified and anointed with the Holy Spirit"; of a being compounded of Deity and humanity, in order that the union of Deity might exalt a sacrifice in which, however, only the human nature suffered; of Christ's thus "purchasing from God" those whom God "had given" to him from all eternity; and finally, we read that the death of Christ is made to stand as a substitute or equivalent for the eternal torments and the remorseful heart-sufferings of millions of condemned sinners. If we pass by these confused and inconsistent terms in the old formula of the doctrine of Redemption, our attention is fixed, and our protest is raised, by the following sentences in the Confession: "Christ underwent the punishment due to us"; "enduring most grievous torments immediately from God in his soul," "he hath fully satisfied the justice of God," and "he hath purchased reconciliation." The statements and inferences of doctrine in these sentences formerly constituted the staple matter of Calvinistic teaching concerning the redeeming work of Christ: they present to us the essential, the peculiar, the characteristic features of Calvinism. One who honestly assumes the name of a Calvinist will unflinchingly accept these essential elements of his creed, and will make no adroit attempts to evade them. Any one who takes the name of a Calvinist, and yet endeavors to soften or explain away the manifest meaning of these sentences will certainly act more candidly if he will change his own name, which he is at liberty to do, and give over trifling with written formulas, which he is not at liberty to do. Of late the sharper phraseology, the positive and unqualified statements which we find in the above sentences, have yielded to a less direct implication of more or less of their substance, and to an infinite variety of softening constructions put upon them.

If, in the course of this controversy, some nominal Calvinists had not ventured to deny the truthfulness of the representations made by Unitarians as to the essential views expressed by Calvin himself, one would hardly suppose that any question could be raised on this point. The following sentences, all drawn from the sixteenth chapter of the second book of Calvin's Institutes, are a fair exhibition of his theology on this point: "That Christ has taken upon himself and suffered the punishment which by the righteous judgment of God impended over all sinners; that by his blood he has expiated those crimes which render them odious to God; that by this expiation God the Father has been satisfied and duly atoned; that by this intercessor his wrath has been appeased; that this is the foundation of peace between God and men; that this is the bond of his benevolence towards them." "Indeed, we must admit that it was impossible for God to be truly appeased in any other way, than by Christ renouncing all concern for himself, and submitting and devoting himself entirely to his will." "For we ought particularly to remember this satisfaction, that we may not spend our whole lives in terror and anxiety, as though we were pursued by the righteous vengeance of God, which the Son of God has transferred to himself." "For the Son of God, though perfectly free from all sin, nevertheless assumed the disgrace and ignominy of our iniquities, and, on the other hand, arrayed us in his purity." "Christ at his death was offered to the Father as an expiatory sacrifice, in order that, a complete atonement being made by his oblation, we may no longer dread the Divine wrath." "If Christ had merely died a corporeal death, no end would have been accomplished by it; it was requisite, also, that he should feel the severity of the Divine vengeance, in order to appease the wrath of God and satisfy his justice. Hence it was necessary for him to contend with the powers of hell and the horror of eternal death." "Christ suffered in his soul the dreadful torments of a person condemned and irretrievably lost." "And, indeed, if his soul had experienced no punishment, he would have been only a Redeemer for the body." "Whence we may conclude what dreadful and horrible agonies he must have suffered, while he was conscious of standing at the tribunal of God accused as a criminal on our account." *

The Assembly's Catechism tells us that "Christ was a sacrifice to Divine Justice." The old divines, who

* That we might not intensify by our own version any of the expressions used by Calvin, we have adopted the translation of the Institutes published by the Presbyterian Board at Philadelphia.

made the Catechism the expository rule of their faith, were wont to receive its statements literally. They held themselves bound to an unflinching fidelity to its doctrines. We will take, as an illustration of this remark, the example of that pious Puritan minister, John Flavel, son of Rev. Richard Flavel, who entered upon his work in Dartmouth, Old England, just two centuries ago, and whose devotional spirit and writings have made him a favorite among the disciples of Orthodoxy to this day.* He published an Exposition of the Assembly's Catechism, and had no distinction among his brethren as one who forced it beyond a fair construction of its doctrinal statements. It will be seen by a few extracts from his sermons, how boldly and literally he was disposed to accept all that was implied in the Calvinistic view of the Covenant of Redemption. Our extracts are made from the folio edition of his works, Edinburgh, 1731. It should be observed that he aims to support all his positions by references to texts in Scripture, made after the usage of his time, without the slightest recognition of any just principles of biblical criticism, and with an entire disregard of the connection in which the passages quoted stand in the original.

Flavel's third sermon is on "Christ's Compact with the Father for the Recovery of the Elect." Isaiah liii. 12.

"Doctrine, that the business of man's salvation was transacted upon covenant terms betwixt the Father and the Son from all eternity." "The substance of this Covenant of Redemption is dialogue-wise exprest to us in Isaiah xlix. Having told God how ready and fit he was for his service, he will know of Him what reward he shall have for his work, for he resolves his blood shall

* The late Dr. Alexander, the Princeton Professor, wrote, "To John Flavel I certainly owe more than to any uninspired author." — Life, by his Son, p. 47.

not be sold at low and cheap rates. Hereupon the Father offers him the elect of Israel for his reward, bidding low at first, (as they that make bargains use to do,) and only offers him that small remnant still intending to bid higher. But Christ will not be satisfied with these; he values his Blood higher than so. Therefore he is brought in complaining, '*I have labored in vain, and spent my strength for naught.*' This is but a small reward for so great sufferings as I must undergo; my blood is much more worth than this comes to, and will be sufficient to redeem all the elect dispersed among the isles of the Gentiles, as well as the lost sheep of the house of Israel. Hereupon the Father comes up higher, and tells him He intends to reward him better than so." "The persons transacting and dealing with each other in this covenant are great persons, God the Father, and God the Son: the former as a creditor, and the latter as a surety. The Father stands upon satisfaction, the Son engages to give it." "And forasmuch as the Father knew it was a hard and difficult work His Son was to undertake, a work that would have broken the backs of all the angels in heaven and men on earth, had they engaged in it, therefore He promiseth to stand by him, and assist and strengthen him for it." We read that the Father also agreed to furnish Christ with all the necessary qualifications for his work, and to reward him for accomplishing it. "The Father so far trusted Christ, that upon the credit of his promise to come into the world, and in the fulness of time to become a sacrifice for the elect, He saved all the Old Testament saints, whose faith also respected a Christ to come." (pp. 6, 7.)

In the next sermon, on John iii. 16, we read:—

"God's giving of Christ implies his delivering him into the hands of justice to be punished: even as condemned persons are by sentence of law given or delivered into the hands of executioners. The Lord, when the time was come that Christ must suffer, did as it were say, 'O all ye roaring waves of my incensed justice, now swell as high as heaven, and go over his soul and body: sink him to the bottom; let him go, like Jonah, his type, into the belly of hell, unto the roots of the mountains. Come, all ye raging storms that I have reserved for this day of wrath, beat upon him, beat him down. Go, justice, put him upon the rack, torment him in every part,'" &c. (p. 9.) This terrible vengeance is represented as but fulfilling what the Father in the compact had announced to the Son, thus: "My Son, if thou undertake for them, thou must reckon to pay the last mite; expect no abatements; if I spare them, I will not spare thee." (p. 8.) "To wrath, to the wrath of an infinite God, without mixture, to the very torments of hell, was Christ delivered, and that by the hand of his own Father." (p. 10.)

With equal plainness does this earnest and outspoken Calvinist insist, in his eighth sermon, that God could not exercise his mercy without satisfaction to his justice. "He, therefore, that will be a Mediator of Reconciliation betwixt God and man, must bring God a price in his hand, and that adequate to the offence and wrong done Him, else He will not treat about peace." (p. 21.) "Our Mediator, like Jonah his type, seeing the stormy sea of God's wrath working tempestuously, and ready to swallow us up, cast in himself to appease the storm." (p. 22.) More distinctly still we read in the twelfth sermon: "The design and end of this oblation was to atone, pacify, and reconcile God, by giving him a full and adequate compensation or satisfaction for the sins of these his elect. From this oblation Christ made of himself to God for our sins, we infer the inflexible severity of Divine justice, which could be no other way diverted from us and appeased, but by the blood of Christ. And though he brake out upon the cross in that heart-rending complaint, 'My God! my God! why hast thou forsaken me?' yet no abatement: justice will not bend in the least, but, having to do with him on this account, resolves to fetch its pennyworths out of his blood." (p. 35.) In the fourteenth sermon Flavel says: "Only the blood of God is found an equivalent price for the redemption of souls." (p. 41.)

Conformed to these representations is Flavel's description of the actual sufferings endured by Christ, thus: "The wrath of an infinite, dreadful God beat him down to the dust. His body full of pain and exquisite tortures in every part. Not a member or sense but was the seat and subject of torment." (p. 88.) "His cry was like the perpetual shriek of them that are cast away for ever. Yea, in sufferings at this time in his soul, equivalent to all that which our souls should have suffered there to all eternity." (p. 102.) "As it was all the wrath of God that lay upon Christ, so it was wrath aggravated in divers respects, beyond that which the damned themselves do suffer." (p. 106.)

One other quotation will prove that the author did not believe that God would grant to Christ anything beyond the covenant as it embraced the *elect.* The extract is in strange contrast with admissions made by eminent champions of Orthodoxy at the present day, in allowing an unlimited atonement and the efficacy of Christ's death for millions who have or have had no knowledge of him. It is from Sermon XV.: "Hence we infer the impossibility of their salvation that know not Christ, nor have interest in his blood. Neither heathens, nor merely nominal Christians, can inherit heaven. I know some are very indulgent to the heathen, and many formal Christians are but too much so to themselves. But union by faith with Jesus Christ is the only way revealed in Scripture by which we hope to come to the heavenly inheritance. I know it seems hard that such brave men as some of the heathens were should be damned. But the Scripture knows no other way to glory but Christ put on and applied by faith. And it is the common suffrage of modern sound divines, that no man, by the sole conduct of Nature, without the knowledge of Christ, can be saved." (p. 44.)

Thus the old Calvinistic construction of the doctrine was, that the obedience of Christ takes the place of our lack of obedience; that he became to God the personal substitute for condemned sinners; that by the imputation of our transgressions to him, he endured the suffering threatened upon us; and that, by bearing the just penalty of an outraged law, he discharged our indebtedness to it, and purchased our redemption from the Lawgiver. It would be possible, if time and space allowed, to trace by a chain of quotations from Orthodox divines the course of softening and modifying speculations which have reduced the old doctrine to the mildest form of the governmental theory, presenting the elder Edwards and Dr. Hopkins as the mediums for working the prominent changes in the use of terms or in the construction put upon them. We might thus easily exhibit, were it worth our while, all the shadings off, if we should not rather say the shadings over, of the old doctrine. Edwards very ingeniously remarks: "Most of the words which are used in this affair have various significations."* The following sentences from this eminent divine will exhibit his views of "the work of Redemption": "There is no mercy exercised towards man but what is obtained through Christ's intercession." (p. 26.) "For when man [Adam] had sinned, God the Father would have no more to do with man immediately; he would no more have any immediate concern with this world of mankind that had apostatized from, and re-

* Works, edition of 1808, Vol. II. p. 190.

belled against him." (p. 27.) "All is done by the price that Christ lays down. But the price that Christ lays down does two things. It pays our debt, and so it *satisfies*. By its intrinsic value, and by the agreement between the Father and the Son, it procures a title to us for happiness, and so it *merits*. The satisfaction of Christ is to free us from misery, and the merit of Christ is to purchase happiness for us." (p. 190.) "The satisfaction of Christ consists in his answering the demands of the law on man, which were consequent on the breach of the law. These were answered by suffering the penalty of the law. The merit of Christ consists in what he did to answer the demands of the law, which were prior to man's breach of the law, or to fulfil what the law demanded before man sinned, which was obedience." (p. 191.)

There is a savor of good old Mr. Flavel's view of the "covenant work" in the following account given of it by the excellent Dr. Hopkins: "It is evident from Scripture, as well as from the nature of the case, that there was a mutual agreement and engagement between the Father and the second person of the Trinity, respecting the redemption of man, by which the distinct part which each person in the Trinity was to act was fixed and undertaken. This mutual agreement is of the nature of a covenant and engagement with each other to perform the different parts of this great work which were assigned to them. This is an eternal covenant without beginning, as is the existence of the triune God, and as are all the divine purposes and decrees. The second person was engaged to become incarnate,—to do and suffer all that was necessary for the salvation of men. The Father promised that, on his consenting to take upon him the character and work of a Mediator and Redeemer, he should be every way furnished and assisted to go through with the work; that he should have power to save an elect number of mankind, and form a church and kingdom most perfect and glorious. In order to accomplish this, all things — all power in heaven and earth — should be given to him, until redemption was completed. And then he should reign in the exercise of all his offices as Mediator, in his Church and kingdom for ever." After quoting passages of Scripture by the old method to authenticate these views, Dr. Hopkins adds: "Though in the passages of Scripture which have been mentioned, and others of the same kind, the third person in the Trinity, the Holy Spirit, is not expressly mentioned as covenanting or engaging to perform any part of this work, yet he is necessarily understood as concerned and included in this covenant, as he is in the Holy Scripture everywhere represented as acting an equal part in the redemption of man, and therefore must be considered as taking that particular part by consent and agreement." * Were it not for the more dramatic view of the "covenant," not between God and man, but between the Father and the Son, which we have already quoted from Flavel, and which might be paralleled from other divines, we might affirm that Dr. Hopkins was not wholly destitute of the imaginative faculty in having conjured up the above conceit, for which the Bible is not responsible. His ingenuity in apologizing for the apparent neglect of the Holy Spirit is not the least striking element in his description. He is explicit in stating a limited atonement, limited at least in its actual work. "Redemption," he says, "does not extend to all sinful, fallen creatures, but many are left to suffer the just consequence of their rebellion in everlasting punishment. It is expressly and repeatedly declared in divine revelation, that a part of mankind shall be punished for ever." (p. 248.) Anticipatory

* Professor Park's edition of Hopkins's Works, Vol. I. pp. 356 – 358.

hints of the "governmental theory," as now held by a philosophical school of Orthodox divines, are to be found scattered over Dr. Hopkins's pages. He speaks of what is consistent or inconsistent with "rectoral righteousness." He says: "The sufferings of Christ answer the same end with respect to law and divine government, that otherwise must be answered by the eternal destruction of the sinner." (p. 328.) He says the blood shed upon the cross "was the blood of God." (p. 282.) Dr. Hopkins is generally very scrupulous and careful to sustain his own strongest assertions by references to passages of Scripture, which, however strangely or fancifully he may quote them, and however unjustifiable and inapplicable the use he makes of them, prove at least his fair intent to bring his assertions to a true test. But for one of his boldest assertions, that which covers one of the vital and most disputable points in the whole discussion of the atonement, he alleges no Scripture authority. Thus he says: "*It was in early times expressly declared* that sacrifices and offerings were not desirable, or of any worth, in themselves considered, and that God did not institute and require them for their own sake, as making any real atonement for sin; *but that this should be made by an incarnate Redeemer*, to whom they pointed as types and shadows of him." (p. 325.) The good doctor drew wholly on his imagination here, as regards the statement which we have put in italics. It was in early times expressly declared and emphatically reiterated, that sacrifices had no value except as they indicated penitence and piety of heart. Obedience was better. The Jewish sacrifices were subordinated to contrition, mercy, faith, and amendment of life,—*never in a single instance to another prospective sacrifice*. Scripture has not a word to this effect.

The favorite form under which the old doctrine is now advocated by the advanced party among those who claim to represent the ancient Orthodoxy of Congregationalism, is called technically "the Governmental Theory." We will cite a quite recent and very clear statement of it. Dr. Pond, in the article above referred to in the "Bibliotheca Sacra," states, as the first reason for the necessity of Christ's agency in reconciliation, that which all Christians will heartily accept, namely, that it "was necessary in order that sinners might *be humbled and brought to repentance*." He might have quoted many beautiful Scripture sentences in proof of this statement, as every doctrine that is really Scriptural may be expressed more beautifully and forcibly in that than in any other language. Thus: "It behooved Christ to suffer and to rise from the dead, that repentance and remission of sins should be preached in his name among all nations." (Luke xxiv. 46, 47.) "God, having raised up his Son Jesus, sent him to bless you, in turning away every one of you from his iniquities." (Acts iii. 26.)

But, adds Dr. Pond, "This necessity for the atonement is not, after all, the most urgent and fundamental. There is a necessity greater than this. We remark, therefore, the atonement of Christ was necessary to sustain and honor the broken law of God, to vindicate his authority, and satisfy his glorious justice." Now we see how easy it is for the believers of this theory to state it intelligibly and boldly. But how comes it that they have to state it in words and phrases of their own? If the sacred writers had wished to state it, nothing would have been easier. But where is there a sentence within the covers of the Bible that can be quoted as explicitly advancing it? We do not hesitate to say, with all the frankness and positiveness of full conviction, that there is not a line or a phrase of Scripture that affirms such a doctrine. Divines have to state it in their own terms, because Scripture terms fail them. Of course we are well aware that there are passages in the Bible which are constructively and inferentially turned to support this dogma. But the constructions and the inferences are the very matters in debate. Having entered our distinct protest here, with an honest and sufficient reason for it, we must follow the reasoning which proceeds *on a human formula.*

Dr. Pond argues, it is necessary for God as the Supreme Ruler "to sustain law. He must not suffer his law to be trifled with and trampled on. He must maintain it inviolate in all its strictness and strength, its authority and purity, or his government of law will be subverted and overthrown." The law, he adds, can be sustained by punishing the transgressors as they deserve, by inflicting upon them the threatened penalty, and only in this way, unless some expedient can be devised by which the honor of the broken law, and the display of God's righteous regard for it, and all the ends of government, can be secured as fully, as perfectly, as they would be by inflicting the penalty. Without some such expedient, to pardon and save sinners would be a moral impossibility, intolerable under the government of God, inconsistent with its stability, its perfection, and even with its continued existence. The Professor does not stop to weigh the balance between the two conditions under which the law may be duly honored, nor to decide by which of the two the ends of law, and the very idea of *Law*, may be vindicated. One of these is, the repentance in dust and ashes, in deepest contrition, of those who, having broken the law, have already suffered from it and by it, and who now honor it by suing with imploring hearts for forgiveness; taken in connection with the tribute also paid to the law by the sufferings of those who break it and do not repent. The other condition is, the visiting the penalty of a broken law on one who has not broken it, but has honored it in all its provisions. Which of these two conditions wins the nobler tribute, the more adequate satisfaction to an outraged law? Let the parent ask the question as it applies to family discipline. Are its ends better answered to him by the kneeling contrition and the importunate appeals for forgiveness of an erring child, or by requiring, or even allowing, an unoffending brother or sister to submit to a punishment? Would the parable of the prodigal son win a new attraction for our hearts, an enhanced power over our consciences, if the father had been represented as scourging the elder son before he embraced the younger?

Dr. Pond proceeds to argue, that the agency of Christ offered an expedient alternative to the suffering of sinners, for sustaining law,—not, however, through his perfect holiness, nor through his perfect obedience to the divine law, the merit of which obedience is imputed to us, as the old doctrine affirmed,—but *through his sufferings and death*,—"in the shedding of his blood." In pronouncing upon the mode of the *efficacy* of Christ's death, "the *manner* in which it *availed* to make an atonement for sin," he rejects that element of the Catechism doctrine which teaches "that Christ by his suffering for us literally *paid our debt to divine justice*," or that "he met *the strict and proper penalty of the law*," as the fulfilment of these conditions would have required that Christ should have been the subject of the most hateful and painful passions, stings and reproaches of conscience, dissatisfaction with God, and the pains and agonies of the bottomless pit in eternal death. These Christ did not suffer. But he answered "the ends of justice." "His death was *vicarious*. He died as a *substitute*." "He endured, not the proper penalty of the law for us, but an adequate *substitute for that penalty*." "He offered *a fair and full equivalent* for the everlasting sufferings of all who shall be finally saved." In this view, Dr. Pond finds the reason why "Christ must have been just such a personage, God and man, divine and human, as he is represented in the Scriptures. Had he been a divine person only, he could not have made an atonement, because the divine nature cannot suffer and die. And had he been a human person only, he could not have made an atonement, because he would have been unable, without the divine nature, to endure the requisite amount of suffering, and he would have lacked that personal dignity and glory which impart such a value and efficacy to his death."

Now, if without the least feeling of disrespect to the writer of the last-quoted sentences, but with the simple purpose of expressing how tortuous is the idea which they present to our own minds, we may venture to paraphrase them, we must say that they seem to us to intimate that Christ's human nature needed the divine element, because the human nature could not suffer enough; and that the divine nature needed the human element, because the divine nature could not suffer at all. Is Christian doctrine answerable for such devices, or do they come of the brains of men?

Similar to these views of the Bangor Professor are the following, which we find in a recent devotional work, otherwise enriched with some of the choicest and most impressive lessons of Christian piety, conveyed in the most chaste and fervent language. We refer to "The Communion Sabbath," by Rev. Dr. N. Adams. The author says: "God alone was able to expiate the sin of his creatures, by taking man's nature into union with the Divine, in the person of the Word, and making satisfaction to justice by that which He saw to be equivalent in effect to the endless punishment of the race." (p. 34.) The author speaks of Christ as "expiating our guilt." (p. 37.) He also says: "The death of Christ was not a substitute for our crucifixion, but for our endless misery." (p. 63.)

Now if the denial, unreserved and emphatic, of this

view — call it "the governmental theory," or by any other title — of what it was necessary, *in reference to God*, and *to God's law*, that Christ should do, and of what Christ did, to open the way for our reconciliation with our Heavenly Father, — if this denial be indeed a denial of the Scripture doctrine of the Atonement, then Unitarians must needs submit to the charge, and meet it as they can. But not for one moment will Unitarians allow that this is the Scripture doctrine of the Atonement. They find no such doctrine in the Scriptures, but one quite unlike it. It is usual for Orthodox writers against us to assert that boastful reason and obduracy object to this doctrine, because of its humiliating character, because of its affront to human pride! But how differently do men judge of the same things! For ourselves, we must say that we know of no mounting fancy or conception among all the fabulous incarnations of Hindoo or Indian mythology, or among the apotheoses of Pagan idolatry, which offers such an incense to human pride as do some of the shapings of this popular doctrine of the Atonement. The charge against us has always seemed to us to be one of the most perverse distortions of truth which polemical inventiveness could devise. What is there humbling to human pride in the doctrine that God for our sakes (for his own sake, even!) condescended to such a method for our redemption? Were the subject of a monarch in captivity in a foreign land to send home to have a ransom provided for him, and were the monarch himself to go to redeem him, the last effect which we should look for would be that the redeemed captive should feel humbled by the transaction. He would boast it as the highest of his honors. The Orthodox doctrine seems to us, certainly in comparison with our own, to foster a surpassing conceit of human pride. But the implication intended to be conveyed by the Orthodox charge against us is, that we really find their doctrine in the New Testament, or, at least, have a misgiving that it is there, while we contumaciously resist it. Will they therefore give us the benefit of our own most sincere and earnest profession, that, with all the means which they have for understanding the Scriptures, and with as profound a sense of their value, and as single a purpose to know and obey their lessons, we find no such doctrine in them as Orthodoxy teaches?

We have stated that the antagonistic issue opened between Orthodoxy and Unitarianism, after long and full debate, has committed us to the following position: That the Scriptures do not lay the emphatic stress of Christ's redeeming work upon his death, above or apart from his life, character, and doctrine; and that his death, as an element of his redeeming work, is made effective for human salvation through its influence on the heart and life of man, not through its vicarious or substituted value with God, nor through its removal of an abstract difficulty in the Divine government which hinders the forgiveness of the penitent without further satisfaction. All the points now left in debate between the two parties are recognized in this summary statement. A brief reference to them, successively, will exhibit in as summary a way our denials of Orthodox positions, and the reason for such denials, and also the substance and grounds of our own doctrinal belief.

A few years ago Unitarianism was compelled to object that Orthodoxy laid the *whole* emphasis of Christ's redeeming work upon his death, upon his cross, his humiliation, his ignominy and sufferings. Of late the co-ordinate value of the life and doctrine of Christ has been acknowledged by some able Orthodox writers, though essential Calvinism and the formula of the Westminster Catechism made no account whatever of these elements of his redeeming work. His *merits* and *obedience* were recognized as prevailing with God, —

not with man. Still we think that even the fullest recognition which we have ever met on any page of modern Orthodoxy does not do justice to the proportions of Scriptural truth on this point. No conviction lives more sincerely in the hearts of Unitarians than this, that the first erroneous bias of Orthodoxy arises precisely here. God forbid that we should write a word to depreciate the importance, the stress, or the value, in the whole work of redemption, of the cross, the death of Christ. But we do not fear this risk when our sole purpose is, not to compare the death of Christ with any other death, but to insist upon its relative aspect and proportions in connection with all else in him and by him. It is Christ's life, and Christ's character, and Christ's doctrine, which we would not have overshadowed by his cross.

Christ came into the world, as he said, to die for the world, and, in dying, to bear witness to the truth the knowledge and obedience of which would insure eternal life to men. Thus his life, his character, and his doctrine are made the elements of his work. When these were displayed to men, they would bring him to his cross, while by that cross he would draw all men unto him. We have, then, to look to his life, character, and doctrine to find the purpose and the lesson of his death. But, in our view, Orthodoxy does violence to truth by impairing the proportion of its ingredients on these vast and solemn themes. Orthodoxy does not follow the harmony of Scripture in laying equal stress upon all that Christ was and taught and did. We do not charge Orthodoxy with laying too much stress upon the death of *Christ*, but with laying too much stress upon the *death* of Christ. The error of Orthodoxy here seems to us to lie in the same direction as does that of the Church of Rome, in the painful multiplication and obtrusion of its scenical and symbolical pictures of the crucifixion; in its analytic representations of the incidents and instruments of the Passion, as shown in the "Stations of the Cross," and in its elaborate ingenuities for keeping all the agonies of Calvary ever before the eye of the worshipper. The Scriptures do not thus isolate and emphasize the Saviour's sufferings. A misleading effect has been produced by the habit of Orthodox disputants, when arguing upon the cross of Christ, of selecting and bringing together from each separate document of the New Testament all the passages which refer to the death of the Saviour. It is forgotten that those documents were addressed by different writers to different communities, and the impression is designed or left that all the passages entered into each announcement or appeal of the Gospel. Indeed, if one could be content to go through the New Testament for the purpose of deciding by count or by the force of emphasis what one element of the Saviour's whole agency or history is chiefly insisted upon by the Apostles, he would probably find that his *resurrection* takes precedence of all others. Paul does not say, If Christ has not died, your faith is vain; but, "If Christ be not risen from the dead, then is our preaching vain: ye are yet in your sins." (1 Cor. xv. 14, 17.) It was his "hope of the resurrection of the dead," for which Paul was called in question before the Pharisees. (Acts xxiii. 6.) When the Apostle enjoyed the coveted opportunity of addressing Felix and Drusilla concerning "the faith in Christ," the record tells us that "he reasoned of righteousness, temperance, and judgment to come," with no reference to an expiatory offering made by Christ. And when he stood before King Agrippa to proclaim the hope and promise of the Gospel, there was the same silence about the expiation, and the same stress laid upon the doctrine of the resurrection. "Why should it be thought a thing incredible with you that God should raise the dead?" (Acts xxvi. 8.) "Jesus and the resurrection" were the strange things that Paul preached at Athens. (Acts xvii. 18, 20, 31, 32.)

Why, then, it may be asked, if the death of Christ is not made in Scripture to be the paramount and only emphatic incident in his manifestation to men, — why did he so die? Why was not his ministry terminated peacefully, gently, and by some natural process? We answer, at this stage of our argument, — leaving the point for further remark in another connection, — that a suffering end was the consistent termination of such a life and of such a work. The sacrificial character of his death — and we hold his death to have been sacrificial in the highest sense of the word — had been foreshadowed by every incident and element of his manifestation. In the body of flesh, through which he suffered on the cross, he had been humbled, and tempted, and scourged, and buffeted. The hands and feet which he showed to his disciples, pierced by the nails on Mount Calvary, had shared the toils and weariness of his ministry as the servant of all. How far the knowledge of "the decease which he should accomplish at Jerusalem," and of the method of it, may have pervaded and deepened the spirit of all his words and deeds, and given to what humanly we call his character its solitary perfectness and its fulness of heavenward consecration, it would be presumptuous in a disciple to judge. It is written of him, however, that he was himself "made perfect through suffering"; that the crowning grace of his soul was his triumph over mortal weakness; and that by his own endurance of trial he became the consoler and the supporter of those among whom his cross is divided. How much of his fitness for his mediatorial work was secured by his own subjection in the flesh, we know not. But we have the knowledge of his life and ministry, which warrants us in saying that the only consistent termination of his life and work was that which closed it on the cross. His was a public life of outward severities, humiliations, and mortifications. To have ended it in retirement, on a peaceful couch in a private dwelling, under a gentle ministration such as his houseless lot had never shared, would not have been in harmony with its course and consecration. Not with reference to any legal exactions of the Almighty Father, but as addressed to the hearts of men, do we enter into the touching significance of such words as these, from the Saviour's own lips: "The Son of Man *must* suffer many things, and be rejected"; "He *must* be delivered into the hands of sinful men"; "He *must needs* have suffered and risen again from the dead"; and, on the walk to Emmaus, "*Ought* not Christ to have suffered these things, and to enter into his glory?"

In the mean while the reconciling offices of Christ, as they are concentrated under the shadows of his cross, are distributed over the toils and the benedictive services of his life, are manifested in the graces of his character, and are set forth in his counsels, his appeals, his promises, and his personal ministry in the heart of a believer. His touch could heal; his word could forgive and save; his look could rebuke and win; his common converse could make hearts to burn within them; and his dying groan did but *finish* the work he had long been doing. It may be that the greater multitude of his disciples in every age have been won to him by the "power of his sufferings." Indeed, this result would follow, or would seem to follow, from the fact that his preachers have selected for stress and reiteration that single point of appeal. But confident we are, that, without diminution from the attractions of the cross, it may be affirmed that his life and character and doctrine, his grace and truth, his humility and patience and sinlessness, have secured him unnumbered believers in all time. The death of Christ takes we know not how much of its meaning from his life. The blessed power of sympathy in suffering in a world of sufferers, where disciples "must drink of the cup and be baptized with the baptism" of their Master, is an influence which we dare not fathom or bound. We feel, however, that some of the most sacred and potent sway of Christ over the weary, the crushed, the woful and agonized, depends upon the fact, that the holiest and the tenderest sharer of our infirmities was "a man of sorrows and acquainted with grief." There is an intimation which we will not ungenerously force, but which we cannot but follow up in our thoughts as dropped by St. Paul, when, in a mysterious way, he says that he rejoiced in his sufferings, and filled up in his flesh that which was "lacking in the afflictions of Christ for his body's sake, which is the Church." It is as if the Apostle ventured to suggest that he would contribute even his own pains and agonies to fill out the sacred purpose of his Master's sufferings.

We come now to the vital point of the doctrinal difference between Unitarianism and Orthodoxy as regards the Atonement. Since we are now found to accord in the meaning of that word as expressing reconciliation, we accept the condition that the Scripture doctrine which we wish to define is — the agency of Christ in opening and preparing the way for a reconciliation between God and men. Keeping in view what has just been said respecting the whole agency of Christ in his life, his character, and his doctrine, we will now concentrate the issue upon his death. How is the death of Christ made efficacious for human salvation? What is the revealed method of its working to that result? The two parties to be reconciled are man, the sinning child, and God, the kind and righteous and offended Father; man, who is a debtor to the law, and God, whose just due and service have been denied him. Man is in the wrong, not God; man needs to be changed, not

God; for he is ever waiting and willing to be gracious. There is a relation of hostility between the Father and the child, and Christ comes to mediate between them. His death, whether or not it has the chief efficacy, has at least the crowning agency in his mediatorial work of securing reconciliation. But how? Through what instrumentality, method, or process? We recognize two, and only two, directions in which we can look for an answer to this question. Orthodoxy looks in one of these directions, and brings back a report which fixes its doctrine on this subject. Unitarianism looks in another direction, and accepts as a consequence another doctrine. We do not wish to avail ourselves of any dubiousness of language, of any confusion of terms, of any specious assumptions of a deceptive accord in opinions which are in fact radically different. We aim for candor, and we would rather overstate than understate our difference with Orthodoxy on this point. Clear-headed, out-spoken, frankly avowed conviction is what we all need here, — what the interests of truth, what the hopes of amity and tolerance, even amid differences, are rested upon. Orthodoxy regards the death of Christ as looking GOD-WARD for its efficacy. Unitarianism regards the death of Christ as looking MAN-WARD for its efficacy. If we have not in this distinction fairly and fully stated the whole issue between us, we beg that our error may be ascribed to our inability to comprehend and define the issue, not to any lack of right intent or desire to do so. We believe that we have expressed it fairly. Indeed, it is because we regard the Calvinistic theory in all its shapes and modifications as involving an influence in Christ's death which looks toward God for its efficacy, that we reject it in heart and faith, unreservedly and earnestly, as a heathenish and an unchristian doctrine.

The essential token of the Calvinistic or Orthodox

scheme on this doctrine, whether characterized as a covenant between the Father and the Son, or centring upon the word *vicarious*, or *satisfaction*, or planting itself upon a "governmental theory," is that the efficacy of Christ's death works by its operation upon God, or some attribute of God, or upon some abstract difficulty in which he is involved by the laws of government he has himself established. Orthodoxy interposes a law between God and man which mercy cannot relax, but which only a victim can satisfy. God can freely forgive, but his law cannot freely remit a penitent offender. The essential token of the Unitarian scheme is that the whole operation of Christ's mediatorial death is upon the heart and life and spirit of man. We cannot confound or merge this fundamental distinction; it reaches deep; it rises high. Though Unitarianism may not undertake to fathom, or comprehend, or give expression to all the mysterious influence and efficacy and mode of operation upon man and man's soul and destiny, though Unitarianism is free to acknowledge an unexplained and inexplicable agency in the sacrificial death of Christ, it nevertheless looks for it *all* in the direction of humanity, not in the direction of the Deity. We are ready for ourselves to go all the lengths of mysticism and mystification on this point, and to yield to the feeling of being on unsounded waters beneath unfathomed depths of ether. We are cheerfully willing to admit that God has comprehended influences in the sacrificial death of Christ which are designed to be efficaciously felt and mercifully availed of by us without yielding to the solution of our understanding. We can even accept some statements which we find in Orthodox pages about "a satisfaction made to law," by simply construing them as applying the sanction and penalties of the law to us through the sufferings of Christ for sin. We can accord well with the following remark of the great Bishop Butler: "How and in what particular way Christ's death had this efficacy [obtaining pardon], there are not wanting persons who have endeavored to explain; but I do not find that the Scripture has explained it. And if the Scripture has, as surely it has, left this matter of the satisfaction of Christ mysterious, left somewhat in it unrevealed, all conjectures about it must be, if not evidently absurd, yet at least uncertain." * We too would be willing to leave the matter unexplained. But our protest against the Orthodox scheme is, that, instead of ascribing the intelligible or the mysterious efficacy of Christ's death to its uses for offending, sinning, and repenting man, it makes a revolting dogma, or a needless device, and follows the sacrifice of the cross into the skies, as setting matters right between God and his own attributes of Justice and Mercy.

We are sensitive to any blurring of the dividing line between the God-ward or the Man-ward working of the efficacy of Christ's whole mediatorial office. We ask no compromise of opinion, we will make none whatever. We are impatient of any confusion of terms, any intermingling of distinctions, on this point. Reconciliation involves two conditions, — repentance in the offender, forgiveness on the part of the wronged. Or, if we add to the condition on the one side, we must qualify the grace on the other. If we require that the offender must not only repent, but make reparation, then we must recognize in the other party, not simple forgiveness, but the exacting of a satisfaction. As God is revealed as forgiving iniquity, he consents to forego satisfaction; and as man is unable to make reparation, he is required to offer penitence. We cannot attribute forgiveness where repentance and reparation are both demanded, for then the remission is not of grace, but by

* Analogy, Part II. Chap. V.

payment. We can neither fetter God's administration with laws which restrict his prerogative of mercy, nor take the benignity out of his forgiveness by attaching a purchase to its exercise.

Unitarianism, in opposition to Orthodoxy, maintains that the death of Christ, so far as its efficacy is distinctly defined, is instrumental to our salvation through its influence on the heart and life of man, not through its vicarious value with God; and also that revelation does not acquaint us with any obstacle in the method of administration which God has established as his government, which prevents his exercising mercy to the penitent except through the substitution of a victim to law.

And here, for the sake of averting an erroneous and an injurious judgment often visited by Orthodoxy upon our views, let a simple statement be strongly made. Orthodoxy, not through warrant of anything which Unitarianism proclaims, but by one of the unkind arts of controversy, attempts to confine our construction of the atoning death of Christ to the power and service of an example. We protest against the charge: we repel it. What some Unitarians may have recognized as a subsidiary and incidental lesson from the cross of Christ, ought not to be thus represented as exhausting our view of it. It is not our doctrine that the death of Christ becomes efficacious to us as an example, or even that it is especially needed or available in that direction. Christ is to us a victim, a sacrifice: his death was a sacrificial death. Its method and purpose and influence fix a new, a specific, a peculiar, an eminent meaning to the word *sacrifice*, when used of him. Indeed, the highest and most sacred signification of the word ought for ever to be associated with *his* sacrifice. But, in conformity with that deciding distinction already made as settled by the terms of a God-ward or a Man-ward intent in the cross, we regard Jesus as a sacrifice *for man*, but not as a sacrifice *to God.* The difference is an infinite one, as indicated by those two prepositions attached respectively to the creature and the Creator. We regard Christ as a victim offered by human sin for human redemption; as one who could not have been our Redeemer but by being "faithful unto death," and as a willing sacrifice for our redemption. He was led as a lamb to the slaughter, and his murderers, as the Prophet had foretold that they would, had wrongly "esteemed him stricken, smitten of God, and afflicted." (Isaiah liii. 4.) But instead of being "stricken of God," he was "wounded for our iniquities." "He tasted death for every man"; not *eternal* death, but death. He was nailed to the cross to secure our salvation, but not to make reparation for our sins to God.

If reconciliation between man and God be the object of the death, as of the life, the character, and the doctrine of Christ, the process for securing that reconciliation requires that the party who has been wronged shall announce first on what terms he will grant it, and that the offending party shall then yield to those terms. Men are the party in the wrong; they are to be brought to a sense of their sin, to be made acquainted with the terms which God proposes for forgiveness, and induced to comply with them. So complete has been the perversion of the simple Scripture terms of reconciliation which Orthodox views have for ages made current in the world, that there has been an actual inversion of the relations of parties. How frequently do Orthodox writers, as if wholly unconscious of the strange liberty which they take in wresting Scripture, allow themselves to speak of Christ as "reconciling *God* to us," instead of following Scripture, which always speaks of Christ as "reconciling *us* to God"! Indeed, the second of the Thirty-Nine Articles of the Church of England, as also of the Episcopal Church in this country, speaks of Christ's manifestation as designed "to reconcile his Father to us"! Such are the risks of false doctrine.

What, then, are the terms of reconciliation which God announces through Christ to men? The terms on which God offers forgiveness are such a faith in Christ as will lead us to realize his doctrine of our sinfulness, our hostility and alienation from God, and our consequent state of danger and condemnation; and further, such a faith in Christ as will persuade us of his authority to promise forgiveness on our repentance and future obedience, while at the same time we avail ourselves of those conditions and yield to the constraining influences of God's Holy Spirit. These are the terms which Unitarianism recognizes for reconciliation to God through Jesus Christ. If God will give us grace to fulfil these conditions, we will compound with ourselves for all anxiety about every "Governmental Theory" which the fancies of theologians can conjure up.

Orthodoxy recognizes these same terms of reconciliation, but adds to them another, looking, not man-ward but God-ward, for its necessity and its efficacy. Orthodoxy argues that violated law requires not only such a recognition of its authority as is offered to the lawgiver by a penitent offender, but also a victim, an expiation, to sustain and vindicate its honor. As God is the representative of that law, he requires that a substitute suffer for the penitent offender in order thus to sustain the authority of law. Christ was that suffering substitute to outraged law for us, and one of the effects of true and saving faith in him is to make us partakers in the merits of his God-ward sacrifice.

As Scripture affords not a single sentence which, even by the aid of a gloss or a false construction, can be used as a formula for stating *all the elements* comprehended in this Orthodox dogma, we will present some of the simplest announcements of it which we have found in the writings of theologians. Bishop Butler, all whose words seem to have been weighed in the scales of a calm and cautious wisdom, says: "Some have endeavored to explain the efficacy of what Christ has done and suffered for us, beyond what the Scripture has authorized; others, probably because they could not explain it, have been for taking it away, and confining his office as Redeemer of the world to his instruction, example, and government of the Church. Whereas the doctrine of the Gospel appears to be, not only that he taught the efficacy of repentance, but rendered it of the efficacy which it is, by what he did and suffered for us; that he obtained for us the benefit of having our repentance accepted unto eternal life; not only that he revealed to sinners that they were in a capacity of salvation, and how they might obtain it, but moreover that he put them into this capacity of salvation by what he did and suffered for them, — put us into a capacity of escaping future punishment, and obtaining future happiness." He had before recognized it as among the teachings of revelation, "that the rules of the Divine government are such as not to admit of pardon immediately and directly upon repentance, or by the sole efficacy of it." He afterwards adds, in reference to the supposed Scriptural view of the purpose designed in Christ's sufferings, "Its tendency to vindicate the authority of God's laws, and deter his creatures from sin, has never yet been answered, and is, I think, plainly unanswerable; though I am far from thinking it an account of the whole of the case." "Let reason be kept to, and if any part of the Scripture account of the redemption of the world by Christ can be shown to be really contrary to it, let the Scripture, in the name of God, be given up; but let not such poor creatures as we go on objecting against an infinite scheme, that we do not see the necessity or usefulness of all its parts, and call this reasoning." *

This moderation is the very majesty of wisdom. Let us see what the modern Orthodoxy of New England says on the same point. Dr. Woods tells us, that "all the influence of repentance results from the death of Christ. Repentance is a means on our part of obtaining the good purchased by Christ's death." "Christ's death was appointed by God as a substitute for the punishment of sinners; it answered the same purposes; it made substantially the same display of God's attributes and the principles of his government, and has the same efficacy, though far superior in degree, to promote the permanent welfare of his kingdom." "A brief definition of the Atonement, then, might be given in some such manner as this: It is Christ's obedience unto death, even the death of the cross in the place of sinners, for the purpose of vindicating the violated law, manifesting the righteousness of God, making expiation for sin, and procuring forgiveness, sanctification, and eternal life for all believers." † The strange confusion of ideas and terms which necessarily attaches to the Orthodox theology, presents a specimen of itself in the following sentences, when compared together. In his Eighth Letter to Unitarians, Dr. Woods says: "God would never have saved sinners, had not Christ interposed and made an atonement." Yet in his Ninth Letter he says: "It is uniformly the sentiment of the Orthodox, that the origin, the grand moving cause of redemption, was the infinite love, benignity, or mercy of God."

Very frequently we find the point of the Orthodox doctrine thus sharply presented: "Repentance is the *condition* of forgiveness with God, but the death of Christ

* Analogy, Part II. Chap. V.

† Dr. Woods's Works, Vol. II. pp. 404, 453, 463.

is the *ground* on which that condition is effectual." "The *ground* of salvation is the completed work, the atoning merits of our Lord Jesus Christ: the *condition* of their bestowal on an individual is repentance." Such formulas as the following we might quote from many writers: — "The sufferings and death of Christ were necessary to make the exercise of the divine mercy to men consistent with the maintenance of divine justice." "Christ died for the purpose of removing an obstacle in the divine government, in the way of extending pardon to the penitent."

The Orthodox doctrine of the Atonement may, therefore, be regarded as concentrated now upon this "governmental theory," and as standing or falling with the proof or the failure of proof that this theory, owing nothing to the wit or fancy of man, is positively and clearly taught in the Scriptures. We have seen how positively and clearly its believers can state it, and this raises our demand, that, putting aside their own formulas, they should offer us instead "the law and the testimony," *and give us at least one text which includes all its essential terms.* It is something, however, to have the old shapings and concomitants once attached to the doctrine, as by good Mr. Flavel, withdrawn from our current religious literature. Those who, as professors in divinity schools, and as men of eminent distinction as theologians, are educating a new generation of ministers, will very soon introduce more or less important modifications in the popular belief by different constructions of this governmental theory. The fluctuations and tonings down of opinion which have reached that form of doctrinal statement are not likely to stop with it. If with due modesty we may intimate a conviction which the tendencies of thought, with some recent striking examples of the result of those tendencies, lead us to hold in strong assurance, we will say that this legal view of

Christ's death must and will yield to a profounder Christian philosophy. Its best recommendation, its strength, consisted in the relief which it afforded to Orthodox believers when they were pressed by the objections to a more repulsive theory. It still has a strong sway over the sentiments; it will fail when tested by textual criticism and the logic of truth. Within the month, we have read three very able arguments against it by men who were educated to defend it, from three such different quarters as the Scotch Church, through J. McLeod Campbell, the English Church, by Mr. Jowett, and the Baptist Church in this country, by Dr. Sheldon. We must devote our little remaining space to a brief mention of a few of our many objections to this last phase of the old Orthodox doctrine of the Atonement. It might seem needless, yet, to avert misunderstanding or misrepresentation, we will here remind all readers, that we are not bringing our reason to bear against a doctrine of revelation, which may God forbid our ever doing, but against what we pronounce to be a human dogma constructively ascribed to revelation. It is against the Orthodox formula that we reason, — the formula which affirms that God, in order that he may exercise mercy towards the penitent, requires or accepts an expiatory offering made by innocence to his own law.

A governmental theory implies, in this use of the phrase, a law which restrains, or at least regulates, the perfect freedom of the working of the Divine administration over men. It was a prime essential in revelation to make known this theory to us if it be true. But where are we to look for it in the explicit teachings of Scripture? What sentences, what single sentence, can be quoted as offering a direct, or even an indirect, intimation of it? Not one! This fettering himself with conditions of his own law, within which alone God can exercise the pardoning prerogative of a Supreme Monarch, must either have always attached to the Divine rule over men, or it must have been introduced in connection with the revelation of the Gospel by Jesus Christ. Now any single case by which, on the authority of inspiration, full forgiveness was promised on simple repentance, without reference to any implied or reserved condition, would prove that the Divine administration, as revealed to men, did not always recognize this limitation of the prerogative of mercy. Will any one venture to assert, that there are not many such cases plainly brought before us in the Old Testament? But when we allege any such case in which forgiveness is explicitly promised to repentance without a hint of any reserved condition, Orthodoxy makes a bold interpolation to meet the straits of its own theory, and urges that prospective faith in the mediatorial sacrifice of Christ was still the implied ground of the forgiveness. What violent dealing with Scripture would be necessary for the sake of interpolating this theory, will appear if we attempt to make the required insertion into any text. Thus, when Ezekiel says that a wicked man turning from his iniquities shall be forgiven and shall live, we must supply the words, "through the efficacy of a sacrifice which the expected Messiah is to offer to God." The emphatic sentence, "I will have mercy and not sacrifice," must be made to read, "I will exercise mercy *on condition of* a sacrifice." Jesus Christ emphatically announced the pardoning methed of God's grace for penitent and renewed sinners, as exercised independently of any agency of his own. This method must, therefore, have been applicable to, and available for, those who lived before it was confirmed by his announcement of it. It must be as available for those who might never know of his announcement of it, as for Christians who receive it from his Gospel. It is in strict conformity with this view, as we learn from the Jewish Scriptures, that there was no other condition attached in the former revelation to the promise of Divine forgiveness than penitence for the past and subsequent obedience. What else is the significance of such beautiful passages as the following, which gem the Old Testament: "To the Lord our God belong mercies and forgivenesses, though we have rebelled against him." (Daniel ix. 9.) "He that covereth his sins shall not prosper; but whoso confesseth and forsaketh them shall have mercy." (Prov. xxviii. 13.) "For thou desirest not sacrifice. The sacrifices of God are a broken spirit." (Psalm li. 16, 17.)

Such were the explicit and benignant terms on which the pardoning prerogative of God was exercised before the mission of Christ. If we had only the Old Testament to instruct us, it may safely be affirmed that not a single believer or reader of it would imagine a governmental theory as standing between God and the exercise of his sovereign mercy. Christ came from God to proclaim a free and universal Gospel from the Father of all, to extend the blessings heretofore restricted to Jews to all the nations of the earth. In announcing the terms of the Divine forgiveness, did Christ introduce any alteration in those which were in force before? Did he take from them or add to them? In proclaiming anew the Divine mercy, did he make our enjoyment of it depend upon anything that he was himself to do or suffer with a view to satisfy God? Is his mediation, besides its manifest purpose of bringing us to repentance, designed to complement the deficiencies of that repentance as a tribute to the Divine administration? Did the death of Christ manifest that God had imposed a new condition for the exercise of his free grace? No! There is no evidence that Christ uttered one word about this governmental theory. It certainly does not appear in any case in which he himself announced forgiveness to the penitent. It is not recognized in the Parable of the Prodigal Son. We do indeed read in that parable of the killing of a fatted calf, in connection with the forgiveness and welcome of the repentant profligate; but it was to heighten the joy of a festival, not as the victim of outraged law. We find no hint of this theory in the Lord's Prayer, which teaches us to look for forgiveness from God on condition that we forgive others; nor any hint of it in the absolution of the penitent woman, who was forgiven much because she loved much, and loved much because she was forgiven much. And let it be observed with emphasis, that if Christ impaired or restricted the terms of free forgiveness in the older dispensation, the Gospel, instead of being a freer and a wider, becomes a narrower covenant. The attempt to evade this objection by assigning to the penitents of the old dispensation a prospective faith or an anticipated interest in a sacrifice to God's law, to be offered by Christ, is a mere device of theologians, — a pure figment of their own fancy.* The governmental theory is compelled to cover with its benefit Jews who cannot be shown to have had any knowledge of it, and then it stands perplexed as to what it shall decide concerning the fate of the heathen, who certainly had no knowledge of it. This is indeed a sore perplexity to Orthodoxy. We take the substance of the sublime revelation made through Peter concerning a heathen man, — "Of a truth I perceive that God is no respecter of persons; but in every nation he

---

* A fair specimen of the ingenuity of theologians in supplying the omissions of Scripture by the baldest inventions of their own fancy, is offered in the following sentence from the younger Edwards: "Did not Abraham and all the saints who lived before the incarnation of Christ, *and who were informed that atonement was to be made for them by Christ,* sincerely *consent* to it and earnestly desire it?" (Second Sermon on Grace consistent with Atonement. New Haven, 1785.) We do indeed read of those who "desired" to see and know in what the scheme of Revelation was to issue, without being gratified. But Edwards tells us that they not only knew, but *consented* to it!

that feareth him and worketh righteousness is accepted with him" (Acts x. 34, 35),—as declaring a method of the merciful rule which our Father in heaven exercises over his children, independently of any grace won for them by a meritorious offering from Christ. It proves, at any rate, that God could show mercy to those who had never heard of Christ, and who had no conscious sense of obligation for his death. But Orthodoxy is confounded here by its own inventions. We have seen how decidedly Mr. Flavel and Dr. Hopkins utter themselves as to the hopelessness of the heathen. Bishop Butler was wiser on this point. In a note to the chapter which we have already quoted, he deprecates the inference, from anything that he says, "that none can have the benefit of the general redemption, but such as have the advantage of being made acquainted with it in the present life." We find, too, that Orthodox theologians of the present day, who by the solvent of their philosophy make their creed elastic, are quite willing to allow that the expiatory sacrifice of Christ, as a legal offering, will impart its fullest benefits to multitudes who have had no knowledge of it. But what this admission gains in one direction it loses in another. For it is an express recognition that repentance is the actual condition of salvation for many, and the sole ground of it as known to them; that the death of Christ is so exclusively legal and Godward in its efficacy, that no motive or sentiment drawn from it is absolutely essential for its operation to the benefit of men; and also that the mediatorial office of Christ in heaven bears no definite relation to its scope on the earth. Now, if that expiation can avail for multitudes who are ignorant of it, and who draw no conscious motive or impulse from it, why should it be wholly nugatory, or even condemnatory, as it is said to be, for those who, finding every other grace in Christ, cannot believe that God required or that Christ made any legal expiation for them? Besides, the theory in this point of view is liable to much of the objection urged by Protestants to that of the supererogatory merits of the saints, by which a large balance of excess of merits was supposed to be set against the account of the eminently pious, and to be available to supply the deficiencies of those for whom these saints would intercede with God. Orthodoxy, in its milder moods, gives promise of salvation to the heathen, not from the unexhausted fulness of God's fount of mercy, but from the infinite balance entered upon the ledger-book of heaven to the atoning merits of Christ.

If it be asked, Why, under our view of the Gospel as proclaiming essentially the same message of free forgiveness on repentance which the elder dispensation announced, we should depend on Christ at all, and why we do not revert to the Old Testament Scriptures for our teaching? — we answer, that we are not Jews, but Gentiles, and that as Gentiles we receive the doctrine which we teach from Christ, as resting upon his authority. He is to us what the Law was to the Jews. And this doctrine is, after all, the real point of harmony between the two dispensations.

Looking with a keen and earnest scrutiny into the terms of this governmental theory, we try them by the tests of Scripture, the logic of truth, and the uses of piety. The theory involves two conditions, both of which must be united in its statement, and be authenticated as its warrant: —

First, that suffering of an intense character must in some form or shape be offered by the guilty or the innocent as a tribute to the violated law of God; and that Divine mercy cannot possibly remit this penalty without making grace overthrow righteousness.

Second, that the death of Christ, by a method and in a compound nature which so intensified his agonies for a few hours as to make them an equivalent for the eternal woe of a doomed race of human beings, *is looked upon by God* as offering to him and to his law that needful penalty.

From the first verse of Genesis to the last verse of the Apocalypse, the Bible will be searched in vain for a sentence which expresses either of these two terms of the governmental theory. The search for a sentence which contains them both may therefore be pronounced hopeless. Give us one such sentence from the lips of Christ, or by authority from him, and we will accept the theory as of revelation from God. The Bible knows nothing of a Divine Mercy bound in the chains of Legality. Mercy is there represented as the supreme attribute of God, and not as needing a device to compensate its relaxing of judgment. The limitless expanses of the universe, the unmeasured space up from the earth to the heaven in one direction, and from the east to the west in another, are made the dimensions of its scope. "Mercy rejoiceth against judgment," and rejoiceth over it, — not one word being interposed about legality. The God who from the infinite fountain of his love can forgive, can from the mildness of his sceptre remit.

We object to the governmental theory, that it is altogether an inferential, constructive theory, artificially wrought out by the brains of theologians, not distinctly revealed nor directly taught in the Scriptures. Take the simplest form of language in which it has ever been stated, and observe how far short of its assertion any passage of the Scripture will fall that may be quoted in proof of it. We grant that Orthodoxy, by the aid of *inference* and *construction* and *ingenuity*, can make out an argument of considerable plausibility in support of this theory. By culling and bringing together scattered texts of Scripture, and relying upon the associations which for a length of time have been attached to them through the sharper view of the doctrine of the Atonement, and then by skilfully arranging these texts and assimilating their repelling elements by a logic quite natural to theologians, a marvellous show of apparent authority may be claimed for the theory. In practised hands, guided by an earnest heart and a mind already prepossessed by Orthodox influence, the theory admits of quite a forcible statement. When subtilty of reasoning, and partiality of interpretation, and ardent piety qualified by the restraints of dogma, engage upon this theory, the result even looks formidable to some who feel that they are held to withstand it. The strength of the theory now lies in old associations attached to texts under the influence of another view of the sacrificial doctrine. A perfect mosaic-work of symbols, phrases, and sentences, picked from between the covers of the Bible, polished down and filled in and held together by the cement of human ingenuity, is made to produce, by a highly artificial process, such a representation as will answer to an immolated victim who is pleading with Heaven, not with earth. Certain glowing Orientalisms of speech which have a free and lofty spiritualism, and some ritualistic images of quite a different tone, are wrought together, and petrified into hard literalisms, and stiffened into forms which, when reproduced in our own language, are false to the truth. As Mr. Jowett has remarked in his Essay on the Atonement, — so significant a production as coming from an Oxford theologian, — "Where the mind is predisposed to receive this theory, there is scarcely a law or a custom or rite or purification or offering in the Old Testament which may not be transferred to the Gospel." It has often been cast as a reflection upon Unitarians, that in their discourses they have allowed some of the sacrificial terms applied to Christ in the Epistles to fall out of their common use. We know not but that the censure has the apparent justification of fact. But if so, it would be averted by those whom it concerns, by the plea, that, though Unitarian theologians find no difficulty whatever, nor the slightest embarrassment, in the real significance of such terms, they do believe that very erroneous associations have warped and perverted them for popular use. Mr. Jowett has admirably indicated the process by which the writers of those Epistles through force of their own previous associations with the shambles and altars of sacrifice, were led to cast some of their Christian conceptions in the mould of their own former ideas. If to this fact — a fact which critical Scripture students will less and less be disposed to question as their noble toil advances — be added an allowance for the associations which Calvinistic theology has connected with the sacrificial terms of the Epistles, we should find it no difficult work to justify a temporary disuse of some phrases of misconstrued Scripture. When popular views have been recast, and popular belief has been conformed to the Scriptural doctrine, old language and old imagery may suggest their true meaning.

But we have dropped that plea in defence of others; for ourselves we do not need it. We also have gathered together every sentence from the New Testament, and from the Old too, which Orthodoxy works into the mosaic composition and statement of its governmental theory. We have the fair transcript before us. We know, we think we know, the force and meaning of such sentences, and the significance of most of them. And again we say, that they do not contain or intimate either, much less both, of the two conditions stated above as entering into the governmental theory. It is claimed that the Orthodox have a great advantage over us in this, that while we have to make a somewhat vague and undefined statement to express the mode of efficacy of the death of Christ, they are able to state it very definitely.

True. But while *they* have to state it in terms and phrases and formulas of their own, instead of allowing *Scripture* to state it for them, the advantage on their side is at least neutralized. We had rather take refuge under the large ambiguities of some Scripture phrases, than define them rigidly by adding phrases of our own. While we have laid down our pen within the last hour, we have read the following sentence in the columns of the week's paper of our "Congregationalist" brethren (May 2): "The Lamb of God, slain for the *forgiveness* of human sins." The sentence is a very definite one; but it is equally unwarrantable as a most startling perversion of Scripture.

The Bible teaches us that the whole plan of redemption, with all its incidents and stages, was contemporaneously arranged in the Divine mind. It was a continuous scheme slowly developed to the knowledge and experience of man. Inspired prophets caught anticipatory glimpses of stages in it which were not to be realized till long after their day. The scheme was to culminate in a suffering Messiah. The Lamb was slain, his death was foreseen at the very commencement of the dispensation: "before the foundation of the world." Now the fact that the scheme *results* in the death of Christ has led to the inference that the death of Christ under a legal view of its purpose was really the *substance* of the scheme, and that, as no stage of it had any significance except what it derives from the result, so the legal view of the death of Christ is in truth the whole substance of the scheme of revelation. If this is not an inferential and constructive theory, we should be at loss to find one among all the conceptions of human brains. We believe that each step and process in the scheme was complete in its operation for its own date in time, and for the subjects of it. The old Hebrews did indeed "drink of the spiritual rock which followed them, which rock was Christ," but it was because the virtue of the whole scheme was concentrated in every element in it. "The mystery which had been hid from ages and generations" was the result which was "made manifest" only to Christians; but its blessings were not deferred till its disclosure, nor made dependent on the method of its disclosure.

Orthodoxy enters into an elaborate argument to prove that the sacrificial offerings of the Old Testament were all typical of the great sacrifice, and took their validity from that. How inconclusive and defective and inconsistent that argument is, will, we think, appear to every one who will examine it without prepossession. It fails at the application of each test of criticism, evidence, authority, and analogy. Not the most distant intimation is given in the Old Testament that the ritual sacrifices looked beyond themselves to an anticipation of the sacrifice of Christ. Not a word can be quoted from Lawgiver, Prophet, or Priest, to prove that such a reference was had in view. The aim and efficacy of those sacrifices were complete in themselves; and a close study of all that is enjoined in connection with those sacrifices will persuade us of the very slight importance attached to them except in a ceremonial way. They are not invested with the awe, nor set forth with the solemnity, which would belong to them as the shadows cast back from the cross. The only one of all the offerings of the Jews which was said to "bear the sin of the people," was not immolated, sacrificed, or slain, but was sent off into the wilderness. It is remarkable, likewise, that the Levitical sacrifices were enjoined in a routine way, without the slightest reference to the state of mind or feeling with which they were offered. It was not them *and repentance*, according to the priestly ritual, but *them* alone. The Prophets seem even to have stood as protesters against the Priests in this matter, in insisting upon the worthlessness of the offering except as it indicated a contrite heart, which was the better of the two. But what the Prophets thus insisted upon as the greater, namely, humiliation, contrition, and repentance, the governmental theory would persuade us were all secretly subordinated to a prospective sacrifice. When we quote to our opponents the sentiment approved by Jesus, — that to love God and one's neighbor "is more than all whole burnt-offerings and sacrifices" (Mark xii. 33), — the reply is, "that is the very loftiest and most exacting demand of the Law, exhaustive, impossible of obedience by us, and therefore, as we do not come up to it, we need a sacrifice for us." No! we rejoin. We need mercy. In no instance recorded does Christ make a retrospective reference to the effect that he is giving efficacy to the repentance of penitents under the old dispensation. Nor can any assertion be quoted as from him, that under all circumstances, whenever and wherever a sinner is redeemed and saved, it is on condition or in consequence of his death.

Yet not only from the Jewish, but even from the heathen sacrifices, would Orthodoxy draw types and foreshadowings of a great legal victim. The foul and impious offerings of Paganism, brute and human, with all their revolting horrors, are made to yield one gleaming ray of pure light as testifying to the strong instinctive conviction of the human heart that God must be approached, even by penitence, with a propitiation. When we attempt to bring home to our thoughts the fearful reality intimated in this incidental illustration of the governmental theory, so intense is the horror which it excites, that, were it not for the restraining influence of Christian respect for those with whom we differ, we should charge them with confounding the purest and holiest element of the Gospel with the most hideous element of heathenism. We utterly and almost indignantly reject this dreadful fancy. We reject it alike in its use of heathen and of Jewish sacrifices. It seems to us a most degrading view of the redeeming work of the holy Jesus to say that his final offering of love had been foreshadowed for ages in the sacrifices of brute beasts. Strained visions of prophets and kings, longing hopes of devout hearts in humble scenes of life, and angelic anthems ringing their symphonies in the ears of shepherds, are the befitting heraldings of "the desire of all nations." But the bloody shambles of fed beasts and the reeking altars of a blinded idolatry, are images which no transfiguration can elevate into types of the Lamb of God.

God had forbidden the Jews to offer human sacrifices, as abhorrent to him. We tremble as we ask the question which forces itself upon us, — Would God signalize the abrogation of the Jewish code by offering for men a human victim, and thus make the crowning act of human sin the essential condition for the expiation of all sin? It is Mr. Jowett of Oxford who uses the words, "the greatest of human crimes, that redeems the sin of Adam by the murder of Christ."

We have said, that we had before us all the passages from the Bible which connect our redemption with the sufferings of Christ, and that we had weighed their import, without finding in them either, still less both, of the terms involved in the governmental theory. We are not about to quote those passages to show how each of them falls short of authenticating that theory. With the briefest glance over specimen passages of such a tenor, we gather sentences like these: — "he hath borne our griefs"; "he was wounded for our transgressions"; "the chastisement of our peace was upon him, and with his stripes we are healed"; "his soul" [his life] was made "an offering for sin"; "he bore our sins"; "he purged our sins"; "he suffered for our sins"; he died "for the remission of our sins"; he "laid down his life for us"; "he redeemed us to God by his blood" [his death]; "he gave his life a ransom for many"; "he was delivered for our offences"; "he is the propitiation [the mercy-seat] for the sins of the whole world." But where in all these sentences, looking *man-ward* for all the solemn and sacrificial efficacy of the sufferings they express, do we find any intimation of a God-ward design, necessity, or working of a legal expiation? We read, "Behold the Lamb of God, which taketh away the sin of the world." It is the *sin* which he takes away. But the governmental theory would require the passage to read, "who taketh away the *punishment* of the world." We read, that "Christ hath redeemed us from the curse of the Law, being made a curse for us." (Gal. iii. 13.) Leaving unnoticed the confusion caused to our minds by the use of the word Law to define both the Mosaic and the moral law, which makes us uncertain whether the Apostle meant more than that the death of Christ relieved Gentiles from subjection to the old legal code, we remind ourselves that it was man, not God, who made Christ "a curse," and treated him as if he were accursed. We read, "For he hath made him to be sin for us, who knew no sin." (2 Cor. v. 21.) The Rev. A. P. Stanley, of Oxford, Canon of Canterbury, in his recent work on the Epistles to the Corinthians, construes the passage thus: "He was enveloped, lost, overwhelmed in sin and its consequences, so far as he could be without himself being sinful." And he paraphrases it thus: "The object for which He devoted the sinless One to the world of sin was, that I, and you with me, might, through and with that sinless One, be drawn into the world of righteousness." The scholarly works of Jowett and Stanley are most profitable study for those who are resolved that the Apostles shall not use a single trope, or other rhetorical figure, without having it urged into a literal interpretation. If a thousand passages of a tenor similar to the above were to be quoted from Scripture, they would all fail of conveying, by any fair interpretation, an idea of Christ's death as a sacrifice *to God.* There is indeed one passage which speaks of Christ's offering for us as "a sacrifice to God." But the very aroma of the phrase connected with it relieves it of its literal construction. The sacrifice of Christ must have been of such a nature, that we can regard it as "a sweet-smelling savor" to God. (Eph. v. 2.) The song of the redeemed in the Apocalypse to Christ is, "Thou wast slain, and hast redeemed us to God by thy blood [thy death]." (Rev. v. 9.) This is the burden of the whole Gospel strain. But where do we find in it an intimation of the legal theory of a substituted victim to God? It is characteristic of all the figures of speech used in the Scriptures, that they are constantly varied, played upon, presented in changing aspects, balancing and mutually explaining each other. Christ is not only called the Redeemer, but also the *ransom money;* not only the payer of our debt, but also the *price* of our discharge; he not only bears or takes up, lifts and carries, our *sins*, but he also bears our *diseases.* But who would force either of these terms to such an interpretation as would compel us to say that Christ became palsied, deaf, and blind, in the process of relieving human maladies? The very variety of the symbols and images used concerning him indicates that they are symbols and images.

If we submit the governmental theory to the test of logic, we find it assailable and vulnerable at the very points in which it most needs to be strong. It may be a misconception of our own, but we think we discern in most modern statements a shrinking from a full, direct, unqualified expression of it, while affectionate and deprecatory phrases are connected with it. Now if it is to be asserted, let it be with all the frankness and boldness becoming a fundamental theory of the relations between God and man. To our minds, the title of legality, the very idea and substance of law in the sense of equity, are perverted in the theory. We are told that the law is outraged, and the sanctions of justice are defied, if the guilty, even when penitent, are freely forgiven. But into our very idea of law enters the condition, that the penalties of its violation, if inflicted at all, shall be visited on the transgressor. Which contingency would the more peril our reverence for law, the remission of its penalties, or the infliction of them on the innocent? Etymologists derive our word *mercy* from the Latin *merces*, a reward or payment; and they tell us that the connection, which is in fact a separation, of the meanings is to be explained thus, — that when the next of kin to a murdered person received a money equivalent for the murder, he yielded to the payment and returned mercy. It is a most tortuous definition, and is, we think, in this respect, similar to the working of the governmental theory. When Orthodoxy fetters God's exercise of mercy by the restraints of his penal law, it forgets that the Divine Lawgiver can harmonize his own laws of justice and of mercy. Mr. Jowett says, in his Essay on the Atonement, that the theory affirms "that there were some impossibilities in the nature of things which prevented God from doing otherwise than he did. Thus we introduce a moral principle superior to God, just as in the Grecian mythology fate and necessity are superior to Jupiter." He also says, that the view of the sufferings of Christ, as a sort of "satisfaction to God," "interposes a painful fiction between God and man." Orthodoxy makes the difficulty which it professes to find for God in looking for a device for mediating between his mercy and his justice. Not regarding penitence as a competent mediation, it interposes a victim. The Apostle speaks of God's being "just, and the justifier of him which believeth in Jesus," as if the two assertions were identical. Orthodox pleaders are in the habit of interpolating the word *yet* in the sentence, thus, "and *yet* the justifier," &c., as if the two assertions needed reconciling. Even Professor Stuart makes that interpolation when he quotes the passage.

We shrink from following the lead of Orthodox disputants into the dread audacity of seeking to define and measure the degree of intensity in the sufferings endured by Christ. Sure we are, that no statement of Scripture presents the question of the *amount* of those sufferings as deciding their *purpose*. If there be one point in this controversy which, from the shock it causes to our sensibilities, we should pronounce to be forbidden ground to all parties, it is this. We have much of bold and offensive assertion upon it, copied from various writers lying before us, but we forbear to transfer it to our pages. Calvin, arguing from the Saviour's momentary dismay, that his sufferings were more than human, says: "What disgraceful effeminacy would this have been to be so distressed by the fear of a common death, as to be in a bloody sweat, and incapable of being comforted without the presence of angels!" * But the younger Edwards emphatically declares that the suffering "was barely that of the *man* Christ Jesus," as "the Eternal Logos was not capable of enduring misery." † And yet there is something vital to the theory before us dependent upon the ascribing an intensified degree of suffering to Christ, in order that his suffering might be of infinite value. The Orthodox dogma is to us hopelessly confused here by variance of testimony and definition among its general advocates. Some, with Calvin and Hopkins, tell us

* Institutes, Book II. Chap. XVI.
† Third Sermon on Atonement and Free Grace.

that God died. Others tell us that this is impossible in fact, and unallowable in statement, while, like Dr. Pond, they ascribe some influence from the Divine nature to what was endured in the human nature of Christ. But Orthodoxy perils its theory by definitions and explanations. What was it for God to pass through the show of dying as a man? It could not be real tragedy. Was it a drama? No! It was *real* in what it was, not fiction in anything. The pleading petition of Christ, "Father, if it be possible, let this cup pass from me!" is to us inexplicable, if Jesus had entered into a covenant with God by the terms of which he knew that the removal of an obstacle in the way of the exercise of Divine mercy to all our race depended upon his sacrifice to God. The petition needs no explanation, if, in conformity with the view we have presented of the consistency between such a close of his ministry and its whole tenor, Jesus for a moment addressed to his Father the struggle of his own spirit, "Must I drink of this cup?"

If we wished to make an exhaustive statement of the objections to be offered against even the consistency of this legal theory with the elementary principles and the majestic equities of true law, we should need the space which we have already used. Especially should we urge with earnestness, that forgiveness on penitence does not in any case peril the authority of the Divine law. One who has truly repented needs no dramatic offering to impress him with an adequate sense of the evil of all sin. His own breast is the best testimony to him. The forgiven penitent is not harmed by the exercise of mercy toward him; the impenitent sinner is not hardened by the announcement of mercy to the contrite. All the attempted analogies which Orthodoxy tries to institute between school discipline, or human tribunals, and the Divine administration, fail at the most important points. Of course, a judge on the bench of a human court cannot discharge a professedly repentant criminal. The judge cannot know if the penitence be sincere, nor has the criminal sinned in matters which injure only that judge, nor does the judge make or execute the law. But do we err in intimating that, if by any infallible test human tribunals could know what criminals of every degree had thoroughly turned from all wickedness to righteousness, the voice of the merciful in a community might plead for their discharge? An analogy drawn between the parental government of a household and the Divine administration would give us the best illustration of what a mild but firm method of law and benignity requires. A kind parent asks only for contrition in an erring child. He forgives the penitent. His law is satisfied.

What shall we say, too, of this legal theory, as respects the terms by which God is to forgive all the sin that is ever henceforward to be committed by the unborn millions of our race who shall live on the earth? God has already received the funded payment which shall make their repentance available for forgiveness, says the theory. All coming sinners are to plead an interest in the past sacrifice of Christ. The victim which was by anticipation available for the penitents of old times, is by retrospection available for all future time. "How am I to be forgiven for the sins I may commit next year?" asks one who hopes that up to to-day he is pardoned. "Draw upon the infinite fund of purchased grace," is the answer. Not in irony, not for offence upon the cherished convictions of any disciple, but in serious perplexity, in troubled anxiety, do we express something beyond mere misgivings here. And in the same spirit, deprecating intended offence, we utter what comes to our thoughts. When Tetzel, the broker of the indulgences sent forth by the Pope, sold for money tickets of pardon for past sins, Roman casuistry might plead that the pardon granted by them was merely a remission of ecclesiastical penalties. But when he proposed to furnish for a graduated scale of prices tickets which should absolve offenders for any sins they might in future commit, his traffic presented itself to Luther in the shame of its full enormity. We disclaim utterly any analogy here with anything in the legal theory. We adduce the instance merely to define this one objection, that sins which are virtually forgiven before they are committed must lose something of their dread for the conscience, while repentance for them is divested of something of its imperative necessity as the operative condition of pardon.

We have but a word to utter in conclusion bearing upon the relation between the governmental theory of Atonement and the uses of piety. No word of ours shall question the testimony of the believers of that theory, as confessing to its power over their own hearts. Into the sanctuaries of human breasts we will not intrude, certainly not as disputants. We challenge an oft-repeated assertion simply as it indicates an attempt to monopolize a disciple's love and reverence and gratitude to Christ, and to insist that the grace of his reconciliation shall flow to the human heart only in one channel. It is claimed that the Orthodox view of the Atonement is pre-eminently, almost exclusively, favorable to true Christian piety; that from contemplating Christ as such a sacrifice for such an intent, and as making by such a method our peace with God, the heart is most profoundly penetrated with horror for sin, with a sense of the need, the cost, and the value of redemption, and that the fervor and glow and gratitude of that heart are thus most effectually kindled toward the Saviour. Be it so to all who can thus testify. They cannot love Christ too much, whatever be their view of the grounds or method of that love. What he has done for us admits of no measurement, and it is for what he has done that he claims the full tribute of our hearts. But may we suggest, not from theory, but from the recorded experience of Christians of various communions, that Christian hearts have chosen different central truths, different symbols of piety, different images and objects out of the rich treasures of devotion to set before them in their various shrines and oratories? The Roman Catholic exalts beyond all other sacred and fond objects in his heart, the Virgin Mary. Her graces and sorrows, her sword-pierced breast, her motherly office for God, her queenly prerogative in heaven, and the prevalence of her intercession, have made her to millions of professed Christians the fountain of their piety, the altar of their worship, the sweet assurance of all their faith. The most acute dialectics of the most skilful apologists of Romanism cannot make clear to the least prejudiced of Protestants how "devotion to Mary" differs from what the Christian owes to God. Again, the mystic pietist finds the central theme of his devotion, and the fullest nourishment for his spiritual affections, in the "Divine Love." His highest moods of peace and joy and faith are ministered to when he yields himself to the fruition of the sentiment to which he gives expression in those words of unfathomed meaning. Other types of Christian piety, comprehending larger or smaller numbers of affiliated souls, engage the inner choice of classes of Christian disciples, according to the delicacy, the culture, the depth, the intelligence, or the refinement of their whole being. It is unwise and unsafe to attempt to concentrate the whole motive energy of piety upon any one truth or element of a universal religion. Each grateful heart is free to express its own experience, and to indicate the point of view in which the Gospel scheme gathers for itself the brightest beams of all the light that it reflects from heaven. But beyond this expression of personal experience, we question the right of any heart to give rules for the method of spiritual radiation to other hearts. And especially would we object to any theory which makes a formula upon the method of reconciliation through Christ to monopolize or to exhaust the compass of the Gospel influence over the various sympathies and exercises of human hearts.

And now we have to confront the conclusion to which our long, and we fear wearisome, debate has brought us. Orthodoxy, not willing to allow each believer to interpret to his own mind and heart the Scripture method of the efficacy of Christ's reconciling work, insists that its own constructive view expressed in its doctrinal formula must be accepted as the condition of acknowledged Christian discipleship. Because we reject this constructive view, we are pronounced to be outside of the pale of Evangelical communion. We regret the decision. We regret it on account of the Orthodox themselves, for it compels us to qualify our respect and affection for them, seeing that they usurp a right which their Master and ours never gave them, and seeing that they prove faithless to their own Protestant principles. We regret the decision on our own account, for we should love to share the sympathies, and to participate in the labors and hopes and noble enterprises of those whom we still regard as brethren in Christ. We regret the decision, but we will not mourn over it. It has no ecclesiastical penalties to visit upon us for which we care one straw. It has now no inquisition, no ballot-box even, to turn its dogmatic test into a torment or an annoyance. It cannot deprive us of Christian fellowship, for whatever we may say of numbers, we have a fellowship of our own, of men and women, who, while they consent to reject in every shape and form the dogma of a God-ward efficacy in the living or the dying work of Christ, accord in a better and a more tender view of the great Redemption, as devised by the love of God, and perfected by the love of Christ. We too love him because he laid down his life for us.

UNITARIANISM AND ORTHODOXY

ON

THE SCRIPTURES.

UNITARIANISM AND ORTHODOXY

ON

THE SCRIPTURES.

No controversial discussions concerning the doctrines of Scripture can be thoroughly pursued without involving sooner or later an incidental controversy upon the authority of Scripture, and the right principles of its interpretation. At whatever point an issue bearing upon this subject is raised, it leads on step by step to all the questions opened by biblical criticism. The character and composition of the Bible as a whole; the nature of its contents; its age, sources, and authors; its natural and its supernatural, its historical, prophetic, and spiritual elements; its relations to other literature and to the demonstrative and physical sciences; its exposure to assaults upon its credibility; and its means and methods of defence,—all these large and perplexing themes present themselves for treatment by the aid of such powers as belong to the human mind under the guidance of a various and progressive culture. Nor does even this specification of some of the more important elements of a necessary task exhaust all the incidental topics which enter into it. The more thorough and deliberate and microscopic the criticism, the more abundant and suggestive appears the material of it. Delicate questions about the exact meanings of words in ancient languages, and even in our own, and about the translation of words and phrases from dead into living tongues, are to be debated by scholars, who must afterwards set forth the results of their study in a style intelligible to the unlearned. The figurative uses of language, idioms, Orientalisms, and metaphors, complicate the discussion. And crowning all comes the great theme of Inspiration, — the meaning of the word, the evidence of the thing, the compass and extent of its influence, — whether it covers all the contents of the Bible or only a part of them, and what part, — whether it was confined to the original writing, and so has been impaired by the risks of time, of manuscripts and their translation into various languages, or whether the gift is of such a nature that its fruits are essentially preserved in every faithful transcript and version of the record.

Some unreflecting persons complain, at the very outset, that such a multitude of questions of such a nature should be opened at all, to perplex simple understandings, to impair in any way the confidence with which people love to read the Bible, to peril the authority, or to bring under debate the truth or value, of any of its contents. The same persons are apt to charge these consequences upon the Unitarian Controversy, and to hold Unitarians answerable for an unfair dealing with the Scriptures, tending to unsettle their Heaven-authenticated claims. In this topic of controversy between those once brethren, as well as in the discussion of the great doctrinal questions to some of which we have devoted many pages, the leading aim and purpose of Unitarians was in part misunderstood and in part misrepresented. The views of Scripture, and of the proper way of treating it, to which they were brought in the exercise of their best intelligence, as honest thinkers and careful students, were represented by their opponents as wanton and daring results of a spirit of pride and unbelief. Unitarians adopted their opinions from the compulsory influence of facts and arguments, whose force they could not resist. They did not hold and advance their views because their inclinations misled them, for they felt that they were yielding to the simple force of truth, the straits and necessities of the case. We have therefore first of all to remind ourselves how such questions as relate to the authority and the right interpretation of the Bible were naturally and necessarily opened in the controversy, how just the grounds of them were and are still, and how, when they have been opened, candor and truth require that they should be met. Wise and considerate men have often been perplexed when confronted with the consequences of their own theories; and though it may be a token of courage, it is certainly no proof of wisdom, to regard such consequences, when of a very perplexing or alarming character, with entire indifference, and as wholly without force against our theories. Whether in the adoption of a principle or a theory we should have in view the inevitable consequences, the practical effects, which will follow from it, is a question on which those who have concerned themselves with it have been divided; the dividing line being generally drawn so as to commit all mere theorists to a disregard of consequences, while those who have been compelled to face consequences have insisted that they should be had in view in the formation of theories. It will be found at the close of our present discussion, that the main issue between the Unitarian and the Orthodox views of the Scriptures, and the proper way of treating them, centres around this question: Shall we start with a theory about the inspiration, the authority, and the infallibility of the Scriptures, which recognizes the qualifications and abatements and embarrassments that will be sure to confront us as we meet the trial of that theory, — or shall we assume the very highest position possible, and then ingeniously contest, or grudgingly allow, the various objections of a fair and reasonable character which invalidate our position? Shall we form our theory in view of certain facts which we must sooner or later deal with in verifying our theory, — or shall we adopt a theory which will compel us to deal uncandidly or unsatisfactorily with facts that are plainly inconsistent with it?

When the Unitarian Controversy commenced here, it found prevailing in the popular mind, so far as that was in subjection to the popular theology, an almost idolatrous estimate of the Bible. This popular view of it allowed no discrimination in the value or authority of its various contents, and would scarcely tolerate any debate which went beyond the apparently literal meaning of the English version. In their use of the Bible, the people recognized no right of choice, no range for discrimination. It was all Bible. Indeed, a reader of the old tracts and sermons of our fathers is led to the persuasion, that they spent the hardest toil upon the least profitable portions of the Scriptures. That they found those portions edifying, only proves how diligently they wrought upon them. Very many of their devoted ministers are known to have spent years of industrious zeal in writing extended expositions or commentaries upon the whole Bible, or upon its larger or smaller compositions. A few specimens of such comments on books or chapters are in print, but no complete work of the kind from their pens has ever been published. Cotton Mather's voluminous exposition still lies in manuscript in the cabinet of our Historical Society. Several generations of ministers, in the full sincerity of their own earnest faith, had inculcated a view of the Bible which modern opinions regard as superstitious. They had fostered this view, and insisted upon it as vital to faith and the ends of edification. To what extent this estimate of the Bible in the minds of believers was balanced by, or even accountable for, a lurking or a full developed scepticism and unbelief in the minds of others, we of course cannot know. Our knowledge of the workings of human nature and the facts which experience presents us in our own day of free, outspoken dissent from the popular belief, would warrant the inference that multitudes of the inquisitive and the restless in mind entertained misgivings, though they might keep silence about them. It would seem that the common rule applied here as in other matters, that when the standard of belief made an excessive and arbitrary exaction, a readiness to recognize it on the part of some was offset by an immoderate rebellion to it on the part of others. Much of the confessed and latent unbelief of our day is the costly penalty paid by a grown-up generation for the austerities and exactions with which faith was connected in the training of their childhood. But as the popular view of the Bible was made the standard for belief, all who for any reason could not accept it were left to make such abatements of it, or to find such a substitute for it, as they could, practising meanwhile such reserve of tongue as prudence or fear might dictate.

It is a remarkable fact, that, in all the voluminous and unfinished discussions which have been pursued on this high theme of the authority of the Bible, the witness whose testimony is of chief relevancy and importance has received the least attention. All other tests and arguments have taken precedence of that which would bring the Bible to a trial through its own claims and contents. Common sense suggests that no reason for demanding for it the reverence and faith of men could possibly be offered from any external source or any subordinate grounds, which would compare in cogency with its own internal warrant. How far the old popular view of the authority of all the contents of the Bible is warranted by *any claims set up for themselves*, is a question which, to our knowledge, has never been tried thoroughly and candidly by a discussion unbiassed by any other considerations. We must defer any dealing with that question until we have briefly noticed some of the extraneous, incidental, historical, and conventional influences which helped, at least, very effectively to support, and, as we sincerely believe, to originate, a view of the contents of the Bible, as a whole, that is not warranted by any claims which they advance for themselves.

The Bible has been a book in popular circulation, free to the use of all Protestant readers, for a little more than three hundred years. For the greater portion of that time, and for all but a very small fraction of the masses of its readers, it has been perused and interpreted under the restraints of some external, ecclesiastical, or doctrinal teaching. For long ages after its contents had been gathered, it was withdrawn, kept back from popular use, in part from the policy of the priesthood, in part from the necessity of the case, as its cost, when written on parchment, was heavy, and those who could read were comparatively few. The Bible, indeed, was never in the possession of more than a very few private owners until after the Reformation. Before the Christian era, a few wealthy Jews might have copies of parts, or even of the whole, of the Old Testament made for them by the Scribes; but the families of Israel looked to the temple and the synagogues for their knowledge of its contents. Faith then came wholly by hearing, not from reading. When the two Testaments had been united in one or more volumes, copies were so rare that they were not found in the libraries of all the churches, convents, monasteries, and universities. Occasionally, the choice cabinet of a monarch contained a copy. That the Christian world could have kept its faith and worship so long without depending upon the popular use of the Bible, would, after all, be the most effective argument in support of the policy of the Roman Church in its prohibition of the Bible, were it not for the counter argument which Protestants would instantly advance, in urging that the faith and worship which prevailed while the Bible was hid away were not consistent with Christian purity and truth.

Luther and Erasmus parted friendship at the Reformation, when the former, in resolute opposition to the judgment or the fears of the latter, resolved upon the translation of the Scriptures into the common tongue, for the free use of his countrymen. The knowledge that there was such a volume as the Bible, the difficulty of procuring it, the excitement raised by the expectation of it, the fact that it was identified with the Protestant cause, in antagonism with all the corruptions and inventions and additions of Romanism, made the multitude most eager to obtain it. Considering that, as Luther said, "the Papists burned the Bible because it was not on their side," we can hardly over-estimate the zeal and longing of the people to secure it. The license included on the title-page of our English Bibles, though passed unnoticed by many readers, tells a burdened tale. "Appointed to be read in churches," is the royal warrant which goes with the once forbidden book. When that warrant first accompanied a version in our own tongue, every one who could obtain a Bible was free to possess it, and all who had the precious gift of knowledge might read it. To read it was to interpret it in some way. And what a valued possession it was is hardly to be realized now, as the flood of literature floats by us. What an intense and deep joy has been experienced by millions of hearts over that book! Not only must it "be read in churches,"—it might be read in homes, by the way-side, anywhere, everywhere. As the larger portion of the people of England were then unable to read, others who had the gift would be to them the medium of its joy and instruction. We can paint to ourselves many impressive and touching scenes of which it was the centre. It took the place and performed the service of priest and altar, of confessor and teacher, of counsellor and judge, to thousands of persons. It repeated the Pentecostal miracle of preaching the Gospel to every one in the tongue in which he was born. It represented in the household all the sanctities connected with the Church, the Sabbath, the grave, and the hope that extends beyond it. We still see, in some of the rural parish churches of England, the solid folio Bible held by a strong ring and chain to the reading-desk as in days of yore; when, after the hours of public worship, the minister having retired, simple villagers, with grave and reverent mien, gathered around some old man or woman, or some youth or maiden rich in the blessings of the mind, and listened to the precious pages. Every one of those pages was a revelation, and we may be sure that such perplexities as the narratives now present, not of scholarship, science, or criticism, but from the questionings of an unsophisticated mind or heart, received as fair and full a solution as the best wisdom of the world has ever since given to them. For nearly a century and a half portions of Wickliffe's translation had been read in English rural homes by wandering apostles of the new light, and each multiplication of copies in that or in subsequent versions extended the circle of readers and hearers. We may infer that, to those who had been trained on monkish legends and lore, the Bible was of easy learning, offering but rare occasion for raising distinctions in its contents.

It could not be but that such a book, so demanded as a designed gift from Heaven, so prized, so used, as a substitute for poor superstitions and services performed in a dead language, would draw to itself the deepest, fondest, purest attachment of human hearts. It was living truth conveyed in the language of household life, that gave to the lessons of the Bible their sacred charm and power. For of all the reproaches, stern or gentle, visited upon the policy of the Roman Church, the most withering of all must be confessed to be this, that the very language which she chose for all her services became a dead language; her piety could not keep alive the tones and forms of her speech, and the spell of delusion which was laid upon her withheld her from change. The Bible was found worthy of all the affectionate trust which it received, and affection and confidence alone in it, however unlimited, never harmed and never can harm any one. Only when the mind — the curious, searching, debating mind — asserts its own prerogative, does that unlimited confidence begin to falter, and need to be confirmed or restored by some deliberate methods of inquiry and discrimination.

But the piety of New England, and of those in the Old World who were in sympathy with the faith that was first nurtured in this wilderness, accepted the Bible — the whole Bible — in the fondest reliance of the whole heart and mind. Every family owned a Bible, and every member of each family read it, studied it, or heard it and revered it. All were either teachers or taught by it. Children were named after its worthies. Occasionally, too, names were borrowed from it in baptism of those who were not among its worthies, on the ground, perhaps, that being in the Bible, no matter how poorly they figured there, was warrant enough for perpetuating them. Precedents, examples, and warnings were quoted from the Bible, as from the whole world's history of all past ages, and from the Sibylline prophecies of all that was to come. The Bible was actually accepted here as a statute-book of civil and criminal law till a code could be deliberately framed; and when a code had been digested, Bible legislation furnished its basis and its penalties. It was well-nigh forgotten that the Bible was not written in English, and that it had ever been translated. The intermediate agency of men, in penning, gathering up, authenticating, transcribing, and transmitting its contents, was well-nigh lost sight of; and as God was the leading subject of the book, its authorship was directly referred to him.

It is easy to understand how ill those who had been educated under this warm, confiding, and entire reliance upon the letter of the Bible, would bear the first bold dealings of criticism with it, however cautious or reverent might be the language of such criticism. Painful and startling was the first experience of this kind. When the natural popular feeling against the intimations of criticism found expression through the teachers and defenders of the popular theology, it was to have been expected that some severity of judgment should have followed. Those who began to discriminate between parts of the Bible, — to raise questions about the relative value and authority of its several contents, — to suggest new renderings of important passages, and to intimate the possibility of error introduced by time or chance in successive copies, or even into the original, by lack of knowledge or false reasoning, — those who opened here these now familiar "offences," were prepared to be misunderstood. They had great reason, however, to complain of being grossly misrepresented. Time, with its wonderful revolutions, has realized a signal triumph for our early Unitarians in this direction. As we shall show before we close this essay, those who claim a doctrinal succession from the assailants of Unitarians have accepted, ratified, and indorsed to the full all the positions taken by those who bore the odium of first reducing the popular idolatry for the letter of the Bible. We utter boldly the unqualified assertion, and stand ready to maintain it in the lists of fair scholarship, that all the leading and essential canons of criticism, and all the qualifications and limitations which the most esteemed Unitarian divines applied to the Scriptures, have, within a few years, been recognized as just by eminent writers in various Orthodox communions. The American Unitarian Association has now in preparation a Commentary and Exposition of the New Testament. Such a work, covering both Testaments, might be made to the perfect satisfaction of our fellowship, every line of whose necessary comments and dissertations should be compiled from nominally Orthodox volumes. As we survey the crowded pages now before us, containing carefully culled extracts embracing admissions and assertions from distinguished Orthodox divines in the field of biblical criticism, and then recall how Unitarians were once abused for saying the same things, we feel a profound respect for men who nobly led on a work of consecrated toil and manly courage in the spirit of Christian fidelity to truth.

But the protest first raised against the ventures of criticism was earnest and foreboding; doubtless, too, it was sincere, however wise, discreet, and just — or the opposite of all those epithets — it may have been. The appeal, in censure and protest, was in substance and tone as follows: — If you cannot substantiate your new views by the letter of the English Bible, just as we and our fathers have been reading it for centuries, give up the matter. Stick to the letter as it stands, and accept the established authority. The wise and good have found nutriment for their piety in a faith

20 *

which never looked behind, beyond, or under the English version, and you will become no better than they were, — no wiser, no more enlightened in the truth, — by meddling with a jot or tittle in the text. Forego the exercise of your bold reason, your proud imagination. If you find difficulties, humble yourself before them: you ought to expect difficulties, and there is a merit in succumbing to them, while it is wicked to practise your ingenuity upon them. Question everything else, if you will; let philosophy, and science, and politics, and trade, and social theories hang all in the wind, as open debates, as themes to try all your wits; task yourself on these as you please; exercise your fancy, your zeal, your spirit of opposition, your eccentricity, your obstinacy, as you will upon them; but leave us the Bible untouched, unchallenged. There ought, at least, to be one thing sacred from dispute, from cavilling, from tricks of debate, from ingenious speculation, from the assaults of human pride, which so readily pass into scoffs at what is to be revered. The interests of religion require and demand this reservation of the Holy Scriptures, and of every line which they contain, from all such presumptuous risks. It is the condition on which alone they can be of best use — of any real, edifying use — to simple men and women. You cannot press any such treatment as you propose upon the Bible, without at once raising unfair distinctions between Christians as regards the terms of salvation and a knowledge of those terms. But scholars are here entitled to no prerogative beyond the unlearned. We all stand on a level before that book; we have no right to judge it, for it is to judge us. Let it remain respected, revered, holy. As the Heaven-appointed style of an altar required that no tool should be used upon it, so the Bible should stand free of any profaning touch from man. Yield to it and secure to it such an unqualified regard, that, wherever any one opens to it, he may feel sure that he is reading what was writ by God, that the plainest sense of it is the truest, the literal meaning the right meaning, and that the Holy Spirit is addressing him in every sentence.

Such was the appeal made in behalf of the Bible against those whose questions and critical processes were met by intimidation or foreboding. The plea was spoken in various tones of kindness or severity, of courtesy or insolence, and it was enforced by various measurements of breadth or narrowness of intelligence, against those who first opened here the now familiar discussions, critical, philosophical, or sceptical, concerning the contents or the authority of the Bible.

From the tone and temper in which this plea has often been spoken, one might suppose it was addressed to some reckless and ruthless men, utterly indifferent to religion themselves, and bent only upon unsettling the faith of others. That those who were thus remonstrated with had an interest of their own at stake in the Bible fully equal to that of any others, and were as heartily and vitally concerned in all the questions thus raised, is but the suggestion of common sense. For who is there that connects his own hope and faith with the Bible, but would rejoice with all his heart and mind to yield to this appeal in all its warmth and earnestness? Are we not all equally interested in a revelation from God, in the volume which contains it, in asserting its authority, and in maintaining the infallibility of the record, if it be infallible? It is preposterous for one class of believers, who are ready to blink all biblical perplexities for themselves, and to offer unsound and inadequate explanations of them to the weak, the confiding, and the credulous whom they may influence, to address another class of their fellow-men, who give proof of honest motives, as if they were seeking to discredit the Bible because they opened their eyes to obvious difficulties in it. It is as if one set of mariners should rail at another set for attempting to speculate upon, calculate, measure, and allow for the variations of the compass, — the compass on which all alike depend, and by which all alike are glad to steer. Is there an honest and sincere person on the earth who would not be grateful for an infallible Bible, or who would be disposed to pick flaws in it? Are those who have given years of scholarly toil to the study of the Bible — all unrequited except as the result has cleared and strengthened their own faith by reducing alike their superstitious prejudices and their doubts — to be assailed as a set of religious Vandals? And if, as the deduction of intelligent and fair biblical criticism, it should appear that, within a few very definite restrictions and qualifications, a few guards of caution, and a few allowances for manifest error, the Bible is entitled to the character for infallibility which popular belief has set up for it, would not the critics who verified and proclaimed the fact be the heartiest sharers in the confidence it would afford? When the variations of the compass have been reduced to rule, its guidance is followed as implicitly as if it were subject to no variations. Let the highest standard be set for the authority and the infallibility of the Bible which honest truth will allow, and we may safely affirm that there is not a single right-minded person in the community who would turn coldly away from it, or willingly do or say anything to detract from it.

But the very occasion for making such an appeal is an intimation that it relies not wholly on fact, but somewhat on feeling and fear, and on a conscious misgiving as to its entire validity. The appeal could not avert criticism, and it cannot stifle it. Doubt and inquiry had the start of the appeal, and had already preoccupied the ground. The strife began at this very point. Apprehension got the better of courage, and remonstrances, often charged with abuse, were substituted for arguments. The question forced itself upon trial, not whether the Bible could be rescued from the scholar's or the sceptic's touch, but whether it could fairly and fearlessly stand the test, which it ought not for one moment to dread, if it were worthy of the confidence claimed for it. If God had written it, his hand and mind might safely be left to vindicate their work. If it had passed unharmed through the risks of ages, of transcription and translation, it need not quail before the dictionary, the grammar, or the commentary. The explorer of the Egyptian catacombs, the curious antiquarian digging away the sand from the plains of Assyria, or marking out the sites of the seven churches of Asia, could not discredit the record. The chronologist by old-world cycles, eclipses, and royal dynasties, the geologist gathering up the medals of creation, the mariner on the Mediterranean, and the traveller through Southern Italy, would never unsettle the Scriptures of Moses or Paul. The timidity of the champions of the Bible would bring its claims into peril far more than would the boldness of its challengers.

So far as the discussions connected with the Unitarian Controversy are had in view, we feel at liberty to say that Unitarians as a class have made a loyal recognition of the paramount importance of true Scriptural knowledge by the labors they have spent upon the original text, and by their scholarly zeal to authenticate and interpret it. In view of facts, of which unfortunately the evidence is painfully abundant in current religious literature, it is the sincere conviction of Unitarians, uncharitable as the confession of it may seem, that many Orthodox writers, for the sake of sustaining unimpaired the authority of the Bible, deal disingenuously with difficulties to which they really cannot close their own eyes or those of common readers. Orthodoxy attempts to hide from observation, or to make too light of, some of the perplexities which the Scriptures present to many conscientious and serious persons; while the obtrusion of these perplexities is regarded by the Orthodox as proof that they cannot be proposed by any really conscientious or serious person, but indicates of itself a depraved heart. The Orthodox in general insist that faith in the Bible, and love for it, should shut the eyes of all readers to the misgivings which their theory of its infallibility creates, and should reconcile them to encounter, unexplained and unrelieved, every embarrassing suggestion. It is claimed that the same Christian submission which reconciles us to bear bodily affliction and bereavement from God, ought to make us docile and tolerant over the seeming flaws in an infallible record. We are asked not only to accept the Bible under the highest character which we can intelligently assign to it, but as burdened with claims which Orthodoxy has set up for it; and in trying to uphold these claims Orthodoxy does not deal fairly with many of the difficulties which, *not the Bible*, but the *Orthodox theory* of the Bible, presents. Orthodoxy gives the Bible a weak side at that very point where it takes up the championship of the Bible.

We will now frankly state the position which Unitarians have in general affirmed, which they have maintained against many opponents, which they believe those opponents must and will sooner or later be compelled to accept, and which has in fact within the last quarter of a century received either an outspoken or an implied recognition from the most competent biblical students of various Christian communions. It is, that the prevailing popular view of the authority, the inspiration, and the infallibility of the Bible, has been superstitiously attached to it, that it did not originate in the Bible, is not claimed by the contents of the Bible, and cannot be sustained by any fair dealing with them; while the special pleading, the subterfuges, the artifices, the evasions, the forced constructions, and the actual violence to truth and fact, needed to uphold the popular view, are the very scorn of many intelligent persons and the grief of many pious persons. That position stands attested by overwhelming truth, and he who is competent to pronounce upon it must be something more than a bold man, and something worse than a weak man, who will now venture to question it. Is it now the pride of reason, the rebellion of a sinful heart, the entering into a controversy with God, which has instigated biblical criticism, and led Unitarians to adopt those general views about the composition, the authority, and the inspiration of the Bible that are identified with their position in this controversy? Let us try to answer this question.

We regret again to have to say, that an unjust aspersion was cast upon the motives of those who, in our doctrinal discussions, advanced the usual and now very familiar terms of biblical criticism, in suggesting the possibility of error, of mistranslations, perversions, and corruptions in the text of Scripture. It is to be granted that such suggestions may be made in the spirit of cavilling, of hypercriticism, of contempt and poor conceit of mind. But they may also be prompted by the highest conscientiousness, by the most intelligent candor, and by a most reverent and sincere intent. The instigating motive and spirit of them must be inferred from the characters, the professed design, and the language of those who offer them. It requires but a little discernment to distinguish between a reckless and a captious disputant, and an honest, humble doubter over perplexities, — though both may ask the same questions and make similar assertions. But the charge quite confidently and indignantly uttered against the Unitarians in pages of "The Panoplist" and "The Spirit of the Pilgrims" was in substance this: "You are flattering the pride of human reason, you are judging the word of God by your own prejudices, and making your own taste or intelligence or conscience the measure and test of revealed truth; you wish to warp and twist Scripture, to perplex the unlearned, and to unsettle the foundations of faith and reverence, leaving us all to the mercy of private judgment and a sort of freedom which Protestantism never contemplated."

In answer to this aspersion upon their motives, Unitarians replied, in general, that it was unjust and bigoted; that in the issue they would be found to be the wiser friends of the Bible; that the object which they had in view in proposing some discrimination in the contents and the popular estimate of that book, and in arguing for certain textual constructions and emendations, was simple truth, to meet the actual emergencies and exactions of the case; that the Scriptures were exposed to harm and to abuse, were open to honest criticism as to a safeguard, and that the human elements in them were subject to examination and revision by the human faculties. They also urged, that, whatever was the authority of the original inspiration, unless we were prepared to claim that all transcribers, translators, and printers of the Bible, as well as the collectors who first pronounced upon the canonical documents, were divinely watched over, restrained, and helped, there must have been risk of error and consequent material for criticism. Whether Unitarianism or Trinitarianism would gain or lose by the processes proposed, was an issue entirely subordinated to the Christian scholar's loyalty to his appropriate work.

Thus the whole question concerning the authority, the inspiration, and the interpretation of the Bible was fully opened, though prejudiced in the tone of its discussion by this unfair imputation of motives. In conducting their arguments, founded on textual criticism, Unitarians suggested the following and similar considerations: — That some books and some portions of books in the Bible are of doubtful authority, and probably spurious; that the collection is of a miscellaneous character, of unequal value, credit, and present authority; that science, history, chronology, geography, and even morality and piety, can propose valid objections to more or less important contents of the Bible, if the *letter* is insisted upon and a *plenary inspiration* is claimed for it; that inspiration could not be ascribed equally to all its contents, and was not needed in some of them, while the nature and measure and proof of inspiration itself were all unsettled and difficult of determination by any formula; that the writers used Orientalisms and figures of speech, exaggerations and metaphors, which would mislead us if rigidly interpreted into more literal forms of language; that what Christ said is more authoritative than anything that comes from any other source; that he may have conformed in language to views and conceptions then prevailing in the world, without always authenticating such views and conceptions as his language implied; that possibly his own words had sometimes been misunderstood or misreported, or affected by transcription or translation; that there are discrepancies, even in the New Testament, which cannot fairly be reconciled into a perfect consistency with the entire infallibility claimed for the writers; that the strict rules of logic were not always observed by the writers in their reasoning; that they were liable to mistake if they went out of the range within which their inspiration was limited; and that on one point at least the Apostles were manifestly in error in expecting the end of the world in their generation, and in speaking of it as certain.

When the controversy, leaving these broad fields, was concentrated upon some specific issue, a dispute was raised as to the proper province of reason in dealing with the Bible and its contents. Unitarians insisted upon an undefined, but still a real and legitimate faculty in a human being, not to judge Divine Truth, but to judge upon what other men offered to it as Divine Truth, — upon its message and its vehicle, upon its consistency with reason and with the elementary constitution of that nature which God had given and which God addressed. Unitarians accord with the judicious Hooker in a belief in "the primary revelation of the human understanding." Holding to this as, though a vague and undetermined, still a vitally essential right, some Unitarians have been wont to express themselves very strongly to this effect: If the Bible could be proved to teach this or that doctrine, professedly drawn from it, so inconsistent with its other contents, with the attributes of God and the nature of man, and so shocking to human reason, then the necessary inference would follow, that the Bible is not from God. Unitarians were replied to by their opponents, that, *if* a book advancing the claims of the Bible were found to contain such monstrous doctrines, its Divine authority would of course be perilled. This being yielded as an hypothesis, it was then denied that the Bible had any such contents, and when, notwithstanding, the Orthodox continued to press upon Unitarians doctrines as from the Bible which to the latter had that character and aspect, the revulsion of heart, mind, and soul against them was not allowed to discredit the doctrines or the Bible which was supposed to teach them, but was referred to the pride of carnal reason and a haughty heart. The doctrines, nevertheless, came from God, and were good doctrines, and the Bible was all the more precious for teaching them; and until a man could choke them down, he was unmistakably in a hopeless state of reprobation.

When the discussion reached this point, it was a blessed thing for both parties that there was such a door of relief opened as that of biblical criticism. God be thanked for the understanding he has given to man, as well as for the inspiration he has given to his Word; for the faculty to interpret, as well as for the oracle; for the certain expounder of its uncertain sounds. The great question presents itself, What doctrines does the Bible teach? So that, beside all the broad issues relating to the authenticity and authority of the different books of Scripture, there came in for discussion a large range of topics connected with interpretation. The direction of these discussions and the spirit brought to them may be inferred from the following instance. There appeared in "The Spirit of the Pilgrims"* a very censorious review of Milman's History of the Jews, written in the spirit of an alarmist. In that review the liberal-minded and intelligent author, though, as a distinguished clergyman of the Church of England, he belonged then as now to a nominally Orthodox communion, was severely handled for venturing to make some concessions of a semi-rationalistic character. The reviewer expresses his own opinion in this sentence: "We know that, of all impossible vagaries of a learned fancy, that of making the Bible a book which infidels will believe is the wildest." This remark is made concerning the efforts of the critic, in allowing for the Orientalisms of the record, to reduce some apparently marvellous, legendary, or exaggerated details to a more credible self-consistency. Suppose now we invert the remark of the reviewer, and say that, Of all the most objectionable

* Vol. III. p. 487.

ways of viewing and treating the Bible, that is the most harmful which fosters infidelity and burdens a vigorous and effective faith in its substantial truth with a slavish bondage to the letter of all its contents. Is not this assertion of ours as true as that of the reviewer? And is not the truth in it as worthy of practical regard and caution from the defenders of the Bible? The advocates of the Bible have found occasion in many cases to be its apologists. They ought to be furnished for both these offices, as were the great ministers of the Christian Church in the centuries after the Apostles. But it is a curious fact, that many divines who have been most ready to write upon the evidences of Christianity have been the least tolerant of the harder tasks of the biblical critic. While those who are already firm and assured in their Scriptural faith of course may look to their religious teachers for instruction founded on their faith, it would seem as if those who are tried by doubts, but are anxious to believe if their difficulties can be removed, deserved some sympathy from the friends and champions of revelation. Some of our divines, however, seem to have acted on the principle, that the harder they made the terms of biblical faith to the sceptical, the more precious those terms would be to the believer.

On the same page of the same review just quoted, we read the following sentence: "Let the defender of the inspiration of the Bible take the highest ground; he will find it easiest to maintain." But what is the highest ground? The writer evidently means by the expression to recommend the boldest assertion, the most unqualified, unscrupulous, and dogmatic assertion, of plenary inspiration. This, however, would be to our minds the lowest ground, lowest in the scale of reason, truth, value, and evidence. Who shall be judge in any case whether an obstinate and rigid adherence to an unintelligent and a reckless theory, or a candid concession to a reconsidered and a reconstructed theory, be the truest ground? — for the truest will be the highest. An issue raised by common sense concerning hundreds of passages in Scripture, asks whether they are to be interpreted *literally* or *figuratively;* and if figuratively, how we are to choose, out of an infinite number of harder prosaical forms of language, a cast into which to compress the poetic figure. Thus, twice does the Bible affirm that the Ten Commandments were "written with the finger of God" on tables of stone. (Exod. xxxi. 18; Deut. ix. 10.) If we insist upon the *letter*, we must say that God took into his hands those slabs of stone, and actually engraved upon them with his own finger the Ten Commandments. But if we yield the literal for *some* figurative interpretation, we have abandoned logic with the letter, and we follow our fancies as they rove in a thousand directions to seek the proper shaping of an image for expressing God's agency in acting through man as an engraver or scribe, a dictator or oracle. How vain, then, is the attempt to trammel such ventures as those of Milman, provided they are reverential, with the broken bonds of literalism! Over and over again we find the Deity represented in the Old Testament as rising early in the morning light, as if, like a man who had a task, he determined to start apace and make a long day of it. No one interprets such language literally. But when we abandon the letter, the alternative is not to insist upon some specific, figurative form, but to launch freely into the expanse of devout and reverent imagery.

Suppose a serious reader of the Bible, with a burden on his mind, comes to his minister with this question: "How can the Bible twice repeat the assertion, that 'David was a man after God's own heart, fulfilling all his will,' (1 Sam. xiii. 14, Acts xiii. 22,) when the same Bible presents David to us as an adulterer and a murderer, and tells us that he was expressly forbidden to build a temple for God, because he was 'a man of blood'?" Doubtless the minister in the age of our fathers would have replied, that "God sanctified all his instruments," and would have let the matter drop there. A minister of our own time would be likely to reply, that the English words "a man after God's own heart" do not convey exactly the Hebraism in the original; which means, more strictly rendered, *a man of God's choice for fulfilling his purpose in one or more directions.* The relief is appreciable and sufficient. But is not this a use of your reason for removing a seeming inconsistency in the record, a trial of your own skill and wisdom to improve upon what your fathers left you? It surely is. Suppose, then, you try the same intelligence upon the popular notion that David's fierce imprecations upon his enemies in some of the Psalms come from inspiration of God, and so are of edifying use in Christian churches for the devotion of Christians at this day. Of the nine verses in that exquisite and heart-moving lyric, Psalm cxxxvii., the first six might have come from a soul kindled by the fire of the divine altar. But what shall we say of the last verse, — "O daughter of Babylon, happy shall he be that taketh and dasheth thy little ones against the stones"?

We can give but a few paragraphs to that element of the great controversy before us which involves the subject of Inspiration, though a volume might be filled by that topic alone. All clear, distinguishing, and satisfactory views on this topic are embarrassed by the unsettled and undefined senses attached by different persons to Inspiration when ascribed to the Bible. The most encouraging reason for hoping that we have made approximation to a true theory of Inspiration, and to more accordance of opinion and belief in reference to it, is found in the fact that we have given over our attempts at a rigid definition of its substance, scope, or limitations.

And yet, till we have something like such a definition, we can argue, advocate, and object to but vague conclusions. Who will tell us, to the content of all, what is meant by Inspiration? We all know what *we mean* to mean by it. We all have a clouded sense of its august, oracular source, its exalted authority, and its intended uses, as abiding in a writing whose words, or at least whose contents, have a Divine sanction. But what rigid exposition can be given of its method, its operation, its limits, its distinguishing marks and tokens? What are the securities of its tenure for human use? Is it restricted to the communication and the sanction of one class of truths, namely, religious truths, and even, by a rigid analysis, to that class of religious truths which we call the highest, that is, the spiritual as distinguished from the moral? Does the inspiration by the Divine Mind of a human mind, as a channel or organ for the communication of religious truth, affect all the views and utterances of that mind, and make all its judgments and opinions infallible? Does this inspiration intermingle with the knowledge and the wisdom derived by the inspired man from other sources? How does such inspiration pass from the mind into speech or writing, using the vocables of a language and its grammatical forms, and words and images which have a variety of significations and associations? Does this inspiration confine its authority to the actual utterances and to the original record made by the subject of it, or is it of such a nature as to admit of being perpetuated unimpaired in a tolerably faithful translation of the record?

The Apostles affirmed, on an occasion when evidence was all important, that two sorts of it were offered in the cause of the Gospel. Thus, "WE are his witnesses of these things; and so is also the HOLY GHOST, whom God hath given to them that obey him." (Acts v. 32.) Here they evidently distinguish between their own testimony as competent witnesses to what they had seen, heard, and known, and the assurance of belief which God gave by inspiration to the obedient. St. Paul often makes a distinction between what he teaches as a man, speaking by his own judgment and prompting, and what he teaches through the Spirit of God. Thus the personal Apostolic testimony is made to be that of independent, veritable eyewitnesses, who had cognizance of facts transpiring within their own observation, and of intelligent judges of truth as to matters level to human comprehension. The testimony of the Holy Ghost stands in some sense apart, as to a degree authenticating what the Apostles knew, and to a degree adding to their knowledge, their power, and their ability to teach, and attaching a demonstration to their testimony. Is there not here a fair distinction between the contents of the Bible as embracing alike what is taught, from human sources, of history, wisdom, moral precept and doctrine, and what came by immediate inspiration from God? And if that distinction be allowed, then Inspiration must be restricted to a portion of the contents of the Bible, while what the book contains of mere human teaching or writing must be subject to the conditions attaching to all the operations of the human intellect.

The old Orthodox theory wavered and oscillated between a *verbal inspiration* and a *plenary* inspiration of all the contents of the Bible, and either epithet attached to inspiration has been the warrant with the Orthodox of all parties for speaking of the Bible as "the Word of God," which, as the careful reader knows very well, has no Scripture warrant for its use.* The usual form of

* In illustration and confirmation of an assertion made on a preceding page, to the effect that all the discriminating suggestions of leading Unitarian critics had recently received full approval from scholars in other communions, who, in a candid dealing with the Bible, have admitted the necessity of

the Orthodox argument is as follows: Christ authenticated the Inspiration of the whole of the Old Testament by referring in confidence to its parts and contents, by quoting it as authority in all cases, and by ratifying its prophecies and doctrines. "Thus saith the Lord" is the warrant of Inspiration for the whole Old Testament. The Apostles of Christ follow in this respect the example of their Master, while the Inspiration which he promised to them assures to their own writings the

---

qualifying popular exaggerations concerning it, we adduce the following very pointed remarks. They are extracted from a volume of sermons, entitled "Rational Godliness, after the Mind of Christ, and the Written Voices of his Church," by Rowland Williams, B. D., Fellow of King's College, Cambridge, England, and Professor of Hebrew at Lampeter. "Above all, let no man blunt the edge of his conscience, by praising such things as the craft of Jacob, or the blood-stained treachery of Jael; nor let the natural metaphor by which men called a sacred record 'the Word of God' ever blind us to the fact that no text has been found, from Genesis to Revelations, in which this holy name is made a synonyme for the entire volume of Scripture; but rather, the spirit is often, especially in the New Testament, put in opposition to the letter; and the living word, as for instance it was spoken by the Apostles, is constantly distinguished from the written tradition of the days of old. Most commonly, in the New Testament, the phrase *Word of God* means the Gospel of Christ, or the glad tidings of the Messiah being come. It should also be noticed, that, while the discoveries of modern travellers do so far confirm the books of the Old Testament as to show their historical character, they give no countenance to any exaggerated theory of omniscience or dictation, but rather contravene any dream of the kind. When men quote discoveries as confirmations of the Bible, they should consider in what sense and how far it is confirmed by them." — pp. 298, 299.

Again: "But above all, the critical interpretation of the sacred volume itself is a study for which our generation is, by various acquirements, eminently qualified. Hence we have learnt that neither the citations usually made in our theological systems, nor even those adduced from the Old Testament in the New, are any certain guide to the sense of the original text. The entire question of prophecy requires to be opened again from its very foundation. Hence, to the student, who is compelled to dwell on such things, comes often the distress of glaring contradictions; and with some the intellect is clouded, while the faith of others has waxed cold. If the secret religious history of the last twenty years could be written, (even setting aside every instance of apostasy through waywardness of mind, or through sensuality of life,) there would remain a page over which angels might weep. So long, indeed, as such difficulties are thought absolutely to

same Divine sanction which they ascribe to the elder Scriptures. The warning, at the close of the last book of the Bible, against taking from or adding to it, is made by the Orthodox theory virtually to cover and to guard the whole volume, and to make it literally the Word of God.*

The Unitarian argues thus, in general terms. The contents of the Bible were not gathered into a volume by either of the writers of it, but by men unknown to

militate against Christianity, the strong necessity which the best men feel for Christian sentiment will induce them to keep the whole subject in abeyance. Yet surely the time must come when God will mercifully bring our spirit into harmony with our understanding. He who dwells in light eternal does not promote his kingdom by darkness; and he whose name is Faithful and True is not served by falsehood. If knowledge has wounded us, the same spear must heal our wound.

"Nor can I close without humbly asking the grave, the reverend, and the learned, whether all this subject does not call for greater seriousness, tenderness, and frankness. Who would not be serious on observing how many men's hope of heaven is bound up with belief in the infallibility of a book, which, every day convinces us, expresses, as regards things of earth, the thoughts of fallible men? Or who is so blind as to think that the cause of eternal truth should be defended by sophistries of which a special pleader would be ashamed? One would make a large allowance for the conscientious anxiety of those eminent persons whose position makes them responsible as bulwarks of the Faith; and who are ever dreading the consequences to which the first outlet of the waters of freedom may tend. But may God in his mercy teach them that nothing can be so dangerous as to build on a false foundation." — pp. 306 - 308.

* The same Episcopal divine from whom we have just quoted so largely thus offsets the common Orthodox notion that the Saviour and his Apostles authenticated and indorsed the whole Old Testament: "Now all these writers of the New Testament appear partly as antagonists of the Old, and partly as witnesses who confirm it. Partly they are antagonists, for even the doctrines of Christ find fault with much that had been spoken of old. He appeals from the law of Moses about marriage to the purer instinct of the heart, as that which had been from the beginning; he refuses to confirm the law of retaliation; and both he and his Apostles, especially St. Paul, turn men's thoughts from the tradition of the wisdom of old time, which was principally enshrined in the Bible, to that life of the soul which comes of the Holy Ghost, and to the ever-expanding law which is both written in the heart, and which accumulates enactment from experience." — Rational Godliness, p. 300.

us. We have no reason for believing that a protecting and guiding inspiration presided over this collection or selection of writings, and we are wholly ignorant as to the degree of care, or the terms and means for authenticating its contents, employed in the work. Some apocryphal or disputed books were excluded from either Testament, and some of the books admitted into the New Testament have from the first been admitted to be of doubtful authority; not so much on the score of their contents, as because they lacked the evidence necessary for authenticating them. The Old Testament bears on its face the appearance of including all the Jewish literature extant at the time of its compilation, and is therefore of a very miscellaneous character, while it mentions and quotes from other Jewish Scriptures which seem to have been lost. We know not the authors of a large number of the books of the Old Testament, and the writers do not all of them by any means claim to have had inspiration. Some of the books relate simply and purely to matters of history, having no concern with doctrine and scarcely any relation to religion. In writing them *honesty* would be the best and the only necessary sort of inspiration. A competent knowledge of facts and a power to relate them would be the full qualification of the writers of a large portion of them. There are also manifest errors and perplexities, inconsistencies and discrepancies, found in a close and careful study of the records, which utterly confound one who seeks to refer them all to inspiration from God.

Still Unitarians, so far from denying, have always affirmed and insisted upon their belief in an inspiration of the Scriptures. They have never given a rigid dogmatical definition of their idea or their belief on this point, because the very conditions of the case prevent their doing so. Again do we have to admit vagueness and indefiniteness into our creed, rather than purchase a rigid formula at the expense of truth, — a formula taken from human hands, under the false guise of a Divine oracle. Our aim shall now be to illustrate this position, — that Unitarianism forms its view of the inspiration, the authority, and the value to be ascribed to the Bible, under a recognition of the allowances and limitations which must be made in qualification of the claim for its Divine origin and infallibility that has been popularly advanced for it; while Orthodoxy nominally clings to and insists upon an unqualified theory of the Divine origin and infallibility of all the contents of the sacred volume, and then by actual compulsion yields certain concessions more or less invalidating its theory. The actual issue, then, between the able biblical critics on either side of this controversy is, as to whether it be wiser and better, more honest and more candid, to make these necessary concessions first or last; to advance one theory in view of the facts that must be recognized, or to advance another theory in spite of those facts. Sooner or later those facts which compel us to qualify the popular view of the Bible must be confronted. Do we not speak a truth, of which the Christian scholars of our day have met much painful and mortifying evidence, when we affirm that the concessions compulsorily drawn out in the course of the arguments proposed by many Orthodox divines in support of the old view of the inspiration and the infallibility of the whole Bible, are made most grudgingly, awkwardly, timidly, and in some cases are ingeniously smothered over in evasive, uncandid, and irrelevant equivocation.

We have a task, in many respects an unwelcome one, before us, but we must perform it as faithfully as we can. The course of our argument compels us to present some specimens from each of the various materials of embarrassment with which an honest defender of the Bible must in our day reconcile his view of the Scriptures.

Protestants have in one respect at least been faithful to the high liberty and to the solemn obligation which they asserted for themselves, the right and the duty of studying the Scriptures with the freest and the most scrutinizing faculties God has given them. Commentaries, expositions, and critical helps without number have been provided. The Bible has had a million microscopes of the intensest power turned upon it. "Reference Bibles," with their curious apparatus, have reduced the theory of interpreting Scripture by Scripture into a literally practical work for thousands of readers. Now let the excellent Dr. Arnold state to us a plain truth in his moderate and guarded way. He says: "It is very true that our position with respect to the Scriptures is not in all points the same as our fathers'. For sixteen hundred years nearly, while physical science, and history, and chronology, and criticism were all in a state of torpor, the questions which now present themselves to our minds could not from the nature of the case arise. When they did arise, they came forward into notice gradually: first, the discoveries in astronomy excited uneasiness; then, as men began to read more critically, differences in the several Scripture narratives of the same thing awakened attention; more lately, the greater knowledge which has been gained of history, and of language, and in all respects the more careful inquiry to which all ancient records have been submitted, have brought other difficulties to light, and some sort of answer must be given to them." *

Dr. Newman, the Puseyite champion of Romanism, in his argument in support of a priesthood, an extra-scriptural church authority, and the doctrine of transubstantiation, illustrates his position that people must be-

* Dr. Arnold's Christian Life; its Course, its Hinderances, and its Helps. Notes, p. 485.

lieve in spite of the difficulties and the seeming unreasonableness of some tenets, by alleging the perplexities of Scripture. Dr. Arnold censures him, because, "with great ingenuity, but with a recklessness of consequences, or an ignorance of mankind truly astonishing, he brought forward all the difficulties and differences which can be found in the Scripture narratives, and displayed them in their most glaring form." * Dr. Arnold says for himself: "Feeling what the Scriptures are, I would not give unnecessary pain to any one by an enumeration of those points in which the literal historical statement of an inspired writer has been vainly defended." † We think this excellent man was greatly mistaken in the opinion which he afterwards utters as to a general unconsciousness or ignorance on the part of the readers of the Bible of the difficulties presented by it when tried by the popular theory; but we must commend his earnest plea, "that, if ever these difficulties are brought forward, let us not try to put them aside unfairly."

The difficulties to which we shall make a brief reference, as specimens of various classes of perplexities and misgivings, are such *only* and *entirely* in view of the popular notion of the infallibility and the homogeneity of all the miscellaneous contents of the Bible. In view of what we regard as a more just and an equally edifying theory of the Bible, they are trivial and harmless.

When, under the best restraints of reverence, intelligence, and a proper self-distrust, we apply the tests of criticism to the various contents of the Bible, we find many tokens of human fallibility, either in the original writers, or at least in the records which have come to us in their present form. It is a relief to us to find, as Dr. Arnold also says he "must acknowledge, that the scriptural

* Christian Life, &c., p. 480. † Ibid., p. 491.

narratives do not claim inspiration for themselves,"* and though, with him, we believe in inspiration in the Scriptures on other grounds, it is a comfort to us to be free to define it to our own minds. As but few of the books claim to have been composed by those to whom they are ascribed, we are left in doubt as to the source of the whole or of parts of some of them. Names are assigned to some places which were not attached to those places till after the death of the reputed writers. In one of the books ascribed to Moses there is a compliment bestowed on him as the meekest of men, and an account of his death, indicating certainly some editorial work, we know not by whom. Admitting the inspiration of Moses, would it necessarily follow that his editor and biographer was inspired? Besides the multitude of historical perplexities presented by the Scriptures, they are embarrassed by much of apparent conflict in their statements with matters of positive science and chronology. Whoever maintains the "plenary inspiration" of the Scriptures, of course commits himself to uphold the perfect accuracy of the writers in every statement which they have made, alike in their incidental allusions and by-the-way remarks, and in their most direct and emphatic announcements. Even if they were not inspired to write on scientific matters, still, if they were restrained or aided by a Divine oversight while holding their pens, they could have written nothing but truth. Now, what heaps of volumes have been composed in attempts to frown down the demonstrative sciences whenever they seemed to threaten a text in Genesis! How much futile ingenuity, how much trivial special pleading, how much absurd theorizing, have been exercised on such matters as "The Six Days of Creation," "The Unity of the Human Race," "The

* Christian Life, &c., p. 487.

Flood," the capacity of "The Ark," "The Rainbow," "The Ages of the Patriarchs," "The Plagues of Egypt," "The Red Sea," "Manna," and "Joshua and the Sun." How was astronomy first resisted as an impious science! When the history of geological science shall come to be written, with special reference to the alarms and opprobriums through which Buckland and J. P. Smith and Mantel and Lyell led on the line of the earth's revelations of its own history, will not Protestantism be regarded as having fully matched the old story of Galileo and his Roman inquisitors? Not the least ludicrous among the incidents to be rehearsed in that history will be the grateful avidity with which a large number of the "*Evangelical*" party threw themselves and their Bibles into the arms of Hugh Miller.

When the Bible presents us with duplicate narratives, or contemporaneous records covering the same time, events, and characters, of course we are urged to a very searching criticism of them. The Books of Samuel, of Kings, and Chronicles are of this character; and when their contents are brought into comparison, they are often found in strange conflict in their statements. Matters which have not the slightest importance, and no sort of connection with the realities or the sanctions of our faith, in themselves considered, are thus exalted into alarms and dangers, if the standard of inspiration and infallibility is set for all the promiscuous contents of the Bible. These books present us with some specimens of a most perplexing nature, under one of the chief class of embarrassments attaching to the narratives of the Old Testament, — the matter of numbers, in stating population, military forces, and amounts of money. It is a comfort to confess, in our confusion and bewilderment, that "we are very ignorant about the Hebrew system of notation," and that old records that have been frequently copied by the pen are especially liable to error in the matter of figures and numbers. When, by command of David, Joab numbered the forces, according to 2 Sam. xxiv. 9, Israel had 800,000 soldiers, and Judah had 500,000; but according to 1 Chron. xxi. 5, Israel had 1,100,000 and Judah 470,000. In 2 Kings viii. 26, Ahaziah, son of Jehoram, was twenty-two years old when he began to reign; but in 2 Chron. xxii. 2, he is said to have been forty-two years old. This latter account makes him to have been two years older than his own father, who died just before the son's accession, aged forty (2 Chron. xxi. 20). In 1 Kings xv. 32, it is said, "there was war between Asa and Baasha all their days"; but in 2 Chron. xiv. 1, it is said, Asa had peace in his land ten years. In 2 Chron. xiv. 3, it is said that Asa took away "the high places" of idolatry; but in the next chapter, verse 17, it is said, "the high places were not taken away." In view of these and similar phenomena, of which he makes a most candid recognition, Professor Stuart very truly says, the critic "has a somewhat formidable task before him; especially if he adopts the theory of plenary *verbal* inspiration."* The Professor also remarks, very naively, in reference to a matter already noticed, that "the statement of numbers occasionally wears the air of something very extraordinary."† It seems hardly credible that the wealth collected by David for the temple should have been what is stated in 1 Chron. xxii. 14, calculated by Dr. Arbuthnot, in his Table of Ancient Currency, to amount to £ 800,000,000. One, too, may be allowed to hope that there is some error in the statement, that a man so wise as Solomon should have burdened himself with a thousand women.

* Stuart's Critical History and Defence of the Old Testament Canon, p. 161.

† Ibid., p. 158.

Similar discrepancies, found by comparing two or more representations of the same events, incidents, and discourses, are now among the familiar themes of discussion in the criticism of the Gospels. The advocate who attempts to reconcile those phenomena with the theory of *Infallibility* in the present form of those records, must task his ingenuity at the expense of his candor.

Take, next, the phenomena presented by the Book of Job. The interlocutors in the discussions contained in that marvellously rich and precious Scripture debate the great mystery of the purpose of evil, its allowance and tolerance by God, and its seemingly unequal, unjust, deferred, and immoderate visitations upon different human beings. The speakers approach and recede from the mystery; they clutch at it, and then quail before it; they offer all sorts of notions about it; and we find in the book arguments affirmed and answered, objections raised and set aside, and a great variety of discordant views intimated or insisted upon. Statements are made in single sentences which are false, wicked, irreverent, almost impious, and are charged to the different speakers whom Job answers, while the Almighty himself is represented as answering Job. Now, wherein lies the inspiration and the infallibility of that book? In all its sentiments, or in a part of them? and in what part? Does the book contain a veritable narrative of real life, or is it an artificial composition, written to convey a great lesson? and how will this contingency affect its being referred to a Divine Source? Mark, now, how Professor Stuart utters himself on the main point: — "Not a few persons appeal to the speeches of Job, Eliphaz, Bildad, Zophar, and Elihu in support of *doctrinal* propositions; just as if these angry disputants, who contradict each other, and most of whom God himself has declared to be in the wrong (xlii. 7 – 9), were inspired when they disputed! The man who wrote the book, and gave an account of this dispute, might be — I believe he was — inspired; he had a great moral purpose in view; but how Job is to be appealed to for a sample of doctrine, who curses the day of his birth, and says many things under great excitement, I am not able to understand. Are we indeed to follow him in the sentiment of chap. xiv. 7, 10, 12? And are we to appeal to his angry friends, who are in the wrong as to the main point in question, for confirmation of a doctrinal sentiment of the Gospel? The practical amount of the matter is, that those who refer in such a way to this book merely select what they like, and leave the rest. They complain, however, in other cases, of doings like to this. They accuse the Unitarians and the Rationalists of very unfair and unscriptural practices, in so doing with other parts of the Bible." * Is not that frank speech from an Andover Professor? We apprehend that, if some preachers who have discoursed upon several texts from Job were to look sharply into the connection of those texts, they would find that they had taken some sentences as Divine oracles, uttered by inspiration from God, which are in fact false and wicked opinions expressed by men.

We have noted the reference made by Professor Stuart to a passage indicating Job's scepticism or unbelief in a future state. Yet it is from Job's lips that the beautiful sentences in the Liturgical Burial Service are taken, "For I know that my Redeemer liveth," &c. (xix. 25–27.) This passage has been read millions of times over human graves, under the impression entertained by Christian ministers, or at least encouraged by them for the comfort of mourners, that Job knew and prophesied of the coming of Christ, and also of the resurrection of the body. Professor Stuart says of the text,

* Critical History, &c., p. 144.

"It is constantly quoted to show the Patriarch's knowledge of a Messiah to come, and of the doctrine of the resurrection, notwithstanding the context, and the tenor of the whole book, are totally of a different nature." * Our readers are, doubtless, for the most part, well aware that a fair and just interpretation of the passage finds in it no such references; but that its meaning conveys the expression of Job's confidence that, *before* his diseased body should be brought to death, his *vindicator*, God, would make his innocence evident to living men on the earth, — a confidence which the event verified. The Presbyterian Dr. Barnes, in his Notes on Job, confesses to us with what a painful violence to fond associations, connected with the old version, he was forced to admit this true interpretation of the passage. Yet the reader who knows the superstitious as well as fond tenacity of prejudices linked with religious feeling, knows very well that a demonstration of an error in such a passage as this in our English Bibles would not persuade to its correction. The passage is a good one for use in an attempt to enlighten such persons — and there are many of them — as cling, with a puerile and sickly fancy, to all the weak supports which use or association has led them to regard as essential or helpful to their faith. They *wish to believe* that God dictated through Job the words on which we are remarking, as found in our English Bible. Suppose, however, they yield to the common-sense suggestion, that the translator happened to give to the passage a construction which it will not fairly admit; will their faith in truth be shaken by the removal of error? Still, let an appeal be made to "the Christian public," to have that passage correctly rendered, and what a storm would ensue in "the religious journals"!

---

* Critical History, &c., p. 409.

A remark similar to that just made, in reference to the false and irreverent sentiments advanced in some sentences of the Book of Job, is equally pertinent — is indeed more emphatically applicable — to the Book of Ecclesiastes. Taking that composition as an essay on human life, in which the writer tells us how he was led on through sensuality and scepticism, with their temporary lures and mottoes and maxims, to the conclusion of all wisdom in the fear of God, we find the work to be of exalted value to us, a treasure and a guide. But in what sense are we to attribute inspiration to it? Are its sentiments inspired, or only its moral? Or shall we say, as Professor Stuart says of Job, that "the man who wrote it was inspired," allowing the inference that *what he wrote* is not inspired, — that *not all* which his pen put down partakes of his inspiration? When preachers take texts from that strange compound of Epicureanism and piety, what must they do about the old theory of an infallible inspiration?

In the Prophecy of Jeremiah, xxii. 24, 28 – 30, the Prophet says he was solemnly moved by God to utter a most fearful malediction on Jechoniah; he was to be cursed as childless, with no posterity to sit upon his throne. What are we to say, then, when, on turning to the genealogy of the Saviour, in Matthew i. 12, we find this "childless" man appearing as a parent, and holding his place in the ancestral lineage of the Messiah? What meaning or limitation has an infallible inspiration here? Again, the Book of Daniel, which reads as a wondrous prophecy of future events, is, with scarcely a shadow of doubt, a history of events that had already transpired cast into the form of predictions. If there is inspiration here, it would therefore seem to be of the *memory*. The Book of Esther, making no mention of God or of divine doctrine, seems to have been composed simply to account for the introduction of a fourth Jewish feast, — that of Purim. Professor Stuart makes a very impressive statement of the difficulties in the way of receiving some of the contents of this book even as veritable history, still more as inspired narrative. Yet through force of considerations satisfactory to his own mind, he concludes that we ought to regard it as in some sense inspired. The Song of Solomon is an utter scandal to many readers, and their offence at it is aggravated rather than relieved by the hard and far-fetched device of some fanciful commentators, who, without a shadow of reason, profess to find in it a fond portrayal of the love of Christ for his Church, under the guise of an amorous Jewish ditty. Professor Stuart's lucubrations on this matter are among the most extraordinary utterances which the book has ever called forth; their squeamishness runs into pruriency. The unblushing presence of that "Song of Songs" in the Old Testament is enough to make all theologians and divines — to say nothing of unlearned Christians — grateful for each announcement and repetition of the suggestion, that the Old Testament *probably* embraced all the extant Hebrew literature.

Still another class of perplexities present themselves to our minds when, in view of the theory of an infallible inspiration, we attempt to form a satisfactory idea about the relation between the Old Testament and the New, as regards quotations from the former in the latter, represented as the fulfilment of prophecies. The allowance of the principle, that the New Testament writers often quote from the Old, and use the phrase "it was fulfilled" merely for *illustration* and by *accommodation*, without implying prophecy, is an adequate solution of all the difficulties in the case. But this principle is so undefined in its applications as to leave the popular theory of the Bible at strange hazard.

Quite a courageous announcement of the principle was made by Dr. Hey, a Divinity Professor in Cambridge University, England, as follows: "One thing which has occasioned difficulty is quotations of prophecies being introduced with '*that it might be fulfilled*'; but this is mere idiom; it means no more than *à propos* does in French, or than our saying, 'I dreamt of you last night; now I meet you, the dream is out.'"* Stuart seems to admit the same principle, in recognizing quotations in which the fulfilment "consists in the striking points of resemblance." †

A still graver question presents itself when we ask if it was possible for the Christian Apostles, the writers of the New Testament, to fall into mistakes incidentally at least connected with the substance and history of the Gospel religion. We shall shortly note some remarkable concessions on this point from the pens of the ablest modern scholars and critics in nominally Orthodox communions. But we have in view now the matter of infallible inspiration. When Peter and Paul differed, that is, in plain English, quarrelled, about the Judaizing element which some wished to connect with the adoption of the Gospel by the Gentiles, when Paul "withstood Peter to the face, because he was to be blamed" (Galat. ii. 11), on which side was the *inspiration?* If with both of them, as we believe it was, it must have consisted with *fallibility* in one of them. To what limitation must Paul's inspiration have been subject to account for the fact that he did not know that it was the high-priest whom he had just rebuked? (Acts xxiii. 5.) How are we to account for a fact of which the fresh pages of an Andover periodical now before us remind us, that "Matthew says that our Lord ate his Last Supper with his

* Lectures in Divinity, Vol. I. p. 259.

† Critical History, &c., p. 340.

disciples on the evening of the Passover, and John that he ate it the evening before the Passover?" *

Now is the question, whether God has made a revelation of religious truths to the world, to be burdened with all these perplexities, or to stand clear of them? That question is to be decided by the possibility and the success of an attempt to reconstruct, not a rigid theory, but a satisfactory view of the authority, the inspiration, and the value of those various records which are contained in the Bible. "Perhaps," says the author of "Rational Godliness," "a greatness and a place not far from the Apostles in the kingdom of heaven may be reserved for some one who, in true holiness and humility of heart, shall be privileged to accomplish this work." †

All these suggestions of perplexity, with all the specific materials of them, may be sadly exaggerated, or they may be regarded as of very trifling consequence. The way in which they ought to be dealt with after they have presented themselves to our notice, offers, after all, the most essential difficulty in the case. Unitarians believe that they may be reasonably, fairly, and candidly disposed of, in perfect harmlessness to our faith. Unitarians also affirm that these perplexities have been aggravated by being blinked or denied, by being treated with shirks and evasions, with forced constructions, and with alarming appeals and remonstrances, as if faith were perilled by recognizing or discussing them. It is our own conviction, that pages may be found in some works written in defence of the Bible actually more prejudicial to a healthful faith in its blessed revelations than anything that can be found in infidel works. Worse than all the difficulties presented by the Bible are many of the crooked and jesuitical pretences for their solution. There

---

* Bibliotheca Sacra, July, 1856, p. 678.

† Page 307.

are precious works in our language, erudite, reverential, and honest, chiefly from the pens of those whom, in the best sense of the epithet, we may call *Liberal* Christians, in which most of the perplexities which we encounter have been treated with caution and wisdom. Grotius, Le Clerc, Locke, and Lardner, and many of the contributors to that admirable repository called Watson's Tracts, collected and indorsed by the excellent Bishop himself, have anticipated and dispelled our fears in the direction of biblical criticism.

Solemn, therefore, is the obligation to which truth commits all those who in this age of the world would defend an intelligent faith in the Bible, to announce only such a theory concerning its authority and its divine inspiration as is consistent with its own contents. The strong must in many things bear the infirmities of the weak, but ministers and theological teachers have had many a serious warning against that extreme deference to old wives' fables and old wives' prejudices which many of them have exhibited in attempting to gloss over such phenomena of the Bible as they were afraid fairly to recognize. Do not the strong, those who will be strong in unbelief and in hostility to the sacred mysteries of faith if they are fed on the husks of superstition, deserve some regard? Are all the secret strivings of the robust and inquisitive and sceptical to pass for naught, that the silly notions and the anile prejudices of those who are willing to pin their faith upon the assertions of a narrow-minded religious exhorter may be kindly fostered?

But we have solid material yet to work into this essay. We revert to the fundamental question of Inspiration. The Orthodox theory is untenable; it is burdened with mischief. Over and over again it quotes the misused text, interpolated with a word which turns its noble truth into a falsehood: "All Scripture *is* given by inspiration of God, and is profitable," &c. 2 Tim. iii. 16. The inference drawn from this perverted text is, that all the promiscuous writings embraced in the Old Testament were dictated by God. Common sense might suggest even the grammar rule to be applied to this passage as meaning, "Every divinely inspired writing is also profitable," &c.

Professor Gaussen, of Geneva, may be taken as the living representative and advocate of a theory of Inspiration which was maintained by the Orthodox at the origin of the Unitarian Controversy here, but which may now be pronounced as utterly discredited by all scrupulous and competent biblical scholars. We leave to those who are concerned in the more than equivocal case presented to us to reconcile the ostensible public approbation which the Orthodox party have extended to Gaussen's work, with what the leaders of that party must know to be untenable in its main positions.* The following extracts will show with what a recklessness of consequences this modern Genevan divine ventures to affirm positions which common sense falsifies. Speaking of the writers of the Scriptures, Gaussen † says: "Whether they record mysteries antecedent to creation, or those of a futurity more remote than the return of the Son of Man; or the eternal counsels of the Most High; the secrets of the heart of man, or the deep things of God; whether they describe their own emo-

---

* At least two editions have been published in this country of Rev. E. N. Kirk's English Translation of Gaussen's fuller work, entitled "Theopneusty, or the Inspiration of the Holy Scriptures." This work has been largely indorsed by "the religious journals" of various Orthodox communions around us. The terms of Christian courtesy which we desire to regard in all things restrain the utterance of our own feelings in reference to the policy which attempts to recommend such daring and defiant assertions as those of Gaussen.

† "It is written"; or, The Scriptures the Word of God. From the French of Professor Gaussen. London: Bagster and Sons.

tions, speak of things from recollection, or repeat what has been noted by contemporaries; whether they copy genealogies, or extract from uninspired documents; their writing is inspired; what they pen is dictated from on high; it is always God who speaks, who relates, ordains, or reveals by their mouth," &c. (p. 2.) Again, he says: "We have next to inquire, whether the parts of Scripture which are *divinely inspired* are so equally and entirely; or, in other words, whether God has provided in a certain, though mysterious manner, that even the words of the sacred volume should be invariably what they ought to be, and that they contain nothing erroneous. This we assert to be the fact." (p. 4.) Again: "Jesus said, 'It is easier for heaven and earth to pass, than for one particle of a letter of the Law to fail,' and by the term *Law* Jesus Christ understood the whole of the Scriptures, and even more particularly the Book of Psalms. What words can be conceived which would express with more force and precision the principle we are maintaining than the foregoing? I mean the principle of the plenary inspiration and everlasting character of all the parts, even to the very letter of the Scriptures. All the words of the Scriptures, even to the least letter and particle of a letter, are equal to the words of Jesus Christ himself. Students of the Word of God, behold then the theology of your Master!" (p. 54.) This reckless writer, when proffering to meet the objections which assail his theory, says: "We will begin by acknowledging that, if it were true that there are erroneous facts and contradictory narratives in the Holy Scriptures, we must renounce the defence of their plenary inspiration. But we can make no such admission. These pretended errors do not exist." (p. 81.) Our readers would hardly care to know how a man who is capable of making such an assertion would try to vindicate it in reference to specific cases of difficulty. We can assure them, however, that his method is tortuous and jesuitical in the worst sense.

If our object were to sow discord among those who suppose that opposition to Unitarian views of the Bible is a bond of union among themselves and a warrant for their own common Orthodoxy, we might make some developments here of quite a startling character. But the exhibition would be painful to all who hold the Christian name, to all who love and cherish the Bible as the most precious of our earthly possessions. We will confront Gaussen's views with but moderate rebukes, conveyed, like those we have already quoted from Dr. Williams, by men of highest honor and credit. Professor Stuart's "Critical History and Defence of the Old Testament Canon," which is to be regarded as the fruit of his life-long labors in a beloved pursuit, is a most curious exhibition of weakness and strength, of boldness signified in passing hints, and of timidity manifested in deference to weak sisters and weaker brethren. He makes admissions on nearly every page which are fatal to the positions advanced by Gaussen, though to the uninitiated in critical linguistic skill he appears to plead for the old Orthodox notions of the Bible. His kindly, sometimes humorous, but altogether risky way, of letting out an acknowledgment of the embarrassments of his theory, really invests his work with a sort of mischievous charm. He wrote the work professedly to rebuke and answer views advanced by Unitarians, especially some extreme positions of Mr. Norton that have not found adoption, so far as we are aware, by any other member of our brotherhood. But the kind-hearted Andover Professor has proved himself a prime offender in the same outrages which Unitarians have been charged with upon "a settled faith in the Bible." Notwithstanding some sharp rebukes of the rationalizers, some little positive dogmatism, some cautious salvos, and some unsupported assertions and conclusions of his own, it is utterly impossible for an intelligent reader to close his book without recognizing its author as a heretic of the first water, in view of the old theory of the inspired infallibility of the miscellaneous contents of the Bible. Apart from such acknowledgments of opinion as these, — that Ecclesiastes was not written by Solomon, nor Joshua by Joshua, that Job was probably written during the time of the Kings, that Samuel, Kings, and Chronicles, Esther and Jonah, present inexplicable difficulties to us, and that quotations of seemingly prophetic passages from the Old Testament may be made in the New by *accommodation*, — the whole spirit of his work tends to qualify and chasten, rather than to favor, the fond dream of an infallible Bible.

One of the noblest fruits of a revived zeal in England for critical Scriptural study, is the revision of the Greek Testament, with a most scholarly apparatus, by Henry Alford, B. D., late Fellow of Trinity College, Cambridge, and now a minister of the Established Church in London. There is an honorable frankness in such passages as follow from his pen.

"Christian commentators have been driven to a system of harmonizing which condescends to adopt the weakest compromises, and to do the utmost violence to probability and fairness, in its zeal for the veracity of the Evangelists. Equally unworthy of the Evangelists and their subject has been the course of those who are usually thought the *Orthodox Harmonists.* They have usually taken upon them to state, that such variously placed narratives [as those of incidents and discourses in which the Evangelists differ and appear to have confounded the order of time and circumstance] *do not refer to the same incidents*, and so to save, as they imagine, the credit of the Evangelists at the expense of common fairness and candor. Christianity never was, and never can be, the gainer by any concealment, warping, or avoidance of the plain truth, wherever it is to be found." *

"With regard to verbal inspiration, I take the sense of it, as explained by its most strenuous advocates, to be, that every word and phrase of the Scriptures is absolutely and separately true, and, whether narrative or discourse, took place or was said in every most exact particular as set down. Much might be said of the *à priori* unworthiness of such a theory, as applied to a Gospel whose character is the freedom of the spirit, not the bondage of the letter; but it belongs more to my present work to try it by applying it to the Gospels as we have them. And I do not hesitate to say, that, being thus applied, its effect will be to destroy altogether the credibility of our Evangelists. The fact is, that this theory [of verbal inspiration] uniformly gives way before intelligent study of the Scriptures themselves, and is only held consistently and thoroughly by those who have never undertaken that study. When put forth by those who have, it is never carried fairly through; but while broadly asserted, is in detail abandoned. If I understand *plenary inspiration* rightly, I *hold it to the utmost* as entirely consistent with the opinions expressed in this section. The inspiration of the sacred writers I believe to have consisted in the fulness of the influence of the Holy Spirit specially raising them to, and enabling them for, their work, *in a manner which distinguishes them from all other writers in the world, and their work from all other works.* The men were full of the Holy Ghost, the books are the pouring out of that fulness through the men,—the conservation of the treasure in earthen vessels. The treasure is ours in all its richness, but it is ours as only it can be ours, in the imperfections of human speech, in the limitation of human

* Prolegomena, Chap. I. § IV.

thought, in the variety incident first to individual character, and then to manifold transcription and the lapse of ages." *

We heartily accord with these noble statements. The passages which we have last quoted from Mr. Alford, if they were left without illustration, might be pronounced vague and dubious. We therefore add in illustration of them a passage which precedes them in his own Dissertation.

"There are certain minor points of accuracy or inaccuracy of which human research suffices to inform men, and on which, from want of that research, it is often the practice to speak vaguely and inexactly. Such are sometimes the conventionally received distances from place to place; such are the common accounts of phenomena in natural history, &c. Now in matters of this kind the Evangelists and Apostles were not supernaturally informed, but left, in common with others, to the guidance of their natural faculties. The same may be said of citations and dates from history. In the last apology of Stephen, which he spoke being full of the Holy Ghost, and with divine influence beaming from his countenance, we have at least two demonstrable historical inaccuracies. And the occurrence of similar ones in the Gospels does not in any way affect the inspiration or the veracity of the Evangelists." † Again we say, he speaks for us.

Turning to the passage in Acts vii. 14, 16, where Stephen, as Mr. Alford suggests, "in haste or inadvertence," made these two "mistakes," — of naming three score and fifteen souls instead of *seventy*, and calling the burial-place Sychem instead of *Hebron*, — we find the following manly comment from our author.

"The fact of the mistake occurring where it does, will

---

* Proleg. Chap. I. § VI. † Ibid.

be far more instructive to the Christian student than the most ingenious solution of the difficulty could be, if it teaches him fearlessly and honestly to recognize the phenomena presented by the text of Scripture, instead of wresting them to suit a preconceived theory."

Similar to this is Mr. Alford's comment on 1 Cor. x. 8, where the Apostle mistakes 23,000 for 24,000 (see Numbers xxv. 9): "Probably set down here from memory. The subtilties of commentators in order to escape the inference [of error in the Apostle] are discreditable alike to themselves and the cause of sacred truth."

On Romans xiii. 11 our author comments thus, in reference to the much-vexed matter of the Apostolic delusion as to the immediate coming of the end of the world: "A fair exegesis of this passage can hardly fail to recognize the fact, that the Apostle here as elsewhere (1 Thess. iv. 17; 1 Cor. xv. 51) speaks of the coming of our Lord as *rapidly approaching*. Professor Stuart (Commentary on Romans, p. 521) is shocked at the idea, as being inconsistent with the inspiration of his writings. How this can be, I am at a loss to imagine [then quoting Mark xiii. 32]. And to reason, as Stuart does, that, because Paul corrects, in the Thessalonians, the mistake of imagining it to be *immediately at hand*, therefore he did not himself expect it soon, is surely quite beside the purpose."

It is possible that Mr. Alford may not have looked carefully through all the pages of Professor Stuart's voluminous Commentary; if he had, he could scarcely have failed at being amused or startled by what we are about to quote. When we consider how Unitarians have been berated for saying substantially what we are now to read, we remind ourselves that the odor of Orthodoxy will often neutralize the flavor of heresy. Recalling the horror with which, at the opening of our controversy, the assertion that the Apostles might possibly be mistaken, was received from our side, let the reader mark how frankly Professor Stuart could say the same under the protection of his Orthodox reputation. In his comment on Rom. i. 13 he writes: "One thing is clear, that the Apostles were not *uniformly* and *always* guided, in *all* their thoughts, desires, and purposes, by an infallible spirit of inspiration. Those who plead for such a *uniform* inspiration may seem to be zealous for the honor of the Apostles and founders of Christianity, but they do in fact cherish a mistaken zeal. Those who maintain the *uniform* inspiration of the Apostles, and yet admit (as they are compelled to do) their errors in purpose, word, and action, do in effect obscure the glory of inspiration by reducing inspired and uninspired men to the same level. To my own mind, nothing appears more certain than that inspiration in any respect whatever was not abiding and uniform with Apostles or any of the primitive Christians. [To Jesus only, adds the commentator, was unmeasured and permanent inspiration given.] This view of the subject frees it from many and most formidable difficulties. It assigns to the Saviour the pre-eminence which is justly due. It accounts for the mistakes and errors of his Apostles. At the same time it does not detract in the least degree from the certainty and validity of the Apostolic sayings and doings, when these ministers of the Gospel were under the special influence of the Spirit of God."

"*When they were under*," &c. We draw the reader's attention to this loose but convenient expression of Professor Stuart, but must leave the point without further remark, except the simple suggestion that an admission of a single instance of mistake, or error "in purpose, word, or action" in the Apostles, impairs the inspired infallibility of their teachings and writings, and leaves every reader to draw the line as best he can in deciding the authority of Scripture.

Dr. Arnold candidly yields the point that Paul did erroneously believe and teach that the world was coming to an end in his own generation.* Mr. Stanley, also of Oxford, another of the advanced minds of the English Church, the biographer of Dr. Arnold, and the son and biographer of the good Bishop of Norwich, makes the same admission. Mr. Stanley seems to feel less anxiety in allowing Paul's error here, than in reference to another serious matter. The Apostle, in that precious chapter to the Corinthians on the Resurrection (1 Cor. xv.), asks, "What shall they do which are baptized for the dead, if the dead rise not at all?" (ver. 29.) Mr. Stanley remarks upon these words: "Their natural signification undoubtedly is, 'Those who are baptized vicariously for the dead,' and this meaning is strongly confirmed by finding that there were some sects in the first three centuries, one at least of which extends back to the Apostolical age, who had this practice. From Chrysostom we learn (accompanied by an apology for convulsing his audience with laughter at the account of a ceremony so ridiculous) that, 'after a catechumen [dying unbaptized] was dead,' (implying that it was chiefly in such cases that it took place,) 'they hid a living man under the bed of the deceased; then coming to the dead man they spoke to him, and asked him whether he would receive baptism; and he making no answer, the other replied in his stead, and so they baptized the living for the dead.'" † Here the Apostle evidently adduces the *disappointment* of those who practised such a superstition, as one of the deplorable disappointments of a Christian's faith which would result from the falsification of his doctrine of the resurrection. How could he make such a reference in a way rather to countenance

---

* Christian Life, Notes, pp. 488, 489.

† Stanley on Corinthians, Vol. I. p. 372.

than rebuke the superstition? Mr. Stanley notes the methods to which recourse has been had for "escaping from the difficulty." He himself accounts it to the Apostle's habit "of accommodation to the feelings and opinions" of those whom he addressed, as in "his frequent adoption of reasonings founded on the allegorical interpretation of the Old Testament, in which, indeed, the Apostle may, to a certain extent, have shared himself," &c.

Mr. Jowett, in his work on some of Paul's Epistles, even treats us to an essay on the Apostle's mistake in reference to the end of the world, and other subjects on which he was in error. The discussion is a reverent one, but it goes deep into the heart of a matter vital to this question of inspired infallibility in the teachings and writings embraced in the Bible. The single point of an error as to the immediate conflagration of the world, if confined to its own subject-matter, might seem of limited importance; but the question forces itself upon the thought of a serious and inquisitive reader, May not the Apostle's expectation on this point have affected all his teachings, have colored all his doctrines; and especially, did it not intensify, aggravate, and throw out of just proportions, his relative estimate of a Christian's duty to despise this life, in reference to a life to come? An interest in the affairs of this world, in marrying and giving in marriage, in buying and selling, in providing for and educating one's children, and in establishing the institutions of society on a firm foundation,— an interest in such matters of reasonable forethought, is one thing, if the consummation of all terrestrial concerns is to be looked for within a score of years, and it is a wholly different thing if "the time is *not* short," and "the day of the Lord is *not* at hand." It might not be difficult to show that the alarmed and expectant state, the forced superiority to all worldly interests, and the tone of "heavenly-mindedness," which the Apostle commended to his converts in view of the coming of the Lord while some of his generation were yet alive, have introduced some exaggerated or disproportioned conceptions into the idea of "true piety." Certainly the fact that "the coming of the Lord" may be realized to any one of us individually at any moment of our uncertain lives, will make motives drawn from such a possibility always harmless and always of a wholesome influence over us. Still the question whether the Apostles believed that this world was to be the scene of Christian conflict during unnumbered ages of the slow triumph of the kingdom of God, or that it was to be burned up and its judgment sealed within a score or two of years, cannot be regarded as irrelevant to a discussion of the inspired infallibility of their teachings.

And this question does but logically and fairly open the way to yet another question, which goes deeper into the profound speculations of our modern Christian commentators. Mr. Stanley puts the query in this plain form: "Is the representation of Christ in the Epistles the same as the representation of Christ in the Gospels? Is the 'Gospel' of the Evangelical Apostle different from the 'Gospel' of the Evangelistic narratives?" * We know that some of the fellow-laborers of Paul intimated that he "had not seen the Lord Jesus," that he was not truly an "Apostle of Christ," and that "he taught things contrary to Christ's teaching." The phenomena which indicate diversity of view or doctrine among the Apostles must of course engage our attention. We must remember that the Judaizing party was not confined to uninspired disciples, but involved the heralds of the Gospel also. Therefore it is not wholly without a show of reason that some scholarly critics

* Stanley on Corinthians, Vol. II. p. 276.

have declared, and some unlearned readers have imagined, that when amid local controversies and under technicalities of language the Gospel was preached in Judæa, Samaria, Asia Minor, and Rome, the simplicity of its pure evangelic doctrine was to a perceptible degree impaired. Orthodoxy, on the one hand, objects to what it calls the ingenuities of Unitarian criticism in putting a gloss upon the technicalities or the rhetoric of some sentences in the Epistles; but on the other hand it works up most elaborate and intricate speculations upon those mysterious profundities of spiritual experience and of "the plan of redemption" which it finds intimated in the same sentences. Is it probable, now, that the unsophisticated minds to which the Gospel was offered, "the poor," the "babes in Christ," whether Jew or Gentile, could enter into the philosophy of Orthodoxy? Mr. Jowett, with his very keen, but by no means irreverent method of analysis, goes perhaps a little farther in the direction of allowance for an Apostolic adulteration of the pure Gospel, than even our own brethren might approve. But the issue itself which is covered by all these questions is one that has very momentous bearings upon our present theme, and, while it tasks the noblest powers of an intellect trained in Gospel humility, it refuses to be pronounced upon by dogmatism or by the deprecatory ban of the alarmist.

We hope that we have made it appear that much of all this critical work of studying and testing the Bible stands above any sectarian object, and designs, in the full earnestness of a purpose common to all who love the Scriptures, to sustain their authority, to remove prejudices, to ward off assaults, and to make them more and more precious to the whole race of men. Of course we maintain, because we believe, and may even say that we know, that false doctrine is indebted for some of its credit to erroneous views of Scripture, to unfair constructions of texts. Those who are not familiar with the processes of critical study have no adequate conception of the range over which Scriptural criticism, when intelligent, keen, and thorough, and still reverent, may extend. Many who read the Bible in English come almost to forget that it was ever translated; that when it was translated, it was by men like ourselves, from manuscript parchments written by men like ourselves; that, since our translation was made, many old and very valuable manuscripts have been discovered; and that our knowledge of the original languages and of Oriental history and life has greatly increased. Certainly in view of all these facts one should not marvel that there are materials and grounds for much fair criticism of the English Bible. Nor can an intelligent reader, however vigorous his faith, resist the impression, when perusing those portions, especially of the Old Testament, which are contemporaneous with our earliest classical literature, that the spirit of the writers often presents as *miraculous* what under other circumstances would have been regarded as natural. The religious consciousness of the Jews that they were under a peculiar providential training, may reasonably and reverently be supposed to have dictated much in the records which represents God as nearer to them than to the rest of his children on the earth.

Again, few persons are aware what a range of meaning and interpretation may be covered by some important words and phrases and sentences. The ambiguities of language, its idioms, its duplicated relations to sense and soul, the associations acquired by words from technical use, from prevailing theories of life and truth, and from each one's own private experience and culture, all gather their richest, as well as their most perplexing and misleading materials, about the Bible. Scholars here have an advantage in some respects above the unlearned, but in many cases scholars are baffled. Take, for instance, a sentence from the Gospel which has no connection with doctrinal controversy. Jesus says to Martha, as we read his words, "But one thing is needful." (Luke x. 42.) We ask what the words mean. Now the wisest scholar on the earth cannot pronounce positively, or give us a decisive reason on the one side or the other, for interpreting the passage to mean, "Only one article of food is necessary for me"; or, "Only one thing — religion — is necessary for you." And then there is matter for whole libraries of curious and searching criticism, for learned commentaries and scholarly investigation, in debating the meaning of many words and phrases in the Bible which have been invested with paramount interest by our controversies. Is the Scriptural phrase "Son of God" used to express the peculiar fondness and nearness of a relation of obedient holiness, or an actual "Sonship" in a sense answering to the earthly tie between a father and a child? The sentences, "This is my body," "This cup is my blood," open the issue about Transubstantiation between Romanists and Protestants; but when Orthodox Protestantism has availed itself of a certain method of interpretation in fixing the sense of those sentences, it turns against us when we apply the same method upon other sentences. When the terrified Pagan jailer asks, "What shall I do to be saved?" Orthodoxy supposes him to have been struck with what it defines as *conviction*, and to have been instantly directed to trust in Christ in the sense of an expiation. Thousands and thousands of sermons have been preached under that view of the text. Is the view justified? The words Faith, Salvation, Justification, Election, Eternal, and many more, which either are used in peculiar senses in the Bible, or have been turned to peculiar uses because they are in the Bible, carry with them now an equal weight of importance from doctrinal theology and the science of criticism.

Another very serious question, which is claimed to be exclusively within the province of fair criticism, asks whether the use of certain technical terms, and the reference to certain current views in popular language, by the Saviour and his Apostles, do or do not ratify the doctrines or opinions supposed to be conveyed in such terms and such language. By the decision pronounced upon that question the doctrine of a *Personal Devil*, and the reality of the *possession* of human beings by his emissaries, will be affirmed either to have been substantiated by the Saviour and his Apostles, or to have been only incidentally noticed by them, without receiving any authentication from such notice.

Occasionally, in the works of disputants at the present day who have had a scholarly training, we meet with what seems to us an obstinate persistency in maintaining certain readings and constructions, and certain corrupted texts, which have been fairly and fully condemned on adequate authority. Then we are led to ask, To what end do patient explorers hunt out old manuscripts and edit their recensions, — to what end do munificent donors found libraries and theological professorships, and multiply all the critical helps of grammars, dictionaries, and commentaries, — if from our seats of sacred scholarship are to come renewed appeals to old prejudices, pleas in defence of old errors, and flat denials of any real progress?

We must reach the conclusion of our present task by a statement of the results to which it leads us. We have in our hands a volume which bears to us the highest character for holiness and truth. We receive it as an actual communication from another world; while the alternative of holding right or wrong views concerning the book is made to suspend the question, whether it can be regarded and proved to be precious and authoritative as such an alleged divine gift should be. The Bible has been assaulted by hostile criticism; a standard has been set for it by men, which is denied to be warranted by its own claims or contents; flaws have been found in it which cannot be repaired in consistency with once prevailing views of its infallibility and its verbal inspiration. The close and rigid study and criticism to which modern scholarship has subjected it, have pretty well settled, in the minds of its most intelligent readers, the decision, that some qualifications and limitations must be allowed in abatement of the positive standard that has been claimed for it. It is deemed by Unitarians the part of simple honesty and wisdom to make this concession, and to insist upon its being made. Without forgetting the respect due to those who do not accord with them, and recognizing the honorable motives of some who carry special pleading in support of a crippled tradition beyond what seem to be the bounds of candor or justice, Unitarians hold that an attempt to sustain such a view of the inspiration of the Bible as has been reasserted by Gaussen, subjects the interests of true faith and piety to a fearful risk. The fact that some persons are willing to avert their own gaze from all the real difficulties of the case, will not close the eyes or silence the complaints of others. That the strong and childlike in the docility of faith are ready to believe in behalf of the Bible that full explanations may at one time or another be given to all its historical, scientific, or critical perplexities, ought not to make them obstinate or unjust in slighting the embarrassments of faith for such as may value the Bible as highly as themselves.

Within the last few years we have had offered to us the best fruits of long and anxious discussions upon the authority and the interpretation of the Scriptures. Angry controversies, venturesome scepticism, perilous and reckless audacity in theorizing, have mingled largely, but we must think only incidentally, in the great work of Scriptural criticism. We would by no means undertake to justify the positions which some even of the most eminent among Unitarian interpreters have taken. Far otherwise. Our own humble opinion is, that in general we have made larger concessions to what threatened to be a destructive criticism, than the emergencies of the case have really been proved to demand. For ourselves, we yield only inch by inch, and then only when the necessity is fairly made out, in each instance which qualifies the highest possible view of the authority and the inspiration of the chief contents of the Bible. But when any demand is fairly made out, we pay our homage to truth under the form of concessions to it, not under the form of obstinate denials of its presence. It is with a profound satisfaction that we now find in the works of distinguished scholars and divines, nominally of various creeds, admissions, full, frank, and complete, of views advanced by Unitarians in qualification of the popular estimate of the Bible, and in the general and specific applications of criticism to important texts. Gaussen has indeed received the indorsement of Orthodox "religious journals." Let us see how the mature views of Tholuck, as they are now obtaining currency, will be treated by those who have heretofore given him their love and confidence. Neander has strained the elasticity of Orthodox attachment to its utmost limits by his historical, doctrinal, and symbolic construction of Christian ideas. Bunsen and Tholuck have yet a repute to keep, but if they retain it, let them prize it as generous.

If we bring into close comparison some of the lectures, essays, or sermons of eminent modern writers, Orthodox and Unitarian, upon the inspiration and authority of the text of Scripture, we are struck with the following difference in their tenor,—the difference shall stand as one of great or of little moment, as our readers shall choose. The elaborate Orthodox essay begins, takes its start, opens, with bolder assertions of Infallibility and Plenary Inspiration than we could make, pitched in the old tone, as if announcing the old theory in a way determined to maintain it, stiffly, resolutely, and defiantly. But read on carefully, and you will find admissions cautiously, timidly yielded, forced out by facts which are not to be winked out of sight when such men as Professor Stuart, J. P. Smith, Arnold, Alford, Jowett, and Tholuck have their eyes turned upon them. When you reach the end of the essay, you will find that every allowance has been granted that you think is essential, and that the conclusion is in marked contrast with the beginning. You may think of the text, "Let not him that girdeth on his harness boast himself as he that putteth it off." On the other hand, a similar essay by a Unitarian will *begin* with perhaps an excessive allowance of concessions, — with an admission of all the necessary qualifications and limitations of the claim of inspiration. It will have in view, at the start, the difficulties which are to be encountered. Therefore it will not open so boldly or defiantly as an Orthodox essay. But when it has made its concessions, it will hold resolutely to the main substance, the essential truth, the kernel of the nut which is within the shell. The contents of the two essays will have more in common than we should by any means expect. In some cases we might even conceive that, if they had come from the same printing-office, some labor of *composition* might have been saved by *transposing* and *overrunning* pages or paragraphs. Is the difference of great or of little moment?

We must be supposed to have intimated all through our discussion our own views upon the serious themes involved in it. If any one asks, To what extent must the popular estimate of the authority and inspiration of the Bible, as a whole, be reduced? what limitations are to be defined for denial? what position is to be assumed for rebuilding a new citadel of faith? we can but answer, The Christian scholarship of this and of the next ages will decide those questions. Our province has been merely to redeem these momentous issues from the contempt of a poor sectarian strife.

The most favorable position for the attainment of just views on this great subject is that which is occupied by a faithful and devout Christian minister, who has received the best intellectual culture of his time. The most thorough critical study of the Bible in private, and a daily application of its lessons to the sins and sorrows, the duties and the straits of human life, are the two conditions which must meet and harmonize. The critical study of the Bible, with no reference to its uses "for doctrine, for reproof, for correction, for instruction in righteousness," will be sure to turn the most devout man into the coldest of sceptics. On the other hand, a devout exhorter, with his thumbs and fingers inserted in the Bible ready to turn to any part of it for words which he ascribes directly to God, if his ignorance exposes him to recklessness, and his feeling runs into rant, will make infidels of the majority of his hearers, and fanatics of the rest. The educated and devout minister alone can meet the emergencies of the case. His critical studies, his knowledge of the unbelieving, as well as of the "religious" world, will keep him mindful of the perplexities which faith in its relation to the historical records of a revelation must present, and will lead him continually to draw from his own triumphs over struggle and doubt the wisest aid in dealing with the difficulties of others. His use of the Bible in the pulpit and in the sick-chamber, as the inestimable and inexhaustible source of all holy lessons which have power over the soul of man and can alone sanctify life and cheer affliction, will day by day renew his grateful confidence in the preciousness of the sacred volume. He knows that it is the world's only light, law, and hope. The very conventionalities of his office, the very straits of his daily and weekly duties, require that those to whom he ministers should with him believe and love the Bible. The measure of his power over the sinful and the afflicted — and those terms embrace all that live — is proportioned to the vigor of his own faith, and to the depth of his own experimental acquaintance with the truths conveyed in the Bible. He is in every way concerned that faith in it should reach the highest possible height, and that gratitude and reverence for it should know no abatement. For many weary centuries the piety of Christendom was kept alive by the Romish priest without the Bible. It will be hard if that piety cannot live with a brighter and purer vigor through the Protestant minister with the Bible.

Let us have no fear of the work of scholarly and reverent criticism upon Scripture. It is in the hands of men and women who too well know its worth to allow it to suffer from the very inquisition which tests its value. We know nothing beyond what the Bible teaches us in any direction or upon any subject in which it undertakes to instruct us. One barrier is fixed; one limit is certain; one condition, known from the beginning, still stands unchallenged, — the Divine element in the Bible always has exceeded, exceeds now, and always will be acknowledged as exceeding, its human element. The Bible has floated on the sea of human life, below which so much has sunk of the ever-changing interests, and of the ever-changing generations, of men. Or rather it has risen from that sea as an island rock, and has heard the storms of ages, and has been lashed by all the waves that have tossed us and our poor barks. Can we find a better anchorage?

RELATIONS

OF

REASON AND FAITH.

RELATIONS

OF

REASON AND FAITH.

We have carried out, according to our ability, the intention intimated in the first of these papers upon the Unitarian Controversy. We have discussed the bearings of this controversy upon the Scripture doctrines of the nature and the state of man, — of God and Christ, — and of atonement, — and upon the grounds and methods of biblical criticism and interpretation. These large themes have been debated for ages by parties holding different convictions concerning them. The history of opinions on these subjects, a mere review or summary of the cumbrous literature of these discussions, would be nothing more than an extension of materials similar to those with which we have had to deal, in confining our view, for the most part, to the last half-century of the controversy. The controversy on these doctrines has divided those who otherwise would have been friends in all the relations and sympathies of a Christian fellowship, while their conscientious differences upon matters which, in the view of both parties, involve the vital truths of the Gospel, have alienated them widely from each other. These protracted and unfinished discussions carry with them a moral distinct from any of their own specific issues. That moral embraces many serious and practical lessons. This great lesson, especially, stands prominent,—that experience has proved it to be altogether unlikely that all professed Christians will ever thoroughly accord in matters of speculative faith, of doctrinal opinion, or religious observance. There are reasons which compel us to adopt this conclusion. The materials for the formation and exercise of our faith are found in a large book, as to the authority, meaning, and interpretation of which there certainly is room for a wide variety of opinion. Then the vagueness of language, the diversities of intelligence, insight, temperament, sensibility, of mental depth and power, of moral culture and of spiritual apprehension among human beings, would persuade us that it is hopeless to suppose that they can ever *believe* alike in a sense which includes the two vigorous conditions of true faith,—the thinking alike and the feeling alike. The utmost that we can look for in this direction is to divest controversy and all religious differences of everything that is acrimonious and odious and passionate, so that we may at least learn the graces of courtesy, of kind temper, and of charity: so that we may respect sincerity of belief everywhere; for there are tokens which will always prove whether one is sincere, earnest, truth-loving, and really religious in forming and holding his convictions. When wise and faithful and devout persons differ very decidedly in opinion, we must find what relief we can — and the relief is highly compensatory for our anxiety — in reflecting that they also agree in loving the Gospel and the Bible. The most eccentric orbits are all made true to mathematics, because they own a primary attraction.

But, it may be said, to allow sincerity in belief or opinion is one thing, and to attach to it the epithet Christian, thus admitting that the extremest differences of a professed Christian faith come within the safe range of acceptance with God, is quite another thing. It is insisted on the popular side in this controversy, that there is a limit within which liberty of opinion, however sincere, must be restricted, if it would be safe. The human mind, with all its inquisitiveness, its boastfulness, and its love of freedom in its speculations, is but one of the elements to be taken into account in discussing matters of faith. There is the positive authority of Christian truth, which is paramount to any claim of liberty we may set up for the exercise of our reason. Sincerity and zeal, when transfused into speculative opinions, imply that there is some truth of transcendent authority and value in the subject-matter of belief. There must, then, be an attractive power, a compelling sway, in truth revealed by God to compensate and hold in check the tendencies of reason to fly off into independent orbits of their own. The question whether there is anything in revelation which impugns or demands a renunciation of reason, is intercepted by the claim, that, if there is, reason must yield. The champion of the rights of reason will then urge that the help and warrant of reason are indispensable in authenticating a revelation. If reason must thus unavoidably be allowed to judge of the credentials of revelation, a consistency between the two sources and methods of our knowledge will require that what we are called to accept through our reason shall also harmonize with our reason.

The scholastic formula advanced by theologians to meet the conditions of the case is, *Fides ante intellectum;* or, *Faith must precede the understanding in the reception of revealed truths.* As is the case with all such formulas on test questions, so in this, the seeming positiveness and explicitness of the statement made in it are so qualified the moment we proceed to definitions, as to throw us back into the very vortex of debate. The formula, indeed, contains within its own terms all the elements of the controversy which it would decide. What do we mean by faith? and what do we mean by the understanding? Does faith involve an exercise of the understanding, or can it under some circumstances dispense with the aid and resist the suggestions of the understanding? And again, What is meant by the word *precede* in the formula? Does it signify merely that faith should have the start of the understanding, leaving that faculty free to come up with faith, and then to settle all matters of joint interest with it? Or does it signify that faith has a title so to occupy the ground that it may warn off the understanding, and refuse even to hold a parley with it? The formula may be construed to mean that some things must be first believed in order that the understanding may be engaged and qualified to deal with them; or that some things must be believed, in order that the understanding, restrained to its proper province, may not require sensible or demonstrative evidence where faith itself, when its suggestions are listened to, will substitute another kind of evidence, or supply the lack of evidence. And, once more, the formula may be construed as meaning that we must believe some things without the slightest exercise of the understanding, and even in spite of its protests. We might gather a curious category of definitions for this formula from the uses it has been made to serve. There have been boasts of faith, and ventures of faith, and submissions of faith, and sweet and gentle triumphs of faith, all of which have made the various exercises of man's believing faculty to cover a richer field for thought, for story, and for philosophical discussion, than is offered even by science, with all its wealth of interest. The old father of dogmatic theology meant to boast of his docility when he said "he *believed* some things *because* they were *impossible*." That boast becomes the merest commonplace, if it means that the things believed are impossible *to men*, and it is but irreverent folly if it vaunts a belief in things that are impossible *with God.*

But what becomes of the supposed authority in the formula, *Fides ante intellectum*, when, instead of deciding all the issues in the controversy as to faith and reason, it is found to open them all anew? The simple truth is, that there is either sophistry or disingenuousness involved in the expected advantage to be gained from this formula, whenever the motive for alleging it is to affront or deprecate or humble the reason. We have found the formula, *Fides ante intellectum*, "Faith before the understanding," used for a purpose of which we should not exaggerate the outrage done by it to common sense, if we interpret it as saying that *digestion must precede eating;* that we must incorporate and assimilate the nourishment to be drawn from the food of religious truth without any exercise of those faculties, any help from those processes, by which all other crude food passes into sustenance. And when the theologian thus calls upon us to deal with the dogmas which he proposes to us, we may be sure that he means to offer us some indigestible food. When the formula, taken in the sense in which popular theology is thought to have ratified it, is made to accompany any proposition offered to our faith as a doctrine of revelation, it is well for us always to pause and make sure of our ground. "Once admit," says the pleader for faith in spite of reason, — "once admit that God has said this or that, and then, however incomprehensible or confounding it may be, we must believe it." Very true. Most certainly we shall believe it; for the admission that God has said it, would be the highest possible proof of it. But how thin is the veil of sophistry by which the theologian thinks to blind us to the whole amount of the difference between what God says and what God *is said* to say! "*Once admit that God has said it,*" &c. Why, the whole preliminary process, the toil and task of the problem, is glibly slipped over as if it were the merest pastime of the mind. One, at least, of the conditions for securing from us the acknowledgment that God has said or revealed what claims our belief as from him is, that we can believe it of him. If we cannot believe it of God, we cannot admit it to have come from him. Every truth or doctrine or message which we receive as from God is accepted either by an intuitive and spontaneous faith, or by a process in which faith has been won by the exercise of our intellectual and moral faculties. A spontaneous faith by no means restricts its ready reception to what we call the easiest, simplest materials. On the contrary, it loves to take in some of the loftiest and most august objects; it prefers soaring to creeping, and the more sublime and awful and overpowering its themes, the more confiding in general is its trust. But when faith involves a process, and, whether upon a large and free, or upon an intricate and narrow theme, finds itself teased and perplexed, then it has an alternative before it. Either its confidence must be won through processes which the reason regards as legitimate, or it may yield what looks like confidence, but at the loss or sacrifice of the quality in itself which makes it a divinely trained faculty of the soul. Even if in the seclusion of a deep wilderness a being of seemingly celestial nature should appear to us, and with audible voice should declare a message as from God, all the inquisitiveness and strength which our reasoning faculty has gained *by all previous exercises* would engage upon the more or less deliberate trial of the question, whether it was probable that the messenger and the message were from God. We should bring all the reasoning power which we possessed by natural endowment, and all the practised skill and caution and distrust and confidence which we had acquired in its use, to help us to a decision of the understanding, and then as the understanding pronounced, we should believe or disbelieve. Of course the decision of the understanding would be different in different persons, because the range and vigor and processes of the understanding faculty are different in different persons. The credulous, the superstitious, the sceptical, the logical, the prejudiced, the candid, the clear-headed, the wise, and the well-informed, might each hold a different opinion about the supposed heavenly manifestation. If they all believed it to be a heavenly manifestation, they would all believe the message; but whether the one or the other should believe or disbelieve the appearance would depend upon the relations established previously between his faith and his reason, and upon the confidence and training of his understanding. For such appearances have been alleged under various circumstances, and they have been believed in and discredited under various combinations of these circumstances. The history of the beliefs of men is but a history of the relation between faith in its spontaneous exercise, and the various modifications of its exercise under the sluggishness or the activity, the neglect or the culture, the true adjustment or the lawless action, of the elements of the understanding. In some ages and places, and by some persons, that seemingly celestial messenger would have been received, and would now be received, as divine, independently of the tenor of his message. The marvel would satisfy so much of the reasoning powers as were brought to bear upon it, and would accredit it to the faith. In other ages and places, and by other persons, that appearance would have been discredited, and would now be discredited, as a hallucination, or an ocular deception, or a creature of the woods. But to the robust and healthful and well trained in mind of all ages, and of the present day, the tenor of the message would be the main ground for a decision of the reason as to its claims to faith.

Ought not the plea that we must humiliate and prostrate our reason as a condition for receiving through faith a doctrine of revelation, at once to suggest the fear that something unreasonable is to be proposed to us? How is it in other departments of our intellectual, and even of our moral training? Ought we not to suspect, do we not suspect, the temptation, or the counsel, or the pleading which proposes itself to us by first flouting at the natural, instinctive promptings of our own inner being? When any one undertakes to seduce from virtue the pure, the innocent, the unskilled in wickedness, he will begin by ridiculing as prudish prejudices those sentiments of the heart which are silently protesting against his solicitations. And when those instinctive sentiments have been trained by affectionate and healthful care, by parental love and wise teaching, the beguiler insinuates his contempt of those who, instead of indulging their own freedom, are held in the leading-strings of home or conventionalism. Is there not one point of similarity between this flouting at moral "prejudices," and the affronting of the reason of those whom God addresses as reasonable beings? Do we find that natural science, as in its highest range and its widest ventures it trespasses on the realm of religion, requires a prostration of our reason? An attempt is often made to contrast and set in opposition those qualities which are respectively needed in scientific and religious investigations. Humility, simplicity, docility, and candor are represented as peculiarly and especially requisite in the theologian, and the implication is that the scientific man may dispense with the fullest exercise of such qualities. But let the scientific man dispense with them in any measure, let him venture to disregard the least suggestion from them, and then mark how the world will estimate his merits or the value of his labors. Our own professional biases shall not hinder our acknowledgment that divines will not wisely challenge a comparison on this score between themselves and natural philosophers. Who, among the humblest and most docile and most candid students of the Revealed Word, — and it has had many meek and lowly-minded disciples, — can be named as surpassing Newton in those graces of soul? But it is positively wicked to require an abasement of the reason as a condition for the exercise of those graces which are the ornaments of all true wisdom in divine or human science.

But it is said that our reasoning powers have been impaired and vitiated by our descent from Adam after his fall. Dr. Pusey, in a recent sermon opposing views advanced by Mr. Jowett and others,* says: "It is almost a received formula on the evidences of the Gospel, that the province of reason is antecedent to that of faith; that we are on grounds of reason to believe in revelation, in other words, to receive faith, and then on the ground of faith to receive its contents, which are not to be contrary to reason. True, as is urged, since reason is a gift of God, it will not conflict with his other gift, revelation or faith. But then, what reason? Reason such as Adam had it before the Fall, unwarped by prejudices, unswayed by pride, undeafened by passions, unallured by self-idolizing, unfettered by love of independence, master of itself because subdued to God, enlightened by God, a mirror of the mind of God, reflecting his image and likeness after which it was created, a finite copy of the perfections of the Infinite? Truly, no one would demur to the answer of such an oracle as this. A work of God, which remained in harmony with God, must be in harmony with every other creation of

* Christian Faith and the Atonement. Sermons preached before the University of Oxford in reference to the views published by Mr. Jowett and others. By E. B. Pusey, D. D., Rev. T. D. Bernard, M. A., &c., &c. Oxford and London: J. H. Parker. 1856.

God, for both would be the finite expressions of the one archetype, the mind of God. But that poor blinded prisoner, majestic in its wreck, bearing still the lineaments of its primeval beauty and giant might, yet doomed, until it be set free, to grind in the mill of its prison-house, and make sport for the master to whom it is enslaved, — this, which cannot guide itself, is no guide to the mind of God."

The title to the sermon from which this extract is taken is "All Faith the Gift of God." Our readers will have noticed the confusion or the error in the first sentence of the paragraph. The writer changes the meaning of the word *belief*, as defining the *conviction* attained by reason and testimony of the credibility of a revelation, into another meaning, as a *miraculous gift* bestowed by God. But from those grounds and processes of reason by which we reach a faith in an alleged revelation, is it possible for him to exclude all regard to the contents and substance of the message? And again, unless we mean to allow in this transcendent matter one startling exception to the wise law of *adaptation* which we ascribe to God's workings, we must claim that a message addressed to an impaired reason must be suited all the more skilfully and mercifully to the infirmities of that reason. It is bad enough to have to suffer, for the guilt of another, the inheritance of a crippled and diseased reason; but to have what is left to us of its original functions baffled and ridiculed, is to allow us but a very questionable remnant of a divine endowment.

We are not going any farther into the metaphysics or even into the polemics of this dreary controversy. For ourselves, we cannot accord with a sentiment which we have somewhere seen expressed, that "the glory of the believing man consists in the prostration of the reasoning man." We know of no doctrine or precept or promise or declaration in revelation which throws contempt on human reason, or scorns its aid, or does otherwise than appeal to it and invite its companionship as far as it can go. That some truths in revelation baffle our reason, exceed its grasp, and lift it into realms too rare and dizzy for its breath and thought, is a lesson with which we started in our childhood, and are rejoiced to learn anew every day that we live. We do not care to be trifled with by theologians, when, for the purpose of confusing us, they confound the meaning of the word *reason* with the meaning of the word *conceit*. *Reason* is one thing; the *pride of reason* is quite another thing. Our Creator and Disposer has happily — we ought rather to say, fearfully — given us abundant means for distinguishing between the just, the true, and the safe exercises of reason in its healthful action, and that painfully large variety of its workings when impaired by disease, by prejudice, by vice, or any other limitation or perversion. Nor is there any very profound mystery involved in the familiar truth that humility and docility, and self-distrust and confidence in the great Source of reason, with a filial trust and a waiting submission, refine and strengthen the soul's high faculty. True faith exalts human reason, instead of humiliating it.

Every human being who has intelligently received the Christian religion has accepted it either through a process of his own reason, or through his confidence in the reasoning processes of others who have proposed that religion to his belief. Protestantism represents the application of the former of these conditions, — the trial of one's creed by his own private reason or judgment. Romanism represents the application of the latter condition, — that of reliance upon the supposed ability and conscientiousness of others in establishing reasonable grounds for the creed which it offers. When the controversy between the two parties is narrowed down to the essential issue of the whole strife, it is reduced to this question,—whether the rule of faith and life for a Christian allows him to ratify it to his own reason through a proper use of the Scriptures and all the means which throw light upon them; or whether he must rely upon authority, upon an ecclesiastical authority, which is supposed to have at once relieved him of the responsibility of private judgment, and to have secured for him something more sure than such judgment, in the large majority of cases, could possibly attain. Those who yield to such authority may still carry on between themselves a half-amicable, half-hostile skirmish, like that between the Romanists and the Puseyites. Their limited controversy centres upon the tests which the individual reason, surrendered up to church authority, still insists upon applying to the historical credentials of that authority, to the subjects and conditions and measurements of its lawful exercise, to the range of its prerogative, and to the exponent of it in pope, bishops, councils, or convocations. Even within this limited department of the whole issue between authority and liberty, there is material enough, not only for an open controversy between Romanists and Protestant Episcopalians, but also for a sharp strife between the Transmontane and the Cisalpine Romanists, and between the High-Church and the Low-Church Episcopalians. To dispose of all these subordinate contentions requires a faculty like that which one needs in sounding the unfathomed depths of the canon law. Those who forego some measure of their own liberty thus differ as to the terms and limitations of that ecclesiastical submission which they yield to the principle of authority. Protestants, whom consistency commits to an entire rejection of such authority, have found quite as wide a field for their own strifes in settling the terms and limitations for the exercise of private reason in matters of faith. Some forms of Protestantism, after battering the outside defences of Romanism, have removed its engines and weapons into their own peculiar citadel. Protestantism has but slowly and reluctantly come to confront the practical results of its own first principles. It has endeavored to arrest the action of reason at various stages of its inquisitive processes with matters of faith. The Scriptures do not contain a single sentence implying that their lessons are offered to a reason impaired by the Fall. They do affirm that pride, and hardness of heart, and prejudice, and a love of error and sin in individuals gathered in a common crowd, make some Scripture truths offensive and incredible to them. But these offensive and incredible truths are not what the theologian calls the mysteries of faith, they are generally matters of plain common-sense, morality, and wisdom. Individuals in the same crowd would receive gladly the same truths, not by any prostration of their reason, but through a healthful condition of their hearts. Those Scriptures represent God as inviting men to "reason together" with him; they put from him to us the fair question, "Are not my ways equal?" they "speak as to wise men," and bid us "judge" what they say; they ask, "Why even of yourselves judge ye not what is right?" If Scripture truths were addressed to an impaired reason, they would be accommodated to its infirmities; at any rate, they would give us warning to put away the poor remnant of our reason, instead of inviting and appealing to its exercise. The astronomer gives us fair notice that, when he takes us under his tuition, he expects us to begin with a complete inversion of our supposed position as regards the heavens. We must stand upon our heads instead of upon our feet; the east must become west with us, our right hands must become our left hands, and we must set the whole skies on a countermarch that a retrograde motion may show for a progressive motion, as it really is. It would have been easy for revelation to proclaim the same condition, and just as high science constantly reminds us that we must take the testimony of our senses as the opposite of the truth, so might faith have required us to interpret the suggestions of reason by contraries. But it has not required this.

The great question to which all the thoughts and inquiries and controversies of long Christian ages have been pointing is this: Whether there is within our reach and use a religion which will meet the wants of devout, earnest, and thinking persons, — a religion which we can refer to the Supreme Father as its Divine Source and Sanction, — a religion which in the highest and most honest exercise of our own faculties we can approve, and to which we can yield our hearts and lives with manifest evidences of benefit and sanctification? The overwhelming evidence that the Christian world is in possession of such a religion must be supposed to be admitted, not only by all believers, but even by some unbelievers; for the candid and wise of the latter class would not venture to dispute what millions have testified to as a matter of personal experience. But what we wish to mark and to explain is the fact that many candid and wise unbelievers, who will allow the sincerity and the sanctification of others in and by their own faith, cannot of themselves accept that faith under the conditions by which it is offered to them. So strong is the natural need and craving of human beings for the comfort and strength of religion, that, as experience has fully proved, in lack of a religion possessing all the attractions just mentioned, most men will accept a religion that fails in one or more points of that high standard. Men have been found able to believe religions, and some forms of the Christian religion, which did not present to them lofty and generous views of God, which would not commend themselves to the sober inquiring processes of the mind, or touch the deeper affections of the human heart, or have a purifying and exalting effect upon the life. Religions and forms of religion lacking one or even all of these qualities, have engaged the intensest faith of human beings. By some overruling influence which has made sincerity of soul to compensate for heathen superstitions and a grovelling creed, some power of devotion, some impulse of virtue, some nutriment of piety, has come from the very lowest idolatries, from the meanest objects to which the soul has clung. But as mind and heart work their way out of these delusions through the impulses of a purer and a nobler faith, the religious instinct of man is educated, and is made to apply higher and more scrutinizing tests to what is offered to it as a divine religion.

We wish to illustrate our own views upon the relations between Reason and Faith as they have been developed in the controversy of which we have been treating. It will be found that Orthodoxy, assuming the championship of the principles of Faith, has denied the full prerogative which Unitarianism claims for Reason in the study and interpretation of revealed religion. Orthodoxy says that Unitarianism has been found insufficient to satisfy the heart, to feed the life of piety, and has been renounced on that account by some of its disciples. Unitarianism asserts that Orthodoxy insults the reason, and has been abandoned on that account by multitudes of intelligent persons who once accepted it.

It has never fallen within our personal experience to know a single man or woman of fair intelligence and true Christian culture who, having in the full maturity of life received the essential and characteristic views of Unitarian Christianity, understandingly, devoutly, consistently, and in practical fidelity to them, has renounced them for any of the forms of Orthodoxy. If any such case were brought to our notice, we should venture largely upon the risk of being pronounced a bigot in our obstinacy of Unitarianism, before we would yield to the show of evidence that all the conditions thus specified had been fulfilled. We should ask full assurance that our views of the Gospel had once been thoroughly understood, heartily believed, and loyally honored in the training of the character and the conduct of the life. We should require proof likewise, that, since Unitarian views have been compelled to assert themselves against a considerable amount of prejudice and popular opposition, and against a prevailing notion that they are unscriptural, a professed disciple of them should have known something of the long controversy in which they have been involved. We should ask evidence that he had been a Unitarian from personal study and conviction; that he had been able to vindicate his faith from Scripture text and from Church history. Then we should be exceedingly inquisitive as to the occasion, the reasons, and the method of his conversion. If he made large account of his feelings or his heart, as the medium of his conversion, we should be prompted to probe him as thoroughly as possible. There are piques, and passions, and disappointments, and partialities; there are fancies, and there are morbid and despondent sentiments, which may have great influence in such cases. Now we do not say there never has been an instance in which a renunciation of Unitarianism for Orthodoxy would bear all these tests. We say only, that we have never personally known such a case.

We are fully aware of the strength of the assertion we have made, and we have weighed every word in which we have uttered it. We have done more. We have sat down in deep and silent reverie to recall and summon before us, not without the beating of some sad memories in the chambers of the heart, every friend, acquaintance, and traditionary associate in the pure Unitarian faith, and every one who has been the subject of a religious biography, who might be said to have realized the kind of conversion to which we have referred. We find our assertion will stand the test of such a trial. Even the little fellowship of acknowledged modern Unitarians has seemingly suffered much from defections. Our opponents have loved to call it the half-way house to infidelity. It has apparently been so to some who seemed to find in what they took to be Unitarianism a temporary delay in their course of sceptical experience, the first impulse in which they derived from Orthodoxy. We have never, either here or in Europe, furnished the Roman Church with a priest from one of our pulpits, but a few men and women have gone from our communion to her altar-rails. The pages of our own journal once had a contributor, who, having used his strong lance both for and against most of the creeds in heaven and on earth, including our own, is now a Roman knight. But even now, as formerly, is the question asked concerning him, whether he helps or harms the religious cause which, for the time being, he advocates with such a marvellous versatility in logic and philosophy.

Two or three once zealous Unitarian laborers, the promoters of benevolent and even sectarian schemes among us, are now in other fellowships. Either they have more of some qualities, or less of others, than were compounded and proportioned in their former associates. Either they desired a sympathy which they did not find, or they offered a sympathy which was not accepted, and they did wisely to go and seek what they needed where they could find it, and to go and exercise what they had where it would be appreciated. Young girls, too, there have been and are, — and unless there is more fidelity in our churches and families in the work of robust religious training for the minds and souls of the young, there will be many more of that most interesting class in our community to imitate the catching example, — who have found the faith, or rather we ought to say, the mode of worship and the creed of their parents, ineffective for their *feelings*. Our communion, though small, has been free, and we have done so little in the work of *indoctrinating* a new generation, that we have no right to suppose that even half of those who are nominally with us have really any decided faith. As the generation of noble Christian matrons who trained their minds and souls by a religion which fed the thoughts as well as the feelings has been vanishing year by year, we have had no reason to expect their full-formed, consistent, and abiding religious convictions in those of their granddaughters who leave out the *thought*, and have regard only to the *feeling*, which enters into a living and earnest Christian piety. When these young persons of either sex profess to have found in some other communion what they did not find in our own, a kindly suggestion may prompt them to ask, if they did not *take with them* to their new religious refuge some element of a true religious life which they did not *bring with them* to our communion. Unitarian views may not have been congenial with their feelings, because their feelings were not then brought into sympathy with religion in any form. It may have been an empty frivolity, a light-headed indifference, or a lack of such thought and mental discipline as an intelligent faith requires of its disciples, or it may have been a vacuum of heart, or a neglect of the law of practical Christian usefulness, which chilled the growth of piety. It may perhaps be said that a minister is bound to engage the feelings of all who are under his religious care, and that he will rouse in the young and the susceptible those emotions which kindle the religious life, if he really preaches the truth as it is in Jesus. We can only reply, that it is easier to say this than to make it good. There may be a show of religious sensibility, and a manifestation of religious interest, produced under other ministrations of doctrine, which we may regard as debilitating or unhealthful to the spirit, or as a poor substitute for some gentle grace of character, or some robust virtue in the life. At any rate, if a minister tries to preach the truth, those who listen should try to receive it by some engagedness of their own feelings. Then, if they fail of conviction, and satisfaction, and true religious impulse, they may offer their feelings to some different ritual or doctrine. When any one, man or woman, young or old, speaks of having been *converted*, he should remember that the word implies a *former* as well as a *present* belief, a conversion *from* something as well as *to* something. If this suggestion should remind some persons that they held no real religious convictions, and had no earnestness or assurance of faith before they experienced their change, charity will forbid their speaking of themselves as *converts*.

Of course, as it would be invidious in us to specify, in each case of seeming dissatisfaction with Unitarian views, the defect or the bias or the motive or the reason which would explain it without the least discredit to those views, so it may appear like arrogance in us to imply that all defections from our communion may be explained by some process not conclusive of the truth in any such case. But if it be arrogance, we cannot but indulge it. Every case within our own knowledge yields to an explanation which leaves our confidence in the Scriptural truth, the practical power, and the sufficiency of Unitarian views, all untouched. And if that confidence needed to be rallied and sustained under any shock which it receives, the conversions *to* Unitarianism, the manifold tokens of *tendencies* to it, and the constant and amazing assertion of its principles by those who have been trained in all other Christian communions, would more than reinstate our confidence. Our opponents must not suppose us to be mere jot and tittle sectarians in such a way as to claim every nominally Orthodox man who accepts our interpretation of a proof text, or our principles of Scripture criticism, or joins with us in a slight upon the offensive peculiarities and the short-comings of the popular forms of religion. As we are revising these pages, we have chanced to read the criticisms in several Orthodox pages upon one of the most striking features of Mrs. Stowe's new Antislavery novel, a book now in the hands of a hundred thousand readers. Those characteristic features of Orthodox faith and piety which have always been most offensive to Unitarians receive from her pen a most scorching delineation. And so her critics visit upon her in return the sharpest censures. She is accused of "caricaturing Orthodoxy just as the Unitarians do." We leave her to the tormentors. But we gather up the "concessions of Trinitarians," the heresies of commentators, the bold utterances of men who have signed the Thirty-Nine Articles, and the merciless castigations visited upon "Presbyterian ministers and elders" by the pen of a female Beecher, and we say they all mean something. They mean just this, and something more too, — that Orthodoxy is not the *ultimatum* of Christian faith for this world. We do not say that Unitarianism holds that honored place, but we have a strong conviction that Unitarianism, or rather the excellent thing which we mean by the word, and which is infinitely better than an *ism*, is in near proximity to it.

The true and thoroughly trained and thoroughly convinced Unitarian holds that his view of the Gospel is identical with the primitive Christianity of Christ and his Apostles. The New Testament is radiant to him with that sublime and simple system of Divine Truth, the heighth and the depth of which transcend the power of his reason, and often confound the searchings of his understanding, but do no violence to the intuitions or the suggestions of his reason. The deep-sea plummet of the mariner fails to find soundings on the mid-ocean, not because it is not perfectly adapted to its uses, but because its capacity is exceeded by the profundity into which it sinks. If there be shoals or dangerous rocks rising even in the deepest waters, the plummet is as good for its uses there as on the coasts. But the fact that the plummet finds no bottom on the ocean assures the confidence of the mariner in sailing without a continual recourse to it. So is it with reason when engaged upon the truths of revelation. Reason cannot sound their depths because they exceed its capacity; but so far as it can exercise its functions, it meets with no obstruction, no embarrassment. The system of Gospel truths invites the admiring homage of human reason, and casts no reproach and visits no discomfiture upon it. Yet more, Unitarianism insists that it was this very simplicity of the Gospel, this full accordance of its truths with reason, that led to its corruption. Theologians and philosophers, impatient of that naked simplicity which made it level to the apprehension and consistent with the understanding of the common mind, at once tried their wits upon it. All manner of complications of theory and fancy, of creed and symbolism, were introduced into the faith of Christendom. Among all the early heresies, so called, it is evident that the simple Gospel itself was the most odious and unpopular heresy. How transparently clear upon the pages of ecclesiastical history is the evidence, that, from the very year in which the Gospel engaged the interest of speculative minds, it yielded its severe and easily apprehended truths to the cunning processes of philosophy! The pages of Neander are strewn all over with sentences of like tenor with the following: "In Irenæus [himself a disciple of a disciple of St. John] the sufferings of Christ are represented as having a necessary connection with the rightful deliverance of man from the power of Satan. The Divine justice is here displayed, in allowing even Satan to have his due. Of satisfaction done by the sufferings of Christ to the Divine justice, as yet not the slightest mention is to be found; but doubtless there is lying at bottom the idea of a perfect fulfilment of the law by Christ, — of his perfect obedience to the holiness of God in its claims to satisfaction due to it from mankind."* Such sentences intimate to us the steps in the constructive processes of dogmatic theology, the abstruse and fanciful and often the grotesque devices of men's minds to rid themselves of "the simplicity that is in Christ." Whole ages were passed in these constructive processes of theology. When we realize the extent and the sway of that empire which the philosophy of Aristotle once had over the minds of men, we can understand how a theology compounded of the elements of pure Christian faith and the devices of human ingenuity should have taken a strong hold of Christendom. Nor is it strange that processes which had for long ages been working to embarrass and complicate our faith should require time and struggle and controversy for their detection and rejection. While the Unitarian traces out the visible stages of the corruption of primitive Christianity, he learns to expect just such a method for the restoration of it as the experiences of his own brotherhood of believers have verified. He is persuaded that the emancipation of the mind from the bondage of theological systems and formulas, by an intelligent and devout study of the New Testament, is the real explanation of the facts attending the appearance of what are called Liberal views of Christianity, wherever they have been

* Torrey's Neander, I. p. 642.

reasserted. Those who are still in bondage, excellent and honored and intelligent Christians, as many of them are, may lengthen their faces, and say in lugubrious tones that Unitarianism is a fatal heresy, into which men and women are led by the pride of reason and by a corrupt human heart. But there are two sides to this argument, and the Unitarian side, so far from yielding to the defeat which is said to have been visited upon it, marks a steady recognition and triumph of its principles. Let us say again, as we said in opening the series of papers which we are bringing to a close, that we are not set upon the use of the word Unitarianism, nor vindicating all that has passed under the name. We use the term to designate a more or less homogeneous and definite system of opinions about Christianity, which are in open hostility to the Athanasian, the Augustinian, and the Calvinistic construction of the Gospel.

The processes of the Reformation have worked according to a method which common sense and fair intelligence can observe to have been conformed to the natural constitution of things. As ages had wrought in the work of ecclesiastical usurpation, through a proud hierarchy, through an ingenious system of spiritual despotism, through a ritual, a calendar of fasts and festivals, a casuistical code, and through a patient moulding of feudal institutions and political relations into a conformity with its own ghostly rule, so the Reformation could advance only by undoing the work of Romanism in all these specific devices. Every imperfect element in the Reformation, as at present it shows itself to us, and all the lingering lookings-back of prelatists, ritualists, and Puseyites to the old, forsaken, and dishonored Church of Rome, are tokens that a strife for independence has not yet quite satisfied itself that it had no quality of a rebellion against lawful rule. The processes by which a pure, a liberal, and a rational view of the Gospel has been developed, answer at every point to those which led on the Reformation. Had we time and space, we could easily illustrate the parallel.

Let it be allowed to us "to glory" a little, in boasting of what we regard as the glory of our own views of Christian truth. If what we are about to say in illustration of our theme, of the relations between reason and faith, shall seem to some to be rather a vain offering to our own conceit, we will still ask them to bear with us, for we have to bear much from them. Considering that the Orthodox so exalt themselves above us for their humility and docility in faith, for their exclusive experience of the life of piety, and their perfect assurance that they have the seal of the covenant, they can well yield to us the poor indulgence of allowing us to justify, if we can, our "pride of reason." We say then, that when a free and intelligent mind, and a heart devoutly engaged in the search for a vigorous and practical and satisfying faith, combine their efforts in a healthful and just proportion, respecting each other's rights, and supplying each other's weaknesses, the study of the Bible will result in, or tend towards, Unitarianism. This we believe as we believe in our own existence. An unbiased and unfettered mind, intelligent, inquisitive, and well-trained, with a devout and earnest longing of the heart to know the will of God, are the conditions which, united, are favorable to the adoption of Unitarian views, and all the world over, in all time, have developed those views from the Bible. The fact has been verified under a great variety of circumstances. The strongest prejudices of training, association, and interest have yielded in evidence of it. A combination, a fair and just combination, of the elements of intelligence and piety, an harmonious adjustment of the relations of reason and faith, will issue in Liberal Christianity. Let mind and heart be brought to bear upon the contents of the New Testament, and let the proper functions of the understanding and the spirit engage harmoniously in the work, and "Unitarian tendencies" will be developed even from Orthodoxy. Let there be an excess or a deficiency in the exercise of either of the functions of either of those joint searchers in the field of Christian truth, let the felicitous proportion between the elements of intelligence and piety fail in any case, and the result will be different. A disproportioned action of the mental faculties, an indulgence of mere curiosity, or bold inquisitiveness, or a restlessness under a deficiency of logical or demonstrative evidence, will issue in a philosophical scepticism, a cold and unspiritual frame of one's religious nature. Let the spiritual instincts, the emotions, the sensibilities and cravings which furnish nutriment to piety, be allowed to act without the aid of the mind's best workings, and the result will be some form of enthusiasm, fanaticism, or superstition. The most zealous advocates of Orthodox Christianity will go with us in acknowledging these consequences, when either reason or faith is allowed to act by itself in contempt of the other. The controversy between us and them concerns the just relations of reason and faith when engaged upon revealed religion, and the proportionate indulgence to be allowed to the inquisitive intellect and the believing spirit. We give to ourselves what we regard as an adequate and just, as well as a charitable and courteous, explanation of the prevalence of Orthodox views, and of their hold upon the popular faith, when we say that these views won their first acceptance, and now retain their impaired authority, because the mind, the reason, has not been allowed its rightful functions in the province of interpreting revelation. Unreasonable views and doctrines have been accepted on the ground that reason must be humbled in homage to the nobler graces of faith. Our opponents invert this charge, and allege that we indulge the pride of reason at the sacrifice of docility and humility in our faith. This censure takes for granted the supposition, which we by no means admit, but resolutely deny, that revelation proposes to our faith doctrines which confound and cross the suggestions of our reason. Denying that position, we of course insist that Unitarian views engage our intelligent faith because they satisfy our reason and win our hearty belief. If we are arrogant in claiming some of the more profound, intelligent, and cultivated Christians as witnesses to our views, we only display the same unamiable quality in a direction opposite to that in which the Orthodox indulge it, in claiming the more humble and devout of believers for their communions. And what we have said, we repeat, that when intelligent mental culture and discipline, and an earnest spirit of piety, engage in fair and rightful proportions upon the study of revealed religion, the result is Unitarianism, or a tendency to Unitarianism. The prejudices of an Orthodox education have yielded to the free and earnest efforts of the mind to clear up some of the perplexities of its faith. In cases so numerous in our religious biographies, that candor must allow more than Orthodoxy has ever yet admitted on this point, this result has been verified. Wherever that proportionate combination of intelligence and piety of which we have spoken has been found, in a single person, in a village, in a religious society, in a community, in a social or academic circle, or in a nation, there Unitarianism, or a tendency to Unitarianism, has been the sure consequence. Poland, Holland, Switzerland, Old England, and New England present us both with eminent individual names and with general testimonies illustrating that truth. Out of the best-trained Orthodox fellowships in those lands have come men and women, who, often by wholly independent studies and exercises of their own, have espoused a Liberal Christianity. The exigencies of consistency with their own creed compel the Orthodox to maintain that all these lapses are tokens of an inborn depravity which leads the pride of reason to emancipate itself from the humbling doctrines of the Gospel. Those who were regarded as saints, so long as they kept silence and repressed their tendencies and remained in Orthodox communions, simply by acknowledging the results to which faithful Scripture study and religious discipline have conducted them, become all at once the most odious heretics, victims of one of the most subtle forms of depravity. This gross outrage alike upon common sense and upon Christian charity has been well-nigh shamed out of countenance in some places, where it was once boldly indulged; but it occasionally hints even now what it shrinks from proclaiming. Again, persons who have in youth, and under strong excitement, been converted by Orthodox doctrines, and have for years led a religious life under the same influences, and joined in the aspersions cast upon Unitarianism, have in their maturer years, on fuller study and experience, become disciples of the very heresy which once engaged their hostile zeal.

What candid reader of the lives and writings of Dr. Doddridge and Dr. Watts will deny the traces in their religious experience and culture of those influences and tendencies which, in a hundred familiar cases on record, have relaxed the rigidness of an early creed, and led on to a more or less complete recognition of substantial Unitarianism? Were not those excellent men, and others of their contemporaries at that very interesting period in the history of the English Dissenters, inclining towards the views which were adopted by some of their most cherished friends, and by many of those a little younger than themselves, who had been in close sympathy with them? Doddridge's Letters and Expositions contain a great many intimations of this liberal bent and tendency of his mind. There has been a great deal of speculation as to the opinions in which Dr. Watts finally rested about the doctrine of the Trinity. The most significant fact in the whole matter is, that his mind was working so restlessly upon that doctrine, that it is impossible to say what his final opinions about it were. Now, for ourselves, we regard that period in the religious history of England as the most favorable for the manifestation and working of an intelligent piety. Its eminent Dissenting ministers were devout men, faithful pastors, diligent students of Scripture, and thorough scholars. They had been trained under Orthodoxy, but were loyal to freedom in faith. Their tendencies have an emphatic significance, and as to what they were, our opinion is decided past the likelihood of a change, for it has been formed by many delightful hours of Sunday reading given to their writings.

In what direction do the heretical tendencies of the more independent, scholarly, and catholic-spirited men of the Episcopalian, Presbyterian, Congregational, Baptist, and Methodist communions, here and in Europe, develop themselves? We hear again the lament over the subtle depravity of the human heart, the pride of learning and reason! Leaving the judgment of the heart to Him to whom it belongs, we maintain that reason is a gift to be proud of, and learning is an excellent distinction. Of both of them, their possessors ought to be at least proud enough to be moved to use them for the noblest purpose, which is as helpers in attaining an earnest and intelligent faith in divine truth. And if the intelligent exercise of close and inquisitive thought, and the searching tests of reason, while they weaken or destroy confidence in some old dogmas of religion, tend to strengthen faith in the great truths of revelation, we see no sign of depravity in confessing the result. Pride and obstinacy may be exhibited in clinging to old dogmas rooted in education and prejudice, as well as in the confession of a change of opinions. Unitarian tendencies bid fair to become so familiar, that there will be more to bear their reproach and fewer to pronounce it upon them. At any rate, Unitarianism, to those to whom it is a spectre, is one which they have never succeeded in laying. It starts up in strange places, and shows itself under a bishop's lawn, in the robes and surplices of Episcopal clergymen and Oxford Fellows. The same heresy, manifesting itself in a new compilation of psalms and hymns for public worship among the Orthodox Dissenters in England, has opened a sharper controversy in their own fellowship than they have ever waged with us. "The *Rivulet* School," so called, from the title of the new hymn-book, is now said to embrace a large number of the most earnest and able of the reputed Orthodox divines among the Dissenters. The British Banner, and other organs of the Three Denominations, are filled with high-tempered discussions about this constantly intruding heresy of Unitarianism. The current number of the British Quarterly, an Orthodox review, in an article on the Life of the late Dr. Wardlaw, says, in reference to recent Unitarian manifestations among the "Evangelical Dissenters": "It is true, that, in so far as they are at all tangible, these appearances go within a small compass at present. But it is not necessary that these small beginnings should continue small. As the religion of a sect, Unitarianism is feeble, — feebler relatively than it was in the days of Kippis and Priestley [which is not true]; but as a complexion of thought, tending to affect the opinions of reading men on religious subjects, it is widely diffused, and by no means contemptible. The open profession of Socinianism is a very harmless affair; the secret leaven of it, beyond that circle, is another matter." These sentences are quoted in another Orthodox periodical, which adds the following:

"The chief danger from Unitarians is not from Unitarianism embodied in a sect, but from its secret and gradual spread among those who do not adopt the name."

What we have thus so frankly avowed, touching our own opinions as to the conditions of intelligent thought and religious sentiment, which, when combined in fair proportion, are sure to result in the adoption and firm belief of Unitarian views, indicates our hope for the future, as well as our interpretation of the past and the present. Unitarian views of Christianity will advance in a single mind, in a community, and in Christendom, according as that combination and co-working of the ingredients of intelligence and earnest faith exists and strengthens itself. Unitarian views will decline wherever those united and well-proportioned means for attaining satisfying convictions of religion are not brought to their work. According as either reason or faith yields its just office, or usurps the rights of its co-worker, will the question be decided as to what shall serve as a substitute for Unitarianism. If the pride of reason, and the restlessness of the intellect, and the sceptical tendencies of an undevout mind, reject the control and guidance of the spiritual nature, unbelief will find a welcome and a sad triumph. If reason is denied its rights, and is bid to humble itself before dogmas that are insisted upon, notwithstanding they shock and confound the reason, if an intelligent and inquisitive mind is forbidden to try its tests upon the evidences and doctrines of revelation, and if these conditions are yielded by those who are still willing to believe, — then the various forms of the Christian faith which have prevailed under those conditions in past ages will retain or regain their hold. Those who, like some converts from Protestantism to Romanism, say that they do not wish to use their own freedom of speculation, nor to depend upon their own judgment in matters of faith, will turn back to the old

Church because it offers them *authority*. Reason could not receive a more direct slight and outrage than is visited upon it by some who, with this plea, commit themselves to the guidance of a yearning sentiment, a longing for a religious refuge without bestowing due thought upon the rightful grounds of the very *authority* which they value. Reason would suggest, that, if an authoritative church is to be sought as a refuge from the conflicts of speculation and private judgment, the mind should first use its best efforts in testing the claims to such authority. What has the Roman Church to show for its credentials ? What *authority* has it for demanding and exercising its assumed prerogative in matters of faith ? Certainly the *claim* of authority is no sufficient *warrant* of it. Such converts to Romanism as have tried to test the rightfulness of its claims by Scripture and history have not really renounced their private judgment, as they pretend to have done. On the contrary, they have set their reasoning powers upon one of the severest and most serious tasks, and, by resting in the result to which they have been conducted, they have allowed *reason* to settle their relations to faith. Those converts who have submitted to the authority of the Roman Church without challenging the grounds on which it claims that authority, have simply deceived themselves. They can have no assurance of the lawfulness and security of the very authority under which they seek a refuge. A fair and just process of their reason, applied to an examination of the foundations of Romanism, might prove to them that the stupendous fabric is a fraud or a fiction.

Reliable English journals assert that there are three millions, at least, of the full-grown men and women of Great Britain in avowed or real sympathy with the new sect of Secularists. The epithet is preferred to that of Atheists, because of the prejudices said to attach to the latter title, as indicating immorality and recklessness of life, as well as a lack of religious belief. The Secularists, not recognizing a life to come, nor any motives or influences drawn from spiritual or heavenly sanctions, maintain that reason and science are sufficient guides, and that the relations of this life give sufficient warrant to virtue. Here we have reason usurping more than its rightful prerogative, and violently crushing out the natural instincts and yearnings of faith. For even science teaches us that this earth is dependent upon and is controlled by heavenly influences, and would be a wreck if cut off from the resources and the sway of the upper realm. Analogy followed out even by reason, to say nothing of faith, would suggest that man and man's life may need to recognize a dependence upon unseen powers and mysterious influences.

While Romanism thus requires an implicit faith, and Secularism makes an idol of reason, the popular standards of Orthodoxy treat reason with degrees of slight and violence according as they strain or relax the sharper conditions of the Orthodox creed. Dr. Edward Beecher has frankly affirmed that the doctrines of Orthodoxy are utterly inconsistent and irreconcilable with the principles of honor and justice in the Divine government. If this be so, and of course we believe it, then the Orthodox creed must outrage human reason. We cannot believe, without violence to our reason, that our Heavenly Father has called all the human race since Adam into existence with a disabled nature, requiring of them at the same time a holiness which only a perfect nature could manifest, and condemning them to eternal woe because of their inability, either moral or physical, to obey him. Reason protests against such a doctrine; and if it were found in the Bible, the issue would be whether the warrant of the Bible substantiated the doctrine, or whether the doctrine disproved the claims of the

Bible. Orthodoxy pleads that reason must humble itself before such humbling doctrines, and receive them as coming from God. Unitarianism insists that the Bible should be thoroughly tested by reason; that the same reasoning powers which we trust in other matters, recognizing humility, reverence, and faith as guides in their exercise, should sit in judgment upon the doctrines offered to our belief. Finding no such doctrines in the Bible, Unitarianism rests in the harmony between reason and faith, and proclaims that an intelligent piety may live and thrive in what is called Liberal Christianity.

Our opponents assert that there is relatively less of Unitarianism in our immediate neighborhood than there was twenty or forty years ago. It may be so. And it may be that there is relatively less of some other good things here. It must certainly be granted, that, if the old tests and tokens and outward manifestations of an interest in theological speculations and in spiritual truths were fair and reliable, as indicating the real amount of religious faith and zeal in the community at large, there has been a real decline of piety among all denominations. Whether there are not other and better tests of true piety, the application of which would prove an advance in the sentiment and practice of true religion, is a question on which we will not enter. There is a condition, one essential condition, under which Orthodoxy may succeed here or elsewhere in repressing Unitarianism and Unitarian tendencies. It is by persuading men and women to accept a religious creed founded on revelation, with a full consent to forego the freest exercise of their reason, their intellects, in view of the superior demands of faith. Orthodoxy must persuade us that this is necessary, and must induce us to comply with it. It must insist upon the formula, *Fides ante intellectum*, almost in the sense of *digestion before eating*. Orthodox criticism has to admit errors of various kinds in the

Bible, but requires us nevertheless to believe in its plenary inspiration and infallibility. Reason is staggered. Reason must consent to be staggered, that it may pay lawful homage to faith. Orthodoxy requires us to believe that on account of Adam's sin all human beings who have been born since have an impaired ability as regards the demands of God's law, but still are held rigidly to those demands, and are subject to the penalty of disobedience. Reason wishes to ask if God's ways are "equal" in this respect. But Reason is reminded that she has nothing to do with the matter. Orthodoxy requires us to believe that Christ the Mediator, who referred all his power to the Being whom he bade us worship as the Father, is still the very God who he says sent him into the world. Reason is prompted to try to reconcile the terms of these statements, and, failing in the trial, is distrustful. But Reason is told that she is trespassing upon what is beyond her province. Orthodoxy teaches us that penitent sinners could not be pardoned through God's mercy without the vicarious sacrifice of a victim, because the Divine Word had threatened, "*The soul that sinneth*, it shall die!" Reason asks how the Divine veracity is vindicated by the scheme, seeing that the threat is not fulfilled *on the sinner*, but that the penalty is evaded. But Reason is bidden to humble herself before the mystery of mysteries. Reason is even denied the privilege of trying her own rigid methods to discover whether these Orthodox doctrines are really taught in the Bible. Indeed, every suggestion of Reason, to the effect that possibly erroneous interpretations and mistaken notions may have been applied to the Bible, is visited with a reproaching denial. Now if reason in all men and women, here and elsewhere, can be induced thus to forego all its instinctive and intelligent impulses to comprehend and ratify and clear up the subjects offered to faith, and will admit that this is a *reasonable* condition for revelation to require, then Unitarianism will be utterly extirpated. If all our race can be made to assent to that condition, then all our race will be Orthodox Christians. If that theory of faith be the only theory offered, and no one challenges it, while human beings are left free to believe or not to believe on those terms, there will be many Orthodox Christians, but there will also be an innumerable host of "infidels." If we are asked to account for the fact, that the majority of professed Christians have been Orthodox, we answer, that it is because the majority have been persuaded to yield up the freest exercise of their reasoning or intellectual powers in deference to the supposed exactions of faith. In other words, and with a changed application, the same explanation which comforts our Orthodox Protestant brethren under the fact that the majority of professed Christians are Roman Catholics, comforts us also in view of our minority as respects other Protestants. Orthodoxy then can repress Unitarianism by bringing about a change in the proportions of free intelligent speculation and living devotional sentiment, which, when they are brought to bear upon the Scriptures, have always heretofore made men and women to be Unitarian Christians. But after Unitarianism had been thus killed out, it would be sure to reappear in an individual or in a community the moment that reason and faith in fairly proportioned combination and action were freely exercised upon the Scriptures. The result will be as sure as will be the appearance of water when we bring together eight parts of oxygen and one of hydrogen. The condition on which Orthodoxy may thus extirpate the Unitarian heresy may thus be very simply stated, whatever be the probability that the result will ever be realized, or the degree of difficulty in the way of reaching it. Orthodoxy must prevent the birth and the growing up of *the sort of persons*, men and women, that are sure to be or to become Unitarians. Such developments of the intellectual and spiritual nature of human beings as inevitably result in the adoption of Unitarian views by persons otherwise quite unlike each other, must be made impossible. Let Orthodoxy take a miscellaneous collection of persons whose biographies are within easy reach, and who, having been trained under Orthodoxy, became Unitarians; for instance, the biographies of Sir Isaac Newton, John Locke, President John Adams, Dr. Mayhew, Judge Story, Dr. Channing, J. S. Buckminster, Henry Ware, Mrs. Mary L. Ware, Sylvester Judd, and C. M. Taggart. Let the relationship between the inquisitive processes of the well-trained and freely searching mind, and the longing instincts of the soul for a living confidence in spiritual truths, which led the subjects of all those memoirs to become thoroughly convinced, earnest, happy, and consistent Unitarians, be fairly understood. The secret of Unitarianism is bound up in that inquiry. Let Orthodoxy master the secret. Then if Orthodoxy can make such a use of its discovery as to prevent such an exercise of such a relationship between reason and faith in all coming generations, it will annihilate Unitarianism. The process may seem formidable, but it is the only one that is available. Our own opinion is, that Orthodoxy will find labor enough of this kind within its own fellowships, at the present time.

In closing this train of remark, it can hardly be necessary for us to repeat our assertion, that we do not deny the union of the most profound piety and the loftiest intelligence in men and women shining with every Christian grace, whom Orthodoxy claims as among her jewels. Well may she be proud of them, and we will join in paying to them the tribute of our gratitude and homage. Our position has been just this, and no more, — that, when with a humble and devout spirit, yearning for true faith in God as revealed by Jesus, the mind is able and disposed to exercise all its faculties upon the medium and the substance of that revelation, and feels free to indulge its reasoning powers upon everything which is offered to faith, the result is Unitarianism, or a tendency to Unitarianism. We know of no single fact better attested than that, by all our religious literature, and by experience in various parts of Christendom and in all classes of believing men and women. We anticipate the protest, the denial, which Orthodoxy will raise against the assertion. But we calmly and firmly aver, that the grounds of our conviction are such that Orthodoxy cannot shake them.

There has been, and is, something very peculiar in the experience of Unitarian ministers in this and in other communities which has never been sufficiently allowed for. The older members of our societies were all of them in their youth under the teaching of Orthodoxy. Orthodoxy does meet the religious wants, and engage the sensibilities, and satisfy the spiritual cravings, of a class of persons in every community. But Orthodoxy always leaves wholly unreached and unsatisfied another class of persons just as sincere and devout and faithful, — so far as the eye of man can discern, — as are the converts to the old creed. Yet more, there are some who tell us that the balance of confidence, of respect, of neighborly reliance and dependence for the various services of life, is far from being on the side of those who have been sealed by the testimony of Orthodoxy. Some who have had large occasion to draw on the sympathy, the forbearance, the service, and the pecuniary aid of others, in the straits of business, in bankruptcy, in misfortune and sickness, have proclaimed that the "world's people" are found at least as reliable and merciful in such emergencies as "the elect." A communication in the "Presbyterian" newspaper, quite recently, astounded us with the avowal, that it gave no assurance to confidence in a man in the walks of business that he belonged to "an evangelical church." We hope we make no trespass upon fair charity when we simply recognize the fact, that some not severe judges of their fellow-men cannot help believing that there is an element in the Orthodox doctrine which impairs the stringency and the solemnity of individual responsibility. How can a human being believe that he has been ruined by the sin of one, and is to be saved by the righteousness of another, without realizing a shock of confusion in all his ideas of private accountability? For these and other reasons, Orthodoxy always leaves some who are as sincere and devout as its best converts utterly unreached by all its appeals and methods. Some, too, who once accepted its doctrines and adorned its communion, lose their faith in its peculiar elements, and crave a higher, freer, religious life. Now experience has proved that very many who are not satisfied with Orthodox views or who have outgrown their faith in them, and are repelled by them as false and of an injurious tendency, are always made more difficult of religious impression. Their early training has warped or prejudiced their religious nature. They are often made sceptical for life by this process. Their childhood seems dreary to them in memory. Their early religious instruction comes back to them as superstitious and forbidding. Then, too, there is a grotesqueness and sometimes a spirit of grim satire and ridicule associated in the minds of the irreverent with themes and nursery recollections that ought to be bedewed in later life with the very holiest and most melting power for the heart. That strange little primer of the childhood of our fathers was even harder in its association of subjects than in its rhymes. Capital B, standing by the Bible, sustained a noble burden in the lines: "Thy life to mend, God's Book attend." But capital

C came next, with Tabby and her two little victims singing the burden: "The Cat doth play, And after slay." The wit of some young sinner against reverence and grammar added to the legend on capital A, "In Adam's Fall, We sinned all," the strictly Calvinistic comfort: "Christ Jesus come, To save some." Some of the biographies to which we have just referred tell us how sad at heart and almost unbelieving the subjects of them were made, how alienated from the joy and fervor of all earnest, soul-quickening faith, by the form in which Christianity was presented to them in their early years. By the help of an intelligent and a devout study of the Bible they worked their way out of the dreary vapors of a Calvinistic education, and it became afterwards the joy of their lives to indulge the liberty in which Christ had made them free. But our communities still contain multitudes whom Orthodox views have rendered sceptical,—hard to impress religiously. Orthodoxy takes up those of easiest sensibility and conviction, and leaves the hardest subjects to Unitarianism.

We often turn over in our minds the question, whether the number of those who really believe and feel the power of religion — of the Gospel religion — increases proportionately to the increase of the population of Christendom. Of course the answer must be made more or less at random, according to the information and the judgment of those who are interested in the matter. This, at least, may be regarded as certain, that the number of persons in each Christian generation who believe and feel the power of religion *as the result of intelligent conviction from their own study and thought, not from authority, or fear, or superstition*, has been steadily increasing in every age. Religion has been more and more taken from the hands of priests, and men have become their own priests, their own interpreters of oracles, their own sacrificers, their own teachers in sacred things.

Among a million of nominal Christians four centuries ago, there were probably not five hundred men or women who had made the foundations and the substance and the doctrines of their faith matters of their own independent inquiry and thought, through the Scriptures and history, through their nature and experience. The mass simply believed or tried to believe as they were taught, on authority. But now, out of any million of nominal Christians around us, a very large number would be found independent and intelligent thinkers, having more or less "reason for their faith," acquainted with the Bible, and able to sustain an argument for high truth. Unbelief, too, where not connected with gross vice, is more dignified and self-distrustful, less bold and violent and reckless.

We have left but narrow space for noting some of the chief distinguishing conditions of a religious faith which will engage the confidence of devout and intelligent persons, under the present aspects of life.

The first of all the requisites in such a religion is that it shall be Liberal. We *mention* this condition even before that of Truth, because a religion that is not liberal cannot be true. The devout and intelligent demand a liberal religion, a religion large, free, generous, comprehensive in its lessons, a religion expansive in its spirit, lofty in its views, and with a sweep of blessings as wide as the range of man's necessities and sins. This is what is meant by a Liberal Religion, or Liberal views of religion, or Liberal Christianity. An attempt is made at the very start to prejudice this liberal view of religion by giving to it a bad name, and by assigning to it an unsanctified purpose. Some persons would interpret Liberality in a religious creed as meaning laxness, looseness, as making things easy for easy consciences, as letting down the high demands of righteousness, and as taking light and dangerous views of duty and sin and man's future destiny. This is a perversion, a false charge. Under a liberal religion the utmost seriousness and solemnity of feeling, and the strictest laws of moral conduct and religious responsibility, find at least an equal sanction with what they do under narrow, cramped, and illiberal views of religion, if not a higher one. Liberal views of religion do not exclude the just workings of the wrath of a holy God from this world; nor do they by any means require the teaching that death is salvation for everybody, and that there is no state of hell beyond the grave. It is not in order to obtain a license for sin or excuses for folly, or to diminish the pains and penalties of unrighteousness towards God or man, that we demand a large and generous and comprehensive faith. It is that we may free the Deity and his attributes and his government from all those offensive and degrading and enslaving notions which false opinions have gathered about them. It is that we may have a faith that can radiate the whole space up to heaven, and shine benignantly over the earth, and interpret largely and gratefully, seriously and confidingly, the will and purposes of God towards man. We want a faith so generous and forbearing and merciful in its delineations of the Father of our poor, sinning, dying race, that it will shame every mean outrage which we through our own passions inflict upon a brother-man, — a faith that will not only open a loophole for our exit from the pit of condemnation into a psalm-singing conference of saints, but will fling open and keep open the wide doors of a gracious clemency to catch the crowds who can at least be grateful for forgiveness.

Take now two or three illustrations of what is meant by Liberal views of religion, in contrast with the contracted and illiberal views which have prevailed in Christian communities. These millions of human beings who live on the earth in their ever-changing generations, — are they all a doomed race, born in sin, destined to eternal woe, unless rescued by a partial exercise of Divine mercy? Or are they creatures and children of a kind and good Father, born with the nature which he has pleased to give them, imperfect, frail, needing discipline, righteously governed, piteously commiserated, and so to be judged here and hereafter *by what they can themselves admit* is a perfect rule of equity? One of these views is Liberal, the other is Illiberal. One is large, generous, free, *just;* the other is dreary, hopeless, *unjust.**

Then there is the still current form of the doctrine of Election. The word is used freely in the Scriptures, and what the word truly signifies is there too, a Scripture doctrine. But Election is never applied in the Scriptures to individuals as such distinct from a class, and it never refers to a future life. It always relates to the calling

* We have taken much satisfaction, all through this series of articles, in quoting at length concessions from Orthodox sources, amounting sometimes even to rebukes of what have long passed for accepted tenets in the creed of Orthodoxy. Our readers may remember a figure of speech used on the May platforms twenty years ago, by Dr. Scudder, a returned Orthodox missionary, — of a platoon of *heathens* a mile or two broad, and three or four miles long, driving on to the pit of hell, and demanding zeal in the missionary cause to save them. In an admirable article in the North British [Scotch Church] Review for August, 1856, on Christian Missions, some stuff of a similar tenor is quoted from a recent American missionary report. Thus: "Every hour, yea, every moment, the heathen are dying, and dying, most of them, without any knowledge of the Saviour. On whom now rests the responsibility?" &c., &c., — implying that the responsibility of rescuing the heathen rests with men. The Reviewer adds: "Can this be mere *ad captandum* language, intended to draw contributions to the missionary societies? If so, it is very wicked. But if it be really genuine and sincere, how melancholy a fanaticism does it display! We shudder at the accounts of devil-worship which come to us from so many mission-fields. We pity the dreary delusion of the Manichees, who enthroned the Evil Principle in heaven. But if we proclaim that God is indeed one who could decree this more than Moloch sacrifice of the vast majority of his own creatures and children, for no fault or sin of theirs, we revive the error of the Manichee; for the God whom we preach as a destroyer of the guiltless can be no God of justice, far less a God of love," &c., &c.

or the choice of a whole people like the Jews, and afterwards of all who should ever live under the Gospel, to the enjoyment of peculiar privileges here, in this world, during this life. Judgment and destiny were of course made dependent upon the use, the improvement, or the neglect of these privileges. Judas himself was one of the elect. "Jesus said, 'Have I not chosen you twelve?'" But this did not hinder that Judas should "go to his own place." The Jews were the "elect people," because to them was given the knowledge of the will of the true God. They were elected to enjoy the truths of religion and the blessings of a visible Divine government here in this world. But individual Jews were subject to the same righteous judgment for the use of their privileges, as were individuals not Jews for their use of lesser privileges. Future judgment would decide between the faithful and the faithless among even the elect. Christians acceded to the advantages heretofore enjoyed by the Jews as an elect people, i. e. as permitted certain precious privileges here in this world; they were not made sure of salvation in the next world merely on the score of their having been thus favored here. Thus St. Paul tells his converts, that he had prayed for them "lest their election should be vain," i. e. lest they should prove to make an unworthy use of the privileges they enjoyed. How could their election *be vain* if it insured their future salvation? So also he exhorts his converts "to make their calling and election sure," evidently proving that *election* means the enjoyment of opportunities here, on the right improvement of which depended the promised reward hereafter.

But now observe, by contrast, what a shocking perversion has been made of this doctrine of Election by an illiberal theology. It has been interpreted as meaning this: That, ages before we were born, God, of his own sovereign partiality, or—as says the New England Confession of Faith—"out of his mere free grace and love, without any foresight of faith or good works, or any other thing in the creature, as conditions or causes moving him thereunto," chose some of his children for salvation, put their names upon a record, and as these appear in their generations makes them by his Holy Spirit the subjects of renewal and the heirs of bliss. The Confession adds: "This effectual call is of God's free and especial grace alone, not from anything at all foreseen in man, who is altogether passive therein." "The rest of mankind God was pleased to ordain to dishonor and wrath for their sin, to the praise of his glorious justice." After this shocking parody of a noble and reasonable Scripture doctrine had been established in the popular faith, as an element of Calvinism, there arose a question as to the terms and conditions of this election. Arminius ventured to suggest that God *elected* for salvation those who he *foresaw* would improve the means of grace; and that he thus had respect to their obedience and good works. This suggestion, which carries us half-way back to the true Scripture doctrine, was an attempt to let in one ray of reason upon the Calvinistic dogma. But it was denounced as a heresy, and is so regarded to this day, under the name of Arminianism,—the real Orthodox doctrine being that God, in electing the heirs of his grace from all eternity, has no reference whatever to their merits or obedience, but acts entirely according to the sovereign pleasure of his will. Now we call this an illiberal, a contracted, a narrow and unworthy doctrine, besides being a perversion of the true Scripture view of *Election.* It gives us a most illiberal and grovelling representation of God and of his government. In contrast with this, the liberal, the Scripture view is that God knows no such partiality, no such favoritism, but puts each one of his children on an equality as regards the future, by judging them righteously according to the good or the bad use which they make of their various privileges and opportunities.

Then follow this distinction between a liberal or an illiberal theology into the doctrine of the Atonement, or the work of reconciliation by Jesus Christ. Is the efficacy of Christ's death limited to a portion of our race, or free for the advantage of all? Calvinism originally taught a limited atonement. New-School Orthodoxy professes to believe in an unlimited, unrestricted efficacy of the death of Christ as a ground for proffering salvation to all. But how do the two parties explain themselves on this difference between them? The advocates of the limited atonement maintain that Christ's death is of service only to those *whom he actually saves.* The advocates of an unlimited atonement come, in fact, to the same result; for they teach that though all have the offer of salvation through Christ, though all are called by him, yet that the renewing work of the Holy Spirit, which alone can dispose the sinful heart to avail itself of this offer, is wrought only upon the heirs of salvation. The agency of the third person of the Trinity, which is necessary to render the work of the second person of the Trinity of efficacy to individuals, is not as extensive as the benefit of the Atonement. The offer is made to all; but the ability to accept it, to avail of it, is not granted to all, but only to a portion of those who live under the Gospel. The Atonement is *suf*ficient for all; but it is *ef*ficient for only a portion of our race. What, then, is the difference in the real substance of the matter between these two Orthodox parties as to a limited or an unlimited Atonement? Nothing at all. We call their view, then, an element of an illiberal theology. A liberal theology insists that the love and offers of God through Christ should be construed in the largest, freest sense; that the work of the Spirit, which makes the proffer of reconciliation available, should be as unrestricted as the grace of God and the mediation of the Saviour in providing the means of it for all.

Once more, what says a liberal theology, in contrast with an illiberal theology, in reference to the whole work of religion on the heart and life, — the substantial tests and tokens of a Christian character,—the proof that any one is in the way of salvation? An illiberal theology exalts a creed, a speculative opinion, into prominent importance as a test. A liberal theology subordinates opinion to the prior significance of a pure and faithful, a devoted and useful life, conformed to the practical precepts of the Master. Whatever tests we refer to Almighty Wisdom for the judgment of men here or hereafter, must be such as will impress us with a sense of their absolute justice, such as we can ourselves confide in, and can apply rigidly. If our faith in these tests falters, they will bring down all our religion. The progress of independent thought and inquiry applied to religion has brought about much the same results as have followed from political strifes and convulsions, all the world over. It has led men to demand their impartial rights, to insist upon an independence of soul, upon impartial laws, and upon a destruction of all class privileges. There have been forms of religion in the world, and even under the name of Christianity, which have corresponded to all the forms of government, the patriarchal, the priestly, the tyrannical, the despotic, the monarchical, the aristocratic, and the constitutional. The latest struggles and developments of religion demand a pure independency, a democracy. No longer can we ascribe to the Divine rule over us an arbitrary election and reprobation, by which some persons, not one whit different in life and character from some of their neighbors, may claim to have been the subjects of a mysterious change, sealing them for heavenly bliss, while the rest of the world is left to perdition. "A just weight and balance are the Lord's." Thoughtful, earnest, and devout minds now demand a liberal religion. Liberal in the honest, pure, and noble sense of that word. Not liberal in the sense of license, recklessness, or indifference; not in turning the sanctities of heaven into the streets, nor in making a scoff of holy restraints and solemn mysteries. Not liberal as the worldling or the fool uses the word, for overthrowing all distinctions, and reducing life to a revel or a riot. The demand is for a liberality which will leave the soul uncramped and untortured in working upon the solemn problems of divinity, and casting its conceptions of a future state, and interpreting the ways of God to men,—insuring a large, free, strong, and sanctifying faith. Such a faith cannot afford to raise an issue with reason on a single point, so far as their road on the highway of truth will allow them to keep company together. When they part for faith to advance beyond reason, they must part in perfect harmony.

A second prime requisite in a religion that shall satisfy thoughtful, earnest, and devout persons is that it shall have authority,—the authority of positive, reliable truth. It must have a firm basis, a solid foundation. We have learned in this age of the world the utmost limit of man's attempts to work his way by mere human wisdom, by philosophy, by science, or any other exercise of his own ingenuity. We want something better than these, something more stable, more satisfactory, something that has authority. Man is better at guessing than in any other exercise of his faculties; and in accepting the results of his guessing faculty, he often forgets the risks of the process by which he attained them. Man can conjure up all sorts of notions about himself, and about all the mysteries which surround him,—the mysteries in which he lives, of which he thinks, of which he feels the solemn power, and especially of that mystery which he himself is. Man can construct theories of his own about everything, and so about religion, and sometimes he can believe his own theories, and find strength and comfort and hope in them. But notwithstanding all this, a religion which is to satisfy a thoughtful, earnest, and devout person must have authority over and above and outside of his own thinking and reasoning powers, his own guesses or fancies, his own knowledge or wisdom. The inmost soul within him is capable of answering to divine truth; but it must be *divine truth*, not human imaginations or guessings, that will move the secret depths of that soul.

What, then, is the authority of the true Christian religion, and who gave it that authority? The revelation of God's will made by Christ has two chief mediums of addressing itself to us, of communicating to us its lessons, its substance, its design, and its proof. One of these is in the record of the revelation in the New Testament. The other is in the actual presence of the workings and effects of that religion in the world, for ages, — its institutions, its experimental trial, the illustrations of its influence, the manner of its operation in an infinite variety of cases and ways. We search and try according to our ability both these sources of knowledge about our religion, and we ask whether we find in them tokens of a divine authority before which our souls should bow? Can our faith seize on them with a bold and joyful confidence, leading us to say, with the first two disciples, "We have found the Messiah, the true messenger of the Covenant, one whom we can believe and love, and follow as he guides us through this world, with the hope of a purer and a holier life to come"? There is room still left for our speculations and our guesses. All the questions which the mind asks are not settled once for all, when we find something that has for us the authority of heaven-taught truth. We may still debate matters of evidence, and matters of doctrine, and mysteries of faith. There is still a range for free speculation as to the shape or the point at which we will frame our spirits to accept the mysterious, the inexplicable, the supra-rational elements of religion. But the main question after all is, Have we faith? Have we found something which wins and holds our confidence,—something which we can believe, something which we do believe as our lives, something that has authority for us?

We all know that the very foundations of faith are unsettled for multitudes around us, and that on this account the Gospel has not the authority of truth for them. A great many influences may contribute to cause this lack of faith. Ignorance, conceit, bewilderment of mind, honest perplexity, prejudice, the distractions of religious controversy, the varieties of belief and opinion,—all these causes, besides real worldliness or wickedness of heart and life, pride, indifference, wrong biases of character, and obstinacy of spirit, may help to account for scepticism and all irreligion. Various remedies also may be applied to remove these obstacles to faith in the authority of revelation. Good advice, good books, argument, appeal, may all be of service. Still there is a condition paramount to all others, on which alone any one can be made to feel the authority of Christian truth. He must put himself in the attitude of a pupil, at the feet of its Teacher. He must realize the existence within him of a believing faculty, which is to dispose him to receive convictions through his spiritual nature when his mental powers have reached their limits in exploring the field of truth. His heart must be reverently ordered into a humble frame; his ear must listen, that he may be in a state to attend to the voice of God, should God speak to him. He is asking whether there is in this world, available for his use, a doctrine and method of religion worthy of being referred to God as its source, and suited to renew and purify and sanctify all the elements of his own life. That question must be submitted to the personal consciousness and experience of every human being. No one can answer it for another. The answer to it decides for each one whether the Gospel has to him the authority of truth. Jesus taught as having this authority. His hearers could understand him. They felt, they appreciated, this quality of his teachings. They were impressed by the marked contrast between the substance, the tone, and the weight of his lessons, and those which they had been in the habit of hearing from quibbling scribes, and word-splitting doctors, and ingenious lawyers, with all their fanciful interpretations and silly traditions and weak conceits, so debilitating to the healthful energies of a craving religious soul. We want a religion which has *authority*, evidences and demonstrations, sanctions and solemnities, befitting a doctrine which claims to rule our spirits and to guide our lives, to minister to our sins and sorrows, our fears and hopes.

A third and last requisite which we may mention, in a religion that will meet the wants of thoughtful, earnest, and devout persons, is that of a living, practical power to promote true holiness, to work on the springs of character, to foster ardent piety in the soul of a believer, and to cultivate benevolence and virtue in his life. This is the final test of all true religion. There is no more deplorable, dreary thing on this earth, than a lifeless faith, a cold, torpid, indifferent religion. We want a faith by which we can live, which shall be the energy of our own lives, which will continually excite the depths of our being, and move us to fidelity, and be hourly rebuking our worldliness and sinfulness. We want a cheerful faith, — a faith which will make us kind and generous and unselfish and happy. Professed Christians, the church-members in some communions, under some forms of faith, in their way of regarding and treating those who do not belong to them, have seemed to think that a line of separation has been drawn by their creed between them and their fellow-creatures for all eternity. If in a humble and thoroughly self-searching spirit they were to ask themselves what quality the pure eye of God discerns in them to distinguish between them and all others in the allotments of the everlasting retributions of a future life, they might be perplexed to answer the question. The old stereotyped answer, that they rely upon their faith in the merits of Christ, will not do now-a-days, unless it is translated into the intelligible language of practical common-sense. They consider themselves as the saved, and all others as the lost. They resemble those who clutch at the long-boat of a sinking ship loaded with passengers, and row off, leaving their former companions to a fearful fate. Now a religion which regards the vast proportion of human beings as under the curse of God, doomed for ever, may perhaps lead to a sort of holy horror or a dismal pity towards them, but cannot excite a love and tenderness and mercy and devotion like that of Christ.

Not in a censorious spirit, if we know our own heart, but in mortified sadness at seeing the short-comings of a religion which ought to live and act with all the genial energies of a glowing flame of universal love in a community, and attract every well-disposed heart to its high work, would we venture to hint at facts which our own professional biases might dispose us to palliate. Take the body of communicants, the church-fellowship in some of our town or village parishes, where the spirit of an ungenial religion rules supreme, and ask what attraction that covenanted circle has for many generous-hearted, warm-souled young persons of either sex? They know very well that the "Church" includes some most excellent men and women, wearing every winning grace of piety and love; persons whose naturally amiable characters have been called out and refined by pure religion, or have helped to temper the austerities of a repulsive creed. But such persons, unfortunately, do not make up the whole Church, nor furnish the standard which exhausts the prime conditions for admission to it. The young know very well that there are some exceedingly hard, uninteresting, and forbidding members among the foremost in such communions,—sour-visaged, scandal-loving, morose old women, and men whose sharpness at a bargain proves that the eye opened on another world has lost none of its keenness for this. The exercises which engage these fellowships in their meetings have often a clammy or sombre character, a grim and dreary aspect, to the young. And so the "vestry" assemblies for conference, held generally in the cellar of a meeting-house, draw together for the most part those who have long shared all the privileges there offered. The young are not attracted by a religion which makes such an exposition of itself and its prominent disciples. And so the current of the world sweeps by the Church. Hearts that yearn for some kind of fellowship,—fellowship too in works of love, of mutual benefit and extensive benevolence,—the very works which the Christian Church ought to be foremost in instigating and serving,—are driven to organize all sorts of odd-fellowships, and semi-charitable associations. The masses of the tempted, the indifferent, the pleasure-seeking, and the industrious and well-disposed, pass by these basement conference-meetings, catching perhaps the burden of a psalm-tune, but with no drawings to dispose them to enter. When religious movements are brought to bear upon vigorous young men, it is often by a sort of intriguing, scheming policy, which will hardly bear looking at very closely. "Young Men's Christian Associations" are formed; but if we scan one of them in a procession or a meeting, the number of the gray-headed among them opens the unpleasant suggestion, that a too generous interpretation is given to the word *young*, for the sake of showing force and strength. Some zealous ministers will be debating some religious or sectarian project, when a shrewd one among them will suggest, that, after the plan has been agreed upon, it will be well to have it announced and carried on under the auspices of the Young Men's Association. So, after due preparation, the community is informed that the Young Men's Christian Association, in this or that town or city, have determined upon this or that. Painful and mortifying is it to a true lover of his country, to learn how much of unworthy manœuvring and blinding artifice now passes under the title of "wire-pulling." Sadder yet is it to realize, that something of the same ingenuity, under disguises, is availed of to make it appear that pure religion has more real sway in the hearts and enterprises of men than it actually exercises. One result is, that a large body of persons who claim to be the very leaders and supporters of movements undeniably belonging to the work of the Christian Church, boast themselves as come-outers from it.

Here certainly are facts which, without needing the embitterment of a sectarian or a sarcastic spirit, convey a severe reproach to every professed Christian, rebuking him for his own share of blame for a state of things which ought not to exist. We will not concentrate this reproach upon Orthodoxy, and meanly boast that our own faith exonerates us from all participation in it. We feel our own short-comings, we know those of our own religious fellowship, too painfully, to allow even the intimation that Unitarianism has shamed by its vigorous spirit and practice of benevolence all other forms of sectarian Christianity. We may, however, accept, as affording a ray of comfort, what has been visited upon us in censure, — the fact that we have emphasized in our communion the duties of benevolence, philanthropy, practical righteousness, and virtue. When the Rev. H. W. Beecher published last year his large volume of Hymns for Public Worship in his congregation in "Plymouth Church," he was severely assailed by reviewers in his own Orthodox communions for having drawn some of his pieces from Unitarian and other heretical sources. His justification was most significant. He wished his book to embrace hymns adapted for use on occasions of a benevolent, reformatory, and philanthropic character, — hymns baptized in the spirit of a merciful, humane, and loving faith. *For these he was compelled to draw on heretical sources*, the Orthodox collections not furnishing the requisite material. So far as this fact avails, we will use it, in closing, not as a compliment to heresy, nor for a poor boast, but to plead for that much-neglected element in religion, — that which includes the cheerful, the humane, the genial, the merciful, — that which ministers to man's wants and woes in this world, as well as opens the hope of another.

THE NEW THEOLOGY.

THE NEW THEOLOGY.

Much of the interest in religious discussions which, a half-century ago, was engaged in the Unitarian Controversy, is now enlisted in the developments of what is called "The New Theology." Among communions nominally adhering still to the formulas and doctrines of Orthodoxy, are many men of mark and power whom their brethren accuse of heretical tendencies. It is not strange that Unitarians should feel a lively interest in the many developments of the past few years which expose the efforts and struggles of the advanced minds in orthodox communions. They have produced for our perusal and study many laborious volumes and many vigorous essays, laden with the results of profound scholarship, and quickened with the glow of true piety. In no age of the Christian Church has the current theological literature been so attractive in itself, so worthy of extended circulation, so free from the poisonous elements of acrimony and passion, or so edifying in subject-matter and spirit, as in our own time. We confess to finding the materials for our own most profitable hours of thought and study in the fresh theological utterances of some noble-minded and scholarly Christian men who traditionally regard us as outside of the Christian fold. It might be said that our interest is only of that questionable character which loves to mark the tokens of discord or the signs of division in a hostile camp. We may be charged with heresy-hunting for the sake of finding comfort under our own state of exclusion from Christian fellowship. Of course there is a risk of that sort besetting us. We would endeavor to appreciate the kindness which reminds us of our liability to it, and we would endeavor to reinforce our candor, and to overcome our own prejudices, that we may not injuriously or uncharitably interpret any generous concessions of Orthodoxy as affording comfort to our heresy. We may be too ready to claim every free expression of every free mind as a discomfiture of our opponents and an amicable recognition of our own position. But while we would not assume to be secure against the weakness thus recognized, we are conscious of a higher and purer reason for our interest in the developments of the New Theology. We believe it to be among the possibilities of things, that the Orthodoxy which we have rejected may still be of service to us. We should be ashamed to boast of a contempt for all its scholarship, devotion, and piety. The largest modifications of religious or doctrinal philosophy to which some orthodox men are inclined to yield, still keep them aloof from sympathy with us. We are bound, therefore, to read their freest pages with the conscientious and most earnest purpose of rectifying possible errors and supplying possible defects in our own theological system by the help of men who prove their sincerity alike by what they yield in our favor and by what they retain to our reproach. We trust therefore that our orthodox brethren will interpret our interest in the speculative and doctrinal liberalism of which their communions have recently afforded us so many instructive tokens, as attaching but in part to our pleasure at the discomfiture of Orthodoxy, and for the rest to our desire to be made aware of the possible — we will even say the probable — defects and errors of Unitarianism. With this introduction, we proceed to treat of the New Theology. We do not intend to enter upon any elaborate exposition or any learned discussion of the materials which crowd upon us in overwhelming abundance. We aim only for a more popular and simple treatment of our subject.

A New Theology has been in every age of the Christian Church the hope and the object of one party in its fold, and by another party the same title has been used for designating the whole series of successive heresies while in their incipient state. Till the rupture takes place, both parties claiming a common orthodoxy divide between them the epithets *progressive* and *conservative.* The New Theology always receives its first nurture in the bosom of Orthodoxy. Sometimes its early training is most affectionately fostered by those who visit upon its mature development the most bitter hostility. When what has thus for a proper length of time been under subjection and pupilage manifests itself as palpable and full-grown heresy, Orthodoxy discards all relationship with it. Henceforward it must take a name, and the party adopting it must stand by itself, excommunicated, until time or strength or success gives to it that assurance of its own full Christian integrity and authority which it may find in being able to excommunicate a subordinate party that has risen up in its own fellowship. The Roman Church for an indefinite time sheltered a New Theology, which in due course developed into Protestantism. Reaching its maturity and manifesting its undeniable heretical qualities, Protestantism came under excommunication, and it was not long before it found itself strong enough to set up for Orthodoxy within a limited fold and region of its own. Then in turn Orthodox Protestantism began to hear warnings of a New Theology as announcing the aim and hope of a party called Puritans. Puritanism, having reached man's estate, was offered its choice either to be chastised into obedience and submission, or to be driven out to set up for itself. It chose to set up for itself, though under a double sentence of excommunication from pope and prelate. But still the possibilities of novelty in the field of Christian theology were not exhausted. As sentences of excommunication multiplied, the fear of that penalty lost its power to overawe free souls. As the sentence has been annually kept in vigor at Rome against English and all other Protestantism, and no harm has ever yet been known to come from it, it was hardly likely to inspire terror when pronounced by any communion that was already under its ban. It would be as unreasonable to fear a repetition of excommunication, as it would be to fear in one's own person the undergoing of successive capital punishments. So Unitarianism, which ages of corruption had only kept in abeyance from a reassertion of the pure, the primitive Gospel, was for a time the New Theology in the Protestant, Reformed, Puritan, Independent Orthodox Church. Unitarianism engaged in its turn the interest and excited the hostility which attend the last development of organized dissent before it has been visited with excommunication. Unitarianism attempted to reduce the Christian faith, not to its *minimum* as is often affirmed, but to its *ultimatum*, by going back to the primitive substance of the Gospel. There can be no further heresy developed from Unitarianism but the heresy of actual unbelief in revelation, — a heresy, by the by, which is just as possible, and which in fact has as often been realized, under all the other forms of Christian theology.

But when Orthodoxy has rid itself by processes of exclusion and excommunication of the successive heresies which have developed in its own communion into parties capable of an independent life, its warfare is by no means ended. Hardly has the expurgated fold kept its feast of purification before its exercises of humiliation begin again. Heretical processes will still go on within the best-guarded fold, and very soon after it has exorcised its avowed traitors. While excommunicated heresies are frankly labelled with their own assumed or imposed titles, they have to part with that of the New Theology, which they bore before their ejection. That title is always reserved as the designation of the undeveloped views of the progressive party, the embryo and incipient heretics, the lovers of novel speculations and free thought, who in due course of time will give evidence of their presence and industry in the orthodox fold. Thus "The New Theology" is now the title of the more or less perfectly developed and avowed, but not as yet excommunicated heresies, that are known to exist in those communions of Christians which have withdrawn fellowship from acknowledged Unitarians and fortified themselves within their citadels of nominal Orthodoxy.

There is a form of religious faith floating around the communities where Christian thought and sentiment are most active, and giving the most significant tokens of its energetic working in our best theological literature, — to which is for the time being attached the title of "The New Theology." Its opponents in Great Britain have endeavored, with some degree of success, to substitute the title of *The Negative Theology.* We have called it a *form* of faith. But perhaps that is too strong and definite a term to be applied to what has not as yet taken a distinct shape, or set itself forth in clearly stated and systematic views. The popular mind is but very imperfectly acquainted with the facts of the case, as these are known and watched by professional observers. Yet, as we shall attempt to show, this popular mind is one of the chief elements, one of the most important parties, in the interest of the subject. Indeed, it is from time to time a matter of curious speculation with us how the uninitiated readers of the religious journals of our orthodox brethren interpret to themselves the incidental and sketchy references to the developments so constantly brought to their notice. For instances, take the following, selected from a very rich budget of similar cases. The North British Review is established in the championship of Scotch Orthodoxy, and with the design of offering able discussions by the most competent men of subjects which the other quarterlies treat after too free and heretical a manner. That Review wins a large circulation and a high repute, both well deserved because of its sterling merits. In successive numbers we are treated with two noble articles on Missions to the Heathen, and on Dr. Chalmers. Running through both articles, entering into their very stamina and substance, forming indeed the very point and pith of their strength, are unmistakable tokens of opinions held by their writers utterly inconsistent with real orthodoxy. These indications are all the more significant to liberal readers, because they imply and intimate much more than they directly advance, though their assertions and positions are frank and bold to a degree which is startling. We read some of the pages with amazement which subsides into a calm delight over these manifest evidences of progress within denominations which have tried every method to resist it. Here we have a sentence or a paragraph which flings actual contempt on some one of the most positive articles of the creed; and then we have a sly hint or suggestion, the *animus* of which is plainly intended to convey its risky suggestion only to a safe esoteric circle of readers. By and by we watch to see how these bold utterances will be received by the orthodox. The Review tells us it is impious to suppose or to proclaim for the sake of swelling missionary funds that the Heathen will perish because they know not the Gospel. The

Review also challenges the repute of Dr. Chalmers, confesses his incompetency as a great Christian advocate against unbelievers, and affirms the untenableness of his view — the orthodox view — of inspiration. Some of the religious newspapers commend in general terms the contents of the Review. Others, whose editors are more watchful, spy out these alarming heresies, and in little paragraphs of invidious, alarmed, or deprecatory strain, follow a second-hand, diluted, or unfair report of them with their rebuke. Again, the Orthodox Dissenters of Great Britain establish monthly and weekly religious journals in the interest of their cause, and pledged to defend their orthodoxy. They try to select able men for editors and contributors, because the scholarship and the literary standard of the times demand that condition for even moderate success. But these able men are very apt now-a-days to be free, progressive, and independent men. As a natural consequence, these pledged orthodox journals are soon found trespassing in heretical fields. The cry of alarm is raised by men of second-rate abilities and of inferior standing, who however are better than any other men for sounding an alarm. The councils of the fellowship are distracted, our own journals catch up the echo of the strife, and give a very partial and insufficient account of its occasion. Once more, Andover and New Haven dare the venture of applying a new philosophy to old theology. Professor Hodge of Princeton is on the watch for every such venturesome speculator, and he reckons with them forthwith in his Review. The Old School religious newspapers rehearse such portions of the questions at issue as suit their space, their idea of fairness, or their temper. Meanwhile, we ask again, what think the uninitiated orthodox readers about these shootings forth and presages of the New Theology? Something is going on evidently which they do not comprehend. Their leaders and guides are all orthodox still.

They "are all, all honorable men." But they do not seem to understand, or if they understand, they do not indorse, each other. The venerable and honored Dr. Dana, in his vigorous old age, looks with a troubled mind towards Andover, the fond hope of unchangeable orthodoxy in his youth. He is burdened in spirit by a sense of responsibility, but still he finds it impossible to indict a heresy which does not instantly prove an *alibi*. Drs. Tregelles and Davidson are employed to re-edit the orthodox work of Mr. Horne on the Scriptures. They are two of the most competent and distinguished Biblical scholars in Great Britain. The work comes from their hands brimful of such views and opinions as have drawn excommunication on Unitarians. An intense excitement is the consequence. The lesser of the two heretics, Dr. Tregelles, writes a very severe letter against the more heretical Dr. Davidson, his colleague editor, and an incidental development proves that all the pupils of an orthodox school of the prophets have been trained in most alarming defections from the faith by such an instructor. To those who try to get to the bottom, or who without such pains discern the bottom, of all these innumerable tokens of the restlessness, disquietude, and treachery within the fold of reputed orthodoxy, the philosophy of them may be very simple. But to the uninitiated they must be mystifying and perplexing, especially as their leaders decline to give them a full, fair, and unprejudiced view of all the issues thus opened. Yet it may be worth while for these leaders and sentinels of orthodoxy to ask what the consequences will be when some of these secrets can no longer be kept, and the heraldings of dawn are followed by the orb of light itself.

The New Theology is the title assigned in New England to those modifications of Calvinism which were first systematically proposed by Edwards, and which became perceptibly a trifle *newer*, as developed by Bellamy, Hopkins, West, Benton, Emmons, and others. Those names, —which the orthodox in New England cherish with a homage that we of course cannot be expected to offer, except to the character of the men, for their ability, acuteness, and talent seem to us to be almost absurdly exaggerated, — those names would be very gladly accepted by the friends of the New Theology of our day, as a protection for their heresies. But we must modernize that word *New* if it is to take in more recent developments. We will frankly say, that we are not interested in what was the New Theology of Edwards. We are on the track of something newer. Not the *nova*, but the *novissima*, is what engages us. A pupil who should translate *novissima luna* as the "new moon" would need to be told that the words mean the moon in the *last* quarter.

It will be understood, therefore, that we use the title of this paper as defining the as yet not perfectly developed religious system of those who claim to hold the substance of the old orthodoxy, but who have essentially modified its symbolical exposition, the terms for stating its elements, and the philosophical language in which it casts itself. The able and progressive men of whose speculations we are writing would freely admit that they had gone the lengths in heresy which we have just defined. Perhaps some of them who will still claim to be orthodox would confess to having gone a little farther. We wish, however, to be held as uttering therefore only an inference of our own, not an admission of theirs, when we add the expression of our honest and firm belief, that many of them do go farther, some of them consciously, some of them unconsciously. We are convinced that their concessions and modifications of creed reach beyond the mere philosophy of orthodoxy, and assail its doctrinal substance, its very life. We will add, that if this be only a surmise of our own, then there is a vast deal of agitation about nothing in the debates of our most intelligent divines. The vigorous life, the interest of religious thought and discussion, in our day, are almost wholly identified with the concealed or avowed divergencies of belief among those who nominally accept the same creed. The heretics in the Church cause the heretics outside of it to be forgotten.

It may be asked how we know that there is any such restlessness in the larger ecclesiastical folds, any secret modification of old religious opinions working effectually at the sources of thought, though eluding definition? We answer, because we know that there are recognized parties in each of the great orthodox communions, because their newspapers are blindly discussing some suspected and half-acknowledged heresies within the pale of supposed uniformity, and because the more able men, the leaders of thought, especially some of the teachers in the most flourishing theological seminaries, are well understood to have essential differences with each other. It may not perhaps be spoken of as a matter of common notoriety, but all those who would be likely to know are very well aware that there are doctrinal divisions with which tolerance is compelled to bear, because policy forbids a rupture in reference to them. Heretics have learned to cling to their own native folds. They do not go off as they once did. They are not driven off so summarily as they once were. Ecclesiastical discipline, once so bold and incessant in applying its tests, has become very forbearing; because of this reason among others, that it fears to encounter the work which might possibly lead on from a venturesome beginning. There is infinitely more material for such discipline now than there ever was before. Many members of the English Church, who from time to time utter themselves upon the feuds which now distract it, maintain that the real wisdom and sufficiency of its principles are for the first time put to the trial in the comprehensiveness under which it embraces all the creeds and all the scepticisms that prevail in Christendom. This opinion startles some of the living, but we apprehend that the true test of it would be — if it admitted of the application — to imagine some of the departed victims of the old intolerance of that Church to be summoned from their graves and treated with the gentle announcement of that plea. That certainly is the *newest* doctrine of our times.

The question now presents itself, — What scope or material is there for anything that can be fairly called "A New Theology"? How can the old, worn ways of thought, the wrinkles in the world's weary brows, be made fresh again, so that they will receive a new impress? How can the formulas of faith be converted to the uses of a new theological creed? Especially, if this question concerns robust and honest minds, and is to be pursued under the limiting condition that the New Theology is *substantially* the Old Theology, — how can we expect a reward for our pains in trying to track the shape of new impressions on these old ways? We must now sharpen our vision.

Theology is the oldest of human sciences. The epithet *human* belongs as justly to it as it does to any of the sciences; for though the themes of theology are divine, its forms and methods and processes are subjected to precisely the same limitations, through our finite and fallible minds, as are attached to the pursuit of either of the departments of human inquiry. Theology is the human term for expressing the science of divinity. It covers all man's thought, philosophy, and theory about the things of God. We call it the oldest of all the sciences, not only because it enters into the first records of the thought and history of our race, but also because every science which might aspire to an earlier date would be sure to involve the theological views of the minds whose observations on nature, on life, or on man it comprehended.

But what is thus found to be the oldest of sciences has been described by two extreme classes of those interested in it under two most inconsistent epithets. One class has pronounced it to be unprogressive, making no advance upon the elemental substance or materials with which it first started, as the first generation exhausted its discoveries and recognized all its insoluble problems. Another class of students comprehends those who, whether with boasting or complaint, allege that theology is a progressive, unstable science, never permanently settled on its foundation, and continually changing in its substance as well as in its terminology.

Every Christian age has had to recognize something which, rightly or wrongly, has been called "A New Theology." The phrase is suggestive to some of all that is quickening and cheering in the evidence of progress, —progress in the discovery of truth, in every province of human interest. To others the phrase is synonymous with heresy, and what is signified by it is a fright and a bugbear. But can we hesitate to call theology a progressive science? It certainly deserves the epithet progressive if it deserves the title of a science. How can it be otherwise than progressive, seeing that it is cumulative, that it is built up out of theories, that it arrays men in contending schools of opinion, and makes every independent thinker upon it an independent theorist? Of course we must allow for the fact, which is merely disguised in the familiar trick of language that ascribes to the theme of our thoughts the modifications which actually are made only in our own opinions. When we say that theology is a progressive science, we mean that men make progress in their dealing with subjects essentially unchangeable, in their theories about truths which were perfect and assured before a single human mind engaged upon them. In this sense, theology has proved to be the most progressive of all sciences. More startling revolutions of human opinion are to be traced in connection with man's views of the Divine nature, attributes, and government, than are to be recognized as wrought in his views of the physical universe by all the amazing discoveries and processes in the crowded cyclopædias of natural philosophy. And in fact the progress of the natural sciences has been the most effective agency in modifying theological opinions, in subverting dogmas and doctrines of a venerable authority, and in compelling each generation of human beings, as it advanced in civilization and knowledge, to find a higher method, a nobler argument, for vindicating the ways of God to men. Theology, as a science, bears down with it from age to age all that made its themes interesting to the first thinkers, and all that was added to it by their speculations upon it. Originally, theology was the science of Divinity. It is that still, and is besides the science of man's speculations and opinions and theories upon its own original materials. The discussion of Bible doctrines is now hopelessly complicated with philosophy. All in vain, as respects the weight of his warning beyond its probable effect on his young disciple, did St. Paul warn Timothy against "striving about words to no profit,"— against "foolish questions which gender strifes." No age after that of Timothy has heeded the warning. Men cannot do without a philosophy of religion, and all attempts to disconnect religion and philosophy have utterly failed, while those who have most strenuously argued for a doctrinal system nominally drawn from the Bible, and as authoritative in defiance of all philosophy, have been compelled to adopt a philosophy of their own in the conduct of their argument.

Religion brings down with it from all past ages, not

only the records which to those who receive them have a more or less decided authority of infallibility and inspiration, but it comes also laden with the precious or questionable burden of tradition. They may be theoretically right who assert that their Christian liberty makes them wholly independent of tradition, as challenging authority with them in matters of faith. But it is one thing to claim that immunity, and wholly another thing to form our own views under an absolute freedom from the influence of tradition. Tradition passes into the forms of language, into words and idioms and phrases, into versions and translations from one tongue into another. There are expressions, yes, sentences even, in our English Bible, which, in their variations from the exact meaning of the original, carry with them more effectively a traditional construction or authority in the teaching of doctrine, than do any of the most positive decrees of the old councils, or any of the most absolute decisions of ecclesiastical tribunals. It is safe to say that the influence of tradition in doctrine and opinion, and in its associations with the Scriptures and their contents, is the larger element in the faith of even the most ultra Protestants.

Religion brings down with it from past ages some old covenants, creeds, and formulas, and when religion is arrayed and set forth with this traditional garb, it becomes theology. These covenants, creeds, and formulas are of earthly fabrication. They become time-worn and rusty, they get rent and moth-eaten; they need patching; they fade, they become thin, they are outgrown; the faith of the last days cannot adapt itself to them. The Christian Church has always had to concern itself with two very distinct matters, the one being religion, the other being the philosophy of religion. About religion Christians have never had a single dispute or variance among themselves, except on one point; and that has been prolific beyond all statement in debate and strife, namely, as to how religion is involved with the philosophy of religion, that is, with theology, — with an intellectual system or theory of doctrines. Theology means and includes man's speculations and opinions about God, and the things of God, his being, his nature, his will, his revelations, his relations with humanity, his work in Christ. There never has been an hour in the history of the Church when, among those who received the Scriptures as authoritative in their religion, there has not been difference of opinion on all these subjects which constitute theology. When sufficient interest has been felt in these differences of opinion to prompt to an utterance of them, there has been controversy. Then come into use such terms as "the old theology," and "the new theology." "The new theology" has various synonymes, *heresy* being the one most in use and most readily spoken. The title has been borne, as we have seen, by all the successive modifications of opinion which have manifested themselves within the fold called for the time being that of orthodoxy. It is among the very last of the conditions requisite for the use of this title that there should be absolute, or even relative, novelty in the views to which it is attached. On the contrary, the most startling and striking developments made under a fresh modification of theological opinions have generally been but a revival or reassertion of some very old, and often of primitive opinions. When the wrong-headed conservatives of established error at the time of the Reformation wished for a sharp epithet of reproach to visit upon the rising zeal for the study of the Greek literature, they called it "the new learning"; forgetting that their Latin and Teutonic tongues had to translate from Hellenic sources not only the text of their Scriptures, but also the terms and processes of their philosophy. The newest opinions of the wisest Christian theologians often prove to be a more pretentious exposition of the simple views advanced by those who were first trained in the school of Christ. The great interest with which liberal Christian scholars and theologians watch the ever-restless speculations of all the more vigorous minds in the orthodox communions is to be accounted solely to an expectation that primitive and simple truth will thus be reasserted. We do not look for the striking out of a single ray of new truth in theology. Our highest hope is that the murky darkness with which orthodox philosophy has obscured the light of simple Gospel verities may be scattered by the agitations raised in the world of opinion. Time was when Unitarianism was called "the new theology." Orthodoxy, having cast that heresy out of its communion, uses some other title to designate our views, and reserves the phrase for application to such of its own heresies as have not yet been visited with the extreme penalty of excommunication.

We have intimated that what is called "the popular mind" is especially concerned in the development of the new theology. It may be taken as an axiom in the history of religious opinions, that all which tends to complicate and pervert theology by abstruse and unscriptural philosophy has come from the brains of professed theologians, while all the influences which tend to the restoration of the primitive simplicity of our faith find their full sympathy in the minds and hearts of those whose best wisdom is common sense. When Protestantism first won possession of a free Bible, it received with it a philosophy of religion which prejudiced an intelligent study and interpretation of it. That philosophy of religion has ever since complicated the faith of men, and when the reception of it has been identified with a belief in the revelation whose substantial truths it is intended to epitomize, it has exposed a religious belief to all the risks consequent upon the action of the mind. When religion is dispensed by its teachers to their pupils in connection with a philosophical theology, the intellectual element will always be more excited than the spiritual. So long as the mass of people of ordinary culture and intelligence can be interested in the metaphysics of divinity, they may be content to refer the perplexities of an orthodox creed to the difficulties they might reasonably expect to find in the intricate processes of philosophy. But the moment they insist upon having a religious creed which shall stand clear of the more involved problems of metaphysics, then they demand that what they are asked to believe shall be reconciled with reason and common sense. It is not so easy for them to indicate the defects and the unscientific qualities in poor metaphysics, as it is for them to appreciate unreasonable, inconsistent, or incredible elements in a simple religious creed. Now we understand the facts of the case to be precisely these. Intelligent culture and activity of thought in practical directions have induced the result that the mass of people who crave a religious faith and hope demand a better philosophy of religion; or, as the matter more correctly stands in their view, that religion should be distinguished and separated from metaphysics. Let a devout-hearted but clear-minded and inquisitive man, longing for the elements of a religious life to come to him from God in as simple and available a form as light, air, and water, meet with the following sentence, for instance, from the pen of the Old School Dr. Hodge: "A man may be justly accountable for acts which are determined by his character, whether that character or inward state be inherited, acquired, or induced by the grace of God."* If that sentence does not prove a poser even to the clearest brains, our own brains are not trustworthy for judgment.

* Princeton Review, January, 1857, p. 135.

How long divines can expect to carry the faith of common men with them when they write such things as that, is one of the questions for our new theology to dispose of. But no man would dare to write such a sentence were it not for his confidence in the unbounded facilities furnished him by metaphysics, by his philosophy of religion, for evading the common-sense inference from it, — which is, that God, guided by what men recognize as *justice*, may entail a wicked character like a physical disease upon a child of his, and then punish him for its irresistible outgrowth into wicked actions. Such a sentence is admirably adapted to remind us of the large indebtedness of orthodoxy to metaphysics for its boldness in advancing the most outrageous doctrines smothered up in technical language. A leading new theology divine lays down these three distinctive principles: "that sin consists in choice; that our natural power is equal to our duty; and that our duty is limited by our natural power." Here is common sense. To Dr. Hodge, however, it is deadly heresy. Yet he would not venture to assert the opposite of either of these statements in plain, positive language, which admitted of no metaphysical mystification. The demand of "the popular mind" is now that religion be divorced from metaphysical subtilties. Scholars of course interpret this demand as requiring a better system of metaphysics, a new philosophy of the doctrines of revelation. While we may look with but a partially satisfied curiosity to discover the precise shape and amount and degree of the modifications which leading minds in orthodox communions have introduced for softening the sharp features of their system, we have another means of information, very instructive if we use it wisely. We may consult the popular tendencies, the actual state of minds among independent thinkers in the community at large. The new theology has a strong hold upon the convictions and sympathies of large numbers around us. Undefined it may be in these minds, as in the minds or the essays of prominent teachers, but still it is sufficiently apprehended to be available as a creed of living faith and cheering hope, and as a ransom from a night-mare oppression which else would weigh upon the spirit. Our own convictions extend to the length of a firm belief that, within the shattered and no longer defensible intrenchments of disabled orthodoxy, there is under training a party which sooner or later will affiliate with another party, now outside of the fold, to prove the main reliance of the Church when shams and conformities and traditions must sink into ruin.

The new theology then starts with the honest and generous purpose of reconstructing the philosophical method for the statement and explication of the doctrines of revelation. It assumes that the doctrines long recognized as orthodox are substantially true and Scriptural. It flatters itself with the thought that orthodoxy is prejudiced to many serious and intelligent minds, not because of anything really inconsistent or unreasonable in its doctrines, when rigidly tested by the laws of Divine truth or the human understanding, but solely because of its metaphysical exposition. It cherishes the hope that, by recasting or reconstructing the philosophy of the old creed, its sway may be retained and largely extended even to the winning of the allegiance of its open assailants. Whether the new theology can thus spend all its energies upon the philosophy of the creed, and yet spare the creed, is the question of chief interest to us. If our friends who are engaged in this generous enterprise can feel perfectly at ease on that point, and can find an equivalent interest in watching the experiment for reconciling us to the creed through a new philosophy of it, we see no reason why we cannot amicably afford to sustain our present relations, and to divide our hope for the future. The new school divines think that, by recasting the philosophy of orthodoxy and reconstructing its formulas for the statement of the substance of its old truth, they can meet all that is reasonable or plausible in our objections to orthodoxy as a fair exponent of Christian doctrine. We think that these divines cannot consistently pursue the processes involved in their undertaking, much less bring it to a conclusion which will satisfy us, or even themselves, without introducing essential modifications into the substance of the orthodox creed. Now this issue is worthy of our age, and of the scholarship, the sincerity, the piety which is to try it. Let it be honorably and faithfully contested. Let him be considered as putting himself outside of the lists of this fair Christian contest who introduces into the conduct of it a mean motive, or a word of bitter invective. For our part, we are willing to admit that Unitarianism, as it has been set forth by its ablest expositors, has not approved itself to all who have been competent to test it as an adequate doctrinal summary of Christian truth; nor as an exhaustive transcript of the essence of the religion of the Bible; nor as a fair exponent of the phraseology of Scripture; nor even as a system which can draw and engage the religious sympathies of large numbers of persons of various culture and temperament in the great offices of Christian piety. As we said in the first of this series of papers, so we say in this, which is the last, something has proved to be lacking in Unitarianism. It is true that we can give plausible explanations of its supposed deficiencies, or lack of adaptation to a great variety of intellectual constitutions or spiritual temperaments. We may say that the severe simplicity of its doctrinal system is above the comprehension and offensive to the tastes of many; or that the prejudiced hearing which it addresses, or its inability to cope with rival systems more attractive to the mass of persons and more in harmony with the traditions of piety, stands in the way of its fair and deserved acceptance. But the facts of the case, however explained, are facts still. While the defects and shortcomings and failures of orthodoxy, and the amount of positive evil which is directly chargeable upon it, are matters which we have had occasion most painfully to know and deplore, we make no boast for ourselves or for our own system. Well, therefore, may we watch with a generous interest the issue whether the nobler spirits of a nominal orthodoxy can make such modifications in it as will satisfy them and reclaim us. Nor will we be churlish about words. We will allow that good word *substance* its largest possible meaning, when a man who we think believes essentially as we do affirms that he holds the substance of orthodoxy. But still there are certain rights vested in dictionaries, and *substance* must always be supposed to mean some part of the thing to which it is applied, and the substantial part of it too. We may say to our orthodox brethren, in the spirit of Christian candor, that never does a humble distrust of our own possible error in the interpretation of the Gospel of Christ present itself with such a religious earnestness to our minds, as when we read the writings of progressive men in their ranks. Their manly sincerity, their intellectual strength, their independence of soul, their fidelity to conscience in their protests against *some part* of orthodoxy, give a new warrant to the portion of it which they retain. But we can conceive of nothing more utterly ineffective, hopeless, or dismal, than the pleadings of the old school divines of our day in defence of their antiquated system.

It will be understood, therefore, from our remarks thus far, that what we are writing of under the title of the New Theology is not a well-defined, consistent system of qualified or modified orthodoxy, which can be gathered out of the published opinions of one or more eminent men. We shall doubtless have something of that sort before long, and we hope that we may be living to welcome it. No one orthodox writer has as yet ventured to give form and shape to a set of formulas whose language varies from those long received so far as to express the new philosophy of religion. So we have to use the title of this article to designate an undeveloped, unsystematized class of speculations, fragmentary portions of which are to be found in a great many publications, intimations of which are continually presenting themselves in unsuspected quarters, and suspicions of which are known to be far more widely entertained, and on better evidence, than some who are concerned in them care to have made public. This, at least, we are warranted in saying, that, if some of our more acute and earnest theologians are not profoundly exercised by a sceptical spirit in reference to their own orthodoxy, they are trifling with the community, and, what is more, with truth. Clerical scepticism is the root of much of our present religious agitation. Men in the maturity of their intellectual powers, and with the best aids of good scholarship, set to defend and to preach the Gospel, find themselves struggling painfully within the fetters of the creed by which they have pledged themselves. To accept it in its own plain sense, is to them an utter impossibility. They cannot, they do not, believe it in its traditional sense, or in its popular acceptation. They know that the belief which it once expressed, the belief which fashioned the stiff and positive terms of the creed simply for the sake of expressing itself, has not the hold upon the living convictions of Christendom which it once had. The suggestion comes to their minds, that perhaps the substance of the old doctrines may be distinguished from the hard and discredited formulas used for stating them. What Dr. Bushnell calls "the deepest chemistry of thought," is brought to bear upon the perplexity. The creed is subjected to a powerful solvent in the mind. That process it cannot bear without suffering decomposition. The part of it which is digested and made to pass into the spiritual system is then pronounced "the substance of the old doctrine." It ought rather, and more honestly, to be called the substance of what was *true* in the doctrine, for when fair and candid men have thoroughly tried this experiment, they are apt rather to need and seek for the substance of truth in a doctrine, than for the substance of the doctrine itself. Clerical scepticism is a disease under which thousands have suffered who have not proclaimed it, nor, perhaps, manifested the symptoms. But when any professed orthodox scholar undertakes to soften the terms of his creed, or to avail himself of the ambiguities of language for evading its unreasonable or unscriptural dogmas, the symptoms of his inner state are not to be mistaken. Now we say, without any fear of being challenged for the assertion, that the best works in Biblical criticism and exposition, the most vigorous essays on religious themes, the articles of highest character in the religious quarterlies at home and abroad, the most able sermons, and all the other utterances of the most scholarly, earnest, devout, and effective men in the various orthodox communions, indicate opinions and a spirit more or less inconsistent with the formulas of their creed. Take this select religious literature and compare its contents, page by page, with the writings of the old standard orthodox divines, and the contrast will amaze any reader. We will not transgress the rule of charity, and therefore we will explain our charge of the infidelity of orthodox men to orthodoxy as meaning this,—that, if we avowed ourselves to be believers in the substance of the doctrines of the Westminster Assembly's Catechism or of the Thirty-nine Articles, we could not, in consistency with religious or intellectual honesty, write or preach what we find in the contents of a hundred valuable volumes now lying within our reach, bearing the names of divines in the American Congregational and the English Episcopal churches.

If any one should ask in what single volume he may find the most of general or particular information upon this latent and undeveloped heresy of "New Theology," we should have to refer him to a volume written by its ablest and most resolute and unflinching opponent. Dr. Hodge of Princeton is now the most distinguished defender of the old school divinity. Manfully and consistently, with his whole heart's zeal, with an honesty which we must respect, and a power which those against whom he exerts it have to fear, does he take up the gauntlet thrown down by every nominally orthodox man who ventures to try his liberal philosophy on the Calvinistic creed. We think that in every such case, starting, of course, on orthodox premises, he has won a fair and honorable triumph over his opponents. He has recently published a stout volume, in which he collects his Essays and Reviews. There is in them strength, courage, acuteness, exact metaphysical skill, and sound doctrinal teaching, — sound, we mean, according to the creed, not according to the Scriptures. All the New School men who have ventured to publish their heresies pass under his reckoning in separate papers. Dr. Cox's heresy on Regeneration, Professor Stuart's on Imputation, Dr. Beman's on the Atonement, Professor Finney's on several doctrines, Dr. Bushnell's on Christian Nurture, the Trinity, and the Double Nature of Christ, and Professor Park's on Rhetorical and Logical Theology, are all lucidly discussed, and the views of their respective authors are fairly proved to be inconsistent with the formulas of orthodoxy. Now if any one tells us that the Princeton Professor is fighting only shadows, or has spent so much strength upon the mere verbal technicalities which do not concern the substance of the doctrine, he will cast but a poor reflection upon the best efforts of the ablest men among us. We stand by the Professor, for he stands by us, and he verifies what our own common sense teaches us, that the rebellion of free though devout minds against the creed of orthodoxy has carried them far beyond the lawful limits of metaphysical speculation or philosophical explanation, and has made them treacherous to the creed with whose fair, honest, well-understood teachings orthodoxy stands or falls. We cannot believe that this strife between the masters of Christian science is mere child's play. It is a manly conflict, and some new views enter into the challenge.

And the real aim of the champions of this New Theology is a noble and a generous one. They have all our sympathy, while we yield to their opponent only our conviction that he is more consistent than they. Their object is to redeem Christian truth from metaphysical perplexity; to shape the dogmas of the creed into assertions of faith which will bear to be uttered in this modern age of time; to affirm as doctrines only such positive statements of great, solemn verities as will bear to be looked at in the light of common sense, and professed without the blush of insincerity, and offered to earnest, longing minds without calling out a protest from the heart. These men know that all manner of palliations, evasions, and apologies have to be offered in connection with anything like a hopeful effort to propound the orthodox creed to the clear-headed, the mature, and the strong-minded of our times. They have been let into the secrets of official or professional intercourse, by which they have learned that orthodoxy requires of its disciples a denial of the rights of reason, and a tribute of implicit faith inconsistent with the fundamental principles of Protestantism. They will not condescend to practise the hoodwinking and the falsifying essential to the maintenance of such doctrinal opinions as have been discredited by more just views of Scripture, of the nature of man, and the government of God. Their hearts are in open rebellion against Calvinism, while their associations through tradition, fellowship, and sentiment are with orthodoxy. They dread Unitarianism. The bad name which their predecessors gave to our heresy has warned them effectually from much sympathy with us. They have a horror of the calm, cold, languid spirit of Unitarianism, of its bleak and houseless exposure, and of the precipices of infidelity which it leaves unfenced. Still they are not orthodox. It is wrong for them to retain the epithet. The severest condemnation of their inconsistency comes in part from their own forced silence, and in part from the positive sentence passed upon them whenever they dare to utter themselves by those who are really orthodox. They wish to make religious doctrines more intelligible, more reasonable, less bewildering, less shocking, as the announcement of solemn truths embracing things human and divine. "No!" say the men of the Old School, "that is the very thing you must not do, for it is the very thing that spoils religion. The bewildering, the mystifying, the confounding element in it is a large part of its life. Let it alone. The more it baffles your reason, and prostrates your pride of mind, the more devout and evangelical will be its influence over you."

Dr. Hodge fairly states the issue opened by the New School men in their attempt to distinguish between the form and the substance of the truth taught in the creed. He maintains, consistently, that the form answers to the substance, and was chosen as the vehicle to convey the substance by those who really believed the substance. "The main point," he says, "is nothing more or less than this: Is that system of doctrine embodied in the creeds of the Lutheran and Reformed Churches, in its substantial and distinctive features, true as to its form as well as to its substance? Are the propositions therein contained true as doctrines, or are they merely intense expressions, true not in the mode in which they are there presented, but only in a vague, loose sense, which the intellect would express in a very different form? Are these creeds to be understood as they mean, and do they mean what they say, or is allowance to be made for their freedom, abatement of their force, and their terms to be considered antiquated and their spirit only as still in force? For example, when these creeds speak of the imputation of Adam's sin, is that to be considered as only an intense form of expressing the 'definite idea, that we are exposed to evil in consequence of his sin'? This is surely a question of great importance." * "The definite idea" which Dr. Hodge puts in contrast with the creed, is that which he ascribes to the teaching of Professor Park.

Again, Dr. Hodge boldly faces his own orthodoxy in the following sentences. "The origin of sin, the fall of man, the relation of Adam to his posterity, the transmission of his corrupt nature to all descended from him by ordinary generation, the consistency of man's freedom with God's sovereignty, the process of regeneration, the relation of the believer to Christ, and other doctrines of the like kind, do not admit of 'philosophical explanation.' They cannot be dissected and mapped off so as that the points of contact and mode of union with all other known truths can be clearly understood; nor can God's dealings with our race be all explained on the common-sense principles of moral government. The system which Paul taught was not a system of common sense, but of profound and awful mystery." † There is a plau-

* Essays and Reviews, pp. 572, 573. † Ibid., p. 583.

sibleness in the ingenious shaping of the assertions in these sentences. It will be observed that the aim of the new school men is misstated by being exaggerated, if not caricatured, and that the plea of censure against them seeks to strengthen itself by an unfair construction of St. Paul. We do not understand any of those who are interested in the New Theology as asking that the doctrines of revelation shall be so divested of their peculiar characteristics, " dissected," " mapped off," and reduced to the same category as other known truths. Nor do we understand St. Paul as setting "the mystery" of the Gospel in antagonism with common sense. We should hardly have expected of a Christian scholar, holding the position of Dr. Hodge, that he would indorse the popular error in the interpretation of that word *mystery* as applied to the Gospel scheme. He uses it as synonymous with something that baffles reason and confounds common sense, whereas his Master repeatedly asserted that it had been given to those to whom he spoke to know and understand it. The mystery, or rather the *secret*, was disclosed, and the commonest sense was invited to see the simple wisdom, the divine love and mercy, displayed in it. The admission made by Dr. Hodge in the above-quoted sentences will not hinder any one from questioning the metaphysics of orthodoxy in the hope of reconciling common sense and the creed. To proclaim an antagonism between them would be fatal to the world's confidence in the one or the other of them. As it could hardly be expected that the mass of men would give over their reliance upon common sense, they would find a warrant in the assertion of the theologian for distrusting such a "mystery" as was irreconcilable with it. This, however, is to be regarded as one of the results already brought about by the disciples of the New Theology, namely, the drawing forth a confession that the Old Theology and *good* metaphysics cannot be reconciled.

A most striking and startling illustration of the same fact transpired in London some four years ago. Mr. Holyoake, the unwearied and by no means despicable champion of that theoretical and practical atheism called "Secularism," which is thought to be alarmingly rife in England, challenged a defender of revelation to a series of formal discussions. The Rev. Mr. Grant accepted the challenge, and a course of public disputations followed. But the Christian advocate, though an orthodox man, expressly demanded that the subjects in debate should not include the peculiar tenets of orthodoxy. The discussions concerned those points of the Christian belief common to us and the orthodox. These were argued precisely as a Unitarian would argue with an unbeliever, and every tenet peculiar to Trinitarianism and Calvinism was kept out of sight and notice. Mr. Grant did not fear to apply the tests of common sense, sound philosophy, and good metaphysics to the great, fundamental truths and doctrines of the Christian religion, as we regard them. Why, then, should he shrink from their application to what Orthodoxy regards as the life and substance of the Christian system? Again, Mr. Rogers, also in profession an orthodox believer, in his Eclipse of Faith, designed to answer the sceptical and rationalistic views of Mr. Newman and others, has not one single word of pleading to offer in the name of reason and philosophy for any of the special tenets of Orthodoxy. He does use those noble weapons, but only as we would use them, and only in behalf of simple Christian verities. Are we mistaken in our inferences from these striking facts?

It would be but an easy task for us to offer in detail a long specification of the doctrinal difficulties in the orthodox formulas, from which relief is sought in the New Theology. We must confine ourselves to a selection, with but few words of comment. First of all comes up the orthodox doctrine of the Inspiration of the Scriptures. Dr. Hodge says, "The old doctrine of the plenary inspiration, and consequent infallibility, of the written word, is still held by the great body of believers." * Now we will not answer for the great body of believers, but we will affirm that the *old* doctrine, — the doctrine of the creed, — the doctrine proposed, argued for, and accepted even a hundred years ago on that subject, — is not the doctrine of leading orthodox divines at the present day. Nothing but subtle tricks of language as to the meaning of words, nothing but evasions and special pleadings when insurmountable difficulties are encountered, will serve to vindicate an antiquated and exploded superstition on this subject. A Christian scholar knows very well what was understood when the creed defined the doctrine of inspiration by the words *plenary* and *infallibility*. Any competent theologian who tries now to assert the old, stringent claim conveyed by those words, must trifle with truth. The issue raised on this subject is very plain, even to the unlearned; it may all be expressed and set forth in a few words. Each of the Evangelists gives us a copy of the inscription over the cross of the Saviour. Matthew says it was "This is Jesus, the King of the Jews"; Mark, that it was "The King of the Jews"; Luke, that it was "This is the King of the Jews"; and John, that it was "Jesus of Nazareth, the King of the Jews." Now, what was the inscription? Suppose the design were to erect in the most splendid Christian temple a more imposing artistic representation of the crucifixion than was ever yet wrought, and that it was proposed to set the inscription on the cross in blazing diamonds. Which of these four versions — given in a plenarily inspired and *infallible* record — shall the artist follow? The very claim set up for the record suggests the perplexity. No one would be embarrassed by

* Essays and Reviews, p. 539.

it, except when it is aggravated by an assertion which is utterly irreconcilable with it. The inscription could not have been written in all the four ways in which it stands in the Four Gospels. Three of them at least, then, are not *infallible*, unless a trick is played with the meaning of that word. Nor shall we find help in the suggestion that the variations may arise from different ways of putting into English the original words given by the Evangelists. The Greek text presents these variations. Let the same process be tried with the four narratives of the Saviour's resurrection, or with the three accounts given in the Book of Acts of the conversion of St. Paul. Let the structure and contents of the whole Bible be studied in the light of our best wisdom, and let the phenomena which they present be confronted with the fair and honest signification of the terms *infallibility* and *plenary inspiration.* The result must be, either that the meaning of those words must be tampered with, or that they must no longer be used to define a dogma about the Bible as a whole. Honest, candid, and inquisitive Christian scholars and readers of all denominations are confronting this fact. Dr. Hodge may tell us that "the great body of believers" still hold to this or that. The assertion is of very little consequence, whether it be admitted or denied. We have serious facts to deal with. We are asking what the great body of believers of the next generation will have to hold by in this matter. We are asking how those who, as orthodox men, profess to hold the old doctrine of the creed on this point, are to reconcile it, not merely with their speculations, but with the contents of the Bible? It is but poor and miserable dogmatism, heartless and cruel contempt, which would invoke the *odium theologicum* to the aid of a discomfited and discredited superstition against men who are laboring in the utmost sincerity of soul to find a more truthful expression for their faith. The strictures to which we have referred in that remarkable article in the North British Review are a fair exhibition of the incompetency of Dr. Chalmers's views on the subject to meet the facts and phenomena that are to be taken into account. The New Theology has subverted the old theory of the *inspired infallibility* of all the contents of Scripture. We do not believe that it will rest content with quibbling with the two words, but will labor to define and vindicate a new and defensible statement of such a truth as to the authority and value of the Bible as will make it not one whit less precious to us all. For the simple fact is, that the doctrinal formula and the popular belief on this point are cast in a form which does not fit the manifest evidence of the very contents of the Bible. The abatement already allowed in the old doctrine, and hardly contested by any one whose arguments have weight, amounts to this: it distinguishes between the inspiration of the *sentiments* contained in the Bible, and the inspiration of the *writers* who were prompted by God to put those sentiments on record. Thus our New Theology men affirm that there are objectionable and positively false sentiments and statements advanced in the Bible; as, for instance, in the Books of Job and Ecclesiastes; and these cannot in any sense be said to be inspired of God. But still they were none the less *written* by inspiration of God, as God induced and qualified the scribes to put them down as entering into the method of a divine oversight over human errors and follies. There have been some very able statements of this distinction by orthodox men. It is easy to apply it in some cases, but when we come to test it in reference to alleged errors and discrepancies in the writings of inspired men about things within their own knowledge, the distinction is found to labor.

We see that high praise is lavished in some quarters upon the new work on this profoundly serious subject by Mr. Lee.* We think the book will most grievously disappoint those who turn to it for wise instruction and efficient relief. The author seems to understand and appreciate the difficulty and the urgency of his work, for he says: "With reference to the *nature* of inspiration itself, and to the possibility of reconciling the unquestionable stamp of humanity impressed upon every page of the Bible with that undoubting belief in its perfection and infallibility which is the Christian's most precious inheritance, it may safely be maintained that in English theology almost nothing has been done; and that no effort has hitherto been made to grapple directly with the difficulties of the subject." † He intimates his own especial method of argument in the following sentence: "There is one principle which forms a chief element of the theory proposed in the following Discourses, — I mean the distinction between Revelation and Inspiration, — that has never, to my knowledge, been consistently applied to the contents of Holy Scripture, even by those writers who insist upon its importance." ‡ When approaching the close of his work, the author says: "Thus far I have endeavored to lay down principles from which the divine authority, the infallible certainty, and the entire truthfulness, of every part of the Scriptures must necessarily result. To this conclusion many exceptions have been taken; and with some general observations on the nature and foundation of such exceptions, these Discourses shall fitly terminate." § Our readers would care but little to know how an author who could affirm the above inferences from his principles, would meet the facts and explain the phenomena that are utterly inconsistent with them.

* The Inspiration of Holy Scripture, its Nature and Proof. By William Lee, M. A., Fellow and Tutor of Trinity College. New York: Carter and Brothers. 1857.

† Preface. ‡ Ibid. § Page 342.

His work is weakest where it ought to be strongest. He evades what he leads us to suppose he is about to reconcile and explain. He tries to withstand the allowance indorsed by Mr. Alford, another University man, that the Apostles, in quoting the Greek version of the Old Testament from memory, have fallen into mistakes, and affirms that, if this were capable of proof, it would be "obviously fatal to that view of the inspiration of Scripture which I have endeavored to maintain, according to which each and every portion of the Bible is perfect and divine." * He seems to censure Professor Stuart for "having enumerated, *without annexing any refutation*, most of the strong points which De Wette and others conceive that they have established against the Books of Chronicles." † We have no doubt it would have greatly rejoiced the excellent Professor to have *annexed such refutations*, if he had only known where to find them. So much for the matter of Inspiration. The issue raised there is no longer one between the Unitarians and the Orthodox. The New Theology is at work upon it.

The aim of the New Theology in its dealings with the organic doctrines of Orthodoxy is one which we are to infer from a great many intimations of it from a great many different sources. Religion, as it is presented to our minds through the education by which we have received our knowledge of it, comes to us as a homogeneous whole, combining divine and human elements. Our first efforts in theology suggest to us the necessity of distinguishing between these human and divine elements as regards the sources of our knowledge and the substance and authority of the truths supposed to be received through each of them. And then comes up the question, How far off, how deep down, must we begin in attempting to draw this distinction? How radical must the process be? The old

* Page 304.

† Page 393, note.

school men are right in affirming that theological soil does not admit of mere top-dressing to any good purpose, and that its crops cannot be changed by sprinkling seed on the surface. The wisest and most candid inquirer, the least prejudiced and most unbiased student in theology, can never succeed in relieving himself wholly of the constraining influence on his own mind of the system under which he has been trained, and from which he starts when he begins his investigations. He has fixed for himself the meanings of important words. He has formed his associations of sympathy, his prejudices of sentiment, and in large measure his standard of judgment. His present views or prepossessions, his inclinations, and his range of speculation, have been determined by circumstances. He naturally takes his traditional or habitual method for deciding between truth and error as the standard by which his further inquiries are to be regulated. He asks himself whether he is to believe more or less than *what he now believes*. The mould already formed in his own mind gives shape to the new materials which he receives into it. Every workman must find some of the conditions of his work in his materials, and whatever novelties of pattern he may propose will be judged to be improvements or defects according as they are compared with some present pattern. Every theological inquirer starts with a creed, which, up to the date of his first attempt to subject it to a thorough inquisition, has passed with him for a standard and symbol of truth. He soon finds a fruitful, almost an exhaustless and endless task, in settling the meaning of theological terms, in coming to an understanding with others about their use of those terms, in asking whether all who employ them connect the same sense with them. The range within which we may accord in our opinions with others, and yet contend and quarrel hopelessly in our attempts to express our views in common formulas, is a problem which requires vast wisdom and unbounded charity for its solution. Nor are the perplexities which arise from this source relieved by our agreeing to use Scripture terms in our theological discussions. All the terms used in these discussions become technical. They are generally chosen from other languages than our own, and are perplexed with etymological niceties of definition, or they are used in a sense different from that which associates them with common, earthly things. These technical theological terms are adopted as if more expressive or comprehensive in their signification than any which our household speech affords; but certainly one prevailing reason with theologians for keeping them in use is, that they are often so vague and indefinite, and so burdened with double meanings, like old oracles, as to allow those who employ them a considerable range of liberty, and to excuse them from being too explicit. If we take any one of the contested problems in doctrinal or speculative theology, we find it to be involved with terms each of which asks for a re-definition, or a rectification of its popular or scholarly interpretation, before any new writer can profitably use it in discussion. He must at any rate tell us in what sense, and with what limitations, he intends to use each of these test words. Thus, in discussing the question of the freedom of the will, the venturesome speculator must define anew, or choose out of many accepted definitions that in which he intends to use, such words as these, *Ability*, *Motive*, *Freedom*, *Necessity*, *Contingency*, *Will*, &c. He can make no progress till he has done this, and in doing it he has unbounded opportunities for bewitching the simple truth, for confusing himself and mystifying his readers. He may find, after all, that he has but been traversing the same old weary cycle of human thought symbolized to us in the motion of the serpent as it curls on till its two extremities, its beginning and its end, meet together and complete the circle. Our dictionaries grow larger with every revision of them, and while our language is adopting new words, it is also doubling the significations of some of its very oldest words. Professor Whewell opens this whole issue, when he distinguishes between the language of science and the language of Scripture in reference to the needful changes to be recognized by the progress of thought. He says: "Science is constantly teaching us to describe known facts in new language; but the language of Scripture is always the same." * But we have to change our scientific language because we get a better knowledge of scientific facts. As we cannot change the language of Scripture, we have to allow for changes that creep into the meaning of words, and for the associations that may erroneously attach to them; and so, while studying the truths of Scripture, we have to show the variance of our philosophy of them by casting them into new formulas. Then, too, our theology, or our philosophy of religion, must respect the facts and the form of revelation in spite of its perplexities and its seeming anomalies; precisely as our natural philosophy has to respect the mysterious and inexplicable phenomena of nature. Taking all these things into view, we may well understand how complicated is the task of the theologian in attempting to fathom and systematize the profound themes of his study. His attempt resembles, in one respect at least, that of the experimenter who is seeking to sound the ocean depths, and finds that the necessary weight of the plummet and the length of his line become embarrassing to him, and may leave him in doubt whether he has reached bottom.

We find, then, that the aim of the New Theology

---

* History of Inductive Sciences, Vol. I. p. 686.

admits to itself an earnest and determined spirit in the pursuit of such speculative ends as the following, — even at the risk of doing something more than speculate, if it be found necessary to do more. It seeks to reconstruct the formulas for the statement of fundamental doctrines, and to rectify their phraseology. It seeks to secure a more philosophical expression of the truths which these formulas are intended to convey, without any essential variation from the accepted doctrines which are admitted to be announced by them. Again, the New Theology wishes to modify in some cases the philosophy of doctrine, by softening some aspects of some of its dogmas which have been exaggerated in their exhibition, and by reconciling some of its inconsistencies, with a view to a more harmonious system. If all this can be done and leave the solemn old sanctities of the creed to an unimpaired reverence and an undiminished faith, the new form shall be offered as but a better way for setting forth the old substance. But if these speculative processes are found to involve substantial changes of doctrine, what then? Dr. Hodge says, and he writes like a most earnest and perfectly competent witness, that the New Theology cannot even argue for, much less reach, its intended alterations in the philosophy of doctrine, without trifling with and perilling its substance. The doctrines of the Trinity, the Incarnation, and the Atonement ask of the New Theology at least a reconstruction of the formulas for expressing their orthodox teaching. The objection to the use of the word *Persons* in stating the doctrine of the Trinity has been well-nigh universally admitted by our best theologians, for the double reason that the formula does not convey the real idea which they wish to express, and that it does assert something which they do not wish to affirm. Dr. Bushnell has gone beyond any writer, still holding to the repute of Orthodoxy, in challenging not only the language of the formulas, but the contents of them, in reference to the three doctrines just specified. Dr. Hodge says: "He rejects the old doctrine of the Trinity and Incarnation; but he has produced no other intelligible doctrine. He has not thought himself through. He is only half out of the shell. And therefore his attempt to soar is premature." * The difficulty which most Unitarians have found with Dr. Bushnell is,—if we may use the not very elegant similes of the Princeton Professor,—that he is carrying about with him some fragments of his broken shell, and even with that encumbrance soars too high for them. "He rejects the doctrine of three persons in one God," says Dr. Hodge, and "in opposition to such a Trinity he presents and urges the doctrine of an historical Trinity, a threefold revelation of God,—a trinity of revelations." Still, Dr. Bushnell is evidently striving after and intending to hold *the truth*, the Scripture truth, which the makers of the creed endeavored to convey in the formula. We may put in the same claim. Let us understand what Scripture *truth* is conveyed in it, and we too will accept it.

Dr. Hodge says much the same of the "half-ism" of Orthodoxy to which Dr. Bushnell clings in his view of the Incarnation,—as God appearing under the limitations of humanity, without admitting a distinct human soul in Christ, or assigning to him a twofold nature. More positive still is the Princeton Professor in condemning Dr. Bushnell's "Altar view" of the Atonement, "which regards it as designed to produce a subjective effect, to impress men with a sense of God's love," † &c.

But the New Theology does not confine its venturesome speculations to these three doctrines. It grapples not only with the orthodox formulas of the nature, corruption, and destiny of man, but it assails with something

* Essays and Reviews, p. 434. † Ibid., p. 436.

more than metaphysical strength, — yes, even with the logic of common sense, — the doctrines which are adequately expressed in those formulas. Here the aim is to find, if possible, a theory of Free Agency which can be reconciled with the doctrines of original sin and efficacious grace. Edwards's work is built upon a union of the philosophical theory of necessity with the theological doctrine of predestination. The new school of our times, the *novissima*, insists upon regarding the freedom of the will as an axiom, a first truth, whose evidence goes with the statement of it. Is man an *agent*, or an *instrument*, is the question? The new school will have it, that the old school believes in physical depravity and physical regeneration, and that it antedates consciousness by responsibility, and makes us accountable before we are intelligent. The issue is not, as Dr. Hodge insists, with reiteration of phrase, that the new theology denies God's sovereignty in every gracious work; the attempt is made to lift that sovereignty, and to extend its range and workings, beyond the compression of metaphysical definitions. Professor Hodge reflects on the late Professor Stuart for having expressed himself as being shocked by the old school doctrine, "that all men are subject to death, i. e. penal evil, on account of the sin of Adam." The Princeton Professor adds, that he and his brethren believe, "that the grace which is in Christ Jesus secures the salvation of all who have no personal sins to answer for." * But how will this accord with the three following assertions from the same pen, — that "the mere absence of a native tendency to God leaves the soul in moral confusion and ruin"; † and that the withholding by God of those divine communications which Adam enjoyed, but of which God deprives us because of his sin, "is a penal evil, from which, it is true,

* Essays, &c., p. 71. † Ibid., p. 43.

utter ruin results, but it is the ruin, not of innocent, but of fallen human beings"; * and with another statement which Dr. Hodge advances as his doctrine, — that "the sin of Adam is so put to the account of his posterity that they are condemned on account of it, antecedent to any action of their own"? † Here is metaphysical theology with a vengeance, and we repeat our former remark, that no man would venture to offer to us such theology, if he did not rely on the unbounded capacities of metaphysics for mystifying simple truth. Professor Park says, that "it is more difficult to reconcile the New England divinity and the old Calvinism on these subjects than on any other." ‡ Professor Stuart, as Dr. Hodge asserts, tried hard to evade the plain meaning of his own formulas on these points. If we pronounced a judgment in the case, we should assume the office of umpire between two professed advocates of Orthodoxy, an office not excluded from the scope of our charity, but not inviting to our logical skill.

The actual loss incurred by all the millions of the human family through the sin of their progenitor, the actual resources still left in human nature for meeting the demands of God's law, and the mode of adjusting the obligation under which we lie to the impaired ability with which we are born, — these are problems on which, with the help of metaphysics, endless discussions may be kept up between the Old and the New Schools. Professor Park tried the whole resources of his amazingly acute and skilful mind upon these and other problems. He tells us that we may use, in addressing the heart, language and modes of expression which may be true to the heart though false to the mind. We may excite emotions by appeals and statements which the intellect will afterwards dispute and qualify. In a

* Essays, &c., p. 44.

† Ibid., p. 83.

‡ Ibid., p. 630.

word, we may have one theology for the feelings, in their ardent, illogical, earnest workings, and another for the intellect, in its cool, deliberate processes of thought and reasoning. We trust all our readers have perused that Convention Discourse of the Andover Professor to which we have more than once referred. We regard it on the score of what it boldly affirms, and of what it so significantly implies, when taken in connection with its wonderful beauty of style and its marvellous subtilty of analysis, as the most noteworthy contribution which Orthodoxy has made to the literature of New England for the last half-century. That single discourse would win fame for any preacher. It has evidently exercised Dr. Hodge beyond any heretical dose which the new-fangled system has ever administered to him. And the Princeton divine has shown almost equal acuteness in meeting the propositions of the Discourse. He tells us, without any anxiety for seeking soft words, that Professor Park has published "an attack on doctrines long held sacred"; that "he has obviously adopted his theory as a convenient way of getting rid of certain doctrines which stand out far too prominently in Scripture, and are too deeply impressed on the hearts of God's people to allow of their being denied"; and that the aim of the Discourse is "to show how the same proposition may be both affirmed and denied." * It so happens, too, that the doctrines to which Professor Park applies his ingenious method of reasoning are the very doctrines which constitute the life of Orthodoxy. The creed, he says, states these doctrines in a way suited to make them effective in addressing the heart, but the mind can by no means receive them when it analyzes them logically. The old doctrine of our utter ruin, inability, and state of doom is reduced by Dr. Park's

* Essays, &c., pp. 542–544.

intellect to the following logical statement, — "that the character of our race needs an essential transformation by an interposed influence of God." On this nice piece of tamed Calvinism, "cold and deadening" enough to have come from "the most chilling of Unitarian pulpits," Dr. Hodge remarks: "Certainly a very genteel way of expressing the matter, which need offend no one, Jew or Gentile, Augustin or Pelagius. All may say that much, and make it mean more or less at pleasure. If such is the sublimation to which the theology of the intellect is to subject the doctrines of the Bible, they will soon be dissipated into thin air."* The difficulty is, as Dr. Hodge shows, that Professor Park commits to the theology of the feelings, as rhetorical or impassioned statements uttered for effect, the carefully worded intellectual propositions which have been selected for catechisms and creeds as gathering up the substance of the manifold and diversified representations of Scripture. The theory, though seemingly so specious and fair, is pronounced to be radically false, vitiated by a flaw in its premises. It starts from the assumption, than which no assertion can be more diametrically opposed to the truth, that strong feeling is engaged by and expresses itself in metaphorical language; whereas strong feeling uses and demands simple, direct, naked, literal utterance. Thus, says Dr. Hodge, Professor Park adduces the sentence, "God, the Mighty Maker, died!" as one which excited and engaged Christian feeling may utter, but against which the intellect protests; but the truth is precisely the other way. Does not feeling recoil shocked on hearing the sentence, while the intellect by the forced ingenuities of doctrinal constructiveness tries to ratify its assertion? So the Princeton divine affirms that the only grain of truth wrought up in

* Essays, &c., p. 551.

the theory of his brother of Andover is, that the Scripture makes use of metaphorical language, — a fact that was recognized before Dr. Park wrote. The latter divine tells us that "the theology of the heart, letting the minor accuracies go for the sake of holding strongly upon the substance of doctrine, need not always accommodate itself to scientific changes, but may often use *its old statements, even if, when literally understood, they be incorrect*, and it thus abides permanent as are the main impressions of the truth." This, Dr. Hodge says, "is a rather dangerous principle." *

Nor is this all. Dr. Hodge will not allow that these tricks with language are consistent with a real, honest faith in the doctrines announced in the old formulas. And here we come to the only point which has much interest for us in this discussion. Can these earnest and able divines, who stand with us as the prime movers in the yet undeveloped scheme of the New Theology, be regarded as actually holding the substance of the old doctrines? Certainly not, we answer, as we should feel bound to hold them if we professed to receive the formulas under any sense which the fair construction of language will admit. So, too, answers Dr. Hodge. In criticising Dr. Bushnell, he says, "It is very difficult to understand what a writer means who employs a new terminology." † It is difficult. But we are apt to understand or infer one thing, and that is, that such a writer does not believe what is expressed in the old terminology. Dr. Hodge very bluntly affirms that Professor Park's theory "enables a man to profess his faith in doctrines which he does not believe." ‡ Equally grave is the following judgment: "There is a large class of words to which Professor Park attaches a meaning different from that in which they are used by

* Essays, &c., p. 546. † Ibid., p. 325. ‡ Ibid., p. 543.

theologians of the Reformed Church, and he therefore unavoidably misunderstands and misrepresents their doctrines." * And, not to leave anything to be surmised, he adds, once more: "His articles [in reply to Dr. Hodge] are to a great degree characterized by evasions and playing with words." † Yet Princeton must be careful of its consistency, for when its divines are writing with different aims in view, they are apt to utter statements which even metaphysics cannot reconcile. Thus Dr. Hodge says: "The two sentiments of complete helplessness, and of entire blameworthiness, are perfectly consistent, and are ever united in Christian experience"; ‡ and also: "It is one of the most familiar facts of consciousness that a sense of obligation is perfectly consistent with a conviction of entire inability." § But in the Princeton Essay "On the Decrees of God," we read: "Every man of sense feels that he cannot justly be accountable for what he could not possibly avoid." Now the being born in a state of complete spiritual helplessness and of entire inability seems so much like being in a condition which we "could not possibly avoid," that we are at a loss to see how any one can feel that he is entirely blameworthy, and yet not justly accountable for it. But on the question whether "the substance of doctrine" is touched in the honorably waged contest between the Princeton and the Andover Professors, we will allow the former, who unmistakably holds the old theology, and knows what it is, to decide. He says: "To say that the sin of Adam is imputed to his posterity [the Princeton creed] is to express a different thought, a different doctrine, from what is expressed by saying [with Professor Park] that his sin was merely the occasion of certain evils coming upon his race. The one of these statements is not

* Essays, &c., p. 617.
† Ibid., p. 625.
‡ Ibid., p. 36.
§ Ibid., p. 252.

merely an intense, figurative, or poetic expression of the thought conveyed by the latter. The former means that the sin of Adam was the judicial ground of the condemnation of his race, and therefore that the evils inflicted on them on account of that sin are of the nature of punishment. . . . . There is here a real distinction. These two modes of representing our relation to Adam belong to two different doctrinal systems. According to the one, no man is condemned until he has personally transgressed the law. Every man stands a probation for himself, either in the womb, as some say, or in the first dawn of intelligence and moral feeling. According to the other, the race had their probation in Adam; they sinned in him, and fell with him in his first transgression. They are, therefore, born the children of wrath; they come into existence under condemnation. It is now asserted, for the first time, so far as we know, since the world began, that these modes of representation mean the same thing." *

Such are some of the developments of the New Theology. We believe that its latent forces and workings reach deep into the minds of many of the most devout believers and the most efficient Christian laborers in the Church of Christendom. Our friends of the old school warn us against supposing that the restlessness of a few speculative minds, here and there, indicates any failure in the power and hold of the orthodox creed as the generally accepted faith of that Christendom. We ask the liberty of being allowed to form our opinion on that point for ourselves. It certainly is a significant fact, that the very class of men, the more thorough scholars, the calmer, profounder, and more earnest and independent thinkers, who were once the builders up of Orthodoxy, — the constructers of its formulas, — should now be found, in all

---

* Essays, &c., pp. 592, 593.

sections of the Church, engaged upon invalidating the doctrinal views which those formulas have imparted to the people at large. Such influences as are unmistakably working in our higher religious literature will sooner or later become popular, will work downwards. It may then be, that something will be offered to us as Orthodoxy which we shall pronounce to be better far than Unitarianism, — something which we can receive with the same sympathy of soul and cordiality of heart with which we read the writings of those who are constructing the New Theology from the ruins of the old.

The way in which free and venturesome speculations in religious philosophy are received in the communions in which they originate, offers much that instructs, and a great deal that mortifies, a lover of the truth. There are of course canons of good sense and rules of caution to be recognized here; and as far as they will justify a reasonable conservatism of what is established, and a dislike of all that is unsettling and distracting, they may properly be brought to bear against some who love to open all manner of unprofitable questions. There are good reasons why all who believe in any system of religious truth may wish to be left in peace to enjoy its comforts, and to work out its conditions of duty. Especially in any brotherhood knit together by the sympathies and interests which unite a fellowship of Christians, large or small, will dissensions always be grievous. Each member is held bound to keep himself within the recognized formulas and methods of his communion. Any one who opens dividing issues, and pushes his own freedom beyond the limits recognized for liberty, and introduces seditious or revolutionary speculations, will always provoke a more exciting strife than if he assailed his brethren from without. There are eccentric, morbid, and ambitious promptings, which lead the subjects of them to raise schisms in their own fellowships. Occasionally those who would never have attracted attention or won notoriety by a quiet fidelity to duty within the rounds of professional labor, will blaze out into public fame by adopting a heresy or by stirring a strife. There are always, in a large community, enough persons of unsettled mind, or of a restless temperament, and an easy sensibility, to welcome the radicalisms of opinion. Generally, the more startling or defiant the utterance, the greater the throng, and the more keen the interest, which, till the novelty is worn away, will receive it. It is, however, in general, a very easy exercise of common sense in discerning minds to decide whether one who seeks to unsettle an established belief is influenced by a pure love of truth or by a personal impulse, a restless disquiet or a desire of notoriety. He whom the love of truth makes a heretic is modest, gentle, prudent, slow, and considerate. The reckless speculator is rash, contemptuous, and dogmatical. It may be well, therefore, that each fellowship of believers should be naturally jealous of the rise of any heretical speculations within its own communion, when the very fundamentals of its distinctive system are put in jeopardy. It is not all theological hate that is called out and enlisted against free speculations under such circumstances. While some love freedom, others love peace. Those who are supposed to be united in allegiance to a creed, feel as if they were consolidated into a structure; their old traditions, and their venerated authorities among the departed, lying deeply buried for foundations, while all the living members are built by joint and rule into the solid walls. An heretical member makes the whole structure topple. It is dangerous to open a new window through such an old edifice, even if it be only to get more of heaven's own light and air. There is something, too, that strongly resembles presumption, as the disciples of a fossilized creed view the matter, in the attempt of any speculating mind to recast the philosophic or doctrinal formulas of a faith which have stood in honor for long ages.

Allowing all that is reasonable in the protests and the opposition with which the New Theology is received in the communions among whose more advanced members it originates, we have what is unreasonable in such opposition still left to be defined and accounted for. Were the work to our taste, we could open here a rich budget of tempting cases with which to illustrate the matter before us. But our readers know very well how all orthodox communions receive and dispose of the heresies that always have risen up among them. True, these manifest themselves in our day in so many ways, and win so much immunity from the character, position, and influence of those who advance them, that the old inquisitorial processes are somewhat relaxed. It is our firm conviction that much real dissent and free speculation is now held in prudent reserve, enjoyed and indulged secretly, but not divulged. We believe that there is relatively a vast deal more latent heresy in orthodox communions, yes, even among the professors of theological schools, than has ever existed before. We infer this partly from the tokens which manifest themselves, and partly as a natural consequence of the way in which all candid utterances of bolder minds are treated. Orthodoxy visits some of its most bitter censures upon those within its communion who have practised concealment about their lapse from its creed, and who occasionally are entrapped or compelled unwillingly to confess the extent of their heresies. Does Orthodoxy suppose that it hunts out one in each score of these quiet and silent heretics who outwardly conform to its discipline? But then comes up the question, Is this silent dissent, this smothered rebellion, honest? Doubtless the subjects of it are perfectly easy in conscience under their secret burdens. They know the price to their own peace at which they would have to make avowals. They are consistent Protestants to the extent of believing themselves free of all human responsibility in their creeds. They too have distinguished between religion and the philosophy of religion, and have a way of satisfying themselves that they may still hold the substance of a creed though they may object to all the terms by which it is expressed. Finally, these secret heretics among the orthodox consult the edifying and practical interests of religion. They know that schisms and feuds and minor controversies among brethren are ruinous to the temper of those who engage in them, are occasions of scandal, contempt, and unbelief to the world at large, and are so much waste of the resources of true piety. The way in which Orthodoxy treats avowals of free and dissentient opinion in its communion, is a bounty on concealment.

But how preposterous is the attempt made by Orthodoxy to reconcile its demand for an unswerving allegiance to its dogmatical theology with a fair and zealous use of all the new means for the attainment of truth. Take, for instance, the blind and obstinate resistance now made in Great Britain by all orthodox sects, with the exception of a very few of the most intelligent and candid in each, to the proposed revision of our common version of the Scriptures. No one advocates a new translation, an entire substitution of another English version of the Bible. All the acknowledged beauties and excellences of the present version are to be retained. All the fond associations connected with phrase and figure and text are to be respected, except where they are manifestly wrong and misleading. Neither the Saxon vigor, nor the antique quaintness, nor the homely directness, nor the pointed boldness, of the received version is to be sacrificed. The aim is only for a revision, for the sake of amending undoubted errors, removing obsolete words, and letting in light wherever there is unintelligible obscurity. Nor is it proposed to have this revision made under any favored sectarian auspices, to turn it into a job or a scheme for speculators or partisans, or to the service of any cause save the highest and holiest, — the edification of all persons of all classes. The advocates of the measure, being found chiefly in the liberal and progressive party, have the countenance of some wise and good men in all parties. They are all willing that the Established Church, the prelates, the Universities, should have the direction of the work, under a commission from the Parliament or the Queen. Now let any one read the religious journals of the different orthodox sects, which abound in more or less extended references to the project, and which are prevailingly and most doggedly hostile to the measure. Scan their allegations, their arguments, their reasons. Weigh their objections, mark their appeals to prejudice, their evasion of unwelcome facts, their doubtful and false assertions. If the intent of their pleadings, and the subject on which they are spent, did not claim for their writers the tolerance of a respectful regard, simply because a religious feeling, however mistaken, is involved in their opposition, one might be pardoned for using the severest language about them. But compare their opposition to this measure, and the grounds of their opposition, with their professions as Protestants. They call the Bible the Word of God, and claim liberty for all to read it and interpret it in the fear of God, assured of finding in it the way of salvation. They know that, owing to the fallibility and the imperfect means at the disposal of those who translated the Bible from the original tongues, it is not always truly rendered. They know that a large number of new manuscripts are now available for the purpose of securing a more exact text; that the Oriental languages have been cultivated by modern scholars to the very best ends; that the laws of language, the principles of criticism, the manners and customs and history of ancient times, have been so faithfully studied, that the results gained from them must be eminently serviceable in the proposed measure. Orthodoxy in its own way favors all these helps to the understanding of the Bible, establishes theological schools, founds professorships, furnishes libraries, and would emphatically maintain that all these means ought to be of some service, and that an improvement of them must enter into the conditions of Christian responsibility for those who enjoy them. But, marvellous is the inconsistency! Orthodoxy most resolutely withstands the palpable and inevitable consequences of its own principles and methods. The noblest result to which all these appliances of Scriptural knowledge could culminate, would be a more exact version of the Scriptures. But no. The Bible shall not be touched. Its inspiration must not be perilled. The door must not be opened, for it will never afterwards be shut. The Spirit shall pour no more light upon the Word. The detected, exposed, and convicted error, the interpolated corruption, the spurious text, shall not be rectified or expelled. The Word of God shall stand impaired and vitiated, not only by mistakes which man has unwittingly introduced into it, but by marked and evident corruptions, which he knows very well how to purify. Such is the opposition of Orthodoxy to an amendment of the version of the Scriptures in the language of the dominant race and people of Christendom, — a version, too, which has transferred its errors into the versions in all the heathen tongues into which the Bible Society or missionaries have translated it.

What hope, then, can there be for "New Theology," while so stout and blind a resistance is offered to an attempt to relieve the Bible from such errors as man's ignorance once introduced into it, though his own added knowledge is so well qualified to remove them? The hope would indeed seem faint, if our reliance was on anything less potent than the undecaying, resistless energy of truth. There is much indeed to dishearten the champions of that truth. Let any one interested in studying the issue now so intensely working, as far as it has dared to manifest itself, in the orthodox communions of Great Britain, take some pains to inform himself on the subject by reading the volumes which are issued as rapidly as will allow of a perusal. Let him take, for instance, that work of daring impudence and ignorance,—"Bible Revision and Translation: an Argument for holding fast what we have," by Dr. Cumming,—whose popularity as a millenarian preacher in London and whose fecundity in issuing worthless religious books are phenomena of equally astounding character. Of this work the Rev. Dr. Burgess, the liberal and learned editor of one of the best orthodox periodicals of Great Britain,—"The Journal of Sacred Literature,"—says: "If our readers wish to see how far sheer impudence can carry a man in the field of ignorant assertion, let them read Dr. Cumming's book. We scarcely dare write what we think of this production; but we will bring forward two out of the many literary and historical falsehoods which it contains."*

Or take another instance. In the pages of the same valuable and scholarly journal from which we have just quoted, Dr. Tregelles publishes a most disgraceful attack, in the form of a letter, upon his colleague, Dr. Davidson, in the task of re-editing Horne's Introduction to the Scriptures. Our opinion of Dr. Tregelles's scholarship is so high, that the utmost stretch of our charity will not acquit him of insincerity and duplicity in that letter. He must *know* that Dr. Davidson's allowed qualifications and abatements of the popular notion of inspiration cannot be honestly challenged. The spirit of his letter is

* Number for January, 1857, p. 261.

acrimonious and bigoted. His attempt to prove that Wisdom, as personified in the eighth chapter of Proverbs, refers to Christ, is utterly unworthy of him. Dr. Burgess is to be commended for his manly, Christian candor in saying of this letter, to which he gives a place in his journal, that Dr. Tregelles "has but little sympathy with ourselves in the line of argument he has pursued. . . . . We cannot now enter on the subject further, but simply protest against Biblical science being thrown back three centuries by a sort of papal intolerance. The way in which the *Record* has treated Dr. Davidson, and is treating all who cannot indorse its ignorant and bigoted views, is *barbarous;* not only unworthy of a Christian, but disgraceful to a free country."* "The Record" here referred to is the title of a tri-weekly newspaper, published in London, as "a highly remunerative organ" of the Low Church, or *Evangelical* party in the Establishment, and so very acceptable to the corresponding party among the orthodox Dissenters. Some plain words about this notorious and scandalous paper may be found in another of those fresh and earnest volumes of which we have been speaking. Its title is, "Christian Orthodoxy reconciled with the Conclusions of Modern Biblical Learning: a Theological Essay, with Critical and Controversial Supplements." Its author is the Rev. Dr. John William Donaldson, late Fellow of Trinity College, Cambridge. He claims still to hold substantially the essential doctrines of his Church, but there is a bracing vigor of thought, an heroic and earnest sincerity of utterance, and an ability of scholarship, logic, and good sense brought to bear in his work upon the rotten elements of popular belief among Christians, which indicate the fullest development of that new spirit whose workings we have been attempting to trace. He is a master of his theme. Cant, superstition,

* Number for January, 1857, pp. 483, 484.

bigotry, and Jesuitical agencies in religion, receive from him an honest condemnation. He is measured and dignified in assailing views under which he was educated, but which he knows to be discredited by the science and intelligence of the age. As his work has but just appeared, we know nothing of the way in which it has been received; but that way will be stormy. He exposes most ably the pretensions and fallacies and utter inconclusiveness of the views set forth by Mr. Lee in the work on Inspiration to which we have already referred. He spares none of the shams by which timid theologians attempt to cover and evade their own weak points or the heavy blows of their assailants. But his especial wrath is visited upon "The Record," before named. "The malignity and falsehood," "the pitiable weakness," "the calumnious personalities," "the nefarious conduct," "the intolerance, folly, and slanderous violence" of "this wretched journal," are indeed hard terms to be used in describing a religious paper. But Dr. Donaldson offers most melancholy and overwhelming evidence that they are not inapplicable to a journal which meets every man and every opinion, not in sympathy with its own views, with cruel abuse, or ignorant misrepresentation, or spiteful bigotry.

Take one more striking testimony illustrative of the hateful spirit by which the results of independent and serious Christian study and thought are received. The Rev. Dr. Rowland Williams, of St. David's College, Lampeter, the author of that admirable volume of sermons entitled "Practical Godliness," is at present engaged upon a work on "Christianity and Hinduism." This profoundly interesting subject, which may task the scholarship and candor of the ablest mind of our age, with all the best helps of native talent and true culture, has been intrusted to Dr. Williams by the University of Cambridge. He is well aware that his process of treating his subject, the method of argument he will be compelled to adopt, the concessions he must yield, and the results he must accept and commend to others, will cause an intense shock to the prejudices of a blind and narrow orthodoxy. We find a letter from him to Dr. Burgess, in the journal we have just quoted, the object of which is to purify some of the vapors of the cloud which he apprehends with good reason will break in vengeance upon him. We wish that our space would allow us to transfer his letter to our pages. It would convey to our readers more forcibly than can any words of ours a conception of the pains and penalties under which the purest disciples of truth in conflict with popular error, prejudice, and superstition are compelled either to silence and heartless conformity, or made to suffer for their loyalty to a holy cause. One sentence from the letter must suffice. Dr. Williams says: "Experience has taught me that any Anglican divine who will write honestly as a scholar, in our day, does so with a halter about his neck."

But it must not be so. It is so only because the weakest and the most prejudiced yield to what is the most unworthy and unreasonable among the meaner motives that influence them. Such as these, however, profess that a zeal for truth instigates their opposition to all the free ventures and all the honest efforts of inquiring minds. Their cure is in their own hands. They must instruct their own ignorance and yield themselves up to the heart-work of the Gospel. It is not wise to try one's temper or to waste one's time upon these stiff and crabbed worshippers of the infallibility of their own prejudices. A good Providence has appointed that there shall be a change in human generations, and so that new truth shall have new fields in fresh minds. The things which are no longer susceptible to receiving impressions become fossils and get buried, while the glorious and beautiful processes of this still young earth are wrought upon its living germs as they yield to the divine chemistry. He is no true believer, no real disciple of Christ, who identifies the everlasting Gospel with the metaphysical or doctrinal system of any age, — least of all, of any past age. Why, indeed, should we attempt to resist the maturer workings of the human mind upon the dogmas which that mind fashioned in its earlier and less competent efforts? Why should we discredit the views and convictions of our manhood, because they are in conflict with the fancies of our childhood?

Certainly the human mind must ever be allowed to range freely over that wide field of speculative theology whose blank, unoccupied spaces it has itself fenced in and bounded and divided according to its own theories. Our systems, the best of them, are but human devices, and we must be free to assail and reconstruct them. Whatever man's thought has fabricated, however fixed and unalterable the materials which it has wrought upon, will be regarded by each generation of thinkers as something which they have a perfect right to take apart, with the purpose of working over the same materials again more wisely, more truthfully. No one can examine with care the most skilfully constructed system of theology, professedly deduced from the Bible, without being reminded that the system is exposed to fallibility in every stage of its development. The common ground of accordance and sympathy among Christians will in vain be sought for in allegiance to any speculative system. The bad passions which have been enlisted in controversy, the cumbersome heaps of almost worthless literature which have been accumulated in conducting it, and the steady increase of the points of difference which it has multiplied, prove that neither edification nor harmony is to be sought in that direction. And yet, in spite of all that has been said about the resistance of dogmatism and acrimony to every venture made by scholarly and scientific criticism, the spirit of theological discussions has been, of late years, infinitely softened and dignified. This result is the triumph of true Christian sentiment over the hearts of those who are seeking to interpret the mind of Christ. While the life which he manifested and the truth which he taught are admitted to be the best of all our materials for the construction of a system of theology, while the deepest and tenderest motive that incites the inquiries of the intellect is to come nearer to the spirit of his doctrine, we must feel that it is safer to allow than to restrain the liberty of speculative thought. We may or may not find a New Theology, but we shall be better disciples of Him whom we call our Master. That fellowship of Christians with whose doctrinal views our own assured convictions most nearly accord, have had enough of mere liberty. We are content now to forego any portion of it that may need to be renounced, for the sake of a better improvement of its glorious franchise. We therefore look with sincere and unprejudiced interest to the speculative and scholarly labors of the advanced minds in orthodox communions. The first-fruits of the as yet not fully developed or acknowledged modifications which they have already made of their system, are the production of many valuable works which are highly acceptable to Unitarian readers, and the affording of pulpit instruction in all our great cities which is wholly unobjectionable to large numbers of Unitarian hearers. May God's blessing be on their labors, to keep them loyal to Him, to Christ, and to the everlasting Gospel of grace and redemption. If the New Theology shall prove to be so much truer and better than "Unitarianism" as to obliterate the sect, whose visible increase it does withstand, we are ready to welcome it.

APPENDIX.

APPENDIX.

The pages which follow are designed to furnish illustrations or confirmations of the views already presented.

It has been repeatedly intimated in the preceding essays upon some very important themes of a long-continued controversy, that one prominent object of this new discussion of them is to prove how the results of the most advanced Christian scholarship and culture bear on the old issues. If competent and sincere inquirers after truth find, that, after debating their differences, they cannot harmonize them, they ought at least to gain a better mutual understanding of the points in controversy between them. The only desirable objects to be gained by a review and a re-statement, from time to time, of the doctrinal positions which are assumed by antagonistic sects in the Christian Church, are a more distinct apprehension of their differences, a more charitable adjustment of their relations, and a more earnest attempt to reconcile their strife. It would be no unfair condition for those whose liberality provides the resources of Christian scholarship in schools, libraries, and funded wealth, to exact of their favored beneficiaries that they should be bound to reduce these lavish means of intelligent culture to practical uses. The most practical of all these uses is the promotion of a spirit of respectful and fraternal regard between Christian scholars and teachers whose opinions set them at variance. If that spirit is secured, it will help more than will any attainments in scholarship or any skill in argument to insure accordance of belief in the essential truths which make the substance of religion.

As I have aimed in the preceding essays to trace down the discussion of the controverted topics to our own times, I have of course been interested to note how the present representatives of the Orthodox party received what I had intended should be said in candid and respectful terms of them. I am happy to find that I have been regarded by those who have remarked upon these papers as having kept within the limits of propriety, and as having respected my own rules for approving what is useful, and for condemning what is hateful, in controversial discussions.

A series of seven newspaper articles has appeared in the Puritan Recorder, a weekly paper published in Boston, as the organ of the conservative party among the Orthodox Congregationalists, in which I find some courteous and friendly, but still adverse, criticisms upon a portion of the contents of the first five of these Essays. They are dated between September 11 and October 23, 1856. These communications are without a name, but I am informed by good authority that they were written by a distinguished Professor in one of our New England Orthodox Theological Schools, whom I know as a personal friend, and esteem highly, as does the community in general. I have thought it might serve the interest of a sacred cause, which we both should put higher than any sectarian object, to quote here the substance of his criticisms, and to follow them with a few additional remarks. I must respect his anonymous personality, and speak of him as my critic.

I.

DATE OF THE UNITARIAN CONTROVERSY IN MASSACHUSETTS.

My critic opens his comments with terms of personal courtesy to myself as a friend, and with a generous recognition of my attempt to be perfectly candid in a task where candor is sorely tested. I must be content with an expression of my gratitude for all such acknowledgments from an anonymous writer; the proprieties of the case will not allow me to quote them.

The first point which he raises is a matter of date. He holds me strictly to the month and year, which would make the Unitarian controversy exactly a half-century old. Having quoted my opening sentence, he adds the following paragraphs: —

"We are at a loss to account for the time here specified (January, 1806) as the commencement of the Unitarian Controversy in Massachusetts. That there was Unitarianism here at a much earlier period, and that it occasioned more or less of controversy, Mr. Ellis knows full well; but then it was a controversy, like Indian warfare, with an invisible foe. The smart of the arrow was occasionally felt; but the hand that sent it was unseen. Unitarianism was closely concealed, and it was not till the spring of 1815 that it was drawn from its hiding-places, and 'the war was opened as on the tented field.'

"I am not aware that the controversy assumed any new phase or feature in 1806. There had been a sharp controversy in 1804, respecting the appointment of Dr. Ware to the Hollis Professorship of Divinity in Harvard College; but this could hardly be called a Unitarian controversy, since Dr. Ware had never yet declared himself a Unitarian. Nor could he be induced to declare himself, *pro* or *con*, at the time of his election. His 'particular principles, though often asked for, were not disclosed.' 'It was particularly asked, whether he was a believer in that important doctrine, the Divinity of the Lord Jesus Christ; but the reply conveyed no precise or satisfactory answer on that point.'"

To this criticism I answer, that it was the perusal of the very documents which he quotes, on the very matter to which he refers, — the appointment of Dr. Ware to the Hollis Professorship at Cambridge, — that suggested to me the date assigned to the controversy. The date itself is a matter of no importance; nothing that I have written on the subject is made to depend upon the exactness of a date in time. But to a reader of this generation it is obvious that the discussions in the Board of Overseers of Harvard College, and the pamphlets founded upon those discussions, did in fact draw out into direct controversy what had long before been a latent alienation between brethren on points of Christian doctrine. On that occasion Orthodoxy was for the first time openly withstood, in the same way in which it has since been withstood, by a positive refusal, on the part of so-called Liberal Christians, to regard its dogmas and formulas as authoritative exponents of Christian truth.

II.

DISAPPOINTMENT OR SUCCESS OF UNITARIANISM.

The next point made by the critic is more important. He quotes some of my *concessions*, beginning with that on page 6, where I admit that Unitarians have been disappointed in their expectation of a more rapid and extensive reception of their distinctive views. I am not disposed to take back my admission. Unitarianism, in its distinctive, dogmatic form, has not won the visible and triumphant success which its early friends believed, which some of the more sanguine of them predicted, would attend its maturer development. The amazing revelations which presented themselves of the deadness and incompetency of Orthodoxy; the protests uttered in many independent quarters against Calvinistic doctrines; the feeling of inexpressible relief which a more liberal and Scriptural faith afforded to thousands of devout and earnest minds and hearts; and the distinguished position and abilities of those who declared themselves as disciples of the "new views," naturally encouraged the hope that such auspices were propitious of a signal success, in the way in which men generally define success. Success of the kind expected has not been realized, and so far I admitted disappointment. My critic had not space to quote and answer what I wrote concerning a real success and influence, as attained by Unitarianism. Orthodoxy has renewed its zeal. But it has never regained, and it never will regain, its relative strength in this Commonwealth at the time when the old Congregational body was ruptured. With the increase of the population, there has been a multiplication and a subdivision of sects. The old New England spirit of faith and piety works through other than Calvinistic manifestations. Popular influences helped by foreign influences, a perfect freedom in speculation, an extensive prevalence of scepticism, and a zeal for practical reforms and revolutions which has been kindled outside of the Orthodox Church, have brought about changes to which Orthodoxy has been forced to accommodate itself, as utterly helpless to restrain them, and with but moderate power to guide them. In the mean while a conviction, which it would be very difficult, if not impossible, to root out of the minds of well-informed Unitarians, assures them that, through good literature, social influences, and religious teaching, their substantial views have had an unspeakable effect upon the communities where they have been brought into antagonism with old-fashioned Orthodoxy.

My critic shall speak at length in answer to what I have said about the disappointment realized by his own party in their expectations when the controversy opened.

"Mr. Ellis is good authority as to the early expectations and consequent disappointment of the Unitarians. With regard to the Orthodox, he does not seem to be so well informed. 'The Orthodox, on their part, expected that they should succeed in putting down and utterly extirpating Unitarianism, by identifying it with infidelity, and by discrediting all its show of argument from Scripture and Christian history, if not from reason.' (p. 7.) With regard to the expectations here imputed to us, I am sure that they are considerably exaggerated. They are too strongly expressed. We expected no great and startling changes; no general and sudden conversions. We did not expect to 'put down and utterly extirpate Unitarianism.' In all honesty, I affirm, so far as concerns myself, (and I think the same is true of my brethren,) that our expectations thirty years ago were not very different from the results now actually realized. Believing that we had reason and religion on our side, we did expect that the truth would prevail; that our churches would be increased and strengthened. And so they have been. We did also expect, when the din and the smoke of controversy had measurably passed away, that a portion of the Unitarian community would begin to see the truth, and to acknowledge it; would begin to feel and to work their way upward into the region of Evangelical religion. And in this we have not been disappointed, — I trust we have not. We certainly find some reputed Unitarians preaching and writing, on some of the great truths of the Bible, in a strain very different from that which formerly prevailed, — in language not very unlike that of their Orthodox brethren. At the same time, knowing, as we did, the force of prejudice and habit, even upon sincere and honest minds, we thought it likely that another portion of the Unitarian community would maintain their position, as we think they do, with little change, unless it be in the use of terms."

My reply to these fairly expressed suggestions must be brief, and must take for granted some degree of information in my readers as to their subject-matter. Any one who will undertake the hard task of reading the old controversial pamphlets on the Orthodox side will find them to abound in the most scorching denunciations of Unitarians as infidels, and of Unitarianism as bald, malignant, and wicked infidelity, and with the most confident predictions that a very short time would prove these hateful charges, and result in the utter discomfiture of the system. A smile, oftener than a frown, will be excited now by the reading of these spiteful diatribes. Yet they were read in the time of them by some of the most devout and intelligent Christian men and women that have ever adorned our pulpits, our colleges, the courts of justice, the high places of magistracy, the walks of honest business, the humbler callings of faithful industry, and the retired scenes of home. These denunciations and predictions were read as the sentence pronounced by Orthodoxy upon views of which thousands had experimental evidence that they were the truth of God to their souls. I do not understand my critic as denying in so many words that such utterances were made by Orthodoxy, or that the expectations based upon them have been disappointed. I will do my Orthodox brethren the justice of believing that they are glad that Unitarianism has not proved so awful a thing, or come to so dreadful a catastrophe, as they once asserted and predicted. But having read these things in print, indorsed by well-known names, I cannot allow any one to plead that no such opinions and prophecies were once expressed, and that they have not been disappointed.

But the critic, correcting my account of the expectations of the Orthodox, says, they did expect " a portion of the Unitarian community would begin to see the truth, and to acknowledge it," &c. The Unitarians cherished the same expectations concerning the Orthodox, that they too would begin to see the truth. What my critic so kindly regards as tokens of a more serious and Evangelical spirit among a portion of the Unitarians, we are apt gratefully to refer to a better knowledge of our views, and a dropping away of the scales of prejudice among the Orthodox. Our own brethren were always aware that their " use of language not very unlike that of their Orthodox brethren," when dealing with " some of the great truths of the Bible," was regarded as a very remarkable phenomenon by their opponents. Time was when Unitarians were considered trespassers and deceivers, if they ventured to use the dear and consecrated terms and phrases of a traditional piety. The Orthodox imagined that they had monopolized or appropriated even Scriptural epithets and texts, by having assigned to them an interpretation which might claim to be a part of their signification for ever after. It was wicked for a Unitarian to employ the language in which Orthodoxy spoke its own convictions. Still, the Unitarians would not be warned off the sacred precincts. They considered that Bible terms, and even the affectionately treasured phrases of devotional literature, formed a part of the common stock of the language. Orthodoxy now concedes that Liberal Christians feel at liberty, in consistency with honesty, to use such terms and phrases; and, instead of admitting its own error in its former charges of hypocrisy, accounts for the fact by supposing something like a reaction among Unitarians. If a portion of the Unitarian community has become more Evangelical, it is a cause for gratitude. But the supposed result is not to be admitted, even though alleged to the credit of living Unitarians, if it is to be used for the purpose of reflecting a censure back upon some of the earlier Unitarians. There were among them men and women as devout, as Evangelical, as earnestly attached to a Scriptural faith, as are any to be found among their successors.

III.

UNITARIANISM AND TRANSCENDENTALISM.

Another of the expectations which my critic affirms was entertained by the Orthodox was, that *a portion* of the Unitarians would lapse into the infidelity which I have already referred to as the predicted issue of their views for the mass of those who should receive them. The following paragraph is therefore significant.

"There was still another result, not only expected, but expressly predicted. It was predicted by Professor Stuart, and others, thirty years ago, that many Unitarians — the young, the adventurous, the men of impulse and progress — would not long remain where they then were. They would drift farther and farther away from the letter of Scripture and the restraints of the Gospel, until they arrived at the very borders of open infidelity. And neither in this have we been disappointed. We have seen it all verified before our eyes; and Mr. Ellis has seen the same. There are ministers around him, calling themselves Unitarians, with whom he would not exchange pulpits more than we should, — with whom, if I mistake not, the more serious part of his brethren have no longer any Christian fellowship."

The implication conveyed in this paragraph is that the form of scepticism known among us by the misused term *Transcendentalism*, was the natural outgrowth of Unitarianism. This charge has often been boldly made, and more often insinuated. It has no just foundation. Plain facts disprove it. The differences between Orthodoxy and Unitarianism arise from questions of interpretation; questions about the meaning of sacred records whose value and authority are admitted by both parties, and which Unitarians have always shown themselves so zealous to maintain, that they have produced works of acknowledged superiority in defence of revelation and the Scriptures. Transcendentalism, so called, denies a revelation, pronounces its miraculous sanctions to be philosophically impossible and absurd, and subverts the authority of Scripture. The relations between the three parties — the Orthodox, the Unitarians, and the Transcendentalists — on the subject-matter of revelation may be illustrated by a reference to the relations of three other parties among us concerning a political question. We have two large parties divided by a very serious issue touching the organic provisions of the Federal Constitution and the functions of Congress on slavery, and all the debates and agitations connected with it. Does or does not the Constitution recognize and legitimate slavery, and implicate all the States in its allowed existence in some of them, and expose free territory to be overrun by it? Has or has not Congress power to discuss the subject, and legislate upon it? On this issue our two prominent parties are divided. They make it a question of the interpretation of an instrument, through its own plain or obscure provisions and through the known views of its authors. Both parties profess to accept and recognize and honor the Constitution. They are willing to receive its fair and decisive meaning, when intelligently expounded, as authoritative, as binding upon them in all their political relations. They will not go behind the Constitution, nor dispute it, nor resist it. In the mean while a third party presents itself, which declares that the Constitution is pro-slavery, that it implicates all our citizens in the iniquity of slavery, and therefore that it must be denounced and subverted. This third party, therefore, plants itself outside of the Constitution. The two former parties, so far as the parallel is designed to illustrate one point of resemblance, may be regarded as representing the Orthodox and the Unitarians, as divided by questions about the interpretation of records and documents whose peculiar authority, value, and sanctions they agree in venerating. Their disputes centre upon and are to be decided by criticism and exposition. The third party, just referred to, represents the Transcendentalists, who insist that the Bible is committed to an unphilosophical, incredible, and impossible theory of miracles, and that they must, therefore, reject it and plant themselves outside of it. Now with what justice can the Orthodox confound Transcendentalists with Unitarians, and condemn the latter for complicity with the former in a theory of unbelief which comes not from methods of criticism and exposition, but from philosophical speculation?

As a matter of fact, too, Transcendentalism, so called, and even New England Transcendentalism, was not the outgrowth of Unitarianism, but an imported product that had been developed from German Lutheranism. A few young New England Unitarians have attracted attention to themselves in connection with their adoption of that form of philosophical scepticism, because of their eminent talents as men of marked endowments. But very many of the undistinguished Orthodox have adopted the same views independently of Unitarianism. It would be an ungracious office to attempt a statistical estimate of the proportionate addition to the ranks of infidelity which has accrued from Unitarianism or Orthodoxy. For myself, I have no doubt on that point. "Secularism," i. e. Atheism, in England numbers millions of adherents. Its leaders came from under the most thorough Orthodox training. Those who compose its ranks were never under the influence of Unitarianism. But Unitarianism is laboring earnestly, and with better promise of success than any other sect has yet realized, to reclaim the Secularists. Professor Stuart's prediction has not been verified among the Unitarians to the extent of its verification among the Orthodox. Justice Story and Dr. Channing both tell us, in their Memoirs, that Unitarianism saved them from the infidelity to which Orthodoxy had exposed them as young men. What saved them has saved thousands.

My critic receives with kindly reciprocation, and with some remarks which I need not quote, other *concessions* of mine, expressing regrets for the embitterment and arrogance exhibited by some Unitarians in the controversy, and acknowledging some proved deficiency in the *working* power of Unitarianism. I need not meet his suggestion which refers this deficiency to a lack of belief in some Gospel truths, for he has not observed my suggestion as to the more marked deficiency of Orthodoxy. I pass to the closing paragraph of his first paper, which relates to

IV.

THE LEGAL DECISIONS IN CASES OF CHURCH PROPERTY.

"But the most important concession which we find in these articles, is that relating to the old decisions of the courts respecting church property. These decisions are still unrevoked, and the younger portion of the community, Unitarian and Orthodox, may not know precisely what they are. They grew out of the separation between the Unitarians and Orthodox, from twenty-five to thirty [forty] years ago. In the progress of this separation, it sometimes happened that a church and a parish, which had long co-operated in the support of public worship, could agree to do so no longer. The parish would call a Unitarian minister, the church by a large majority would refuse to concur. The parish, unwilling to recede from its vote, would go on and settle the Unitarian minister; and the church, in regular church meeting, and by a strong major vote, would decide to withdraw from the parish. They claimed the right, as a distinct and independent body, and a *quasi* corporate body, to withdraw, and to carry their records and their property with them; expecting, of course, to leave all parish property behind. But the parishes thus left were not content with holding their own property; they claimed also the property of the church. They sued for it, and in repeated instances recovered it. The ground taken by the courts, in opposition to all reason and Scripture, to precedents and history, was, that a Congregational church is a mere appendage of the parish; that it cannot exist separate from the parish; that it may think to withdraw and retain its property, but it cannot do it; that the few church-members which remain are legally the church; or if none remain, the parish may proceed and gather a church, which shall succeed to all the rights of the property of the seceding body. Such was the ground of these decisions, and on this ground church after church was plundered of its property, even to its communion furniture and records. We called this proceeding *plunder* thirty years ago. We call it by the same hard name now. And we solemnly call upon those Unitarian churches, which are still in possession of this plunder, to restore it. They cannot prosper with it. And we call upon the courts of Massachusetts to revoke these unrighteous decisions, and put the Congregational churches of the State upon their original and proper basis. And in this call, the editor of the Christian Examiner, if he is consistent, will not longer fail to unite. For he says: 'We do not feel perfectly satisfied with the legal decisions in two cases, bearing upon the ownership of church property, though we admit that the issue raised was quite a perplexing one.'" (p. 31.)

As my critic has gone so largely into this subject of the litigation concerning church property, and has made such strong assertions in reference to the legal decisions which established what he regards unjust claims, I must make a brief reference to the subject. He has pressed my admissions beyond their reasonable and fair construction. That the issue raised was so perplexing a one, as I have said, relieves the decisions of our highest legal tribunals from the imputation of injustice, and yet makes it not inconsistent for me to add, that I do not feel perfectly satisfied with them. I will state the strongest case possible to illustrate the legal operation of those decisions. Suppose that in one of our best established Unitarian societies, worshipping in a meeting-house built by the voluntary contributions of its members, a portion of them, being a minority, should form themselves into a church body, or fellowship of communicants, under a strictly Unitarian covenant. Suppose that these communicants assess themselves for the purchase of a costly service of communion plate, and that one or more of them bequeath a fund equal to sustaining all the expenses of supporting religious institutions in the parish. Suppose further, that, on the death or retirement of the Unitarian pastor, a majority of the owners of pews in the meeting-house see fit to invite an Orthodox, Methodist, or Baptist minister to become the pastor, and that the members of the church, without a single exception, protest against the measure, insist that the vacancy should be filled by a Unitarian, and, failing to carry their point, retire unanimously, and establish worship and the ordinances in a new meeting-house, hall, or dwelling, within a rod of their old temple. Our Supreme Court has decided that, in retiring, they go as individuals, not as the church body, and must leave or surrender up the recently purchased plate, and the recently founded bequest to the parish within which the communicants had been gathered, to be used by a new fellowship, pledged, as the case may be, by an Orthodox, Methodist, or Baptist covenant. There is no denying that the first aspect of such a decision is that of gross injustice, high-handed oppression, aggravated by virtual sacrilege. And what was the ground of the decision? Simply this, as defined by Chief Justice Parker, in the Dedham case, 1820, that "*a church* cannot subsist without some religious community to which it is attached." I have supposed a case in which a Unitarian church fellowship would be deprived of its ecclesiastical property this very year, by the precedent established by that decision. The illustration will help us to understand how odious and oppressive the decision seemed to some of the Orthodox party when it took effect by favoring the Unitarians in the sharpest crisis of the controversy. Now let us look at the matter under its original bearings.

When a party of men with their families proposed to plant a new town, settlement, or precinct within the limits of this Commonwealth, they addressed a petition to the General Court for a grant of land in the wilderness. Receiving their warrant, and reaching their destination, they proceeded to allot the land, in parcels of upland, meadow, and woodland, to the members of the company, according to a fair rule of division. They set apart the dreariest and bleakest spot, provided it was sandy for easy digging, and worthless for culture, for a burial-ground. Other lots were staked off for the meeting-house, the school-house, the pound, the parsonage, and the ministerial wood-lot. A tax was then levied upon the inhabitants, according to their property, to open roads, to build a meeting-house and a school-house; and a tax was annually imposed to keep these works in repair, and to support the minister and to pay the schoolmaster. So far, of course, no distinction was made founded on church relations. The roads, the meeting-house, the minister, and the school entered into the public burdens. In some cases a church body, the members of which had already entered into a covenant, made the new settlement in their religious capacity, and formed the nucleus of a religious society, which, being joined by new-comers, and by the uncovenanted members of the families of the communicants, laid the foundation of religious institutions in the precinct. The meeting-house, however, was built, and all the expenses connected with religious institutions were defrayed, by the tax on all the inhabitants, as before. In other cases a church body was gathered in and from the uncovenanted membership of a parish or religious society. In all cases, whether the church had been the nucleus of the society, or culled from out of it, it became an *imperium in imperio.* It established its own terms for the admission of new members. As the judgment, charity, and zeal of those who from time to time were in communion dictated, these terms might be lax or rigid, might enter into minute specifications of doctrine conformed to the Calvinistic formulas, or be cast into a more free and general form; might take Calvinism for granted, by using phraseology implying it, or insist upon it emphatically, or else might allow virtually or expressly a greater or less liberty in the range of belief. All the inhabitants were compelled to support and attend public worship, but the right or privilege of a participation in the ordinances was exclusively within the refusal or the gift of those who had already secured the prerogative to themselves. The existing church for the time being, from year to year, and from week to week, had an unrestrained liberty to modify the terms of its covenant. The voice of the majority would ratify any change in its doctrinal definitions, or in the stress of its provisions for making members mutually subject to each other's oversight. True, there was a theory on this matter, reinforced by a platform, and professedly based upon texts of Scripture, which seemed to warrant an assumption of apostolic authority for the New England model. But this did not hinder the prevalence of a great variety of usages as regards covenants, nor impair the actual independency of the churches, nor restrain the freedom of opinion among individual members. If it was thought desirable to alter the terms of any church covenant, to resist an insidious heresy by a more stringent definition of Orthodoxy, or to license an advancing liberality by yielding what Protestantism from the first pretended to claim, — the right of private judgment, — the proposition was made; the vote was taken, and the decision was in force.

The church body, thus established and perpetuated within a parish, received its appellative name from the parish, or the town, or the precinct, in which it was gathered. Sometimes lands and funded property were set apart, and taxes were imposed, by vote of the freemen of a town, on the estates of all inhabitants for the support of "the church" in that town. Individuals, sometimes members of the church, and sometimes not, left bequests for religious uses, the destination of which was variously defined as for "the town," "the parish," "the religious society," or "the Church of Christ," in this or that precinct. Parish property and church property, however distinguished in terms, was in early times designed and used for the same purposes. A question warmly debated between the parties to the controversy referred to in these pages was, whether or not, by the laws of the Commonwealth, the church body, the fellowship of communicants in a parish, composed a full corporation, with corporate powers independent, within its own range, of the parish. Our courts decided the question in the negative. But the merits of the question were complicated by historical and conventional references and usages. It was maintained by one party that the church was of paramount importance, as it called into existence the congregation or religious society, and set up the ordinances for establishing a Gospel work in the precinct. It was replied by the other party, that the church-members had from the first usurped an undue power, which was oppressive, in sacred things, and had gone the lengths of utter tyranny in secular matters by restricting the franchise to communicants. A variety of customs and of statutes had regulated the relations and respective rights of parishes and the churches connected with them. In the beginnings of things here, circumstances alone had disposed of these matters, and the usage had been various. The first law passed on the subject gave the choice of the minister to the communicants, but compelled the parish to support him. Then each party had a right to a separate vote, the church taking the precedence. Then it was provided, that, if the society in any case dissented from and withstood the choice of a minister made by the church, a council from sister churches should be convened, and its decision should be binding on the society if in accordance with the choice of the church, and upon the church if it favored the choice made by the society. Afterwards a concurrent vote, and then a joint vote, seem to have gained prevalence, as a sort of compromise between custom and law. The deacons of a church were, in 1754, constituted a *quasi* corporation, for the sake of holding and administering funds for church uses.

As changes in religious sentiment, and the legitimate exercise of Christian liberty, advanced with the growth and expansion of our communities, it was easy to foresee that difficulties would arise from the relations between parishes and the churches formed in them, when a strife should be opened that was embittered by sectarian passion, and vitiated by a prize in the shape of property. Some of the churches and parishes in the Commonwealth had large funded possessions. The ministerial land and wood-lot, the parsonage, the money at interest, the meeting-house, and the communion plate, had rival claimants. Where the society, the church-members, and the minister all yielded to an extending liberalism in religion, no conflict would arise. When church and society had a prevailing element of liberalism, even if the minister, who had a life tenure of office, remained Calvinistic and rigid, it was necessary only to wait the event of his death to secure a new and liberal pastor, and to relax the terms of the covenant. Where the minister held to an unabated Calvinism, and his church sympathized with him, of course no new members could pass the ordeal of the covenant without acceding to the terms required of a member of the congregation for securing the privilege of church communion. Thus all the parishioners who held liberal views were excluded from the church. The large majority, the whole of the uncovenanted members of the society, might become unorthodox; the church might dwindle to a mere handful, and retain its rigid orthodoxy; and under this state of things a vacancy might occur in the pulpit and pastorate. Of course, the parish, who were to attend on the ministrations, and afford the entire support, by tax or from income of funds, of a new minister, would by vote make choice of one whose religious views accorded with their own. The church might convene and choose a pastor, to whom the parish would refuse a hearing, or might content itself with dissenting from the parish choice. What was to be done? It was clear that the parish had a right to say who should and who should not occupy its meeting-house, derive a support from a tax imposed on its members and from funds in their keeping, and stand in the relation of a religious teacher and friend to them and their families. If the members of the church in the parish, being a minority of the parish voters, withstood the choice of the society, they had the same right to withdraw, and to organize another society, as belonged to any minority of the parishioners, independently of covenant relations. But suppose the church so withdrawing claimed a right to take with it, and appropriate for its new institution, a ministerial fund which had been given in terms designating "the Church of Christ" in this or that precinct or parish. It was comparatively easy to resist this claim, on the ground that the design of the fund was to support the ministry in that parish. But suppose the church, or the large majority of its members, grieved by "the decline of piety," and irritated by an embittered religious quarrel, should turn their backs upon the old meeting-house, and upon its new heretical minister, and, assembling in private dwelling, hall, school-house, or rival temple, should spread the sacramental table with the old vessels consecrated by the faith and fellowship of the dead, or purchased the year before by their own contributions, and should open the record book of covenants and acts of church discipline; have they not a right to this remnant of their traditional privileges, to these peculiar possessions of theirs, in which the parish had no interest, and had never used or touched? Our courts answered this question in the negative. The new minister and the old parish may proceed to organize a new church body, with new deacons, who may institute a legal process against the deacons of the retiring church, to obtain possession of the communion vessels, the church fund, and the records.

I have stated a hypothetical case, with all the aggravations which could possibly attach to it. I will now proceed, not for a controversial, but for an historical purpose, to report the substance of the case which actually came before our courts, and drew out the decision which established the legal precedent. Its date is at a Law Term of the Supreme Judicial Court of Massachusetts, October, 1820. The issue concerned the right of property in certain ecclesiastical funds. For the sake of bringing the case to a decision on the *first principles* which it involved, the point was conceded, — though it might have been challenged and disproved, — that a majority of members previously in communion with the church of the old or First Parish in Dedham had withdrawn, and established worship and the ordinances in another sanctuary. Did the church property vest in the receding body, or in that portion of the fellowship which remained in connection with the old parish?

The church at Dedham had, with great unanimity, liberalized the terms of its covenant previous to the close of the last century, under Mr. Haven's pastorate. The late Dr. Bates, his successor, was regarded at his settlement as one of the *liberal* or *moderate* men, and was chosen as such; the majority of those who elected and were to support him being in sympathy with what, in the then transition process of theological opinion, was called *moderate*. In the course of his ministry he was supposed to have grown more rigid in his views, and he ceased to exchange with brother ministers whom the society had been accustomed to see in the pulpit. When he was dismissed to assume the presidency of a college in Vermont, a strife grew out of the seeds of division which existed in the parish. The measures connected with the choice and ordination of a new pastor set the parish and the church in opposition. The old ecclesiastical usages which marked the action of our societies, having been as variable and unsettled as I have already noted, were found to have been peculiarly so in this parish. Usage afforded no fair or final arbitrament in the emergency. The funded property, which had accumulated from early times, with many additions, was of considerable value. It had been given by portions to the town, the parish, and the church, those three terms being used, in fact, as synonymes to designate the common purposes to be served by these funds. They had been managed at one time by the whole town, and afterwards by the deacons, under the law of 1754, which made them trustees of property designed for religious and charitable uses. When there had been a vacancy in the same parish in 1685, the communicants and the non-communicants, voting together, had invited Mr. Bowles to become the pastor; a general meeting having decided that "the church and town will act together as one." In an election two years afterwards the parish took the lead, and the church followed. In the case before us, the majority of the church opposed the vote of the parish for calling and ordaining a liberal pastor. After much agitation, the will of the parish having prevailed, the disaffected party withdrew from the old meeting-house, and from the ministrations of the new pastor, to set up worship in another place. A suit was instituted by the newly-chosen deacons for the possession of the funds, to which the retiring party laid claim, as lawfully in their administration. It would seem as if a primary point for decision was, whether the majority of the church-members had withdrawn. But, by the advice of legal counsel, the parish, as has been already said, conceded that a majority of the church constituted the opposition to its proceedings. This concession was intended to secure a decision on the first principles involved in the case, and being yielded, it of course entered into the assumed facts, constituting the law question to be pronounced upon by a full bench, not by a jury. It is not admitted, however, that a majority of the church-members actually withdrew from connection with the old parish. The Rev. Dr. Lamson, whose candor and integrity will not be disputed by any one who knows him, and whose knowledge of all the facts of the case, from his own prominent place in them, his possession of the papers, and his intimacy with the parties, makes him our best witness, is very explicit on this point. It was at the opening of his ministry that the litigation occurred. The lapse of nearly forty years finds him still the much beloved and honored pastor of the same parish. In a note to his Second Century Historical Discourses, preached in 1838, he says: "The majority of the old members did not, in fact, retire." "This I believe, from a careful inspection of a very accurate list of the original members, to be a fact." "Of one thing there can be no dispute; that is, that after the ordination there was a larger vote sanctioning the proceedings of the parish than was ever given against them. I make this whole statement after a diligent examination of authentic documents, and ample means of information, and I believe that every part of it can be fully substantiated."

The court, however, adjudicated as if the point conceded, viz. the withdrawal of a majority of the old church-members, were really the fact. Its decision was, that the "Church associated and worshipping with the First Parish is the First Church," and the custody and improvement of the funds were transferred accordingly.* A decision by first principles.

It is unnecessary to revive here the remembrance of the bitter and unmeasured abuse visited upon our highest judicial tribunal for this decision, which became a precedent for other cases. An Ecclesiastical Council in Groton, in 1827, formally challenged the decision. Nor is it my province to enter into a legal argument in vindication, or in denunciation, of the professional judgment of men whom with good reason this community regarded as most conscientious and wise. But as candor has led me to connect with an admission of the perplexity of two of our church cases, an allowance that I "do not feel perfectly satisfied with the legal decisions," and as my critic has permitted himself to write about "the plundering" of churches, I may add a few words of measured explanation.

When the issue arose which was sure to present itself here, as it had presented itself in several of the European Continental nations, and more particularly in Great Britain, in connection with changes in the popular religious belief, it was necessary to settle a principle of law touching funds vested for religious uses. The form of the question in our Commonwealth was, whether church funds belonged to a selected body of persons in a religious society covenanting in a separate fellowship of their own, and belonged to them in such an absolute sense as would admit of their being withdrawn by these covenanted members if they should retire from the society; or whether such funds were to be for ever available to a continuous fellowship, or even to new and successive bodies of communicants perpetuated or arising within the original society. The legal decision ratified the latter alternative. The following reasons suggest themselves in support of the decision.

A "church" can subsist and perpetuate itself only by an

* The case is reported in Massachusetts Term Reports, Vol. XVI. pp. 488 – 522.

organic connection with a "society." The society is the soil for the roots of a Christian vine, supplying the new material to repair waste by death. A church not connected with a society would die out.

Again, it has been found difficult in some instances to settle disputed cases involving the right of membership of religious societies, when depending upon only such tangible conditions as residence, taxation, the ownership of a pew, and occasional presence in a place of worship. But it would be infinitely more difficult to dispose of cases involving the right of church-membership, if large pecuniary interests were in question, and the law were invoked to review matters of church discipline, creed, and covenant. "Church usages" have been so various in different parishes, that there is no common law for authoritative reference in half the cases that do or might arise. Some persons may be members of a church, who are not members of the parish in which it is gathered. Some persons disaffected or not edified in the places of their residence, may go on the Lord's day to participate in Christian ordinances wherever they please. Do such persons become legal administrators of the old parish church fund in the place where they may commune? The majority of the church-members, as found among the living signers of the covenant, in one of our old parishes, might decide in church meeting to-day to emigrate to Kansas. Can they take with them the funds given to the church of their present parish? Some church-members after marriage, or in pursuit of health or business, have removed from the State or the town in which they had entered into covenant relations. They know not how long they may stay abroad, they may expect to return sooner or later, and so they may not take up their church relations; or the church to which they belong may decline to release them, because unable to commend them to the fellowship of any other church in their new residence. Shall these absentees and wanderers be hunted out for the sake of their votes, by proxy or otherwise, when contested questions are closely tried in their old fellowship, and shall they be allowed to present themselves at any time and claim and exercise the privilege? Shall the question as to the choice of a pastor from the Cam-

36 *

bridge or the Andover schools, over one of our old churches and parishes, and the continuance of the funds in its possession, be left possibly contingent upon the answer to a telegraphic message sent to three men or women living in Ohio, whose names are on the church-books?

Again, some church-members have been factiously excommunicated to deprive them of their votes. In other cases, as many members of a society not in communion as have already joined the church, and perhaps a far larger number, may strongly desire the privilege of communion, and in the judgment of charity may be as worthy of it as are any who share it, but may be kept out by arbitrary terms or hostile voters. Many devout and faithful people have been thus notoriously deprived of their Christian rights, because they exercised the same soul-freedom under the profession of which our churches were planted.

Once more. How could a church be identified, except by its connection with a local parish or society? Supposing even the possibility, it has never yet been verified, but always disproved, that a succession of men and women could be found in a town for several centuries who could honestly profess to hold precisely the same religious and doctrinal views held by the founders of their church. It is well known, that those founders laid equal stress upon the measures of an unrelaxed discipline, as upon the integrity of an undiminished creed. It may be fairly affirmed, that, if the original members of our churches could return to their places in the holy assemblies of those who claim to be their successors in doctrinal purity, they would be greatly scandalized at the utter disuse or the mere shadowy remnant of the old, stern discipline, which exacted confessions and administered penalties before the whole congregation. Ecclesiastical sentences were as rigorous as the civil sentences in the early days of this colony, and more galling and humbling. The old church record-books contain something beside the covenant, and the list of those who owned it. Would even our most Orthodox brethren consent to be held to a strict process for the *identification* of one of their churches with a church of the fathers? Surely, the money is not the only consideration.

Our courts recognized as fundamental law, that a church was a voluntary association of some or all of the members within a religious society; and as so far identified with that society, protected and sustained by the corporate rights of that society, that it extinguished itself by withdrawal, and could exist and be perpetuated only by retaining an organic connection with it. Had our courts fallen short of that decision, or adopted any other, they would have involved themselves in all the perplexities of the Canon Law. They would have been forced to assume the functions of ecclesiastical tribunals, to adjudicate on questions of simony, bigotry, heresy, and excommunication. Then, too, acres of territory, and heaps of funded wealth, the lawful inheritance of new generations unfettered by conditions of creed, would have been pledged to obsolete terms and disbelieved doctrines. The Legislature of Massachusetts was saved by her judiciary from the necessity of following the lead of the British Parliament in transferring all the ecclesiastical property of the realm from the use of "Orthodoxy" to the service of "heresy."

Still the case was "perplexing." Still one may "not feel perfectly satisfied," that in every instance the conditions of Christian equity were realized. But do not let us say that the honored and revered men who have adorned the high places of justice in Massachusetts were ever concerned in "plundering churches."

On reviewing what I had written upon the subject of the Church cases, it occurred to me that, in my desire to treat the matter under its general bearings, I might not have done justice to the strength of the legal reasons on which the decisions were based. I therefore submitted the proof-sheet of this portion of my Appendix to a professional friend, with the request that, taking note of what my critic had written in such strong terms upon this subject, he would supply any deficiency of mine in the proper treatment of its legal relations. I have received from him the following remarks: —

"It is true, as you have stated, that in the earlier years of our colonial history the power of choosing the minister, or teaching elder, in a parish or religious society, was vested in the church; but so was the election to civil offices. Church-members alone had a right of suffrage in civil affairs. Afterwards the church and the society had a concurrent vote, and the law on the subject was varied from time to time.

"But to avoid any collision or conflict of authority on this subject, it was expressly provided by the Constitution of 1780, — the fundamental law, not to be changed by the Legislature, — that the parish, or religious society, or town, or district, where the same corporation exercised the functions of a town and religious society, should have the exclusive right and power of electing the minister and contracting with him for his support. The language of the Constitution upon this subject is explicit, as follows: 'Provided, notwithstanding, that the several towns, parishes, precincts, and other bodies politic, or religious societies, shall, at all times, have the exclusive right of electing their public teachers, and contracting with them for their support and maintenance.' And when the Third Article of the Declaration of Rights, containing this provision, was abrogated by amendment in 1833, this provision securing to religious societies the right of election was reinstated, and is now a part of the Constitution of the Commonwealth; except that, instead of the term 'public teachers' in the first instrument, the more specific designation of 'pastors and religious teachers' is substituted. This was accompanied with another fundamental principle, that all religious sects and denominations shall be equally under the protection of the law, and no subordination of any one sect or denomination to another shall be established by law. These provisions constitute the legal foundations of the religious institutions of the Commonwealth.

"The religious society may be a territorial or a poll parish, or organized as a religious society under the statute, and may be of any denomination. Such a religious society is a corporation and body politic, capable of taking and holding property in its own right, for the purposes for which it is organized, which are, the support and maintenance of public worship and religious instruction, providing for all the expenses incident to these duties, as building a meeting-house, settling a minister, providing for his support, and the like. The *Church* is a body of individuals formed within a religious society by covenant, for the celebration of Christian ordinances, for mutual edification and discipline, and for making charitable provision for its own members, and for all expenses incident to these specific objects. The church may be composed of all or of a part of the members of a religious society. It may be composed of males and females, adults and minors; though by long-established usage adult male members alone vote in church affairs.

"Now it is manifest that, under the foregoing provision of the Constitution, the legal voters of the parish alone have by law the power to vote in the settlement of a minister, and the church as an organized body can have no negative. But each male member of the church is usually, if not necessarily, a member of the religious society, and as such has his equal voice with all other members of the society. But in fact and in practice, church-members, being among the most respected members of the society, will ordinarily have an influence, by their counsel and their character, much greater than the proportion which they numerically bear to the whole number of votes. And from the respect due to such a body, as a matter of courtesy, they are usually consulted, and in many instances are requested to take the lead in giving a call to a minister; and, if the parish concur, in making the ecclesiastical arrangements for his ordination, the invitation of a council, and the usual solemnities attending such settlement. This customary deference to the church is all just and proper, and a course which every lover of Christian harmony and order would approve. But if such harmony cannot be maintained, and the parties come to a controversy requiring an appeal to the law, the law must decide these questions of right according to the express provision of the Constitution, and the laws of the land, without regard to sect or denomination.

"Another fundamental principle lying at the foundation of these legal decisions is this: that the church of any religious society, recognized by usage, and to some extent by law, as an aggregate body associated for highly useful and praiseworthy purposes, whose usages and customs are to be respected and encouraged, is not a corporation or body politic capable of taking and holding property. No doubt, in the very earliest times there was some confusion in the minds of our ancestors upon this subject; but ever since 1754, now more than a century, the distinction between church and society has been well known and universally observed. The very purpose of the statute of 1754 was to vest deacons of Congregational churches, and the wardens and vestry of Episcopal churches, with corporate powers to take property for the church, for the very reason that the church, as an aggregate body of individuals, not a corporation, could not by law take property, or hold and transmit it in succession. Since that time, church property and parish property have been regarded as wholly distinct. Church property holden by deacons could not be appropriated by the parish as of right, nor could parish property be used or appropriated by the church. In the Dedham case there might be some doubt raised in the mind of one not attending carefully to this legal distinction. The property originated in grants made to *the church* in form at the very early date of 1660, when, as I have said, there was some confusion of terms; for though it was given to the First Church, it was for the support of "a teaching elder," i. e. a minister, which is peculiarly a parish purpose. The court decided in that particular case, that, by the particular grant, the legal estate, being given to "the church," by force of the statute of 1754 vested in the deacons as church property in trust for the support of a minister, and so was, in effect, in trust for the parish. But the court decided in that same case, that, but for the trusts declared in those grants, the parish, as such, would have no claim, legal or equitable, to the property granted, or the proceeds of the sale of it.

"The effect of that decision was, that the legal estate vested in the deacons as church property, and that the First Parish, as a corporation, had no title to it. And this is manifest from the consideration, that the deacons of the church maintained the action as the recognized legal owners.

"As to which of the two parties in that suit were rightfully the deacons of the church of the First Parish, that was a distinct question. And upon considerations, and as matter of law, the court decided, that although a majority of the members of the First Church seceded and withdrew from the society after they had given a call to a minister, in which the church as a body did not concur; yet those of the church who remained and adhered to the First Parish constituted the church of the First Parish, with the incidental right of removing and choosing deacons, and the deacons whom they had chosen, in place of those whom they had removed, were the deacons of the church of the First Parish.

"The principle, then, appears to be this: that a church is an associated body, gathered in a religious society, for mutual edification and discipline, and the celebration of the Christian ordinances. It is ascertained and identified as the church of the parish or religious society in which it is formed. The church of the First Parish of D., for example, is ascertained and identified by its existence in, and connection with, that parish. If a majority of the members withdraw, they have a full right to do so, but they thereby cease to be the church of that parish. They withdraw as individuals, and not as an organized body. They may form a religious society by applying to a justice of the peace, under the statute, to call a meeting, and a church may be gathered in such society. But it would be a new society, and the church gathered in it would not be the church of the First Parish of D. They might associate others with themselves and settle a minister, but this would not make such society the church of the First Parish. It follows as a necessary legal consequence, that all church property, even a service of plate for the communion, given to the church of the First Parish of D., must be and remain for the church gathered in that parish, and those who may succeed them in that parish, and it cannot go to the use of any other church, or the church of any other society. However desirable it may be by all right-thinking persons, that all such controversies should be avoided, by an amicable adjustment of all such claims upon the principles of the most liberal equity and charity, and with a just regard to the feelings as well as the rights of all, yet, if parties will appeal to the law to decide a question respecting the right of property, even to a service of church plate, the law must decide it upon the same legal principles which govern the acquisition and transmission of property in all other cases.

"There is no case in which it has been decided, in this Commonwealth, that any parish or religious society, acting as a corporation charged with the special duty of supporting and maintaining public worship, have a right to recover property of a seceding church, or of any church of such parish. But the controversy has always been between those members of the church of a designated parish who remain with that parish, and those who secede, retire, or withdraw therefrom, as to which is the real church of said parish. It has been a question of identity, and the decision has gone upon the principle, that, whatever other rights or claims the retiring or seceding members, even though a majority, may have, they could not be considered in law, after such secession, as the church of that parish."

V.

UNITARIANS IMPEACHED FOR CONCEALMENT.

My critic devotes the substance of his second paper to the reiteration of the specific evidence on which the Orthodox party charged some of their former brethren with a *concealment* of their newly adopted Unitarian opinions. If the reader will turn back to page 17, he will note my very emphatic statement, that any one who should attempt to *vindicate* our first Unitarians from the charge of concealment, "would undertake a needless and futile task." I admitted, also, that there was "a show of evidence to support the charge, though not of a sort to fix the slightest stain upon the characters of those who were the subjects of it." The simple facts of the case I considered to be a complete relief from all that was censurable in such concealment, and I remarked, that those who would not admit in their favor the force of these facts were not within the reach of any plea that could be offered. I then added this sentence: "*Not for their vindication*, then, but merely as a matter of explanatory history, will we briefly advert to these facts."

It was with some surprise, therefore, that I read the first sentence of the comments of my critic, as follows: "A considerable part of Mr. Ellis's first article is taken up in the attempt to vindicate the early Unitarians of Massachusetts from the charge of improperly *concealing* their peculiar sentiments." But not to lay stress upon this inaccuracy in my critic, which, in the old-fashioned style of controversy, would have provoked a sharp reply, the facts of the case still stand unquestioned, and I do not find a single line in the comments before me that recognizes or meets them. The critic quotes from a series of Unitarian witnesses the evidences, as he thinks, of their own complicity in the wrong of keeping back a full and frank avowal of their Unitarianism. I admit freely the facts of the case, so far as they are facts, and attach to them the motives by which, as I suppose, they are reconciled with the full integrity and the measure of wisdom possessed by good and intelligent men. The reader will observe the stress that is necessarily laid upon the word *Unitarianism*, in order to the maintenance of the side taken by my critic. The word, after all, — the word with its prejudiced and perverted associations, and the bugbear frights once connected with it, — explains what is most dark about the matter. Had some ministers and laymen, now known to have been what are now called Unitarians, stood up fifty years ago, and announced themselves by that name, they would have misled their friends to a far greater extent than that to which they deceived their opponents by disavowing the name. We have had hundreds of the warmest and most determined opponents of slavery among us who would in any company disavow the charge of being "Abolitionists." And why? Because the conventional use and the associations of the terms attach to it the idea of ultraism, of extreme opinions and measures with which they do not sympathize, and the odium of which they are unwilling to bear. Will it be fair, a half-century hence, to charge upon such persons the dishonest concealment of abolition opinions? The case of the first Unitarians was nearly a parallel one. A few sentences found in the early controversial writings of Dr. Channing will always be sufficient for a lucid exhibition of the whole truth in the case to a candid reader. When the word

Unitarian first came into use here, its signification was quite unlike that which it bears now. It was burdened with the reproaches of ultraism, extravagance, eccentricity, looseness, and recklessness in speculation, and, moreover, it actually defined a form of belief about Christ and his Gospel which, from that day to this, has never had the convictions or the sympathy of the majority in our fellowship. When the epithet was associated with Priestley's materialism and reputed Jacobinism, and with the Rev. S. T. Coleridge's two sermons, "with blue coat and white waistcoat," in the Unitarian chapel at Bath, on "The Corn Laws," and "The Hair-Powder Tax," some of the good people of Massachusetts who well knew they were neither Calvinists nor Trinitarians might well object to recognizing themselves as Unitarians, and still more to proclaiming themselves such. Very many even now who accept, without assuming, the epithet, are willing to do so only because it has been discharged, in the place of their residence at least, of these associations. Perhaps, too, some of these persons, if removing to other places, where Orthodoxy has given a false and slanderous report of Unitarianism, would feel justified in the court of conscience in repudiating the name. And here doubtless we have a hint of one of the most effective reasons which influenced some in disavowing or temporizing with an epithet which they were solicited by their jealous opponents to accept. Orthodoxy had wrought out a very awful delineation of *Unitarianism.* There was nothing too bad for spite or bigotry to say of it. It was worldly, licentious, devilish. It did all sorts of wicked things. It made light of sin. It offered an opiate to accusing consciences. It mocked at the Bible. It ridiculed a change of heart. It argued down a future retribution. It favored "promiscuous dancing," and it "denied the Lord that bought us." It can easily be conceived that Christian men and women, who believed themselves to be as sincere, as earnest, as wise, and as pious as their neighbors who so maligned them, might object to falling into ranks which had been thus described. Some real Unitarians may have thought that a prudent and gradual development of changed views which they themselves were thinking and studying out, in loyalty to the truth, might be wisely protected from an ill name, till the excellence of the views would prove of avail to redeem a good name from unjust reproach. When the people knew what Unitarianism really and essentially signified, and its disciples knew their views under that name, there was no concealment.

It is evident, however, that under this charge of *concealment* some Orthodox controversialists mean to convey something more than the word signifies in any use of it consistent with honesty. It is in fact used by such as synonymous with *deception.* In this form the charge refutes itself. The charge, too, in any form, is carried too far to be sustained, because it is not self-consistent. "Unitarians concealed their peculiar sentiments." Does this mean *all* their peculiar sentiments? Of course not; for then they would have never have been known, or even brought under suspicion. They must have divulged freely and effectively some of their peculiar sentiments, in order to have drawn attention to themselves as suspicious persons. They probably announced most plainly those of their sentiments which they regarded as most peculiar, because most significant of their dissent from popular views, and the most antagonistic to the traditions of Orthodoxy. These were not the jot and tittle matters of verbal criticism or doctrinal logomachy, but the weighty principles of a rational and intelligent faith. There are some peculiar sentiments advanced in the writings of noble Jonathan Mayhew. Yet there is not in them a single line or sentence of dogmatic Unitarianism. Did he practise concealment?

There is a paragraph of my critic's paper on this subject which demands a particular notice.

"We find another admission in these pages, which contains more of truth, possibly, than the author was aware of when he wrote it. 'It is a fact,' he says, 'familiar to all Christian scholars, that Unitarianism has lain *latent* in all ages of the Church. There have always been intimations of its presence, and of its *secret workings*. It has cropped out here and there always.' (p. 30.) The testimony here given is true so far as this: Unitarianism in the Church has always been *latent*, before it has been *patent*. It has worked *in secret*, before it has ventured to appear openly. Thus Irenæus describes the Unitarians of his day, as 'using alluring discourses in public, because of the common Christians'; as 'pretending to preach like the Orthodox'; and as 'complaining that, though their doctrine be the same as ours, we abstain from their communion, and call them heretics.' But he adds: 'When they have seduced any from the faith, and made them willing to comply with them, *then they begin to open their mysteries.*'"

Availing himself of a double meaning in the word *latent*, my critic — shall I say unfairly, or sarcastically? — suggests that I have admitted more of truth than I was perhaps aware of. If he had allowed me to use the word *latent* as I did use it, his own remark would have lost its point, and he would have saved his space for an answer to my assertion. Could he, however, deny, that in every age of the Christian Church, and in every place, when and where Orthodox views may have been popularly or prevailingly received, some of the most intelligent and sincere and devout persons have always held Unitarian views, or been the subjects of Unitarian tendencies? If my critic be indeed a Professor in a New England Theological School, his reading, if not his charity, would prevent his venturing on such a denial. For he would only subject himself by the denial to account for the fact, that Unitarianism had always *manifested* itself under favorable circumstances among the born and educated and honored disciples of Orthodoxy. What is so ready to *appear* must have had a previous *latent* existence. Nor does it consist with what we know by many interesting disclosures of the slow and hesitating processes of honest minds in working their way from error to truth, to describe the slowness and secrecy of the method as a sneaking or artful fear or policy.

I am amazed, however, to find a New England Theological Professor committing himself to such a scholarly injustice, to say no worse of it, than appears in the quotation at the close of the paragraph above. I excuse what is excusable in the wrong, by referring it to a cause which has often violated truth and complicated controversy, — the taking quotations at second hand. My critic credits his pretended extract from Irenæus to Dr. Miller's Letters on Unitarianism. If my critic had taken pains to verify the quotation, he would have crossed out his own indorsement. What dreadful creatures these Unitarians of the time of Irenæus must have been, of whom such hard words could be used! "Using alluring discourses," "pretending to preach like the Orthodox," "seducing" some from the faith, and then opening "their mysteries"! One would suppose the description answered to a sort of Mormons. And in fact it does apply to persons with whom Unitarians are no more concerned than they are with Mormons. Nor does Irenæus speak of Unitarians as such, nor on a matter involving the views of Unitarians. Neither does he use half of the hard words which Dr. Miller ascribes to him. Dr. Miller's professed quotation from Irenæus is one of those gross outrages for so many of which polemics have been made odious. Any one who will turn to the fifteenth chapter of the third book of Irenæus "Contra Hæreses," may see what this pretended account of certain "Unitarians of his day" really is. He is dealing with a mixed mess of Ebionites, Gnostics, and Valentinians. These, he says, having publicly won disciples, "*his separatim inenarrabile Plenitudinis suæ enarrant mysterium.*" Some very excellent Unitarianism might be quoted from Irenæus himself.

The historical list of the *concealments* charged upon these always *latent* Unitarians closes thus: —

"For some reason, this policy of concealment seems to have been common among Unitarians in all ages. They have worked in secret (no doubt with the best intentions) before they have ventured to appear in public. And not only so, the doctrine has perhaps always been most successfully propagated in secret. It has made the most progress, not when standing openly upon its own foundations, but when silently mingling with other sects, and secretly diffusing itself among them. So it has been in other times and countries. So, in the judgment of Mr. Ellis, — and in this judgment we entirely coincide, — it has been here. 'We seemed to begin to decline the moment we began to try to strengthen ourselves. The Unitarian *sect* has hindered the progress of Unitarianism.' — p. 45."

It is even so. Popular Orthodoxy has always been very effective in repressing the utterance of Unitarian convictions, where they have been entertained by comparatively few persons, and the odium of heresy is heavy and stringent. The rule applies equally to the repression of Protestant opinions in Roman Catholic countries. Through force of this rule, thousands of Unitarians in Orthodox communities and societies think their own thoughts, say their own prayers, meditate religious truths by themselves, and hold their tongues, as do thousands of Protestants in Roman Catholic countries.

VI.

GENEALOGY AND INFLUENCE OF UNITARIANISM IN MASSACHUSETTS.

The third of the series of critical papers on which I am commenting challenges some of the views I have incidentally expressed about the successive modifications of religious opinion, which finally resulted in Unitarianism in this region, and about the reflex influence of Unitarianism upon the Orthodoxy which has been in antagonism with it. The writer objects to a statement of mine on page 19, part of which only he quotes, that, "for a whole century before the full development of Unitarianism, there had been a large modification, a softening and toning down of the old theology, an undefined but recognized tempering of the creed." The remainder of my sentence is, "a relaxing of the strain upon faith, and *a compliant acquiescence in that state of things.*" To this it is replied: —

"We think 'a whole century' throws the date of these modifications too far back. It was, however, more than half a century. And whether the modifications spoken of were 'a toning down,' or a toning up, of the old theology, we will not now say. Most people would think they were the latter. They commenced with President Edwards, and were followed up by his pupils and admirers, Bellamy, Hopkins, the younger Edwards, West of Stockbridge, Emmons, &c. In distinction from the old theology, they were sometimes called 'the New Divinity,' and sometimes 'Hopkinsianism.' As they changed none of the facts or substantial doctrines of the old theology, but merely modified some of them, i. e. stated and explained them in a somewhat different way, they are properly called *modifications.* And as the authors of them renounced not one of the five points of Calvinism, they considered themselves consistent Calvinists;

though they did not adopt all the explanations of Calvin, or of the earlier settlers of New England.

"While these changes were going on in one direction, a portion of the clergy, the most remote from the Edwardeans, were sliding off into what was called 'Moderate Calvinism,' or 'Arminianism.' Still, there was no marked division or classification among our ministers, until near the close of the Revolutionary war. At that time, there came to be a threefold division among them, pretty clearly marked, which continued for the next thirty years, viz. the Calvinists, the Hopkinsians, and the Arminians.

"Among the two first of these classes there never was any concealment of their peculiar opinions. The Calvinists, being strictly what the first settlers were, had nothing to conceal, and no motive for concealment. The Hopkinsians, so far from concealing their peculiarities, were rather disposed to make them prominent. They believed them to be improvements upon the old Calvinism of the country, — a carrying of it out in greater consistency, — and they were inclined to make the most of them. The concealment at this period was confined to the so-called Arminians. This was the body which came out at length Unitarians; and without doubt, many of them were concealed Unitarians long before they ventured to declare themselves. It was among these that the concealment spoken of in my last number wholly existed. Nominally Arminians, — a name which, as Mr. Ellis says, has been made to signify almost anything, — they were really, and must have known themselves to be, Arians, Unitarians, disbelievers in the proper divinity of Christ."

I cannot admit that a whole century does throw the date of these modifications too far back. The most cogent evidence that could be brought to bear upon the case has passed carefully under my notice, in reading the writings of some prominent ministers and laymen of a century and a half ago, and in comparing them with those of the first generation on these shores. If the occasion calls for it, I will undertake to gather from writings of the date defined religious phraseology and expressions of religious opinions which stanch and unswerving Calvinists never would have put forth. Though it is only about a hundred years since Mr. Rogers of Leominster was dealt with as a Unitarian heretic, we may well understand that there must have been considerable of *a compliant acquiescence* in a previous gradual modification of doctrinal opinion to have enabled him to continue in the ministry. The dread of stirring up a strife kept back in many cases the avowal of much of the mental dissent from the doctrines of the Catechism; but some were too frank and bold to hide all the proofs of their deliverance from Genevan bonds.

Whether, as my critic pleasantly suggests, the phrase "toning up," or "toning down," is the more applicable to the modifications now in view, depends upon the sort of modifications to which he has reference. I was writing of one class of such modifications; he of another class. I do not trace the genealogy of Unitarianism through the opinions of Edwards, Bellamy, and Hopkins. Unitarians attach very little importance to what is peculiar in the New School of a century or less ago. We take the happy statement of my critic as expressing about the fair truth touching these divines, that "they changed none of the facts or substantial doctrines of the old theology, but merely modified some of them." "They did not adopt all the explanations of Calvin." No. They had grace given to them to realize that Calvinism needed some tinkering. Their successors of the New School have not accepted all their explanations of the explanations of Calvinism. I have therefore referred all along to the speculations and modifications introduced by these New School divines, as tokens only of a restlessness under the obvious meaning of formulas which they professed to receive. A man who apologizes for Calvinism, or trims or reduces its sharp definitions, or tries to make it less revolting to a pious and loving heart, is to us a witness against it. We date the first beginnings of Liberal Christianity here from the time when professedly Orthodox ministers began in their shame-facedness to apologize for Calvinism. They felt that it needed an apology, and this was their first disloyalty to it. The true old Puritan divines would have been roasted before making that confession.

Unitarianism draws its direct lineage, as my critic affirms, and as I had expressly said, through Arminianism; though probably there were hundreds of Unitarians who could not have defined Arminianism, any more than they could have talked Chinese. Now there is not the least need of all this painstaking exactness in drawing the genealogy of heresy. My sole point in the part of my statement quoted was, and is, merely to remind my readers that the responsibility of a change of sentiment from old-fashioned, real Calvinism to Unitarianism, does not rest upon the Christian men and women of any one generation. The influences which are still modifying the opinions of those reputed Orthodox, and which have made thousands of them un-Calvinistic, began to manifest themselves here more than a century and a half ago.

There were, however, single cases, many of them of men and women of independent and earnest minds, who made the whole transition from Calvinism to Unitarianism. We find many such around us now. Every Unitarian minister knows of persons in his own congregation and church who are able to relate with a fervent gratitude the history of their deep religious experience in passing from the creed of the Genevan bigot to the glorious Gospel faith of Christ.

It is to the aforesaid Arminians that my critic says the guilt of concealing their change of opinions is to be imputed. "Many of them were concealed Unitarians long before they ventured to declare themselves." From the turns of expression, the epithets and phrases used in describing these persons, one might suppose that my critic regarded them as a crew of dark, malignant, and cunning conspirators against God and truth, instead of a company of his own brother Christians, erring, imperfect, and frail like himself, but still realizing, perhaps as profoundly as he does, their responsibility to God and Christ, and seeking to know, believe, and obey the truth in the deepest sincerity of their souls. I know that my critic would not use these abusive terms of language of a living friend. Why, then, should he use them of the dead?

There are two or three points which require brief remark in the three following paragraphs: —

"As the real character of these men became more apparent, and the issue to which things were coming could no longer be concealed, a disposition was manifested by the Hopkinsians and Calvinists to drop their divisions and come together; and, without any of the formalities of a compromise or union, a real and general union was effected, embracing the great body (though not all) of the two classes above indicated. Among the visible results of this union was the founding of the Andover Theological Seminary by Hopkinsians and Calvinists, and the uniting of the Calvinistic Panoplist with the old Massachusetts Missionary Magazine. And here we have the origin of what has since been called 'The New England Theology,' or at least of this name for it, — a modification of old Calvinism, and yet not high Hopkinsianism, as this has been held by some of its more recent advocates.

"I make this statement for a twofold purpose; first, to show where the concealment of Unitarianism began; not, as Mr. Ellis thinks, in a 'section of the Orthodox party,' but among a class of men who chose to be called Arminians, while they really were (or many of them were) concealed Unitarians, and came out as Unitarians when the mask was torn off. And, secondly, to show the inaccuracy of another statement in the articles before us, that 'it was Calvinism, — the real concrete system of the Genevan Reformer, — and not the vague and undefined abstraction entitled Orthodoxy, which our predecessors assailed.' — p. 4.

"Who does Mr. Ellis mean by 'our predecessors'? Does he mean Dr. Channing, and Dr. Ware, and Professor Norton, and the early editors of the Christian Examiner? But Dr. Worcester, the opponent of Channing, was ever known as a New England theologian, and not an Old School Calvinist. And Dr. Woods, at the time of his appointment at Andover, was regarded as the special representative of the Hopkinsian interest in that union Theological Seminary, as Dr. Pearson was of the Calvinistic interest. And certainly Professor Stuart and Dr. Beecher, the early assailants of Unitarianism, were never regarded as Calvinists of 'the concrete Genevan stamp.' In short, as I have said before, the Unitarian controversy, divested of all disguises, did not commence till the spring of 1815; and those who then, and more recently, stood forth as the champions of Orthodoxy, were not Old School Calvinists, but those who had imbibed the Edwardean or New England modifications."

As to the truce between Hopkinsianism and Calvinism, which was brought about by the opening of the real Unitarian controversy, it was a matter of policy. All politic schemes are sooner or later followed by a catastrophe. Nor will Andover fail in some way to illustrate old experience on that fact with a new token.

I still insist that a section of the *Orthodox* party, not, however, of the Calvinistic portion of it, brought in the heresy which developed into Unitarianism. To say that the direct transition was made by Arminians, is no sufficient answer to my statement, any more than it would be to object to the statement, that men are grown-up children, by the critical suggestion, that it is not children, but boys, that make men. But there were downright Calvinists who became Unitarians, without stopping for a week in the stage of Arminianism, or knowing that there was such a system of modified Orthodoxy.

My critic fails entirely to make me see the alleged inaccuracy of my statement, that it was the real, concrete system of Calvinism which our predecessors assailed. Those predecessors are rightly apprehended and named by him. And what was the whole strain and burden of their professed intentions? What did they say over and over again, with wearying reiteration, that they were assailing? It was simply Calvinism. It was not the New Divinity. It was not the system which might be lying in the brains or the heart of Drs. Woods, Beecher, and Worcester, or Professor Stuart. Indeed, one of the bitterest aggravations of the controversy was found by Unitarians in the perpetual misrepresentation made of their most positive and earnest profession, that they were arguing against and rejecting Calvinism. They took the Calvinistic formulas and standards. These they quoted honestly. They defined what they regarded as the fair meaning of these formulas, the meaning conveyed through them to their own minds, the meaning which was to them so obviously unscriptural and untrue as to make them earnest opponents of Calvinism. They drew fair inferences from the doctrines of these formulas. They introduced and closed their discussions with repeated and tiresome references to standards. They found the Orthodox with whom they were in controversy claiming the reverent, filial praise of allegiance to the faith of the fathers of New England, — the doctrines of the Reformation, — the doctrines of the Westminster Catechism, and of the New England Confession of Faith. What did it all mean? Did it mean that all these standards should be taken under the reduced or subdued interpretation which they might have in the minds of some gentlemen of Andover, who had not then, *and, we may add, who have not yet*, ventured to put into print citable evidence of the precise degree to which they have impaired the integrity of Calvinism? Our predecessors undertook to give reasons for rejecting Calvinism. They were competent to say what Calvinism taught. They quoted these teachings. And what was the consequence? They were accused of slandering living men, — of caricaturing the faith of living men; they were even accused of misrepresenting Calvinism, till Professor Norton, by his elaborate quotations, made Calvinism recognize its own features. I have not said anywhere, as my critic implies that I have, that those who "stood forth as the champions of Orthodoxy were Old School Calvinists." Some of them were, and some of them were not. If the Orthodox did not defend Calvinism, then they did not defend what Unitarians were assailing. Unitarians understood their opponents as claiming the credit of being lineal and loyal descendants in the faith of the New England fathers, who fastened upon our churches and nurseries the doctrines of the Assembly's Catechism. It is those doctrines that Unitarians assail. How far professedly Orthodox men may have elaborated a system based upon an appreciable modification of those doctrines, is a question of our own times, and to that issue two schools among the Orthodox are the parties. That, however, was not the question fifty, or forty, years ago. The Unitarians believed, and their successors believe still, that there was a great deal of disingenuous, uncandid, and provoking argument and feeling displayed by the Orthodox, in trying in all sorts of ways to evade the blows dealt against Calvinism, by charging upon Unitarians a misrepresentation of the system. Of course it became very evident, as the controversy advanced, that many of the champions of Orthodoxy had no idea of assuming the defence of pure Calvinism. If they had candidly announced this at the outset, and had proclaimed how much of the system they intended to defend, and under what abatements and modifications they would alone be held responsible for it, they would have relieved the controversy of a world of acrimony. But they did assume the defence of Calvinism, and the defence of those specific doctrines of it which were sharply defined in the formulas. Unitarians took them at their word, as holding the pure old dogmas of Geneva. How were Unitarians to know anything about the precise amount and shapings of un-Calvinistic theology, as held by the men whom my critic names? It is only with great difficulty, and with but limited satisfaction, that any one can obtain, even at this day, the knowledge he may crave about the real creed taught at Andover.

Having corrected my supposed inaccuracy on this point, my critic passes to deal with another, as follows: —

"And this leads to another correction in the statements of the article before us. Mr. Ellis supposes that the modifications of old Calvinism, which now are, and long have been, current in New England, are to be ascribed to the Unitarian Controversy; that the Orthodox party, unable to defend Calvinism, as it was, against the assaults of Unitarianism, have gradually modified their system, softened it, 'toned it down,' till it has come to be a more plausible and defensible theory. 'The Unitarian may say, that the old Orthodoxy has been extirpated, as the modern shape and temper of it are greatly unlike the old Calvinism that we assailed, when it was nominally believed and theoretically defended.' 'Unitarianism has had an immeasurable effect upon Orthodoxy in this one direction. Orthodox preaching is, in some quarters, so qualified in its general character, that, if it sounds to the ear as its printed specimens utter themselves to our hearts and minds, we should be quite content to listen to it.' — pp. 7, 41."

The issue opened in this paragraph may be said to be so entirely dependent upon mere opinion and judgment about a supposed matter of fact, as not to be profitably debatable. My critic says that he is "sorry to remove or disturb so flattering an unction as this, or to spoil such a pleasing dream...... It is a pity, certainly, to disturb it; but it cannot be helped. It is all a dream. There is no foundation for it in truth...... We repeat, then, our firm conviction, that the influence of the Unitarian Controversy, in modifying and softening the Orthodoxy of New England, has been inconceivably small. It is an *infinitesimal*, which no theological calculus can reach or compute."

Now, I might quote many highly approved Orthodox testimonies to the fact, that the influence of Unitarianism in New England has impaired the integrity of Orthodoxy here, and sensibly reduced the vigor and pungency of Orthodox preaching. But these testimonies, again, would express only opinions and judgments, though, as coming from my critic's own fellowship, they should have weight with him. It will hardly do, however, to tell a Unitarian, who, by intimate friendships with Orthodox persons, and by a perusal of their writings, has an opportunity of comparing their views, and their tone, sentiments, and feelings, with those which characterized the old-fashioned Orthodoxy, that Unitarian culture and liberality, Unitarian scholarship and philosophy, have not had a calculable effect on Orthodoxy. Boston and its neighborhood are the last places on the earth in which to proclaim that notion. Those who can actually see and feel how Unitarianism finds the greatest obstacle to its denominational extension to lie in the wholly unobjectionable character of very much of the present Orthodox preaching, will be very slow to indorse the averment of my critic. He insists that Unitarianism has brought about no additional modification of Calvinism, beyond what was current forty years ago. "There has been no change among the great body of our ministers in this respect. Or if any considerable change is perceptible, we think it has been in the other direction. Probably a larger proportion of our ministers may adopt the old Calvinistic statements and explanations now, than would have been willing to do so in the early part of the present century." I have copied these sentences of my critic, with the courteous intent of allowing him to say positively what as positively with all frankness I contradict. There has been a change in the tone and in the advocacy of Orthodoxy. There is an essential change in the substance and character of the prevailing Orthodoxy. Orthodox congregations in intelligent communities would not listen now to what were called the old "blue light" doctrines and preaching. My critic suggests that Dr. Edward Beecher be asked whether Unitarianism has had any effect on Orthodoxy. Unfortunately for him, that vigorous heretic has written a book expressly to treat of a method for vindicating Orthodoxy from the reproach which Unitarianism has fairly fixed upon it, and compelled it to face; namely, the reproach of being irreconcilable with principles of rectitude and honor in the Divine government.

VII.

THE ORTHODOX DOCTRINE OF HUMAN NATURE.

The fourth of the series of newspaper articles now under review discusses a part of the contents of the second of the preceding Essays. That Essay, on the controversy upon the Nature and State of Man, was one which, in justice to my subject, I could not have written without reflecting in terms of severity upon the disingenuousness and evasiveness with which some of the Orthodox party shirked — that is the proper word, though a vulgar one — shirked the fairly expressed terms and the fairly drawn inferences from the Calvinistic doctrine which they professed to receive. I think I have given abundant evidence of this unworthy and reprehensible course of conduct in the pages of that Essay. The Unitarians found it utterly impossible to hold the Orthodox to the plain significance of their own formulas. They said they were Calvinists, that they accepted the doctrines of the Puritans, that they held to the articles of the Assembly's Catechism and of the New England Confession of Faith. Very well. This seemed to give a fair starting-ground for the discussion. The Unitarians avowed that they did not accept Calvinism, nor its doctrines, nor the standards just mentioned. They proceeded to define Calvinism, and to quote these doctrines, and they were immediately assailed as if they had been a most uncommon company of deceivers and slanderers. The Christian Spectator, as I have quoted it (p. 57), insisted upon the authorities in the case for charging upon Calvinism such odious views of human nature under God's righteous rule, and flatly denied that the Institutes of Calvin, the works of the Westminster Assembly, &c. contained the doctrine charged upon them. But when evidence which no reasonable person could refute was brought to bear upon these denials, the Spectator, with the most amazing effrontery, affirmed (p. 59): "What Calvin believed and taught, and what any modern Calvinistic authors have taught, are questions of no real importance in the present discussion." How could there be any profitable discussion, as between Christian opponents, when such a sleight as this came in as a token of the irritation of the Orthodox party, and as a sure means of irritating the Unitarian party? The Orthodox were goaded into the heats of passion by being compelled to face the literal terms of their own formulas, unrelieved by the plausible, softening explanations and reductions through which their own teachers presented them. The Unitarians were forced to the conviction, that the Orthodox wished the credit and the security of holding to the creed of the fathers in its undiminished integrity and rigidness; while they were still ashamed, under the light of day, to admit to themselves, what Dr. Edward Beecher has so nobly confessed, its utter "inconsistency with the principles of justice and righteousness in the Divine government."

I endeavored to write about this painful element in the old controversy with candor and moderation. I could not suppress all reference to it, nor write otherwise than rebukingly of the inconsistency and unfairness of the course pursued by the Orthodox. The embittered and malignant spirit which their evasions of their own creed introduced into the controversy will always require notice from the historian of the controversy, as the phenomenon is so obtrusively offensive there. Rather than utter in one manly sentence the avowal, "We do not hold unqualified Calvinism, and will not defend it," the Orthodox preferred to charge upon their Unitarian opponents ignorance, slander, and the most odious vices. This I had to say in order to be true to the relation of facts which there was no disguising. My own personal acquaintance with many Orthodox persons of recent years would prevent my charging upon them my own construction of their professed creed. *I understand them* as avowing their belief, that God calls us all into being with a wrecked nature, holds us to a service which only an unimpaired nature could perform, and dooms us to an unspeakable woe for our shortcoming. This, in the best exercise of the faculties which God has given me, and with all the mastery I can exercise over every bias that might pervert my judgment, — this is the only intelligible view which I can gather from the Orthodox doctrine of human nature. But I would not charge that view upon an Orthodox friend; for I know how angry or uncomfortable an Orthodox person is made by having his own tenets set forth in the frank, strong language of one who rejects them as revolting and impious. An Orthodox believer wishes the benefit of all the palliating, subduing, apologetic phraseology and metaphysics that can possibly relieve the hideousness of his naked doctrine. This benefit the Unitarians, when their controversy was sharp, would not yield to the Orthodox. They insisted that those who professed to be Calvinists, and to defend Calvinism, should face and recognize Calvinism, and not take refuge behind some softened, reduced shape of the grim spectre.

Now my attempt to do justice to this element in the controversy, and to rebuke and censure in measured terms the injustice of evading a fair issue once espoused, has drawn from my critic the following language: —

"And here we are sorry to say that Mr. Ellis's wonted fairness and candor seem, in a great measure, to forsake him. He too often seems heated and excited, and on that account incapable of doing that justice to his opponents, or his subject, to which his unsophisticated good-nature would be likely to prompt him. But we derive one advantage from his misfortune. It will be the less necessary to follow and refute him. Our remarks, in reply, may be very brief."

They are brief, too brief, — so brief as not to meet a single one of my prominent positions in the Essay. He shall have the benefit, however, of addressing my readers for himself. The following paragraph is an ingenious combination of statements to be admitted, and statements that might be questioned. The zeal of the writer has driven him into anachronisms which make him appear uncandid, though I would not for a moment entertain the suspicion that he could be influenced by any other than honorable motives. Yet he none the less makes some of the concessions and confessions which Unitarians drew out of the Orthodox grudgingly, as admissions of their reduced Calvinism, to show as if they had been publicly avowed before the controversy as the terms in view of which it was to be conducted.

"Mr. Ellis begins by affirming that the early 'Unitarians understood and avowed that they were assailing, not the undefined and modified semblance now called Orthodoxy, but *Calvinism*, which had expressed itself in positive formulas, and to which the Orthodox party nominally professed an unqualified allegiance.' (p. 55.) We care not what these early Unitarians 'understood and avowed.' They well knew, and we know, that the current Orthodoxy of New England, in the year 1815, when the Unitarian Controversy properly opened, was not precisely that of the old Calvinistic formulas. To these formulas the Orthodox of that day did not 'profess an unqualified allegiance.' They were willing to accept them, and they did, 'for substance of doctrine,' as the phrase was; but this implies that they were not accepted *ad literam.* Nor were the modifications of statement which they wished to make unknown to the public, or to Unitarians. They had long been exhibited in sermons and in books. They were paraded with some exaggerations in Ely's Contrast, as early as 1811, and of this work an elaborate review had been published in Norton's Repository. All this took place some years before the opening of the Unitarian Controversy. And yet, at the commencement of the controversy, the attempt was made, and is still persisted in, to hold the Orthodox to the letter of the old formulas; and what is worse, to all the '*logical deductions*,' amounting in some instances to the grossest distortions, which their adversaries have been pleased to draw out from them. It was vain for Doctors Woods, and Worcester, and Beecher to say, 'We do not accept your logical deductions, or the old formulas themselves, without explanation.' It was vain for them to state, as they often did, and had a perfect right to do, (and their opponents should have believed them and met them accordingly,) what their explanations and modifications were. They were brought back and reined up to the 'old formulas,' with the appended 'logical deductions,' and must fight for these, or abandon the contest."

Here, it will be seen, is the old charge of misrepresentation, because Unitarians insisted upon taking Calvinism to mean Calvinism. My critic says, he "cares not what the early Unitarians understood and avowed." But they did care. They knew their aims; they had a right to choose their aims; they did choose them; they avowed them. They undertook an assault upon Calvinism, upon the doctrines of the Westminster Assembly's Catechism and of the New England Confession of Faith. They did not undertake to assail the specific theological system of either Dr. Woods, Dr. Beecher, or Dr. Worcester, for the best reason in the world,—they did not know what the system of either of those divines was, and might not have thought it worth their while to controvert the views of an individual. They had no means of knowing, we have no sufficient means of knowing now, precisely how much of consistent Calvinism those divines received or rejected. Dr. Hodge, of the Old School, tells us that the New Theology *does not hold* "the substance of Orthodox doctrine." Unitarians might shrink from this direct giving of the lie to their Orthodox opponents, even at the risk of offending them by charging upon them their own construction of the substance of Calvinism. But there was one privilege demanded by the Orthodox which the Unitarians had no idea of granting them, namely, the privilege of professing to be Calvinists without believing Calvinism. Still less would Unitarians permit any ingenious trickery, under the phrase of "substance of doctrine," to metamorphose Calvinism into something wholly different from Calvinism. There was a sort of scientific passion for keeping the verisimilitude of old fossilized antiquities, which led the Unitarians to insist that Calvinism should not be trifled with even by its assumed patrons. The feeling was similar to that which would protest against the patching out and filling in and substituting, by any of Barnum's fabrications, of a veritable collection of the remains of old saurians and mastodons. As my critic says, "Unitarians well knew that the current Orthodoxy of New England in the year 1815, when the Unitarian Controversy properly opened, was not precisely that of the old Calvinistic formulas." Why, then, did it pretend to be *substantially* what it was not precisely? Why did it insist, in all sorts of persistent phrases, that it held the faith of the Reformers and the New England fathers, and of their Catechism and their Confession? "The modifications of statement which the Orthodox wished to make," were known to the Unitarians. These modifications would either affect the *substance* of Calvinism, or they would not. If they did affect its substance, then Unitarians denied the Orthodox the right to make these modifications and still claim to be Calvinists. If, on the contrary, the modifications did not reach to the substance of Calvinism, then the Unitarians did no wrong in holding the Orthodox to the Calvinistic formulas. It was fair that they should "fight for those, or abandon the contest."

If, as my critic fears, heat and excitement interfered with my candor in reviewing this part of the controversy, he would hardly allow that I am reasonable in objecting strongly to his own course in the remainder of his paper. He quotes some of the strong and pointed statements made by Unitarians and myself, to set forth what we understand to be the substantial Calvinistic doctrine of human nature, and our objections to it. He then adds: "Such is the view of the doctrine of depravity which, through this long article, Mr. Ellis imputes to the Orthodox of New England, and which he labors to expose and refute." My reader has but to turn back to the Essay and see that I *impute* this view to the Westminster Catechism and the New England Confession, which I quote. My critic proceeds: "Nor can it be said (we wish it could) that Mr. Ellis did not know that he was misrepresenting the Orthodox, [I was writing of *professed believers of the creeds quoted*,] for he quotes the following statement of Dr. Woods, made more than thirty years ago: 'If there is any principle respecting the moral government of God,' &c." (See page 65.) I do quote that disclaimer of Dr. Woods. And why? For the very candid purpose which my critic denies to me, of showing that the Orthodox wish to be relieved of the imputation of holding rigid Calvinism. So far am I from affirming that all the Orthodox of New England hold all the views in question, that I took pains to quote from Dr. Woods and others, that they might have the benefit of their qualifying assertions. Strangely enough, my critic resorts to my own pages for quoted passages which he thinks may be adduced as means of relieving the modern Orthodox from receiving my construction of Calvinism. And yet, after I had taken pains to make the very quotations which he adopts, in my desire to deal fairly with the authors of them, I am charged with *knowing* that I am misrepresenting them. This certainly is hard measure. I cite the creeds, I cite old Calvinistic authorities, I state the doctrine drawn from them, and my objections to it. I add some quotations in which professedly Orthodox men advance softened or modified views. My critic quotes my quotations, as available for the very purpose to which I adduce them, and then censures me as if I had failed of this fair course. He takes another of my quotations from the Spirit of the Pilgrims, (see page 98), adduced by me with the same intent of allowing the modern Orthodox the benefit of their own modifications, he continues the quotation a few lines further, and then adds: "These statements of our real belief Mr. Ellis had seen, some of them he had quoted." His piece contains two quotations, no more, and they are transferred as such from my own pages. He is safe, therefore, in saying that I "had seen them." What he means by "some of them" being quoted by me, is pointless; it is probably to be referred to a careless slip of the pen in writing. I have, then, quoted just such passages, the same passages, as he would himself adduce, to show that the modern Orthodox do not hold the constructive view of a Calvinistic doctrine previously presented. And yet my reward is a charge of intentional misrepresentation, as not having done the very thing I have done. My critic makes quotations with which to condemn me; but, with marvellous strangeness, he borrows them from me. All through my Essay, from the beginning to the end of it, I recognize fully the modifications of Orthodox doctrine. See particularly the statement beginning near the bottom of page 59.

I will overlook, and freely pardon, the error into which my critic was thus led, probably by reading wearily and carelessly my long article. But his next paragraph would justify some sharpness of reply from me. By bringing together three sentences, or parts of sentences, culled from a space of twenty pages in my article, and by wholly severing the connection of thought and the line of remark in them, he would present me in the ridiculous light of the following inconsistencies.

"In his remarks upon the quoted statements of our real belief, Mr. Ellis talks variously. In one place, he represents our modifications as 'unintelligible,' and says that, 'singly or together, they do not give much relief' (p. 66). Then he represents them as so evasive and pitiable, as to be a 'scandal to our whole profession' (p. 81). But finally, thinking rather more favorably of them, he says: 'The modifications, abatements, and palliations of which professedly Orthodox writers have felt compelled to avail themselves, in dealing with this doctrine, have been of great service to us' (p. 89)."

I do use all the words jumbled together in this paragraph, and as I use them, and in their connection, I think they have a meaning in them, and that their assertions are happily consistent. I had hoped that the style of controversy drawn upon in such a jumble of an opponent's words was out of date among well-disposed writers. If my reader will do me the favor to turn to the pages from which the critic has quoted words enough to make a burlesque of my statements, and will connect them as I have connected them, I venture to think that he will find the assertions to hold very well together. First, I say, on page 66, that I might have attempted to quote "a series of the ingenious or futile, the actual or only apparent modifications, and attempted modifications, of the Calvinistic doctrine of the nature and state of man." Knowing very well, however, that the metaphysical jargon and the subtle evasions and mystifications employed by theologians of the Old and New Schools in their dealings with this subject, were absolutely *unintelligible* to many readers, I declined the undertaking. I took care to guard against leaving the implication that *much relief* would be found in these modifications of Calvinism, singly or together. They still fail in relieving the Calvinistic doctrine of this unscriptural and revolting element, — that, born with a nature ruined by an inherited corruption, we are still held by God to an undiminished responsibility. So much for the *unintelligible* quality in modern Orthodox speculations, and their deficiency as means for effectually clearing an offensive doctrine.

Secondly, on page 81, I say, and I repeat with emphasis the assertion, that "the lamentable shifts and evasions and subtilties to which Orthodox theologians have had recourse during the last half-century, in trying to evade the plain meaning of this article of their creed, are a scandal upon our whole profession." And a scandal they surely are, — a grievous one; — more scandalous, because of the sacred bearings of the argument, than are the quirks and trickeries, the fallacies and the deceptions, introduced by a class of lawyers into their pleadings. Calvinism proposes to us in its formulas a doctrine which, if words have any clear meaning, asserts, that, as the result of our covenant or federal relation with Adam, we are born with a corrupt nature, and are yet held by God to such a responsibility as could be justly exacted only of an unimpaired nature. Unitarians protest against the doctrine, and reject it. They reject it because it outrages reason, justice, and Scripture. They state their objections, and in this statement they generally include a definition of the doctrine, and a plain, frank description of what is to them its odious and revolting quality. But how are their statements and objections met? Often with a whining and petulant complaint from Orthodox disputants, that Unitarians misrepresent their doctrine, and also with *scandalous* tricks of language and sophistry used in the vain attempt to evade the substance of their own doctrine. Now I have admitted that some Unitarians have caricatured Orthodoxy. But I have also insisted that some fair-minded and candid persons, as Unitarians, have tried to understand the Orthodox doctrine as it is held by its professed disciples, with all the alleviations and abatements of its harsh features of which its friends give it the benefit. Yet these candid inquirers find the same odious and unjust quality in the doctrine. In courteous and emphatic terms they express their dissent, their repugnance to it. What then ought the Orthodox to do? They ought to defend their doctrine or to renounce it. They may claim the privilege of amending phraseology where equivocal or antiquated words, or misleading phrases, interfere with the intelligible announcement of their doctrines. But they can claim no more than this. As frank, bold, unwavering champions of truth, they should stand for what they advance in their formulas. They say, as we understand them, that God requires the tale of brick without the straw; that he demands that a clean thing should come forth out of an unclean, that a corrupt nature should develop into a pure life. If the Orthodox do not say this, then plainly we have no real controversy with them upon so vital an issue as has always been supposed to be involved in the doctrine of human nature. Dr. Edward Beecher, with noble and heroic frankness, has admitted that the Orthodox doctrine includes precisely that odious and shocking quality of injustice, unrighteousness, as ascribed to the Divine Government; and he does more than allow, he *insists*, that Unitarianism rejects and assails it with valid reason and in loyalty to holy truth. But all Orthodox believers will not yield this full justice, nor even the least measure of it, to Unitarians. Some of them charge us with slander, falsehood, and every other unchristian vice, rather than admit that we have the slightest ground for objecting to their doctrine. They would make us the most unreasonable beings in the world, because we reject something that is perfectly reasonable. One would suppose that the intelligence of educated men in this age of the world was equal to the task of interpreting the meaning of a Calvinistic formula. But no! Unitarians prove that they cannot interpret it, simply by rejecting the doctrine conveyed in it. To make this appear, the doctrine has been tampered and trifled with by "lamentable shifts, evasions, and subtilties" on the part of its professed disciples, in a way to amount, as I have said, and repeat, to a *scandal* upon the profession of theologians.

And, thirdly, I have said on page 89, and I also wish to say it again, that "All the modifications, abatements, and palliatives of which professedly Orthodox writers have felt compelled to avail themselves in dealing with their doctrine, have been of great service to Unitarians." And why do I say this? And how do I consider that we have been served in this way? My own pages answer these questions. My critic had only to note what I said in *connection* with the first of the three sentences which he has quoted and jumbled together, in order to have been prevented from attempting to prove my assertions inconsistent. For, on page 66, I had said of these attempted modifications of Cavinistic doctrine: "*They are of service to us* as showing a constant uneasiness under any form in which the old doctrine has as yet been presented, and as indicating how trifling a relaxation of its old terms will be welcomed as a comfort." Again, on p. 61, I had said: "We are ready to grant to the Orthodox the fullest benefit of all the modifications of this doctrine which the most ingenious man among them is able to devise. But we must urge that these modifications *all accrue to our side*, as they relax and soften and qualify the sternness of our old foe, and are yielded or availed of for the sake of mitigating the repulsiveness of the original doctrine."

Thus I have taken pains to put back into their connection the three sentences which, after having suffered violence, were used to prove upon me inconsistency or ludicrous incoherency of statement. Set the three sentences together by their connection, and they affirm these three easily demonstrable propositions: that many of the attempted modifications of Calvinistic theology require such metaphysical terms and subtle distinctions for their exposition as to be unintelligible to many readers, while they still stop short of essentially relieving the reproach of the doctrine; that some of the devices of theologians to evade, and get round, and extenuate and apologize for formulas which they will neither frankly yield up nor boldly defend, has brought scandals upon our profession (I did not include as among these scandals Dr. Edward Beecher's theory for supplementing Calvinism, that, when we are born into the world, we are old sinners under condemnation from a previous state, with a new chance for redemption, as this theory is ingenious, not scandalous); and that every concession, evasion, and modification made in defence of Orthodoxy, whether amounting to much or nothing, is of service to Unitarians, as revealing the restlessness and lack of full satisfaction among the Orthodox.

Most gladly would I have used the space just given to a side issue, in meeting any argument offered by my critic in opposition to the positive points advanced in my Essay. But he has not met a single one of my positions, he has not sought to relieve a single one of the objections which I urge against the Orthodox doctrine, nor questioned a single one of the arguments by which I defend the Unitarian view. His article is wholly given up to statements of the same character as those to which I have already referred. Here are more of the same tenor.

"It is clear from these quotations [those which I have made in my Essay], that Mr. Ellis knew what our statements were, in regard to this doctrine of depravity. He knew what they had been, from the beginning of the controversy to the present time. And yet he persists in urging upon us dogmas which we do not believe, insisting that we must take them, swallow them, and be responsible for them, when we repudiate them, or some of them, as sincerely as he does himself. And this is that of which we complain. Are we not competent to make a statement of our own views? And when we do make it fairly, honestly, and repeatedly, are we not worthy to be believed? Must we be perpetually held up to ridicule and reproach, as holding opinions which are as foreign to us as they are to our accusers?

"Will it be asked again, What do you believe on this painful subject of human depravity? I answer, we believe just what Mr. Ellis has quoted us as believing, in his extracts from the Spirit of the Pilgrims. We believe 'that, since the fall of Adam,' — and, I will add, *in consequence* of the fall of Adam, — 'men are, in their natural state, altogether destitute of true holiness, and entirely depraved'; but 'that, though thus depraved, they are justly required to love God with all the heart, and justly punishable for disobedience; or in other words, they are complete moral agents, proper subjects of moral government, and truly accountable to God for their actions.' — Vol. I. p. 11. 'We do not believe that the posterity of Adam are personally chargeable with eating the forbidden fruit; or that their constitution is so depraved as to leave them no natural ability to love and serve God, or as to render it improper for him to require obedience. We do not believe that God has made a part of mankind on purpose to damn them; or that he compels them to sin; or that he mocks them with offers of pardon on conditions that they have no power to comply with; or that he punishes them eternally for not performing impossibilities.' — Vol. II. pp. 3, 4.

"This statement of our belief on the subject of depravity we made, in all sincerity, almost thirty years ago. In all sincerity, we repeat it now. We cannot but think it intelligible and explicit; and if Mr. Ellis cannot, as he intimates, harmonize all parts of it, we humbly think that we can. It will be seen, at a glance, that it differs most essentially from Professor Norton's statement of the Orthodox belief, and from the extracts above quoted from Mr. Ellis. And this imputing to us of opinions which we do not receive, and then arguing from them as though they were conceded verities, and holding us up to scorn and reproach on account of them; — this is that of which we feel that we have good reason to complain."

After the repeated perusal of the above extract, I can hardly account for the strange misunderstanding which has evidently warped the judgment of my critic. The very quotations from modern Orthodox writers which he credits me with presenting on my own pages, were made by me for the set purpose of giving his brethren the benefit of their own professed qualifications of Calvinism, which he insists that I deny to them. If I had given no such quotations, he would have had reason in his censure. But as I do offer them, and offer them, too, as they are offered by their writers, in mitigation of judgment, what more could I do? My critic says: "We believe just what Mr. Ellis has quoted us as believing, in his extracts from the Spirit of the Pilgrims." Very well. Then I have fairly stated their belief, have I not? Near the close of the extract, my critic says that the Orthodox belief, as just defined by him, differs from Mr. Norton's statement of it, and from statements of it made in some other quotations from me. Very true again; and the statements ought to differ, according to his own showing. For those definitions given by Mr. Norton and myself were of old-fashioned, pure Calvinism, from its formulas and its stanch champions. Some of these my critic says he repudiates as sincerely as I do, and that they are as foreign to some of the Orthodox as to the Unitarians. But this does not prove that the repudiated opinions are not Calvinistic, nor that they were never entertained by the Orthodox, nor that they are not to be fairly inferred by sound and irrefutable logical deductions from the very substance of Orthodoxy. It was against this veritable form of Orthodoxy, namely, Calvinism, easily ascertainable and well understood, and not against its softened, palliated shapings and reductions, that Unitarians first directed their opposition. The concrete, old-fashioned Calvinism of the formulas and the Catechism and the Confession was, I say again, the original target of Unitarianism. They knew what that was, and could get at it. Every subsequent modification and abatement of its doctrinal form or substance — especially those for which my critic pleads in his attempt to state them — has received attention from Unitarians. Their periodicals and controversial essays will afford abundant proof that they have been quite eager to seize upon, yes, even to anticipate and forecast, every heretical development, every modern phase of dissent, from the Calvinism of the standards. Indeed, my own aim and method were to begin with fair quotations from these standards, and with contemporary expositions of them, as furnishing the criteria from which to define the faith of those who accepted them, and the heresy of those who rejected them. After a clear statement of these preliminaries, I endeavored, in reference to each of the great doctrines in controversy, to follow down the course of discussion, and to make note of every substantial or supposed variation from Calvinism made by those who still claimed to be Orthodox. The quotations of which my critic has availed himself for exhibiting his own modifications of the creed, were offered by me in the carrying out of this design. I cannot yet see how I could have pursued a method better suited to meet the wishes of my critic, or the conditions of fair polemics.

Within the compass of the pages now gathered into this volume, will be found a recognition of every modified and softened statement of the leading Orthodox doctrines that has ever passed under my notice. As one of my objects was to prove that Orthodox men had departed from their standards, or tried to evade the full doctrinal significance of them, all such subdued views as my critic wishes to have the benefit of were the very things which I sought to hunt out, and to present in the plainest way. How, then, can he justly accuse me of urging upon him dogmas which he does not believe?

I think, however, that I can appreciate, or at least understand, the reason why my method and course of argument should have called out the expression of such indignant feeling from my opponent. It is simply because I will not allow that the modifications of Calvinism conceded by him and his friends furnish any essential relief of what are to us the unscriptural and revolting features of the system. Most cheerfully would I yield this allowance if I could do so; but I cannot. On the contrary, the statements of my critic are only to my mind another exhibition of the utter futility of such attempts to hold the substance of Calvinism through the softening and apologetic help of a mere variation of phrase in the verbal exposition of it. I cannot allow that my critic has succeeded, where hundreds of good men before him have failed, in reconciling the substance of Calvinistic doctrine about the ruin of our race in Adam, and its undiminished responsibility, with the sense of justice and the gift of reason with which our Maker has endowed us, and which he addresses in the inspired teachings of Scripture. Let him turn from me, and meet the frank avowals of his own brother in faith, Dr. Edward Beecher. Modify Orthodoxy as he may, if he still retains the fiction that God demands a clean thing from an unclean, he retains the Calvinistic dogma which we insist flouts the very foundations of Divine equity. Explicit as my critic says his professed departure from real Calvinism is, I must frankly reply, that to me it is not explicit, that it amounts to little, if anything. It leaves still the outrage which is inherent in Calvinism, — of assigning to us a prejudiced start on an immortal career, of making human life a foregone conclusion at its commencement. The statement still leaves the question, "What do you believe on this painful subject of human depravity?" wholly unanswered, so far as the answer promised or expected is to convey any essential relief from pure Calvinism. With the utmost courtesy, but with frankness, I must reply to my critic, that I cannot reconcile the two terms in which he avows his own belief. After his warm protest against being held answerable for Calvinism, he sets himself to meet the question, "What, then, do you believe?" and I read on, looking to find some generous concession, some *explicit* renouncement of the odious element in Calvinism, some more reasonable and Scriptural exhibition of the relation between man's native condition and his responsibility. But I am grievously disappointed. I cannot reconcile the statement, that, in consequence of the fall of Adam, we come into existence *entirely depraved*, with the statement, that, though thus depraved, we are *justly* required to love God with *all the heart*, and are *justly* punishable for disobedience. How does the doctrinal belief affirmed in those two statements differ from the doctrine of the formula? The two statements appear to us self-contradictory. They involve that gross outrage upon reason and righteousness, of which we complain in Calvinism. To assert, that, though we are born without wings, we are justly punishable by God because we do not fly in the air all the way up to God, is to our minds not one whit more affronting to reason and equity, than to assert that, though born entirely depraved, we are justly punishable for not loving God with all our hearts. Of what character or value must be all the love of an entirely depraved heart? Is pure love, or the love of a pure object, possible to such a heart? I say, then, frankly, as my critic very reasonably fears that I shall say, "that I cannot harmonize all the parts" of his proffered doctrinal statement. I say more, namely, that he himself cannot harmonize them in a way intelligible to other minds. If, further, he asks me to admit that his view differs substantially from what he says that he repudiates, I must decline to make the admission.

But I cannot pass without a word of denial his vehement complaint, at the close of the above extract, that Unitarians hold up him and his brethren to "scorn and reproach" on account of their professed belief. It is the dogma which we subject to that scorn and reproach, as an outrage upon the reason and the sense of justice with which our Maker has endowed us, as an utter perversion of the doctrines of the Bible, and as the occasion of an untold amount of infidelity, first, among those outside of the Church, and, second, among those who have once been received into it. We are, therefore, bound to scorn and reproach the dogma, to try against it every weapon which Christian faith, reason, logic, and zeal can supply. The only modification of the dogma which will be explicit enough for us, will be an entire and honest renunciation of it. There are two ways by which it may be relieved: one is by graduating the claims which God makes upon us to the impaired nature with which, in the course of his providence, we are born into this world; the other is by asserting for us such a degree of unvitiated, uncorrupted moral power, as will enable us to love God with all our hearts. Either of these methods of relief would involve the renunciation of Calvinism. My critic avails himself of neither of them. He asserts entire depravity at birth; he claims for God the whole heart's love; he holds us justly punishable, and by a most terrific doom, for falling short of what, under the conditions, is an utter impossibility.

VIII.

THE DOCTRINE OF THE TRINITY.

The fifth paper in the series upon which I am commenting deals with some few, and those by no means the most important, points suggested in the third of the preceding Essays. It opens with another of those partial representations of my views, which, through the aid of imperfect quotations, attempt to convict me of inconsistency or incoherency of statement. Thus my critic writes: —

"Mr. Ellis does not object to the Trinity on the ground 'that the doctrine involves a *mystery*,' but rather on the ground of 'its utter absurdity.' And yet he confesses that, 'in some of the modern shapings of the doctrine, there is no reason for rejecting it, which would weigh against the slightest good reason for receiving it. But the slightest reason for receiving it is the very thing which is lacking.' If the doctrine be an 'utter absurdity,' it would seem that there ought to be strong reasons for rejecting it, — strong enough to overbalance any and all reasons in its favor. But let that pass."

It is true that I represent Unitarians as objecting to the doctrine of the Trinity, not because it states a mystery, but because it is absurdly inconsistent in the very terms which it brings together for making its proposition (p. 119). I have also admitted what I am quoted as asserting in regard to some of the modern shapings of the doctrine (p. 116). And yet I have not avowed that any force of reasoning would induce me to accept an "utter absurdity." It is the bald, dogmatic statement of the doctrine in the formula, copied on a previous page, which I represent as involving an absurdity. But my critic seems to have skipped the following sentence, in which I pass from the doctrine as advanced and defined in the formula, to the shadowy views of some professed Trinitarians. My words seem plain enough as I turn back to them, on p. 115: "The doctrine of the Trinity has indeed been so sublimated and refined, and so reduced in the rigidity of its old technical terms, that it may now be said to offer itself in some quite inoffensive and unobjectionable shapes."

My critic now favors me with some direct replies, which it gives me pleasure to meet as directly.

"Mr. Ellis objects, first, to the doctrine of the Trinity, that 'it is impossible to state it in the language of Scripture.' And so it is impossible to give a precise, scientific statement of many other doctrines, which Unitarians and Orthodox both believe, in the language of Scripture. The objection proves too much, if it proves anything."

I must try the virtue of a flat denial, if courtesy will allow, in meeting my opponent on so vital a point where an unproved assertion cannot be admitted. I therefore do deny positively that Unitarians receive one single doctrine or tenet of their faith which they are unable to state in the precise language of Scripture. I might even go so far as to affirm, that we receive no doctrinal tenet for which we cannot quote the very words of Christ himself. My critic must have sadly underrated the importance which I attach to the Unitarian objection to the doctrine of the Trinity above announced, if he supposes he can evade its force so easily and dogmatically as he has essayed to do. We boast that our Scriptural faith can express itself in explicit, ungarbled, positive, and emphatic sentences of Scripture. We will receive nothing as vital to our faith which cannot be so expressed. We object to Trinitarianism, and the objection has never been fairly met, and never can be fairly met, that it presents to us, as the groundwork and basis of the whole Christian system of revealed truths, a dogma for which it cannot quote a single comprehensive text. It certainly cannot be alleged that it was any less important for Christ and his Apostles to announce the doctrine clearly and emphatically, than that subsequent Christian teachers should lay stress upon it. What stress such teachers have laid upon it we all know. The doctrinal statement of the Trinity leads off the Orthodox creeds: no vague, inferential implication of the contents of the doctrine is thought to be satisfactory. Doubt about it is dangerous; a rejection of it is fatal. The doctrine is obtruded upon us in its stiffest literal terms, though, strange to say, many of its champions affirm that they dislike its terms, and wish that they could express it more adequately. Here certainly is no backwardness, no hesitation, on the part of those who, believing the doctrine, think it ought to be reiterated and emphasized. Now, how comes it that Christ and his Apostles furnish us not one single announcement of it? If anything can be inferred with certainty as to the belief of the Jews concerning the mode of the Divine existence, it is that they knew nothing of the Orthodox dogma of the Trinity. Surely then we might expect that their first Christian teachers would have been at least as careful to declare it to them as a new revelation of truth, the basis of all Christian doctrine, as modern Christian teachers are to demand a faith in it from their pupils. It will not do to say that the Apostles left other essential Christian doctrines without any direct, explicit statement of them. It is not true. They had a commission from their Master, and they discharged it. Whatever they have not taught plainly, must be pronounced to be no part of their teaching, however positively their successors may have taught it. Peter, who preached to the Jews the first Christian discourse after the Church had risen from the grave of its Founder, told them that "Jesus of Nazareth," "whom they had put to death," was "a man approved of God by works which God did by him," and that God had raised him up. Words could not be more explicit. Yet not from them, and from no other words spoken by the Apostles to the Jews, as recorded, could they have gathered a plain statement of the Trinity. As to the Gentiles, we find traces, among a school of philosophic dreamers, of a sort of Trinitarian conception, far unlike that, however, which Christian divines now receive, though the dogma came into the Church by that channel. No direct announcement of the doctrine was made by the Apostles when they preached to Gentiles, who certainly were ignorant of it, and might claim to be distinctly informed about the first *fundamental* doctrine of the Gospel.

I must, therefore, reiterate the objection which my critic so strangely tries to parry by asserting what is directly opposite to the truth, that Unitarians receive many doctrines as of the prime substance of Christianity, of which the Scriptures make no precise statement. I must do one thing more. I must express my disappointment at the hopelessness of any issue of harmony from discussions in which the main points receive such a slighting treatment. I do not know a more valid argument which could be alleged to a fair and unbiassed mind against the claim of any doctrine to be received as vital and fundamental to the Christian system, than the fact that it is not taught in the plain and earnest utterances of Christ and his Apostles. We know how eagerly Trinitarians would snatch at any Bible sentence which comprehended all the elements of the doctrine. We know that they are at no loss for words and phrases in which to state it. We know how they obtrude it and emphasize it. We turn earnestly towards them, and ask why they are compelled to do this in words and phrases and formulas of their own invention? Why they cannot find a single Scripture sentence which will serve their use? We hope much from reasonable men, when we ask such a question. We are as honest and as earnest as they are. We wish to be reasonable and teachable. We protest that we wish to have the fundamentals of the Christian system in the sufficient words of Christ and his Apostles. And what satisfaction do we receive from our opponents? Such only as we are left to find in a disengenuous evasion of the difficulty that is raised, unless we can accept such a reply as my critic offers to my next objection, as follows: —

"'Again,' says Mr. Ellis, 'a fundamental doctrine ought to be emphatically announced and constantly reiterated.' And we hold that the doctrine of the Trinity — in its elements, its necessary component parts — *is* 'emphatically announced' in the Scriptures. We think it is, not 'constantly,' but *frequently* reiterated, much more frequently than 'the unity of God.'"

That clause, "*its necessary component parts*," comes in very ingeniously. The necessary component parts of almost any doctrine which the human brain could devise, might be found in Scripture, if we admitted the lawfulness of the process for making such a composite of Scripture language as is often brought to the proof of the doctrine of the Trinity. My critic, by that ingenious clause of his, will have suggested quite forcibly to many Unitarians one of their very gravest objections to the admission of the Scriptural character of that doctrine. We first object, that it is not directly taught in Scripture. We next object, almost, if not quite, as triumphantly, to the processes and the dealings with

Scripture which Trinitarians are compelled to pursue in order to get out of it *the component parts* of the doctrine. We pronounce these processes unreasonable, violent, and unfair. They are a reproach upon the science of Biblical criticism. The dislocations, transpositions, glosses, and hard-drawn inferences and artificial reconstructions which make the Scriptures yield up *the component parts* of the doctrine of the Trinity, do not approve themselves to us. Sometimes young school-children, who inherit a championship of Unitarianism and Trinitarianism from their parents, will try these dislocated texts, sentences, half-sentences, and phrases on each other. The vanquished champion of one day will ask of parent or Sunday-school teacher a rebutting text for the next day. The Orthodox child will quote the assertion of Jesus, "I and my Father are one." His opponent will meet him with the petition of Jesus to his Father, that his disciples may be *one*, in precisely the same way and sense. Now we had better leave this sort of doctrinal tactics to children. It may be well for grown men to remember that the *component parts* of a house will not make a house unless they are orderly disposed.

The next objection advanced against the doctrine of the Trinity is, that the three texts on which Trinitarians would most readily seize for its vindication, and which the most ignorant and obstinate among them insist upon bringing forward, are discredited for such a use by all competent scholars. The fact is most significant, as it proves that the Scriptures have been tampered with for the sake of interpolating testimony to a doctrine which was evidently recognized to be in need of testimony. My critic replies thus: —

"Mr. Ellis further objects to the doctrine of the Trinity, that 'the texts which are quoted to support it are peculiarly embarrassed with doubts and questions as to authenticity, exactness of rendering, and signification.' He instances three prominent proof-texts, viz. 1 John v. 7, 2 Tim. iii. 16, and Acts xx. 28, which have been regarded as of a doubtful character. We have no time or need to go into a consideration of these vexed passages here. The history of them proves that, in some of the early controversies respecting the Trinity and the person of Christ, they have been tampered with, either by the Arians, or the Orthodox, or by both. We do not abandon the common reading of these passages, more especially of the last two. Neither are we disposed pertinaciously to contend for it. They may be held in abeyance, for further light, without at all endangering the Scriptural support of the doctrines which they seem to teach."

On this reply I have only to remark upon the evident reluctance of the writer to admit the full force and pertinence of the objection. I should have been glad to have had this cumulative evidence which impeaches the Scriptural character of the doctrine of the Trinity met with a little more candor. Trinitarians are fond of charging Unitarians with interpreting Scripture under a bias, of bringing prejudiced opinions to it, and of explaining away its manifest teachings. The charge seems to us almost ludicrously self-convicting, in view of the stages of pleading through which my critic passes. I must remind him that the text 1 John v. 7 has no part in "the early controversies respecting the Trinity." It did not exist then. As to "holding in abeyance for further light" these texts which the best Orthodox authorities agree in surrendering, we must answer, that life is too short for it, and the claims of progress will not admit of it. The course recommended by my critic seems to me rather like holding light itself in abeyance.

The next paragraph offered by my critic contains a little word-play, of which he and my readers shall mutually have the benefit, so far as the copying it here can avail: —

"Mr. Ellis objects, that 'the Scriptures bear a positive testimony against the doctrine of the Trinity, by insisting upon the absolute unity of God.' But does not Mr. Ellis know, that the unity of God is an essential part of the doctrine of the Trinity, — so essential, that there can be no Trinity (Tri-unity) without it? Trinitarians are not Tri-theists. They hold to the unity of God as firmly, and would contend for it (if denied) as earnestly, as Unitarians themselves. How then can the testimony of Scripture as to the unity of God be regarded as a positive testimony against the Trinity?"

All that I need say in answer to the question here asked is, that the Scriptures, by insisting in variety of phrase upon the single, undivided unity of God, and by affirming, not only that there is One God, but that God is *One*, and by not containing a single assertion of the Trinity, do give a most emphatic testimony against the latter doctrine.

The following, though it seems to open with the promise of rebutting a statement of mine, leaves it valid.

"Finally, Mr. Ellis 'objects to this doctrine, that we know its origin to have been, not in the Scriptures, but outside of them. It was the Greek philosophy of Alexandria, and not the Hebrew or Christian theology of Jerusalem, that gave it birth.' To all this we have only time now to reply, that *we know*, or we think we know, precisely the opposite of what is here stated. We can clearly trace the doctrine of the Trinity, in its essential features and elements, in the Scriptures of the Old and the New Testaments, and in the writings of the fathers who preceded the school at Alexandria. Plato taught no doctrine at all resembling the Christian Trinity. We speak advisedly on this subject. The New-Platonics of the second century after Christ, in their zeal for a general comprehension, *corrupted* the Scripture doctrine of the Trinity, and introduced their corruptions into the Church, and in so doing they laid a foundation for the disputes and controversies of the next five hundred years. What I have here said is a *true historical statement*, which I am prepared to vindicate, whenever called to it in the providence of God."

That my learned opponent *thinks* that he "can clearly *trace* the doctrine of the Trinity, in its essential features and elements, in the Scriptures," I have no doubt. But that would not prove that the doctrine came into the faith of its first believers through the Scriptures. The school at Alexandria and the doctrine of the Trinity both had the same *fathers*. Jewish Platonists were the most efficient corrupters of Christian doctrine through this world's philosophy. Any one who has tried to read Philo has learned a lesson on this point which he can never forget. Though the story in Eusebius, that Philo was acquainted with the Apostle Peter, and that of Photius, that Philo was a Christian, are not reliable, there is evidence enough that some of the Christian fathers were readers and copiers of Philo. My critic says, truly enough, that Plato taught no doctrine at all resembling the Christian Trinity. But still he and his followers speculated about a Trinity, and it was, as we firmly believe on the best sort of evidence, — it was through them that a school of philosophizing

Christians were first misled into a corruption of the simplicity of the Gospel. Every argument, from the most elaborate to the most superficial in character, which has ever passed under our notice, in attempted proof that the Scriptures reveal a Trinity of co-equal persons in the One God, bears on its face unmistakable evidence that it is an argument in behalf of a preconceived and extraneous notion, not a development of plain Scripture doctrine.

The summing up with which my critic closes his attempted refutation of Unitarianism on this point, is as follows: —

"Before leaving the doctrine of the Trinity, I wish to say a word as to the often alleged absurdity of it. Without doubt, the doctrine in question (or something like it) may be so stated as to become an absurdity. To say that each person in the Trinity is God, in the same sense in which they all are one God, would be a contradiction. But to say that each person in the Trinity is in *some sense* God, and that in *some other sense* they all constitute one God, is no contradiction. Here is one tree, one trunk, made up of three distinct and equal branches. Now each of those branches is in some sense a tree, having bark, sap, wood, leaves, and all the attributes of a tree; and yet each of the branches is not a tree, in the sense in which they all constitute one tree. In this tree, as in a great many other things, there are three in one, and one in three; and yet there is no contradiction, no absurdity. And just so — in so far as divine things can be illustrated by created things — in respect to the Trinity. Properly conceived of, and properly stated, it involves no absurdity. For aught that any created being can show to the contrary, *it may be true;* and as God has so revealed to us the mode of his existence, we are bound to believe that it *is* true.

"As to the *quo modo* of the Trinity, or the *manner* in which the three are one, and the one three, here lies the whole mystery of the subject. A thousand questions may be asked with regard to this point, which no human being can answer; which it is presumptuous to try to answer. But as to the *fact* of the three personal distinctions in the one undivided essence of the Godhead, we have a divine revelation, and consequently ought to have no doubt."

We may gratefully recognize it as one among the approved results of a long controversy, if it be that a Professor in an Orthodox Theological School has said in those paragraphs the best that he feels able to say in the way of apology for a metaphysical dogma. We may pertinently ask, Why perplex the simple Christian faith with such a confessedly undefinable, inexplicable dogma? What possible connection can be indicated between the revelation of God's will to man, and the obscuration of the Oneness of God by an inconceivable distinction of personalities in his essence? Why should the subtilty of metaphysics make such a perplexing theory to lie at the basis of a knowledge of God's will? We deny, as positively as our opponents assert, that "revelation discloses the *fact* of the three personal distinctions in the one undivided essence of the Godhead." We find no such fact disclosed in our Bibles. We maintain that it is a direct contradiction to affirm "that each person in the Trinity is in *some sense* God, and that in *some other sense* they all constitute one God." The contradiction is nothing for which Scripture is responsible, but it is a device of human brains. The critic ventures on the perilous attempt at illustration. He tells us, that of a composite thing, a thing composed of parts, we may ascribe the quality and attributes of the whole to each part. We say, no. A branch is not a tree in any sense, and no trickery with language will justify any one in calling it so. A family may be composed of a father, a mother, and a son, but no usage of words will allow us to speak of either of those three parties as in any sense a family. My critic insists that the doctrine of the Trinity, "properly conceived of, and properly stated, involves no absurdity." But what is a proper conception of it? And what is a proper statement of it? Before puzzling our thoughts with the problem "as to the *quo modo*, the manner in which the three are one, and the one three," we ask for a distinct assertion from revelation of the fact itself. There is no such assertion, from the beginning to the end of the Bible, of any such enigma. Our own opinion is, that the presumption is not on the part of those who try to solve the enigma, but of those who have invented it, and who still insist upon perverting the Scripture doctrine of the supremacy of the Father, the spiritual operation of God's spirit, and the subordination of Christ to God.

IX.

UNITARIANISM ON THE NATURE, RANK, AND OFFICES OF CHRIST.

Passing now to the discussion of the point in controversy concerning Christ's nature, my critic makes many specifications of apparent reply, but does not address a single word even of recognition to the thesis towards which I argue. I begin my article on page 107, with the plainest possible announcement, repeated from page 48, of the view to which Unitarianism here commits itself. That is not, as I expressly say, to any definition of Christ's nature, nor to any denial of his Divinity, nor to any bold attempt to measure the distance between him and God in one direction, or between him and man in another direction. It would seem difficult to express in more intelligible terms than are used in the following sentence the sole point to which I address myself; namely, that Unitarians maintain that Jesus Christ is not presented to us in the New Testament as possessing the underived honors of the Godhead, as claiming by himself and by his Apostles the supreme prerogative of Deity, and therefore as an object of worship and prayer, or of our ultimate religious dependence. Plain and prominent as my statement is, and so worded as to comprehend all the essential conditions of Unitarian doctrine, my critic averts his attention entirely from it, and turns to the usual strain of Orthodox pleading from disjointed texts for the sake of mystifying, rather than elucidating, the Scriptures. I must object to this method of dealing with something other than my argument. I find in his criticisms two incidental Scripture quotations, that might be intended to meet my statement, though they are not addressed to it. The first of these quotations is from Revelation i. 8: "I am Alpha and Omega, the beginning and the ending, which is, and which was, and which is to come, the Almighty." He says, "When we hear Christ speaking these words, we cannot doubt that he speaks as God." But waiving the possible question whether Christ or God is represented as speaking these words, we find the form of speech twice repeated as by Christ, with the omission of the words "the Almighty." (xxi. 6 and xxii. 13.) There is a very remarkable fact in connection with the use of these terms of speech which my critic would have done well to note. John says, that he "fell down to worship" the Beingwho spoke these words, and was repulsed with the counsel: "See thou do it not; for I am thy fellow-servant; worship God." (Rev. xxii. 9.) The other quotation is from the words of Isaiah: "His name shall be called the Wonderful, the Counsellor, the Mighty God, the Everlasting Father," &c. for the proper rendering of which the best Orthodox lexicons will afford all the necessary means, though they can hardly be regarded as words in which Christ for himself, or the Apostles for him, claim the underived honors of Deity. And it is from these quotations that I am to consider my plain position as refuted! Will not all the teachings of Christ himself afford us a single passage in which he presents himself as the object of our worship and ultimate dependence? No! For one such passage would be manifestly inconsistent with his reiterated and emphatic assertion of his subjection and subordination to God, his reiterated and emphatic assertion, that not he, but God, his God and our God, his Father and our Father, is the object of our homage, worship, and ultimate dependence. When Christ says that we shall ask him nothing, but shall ask in his name, how are we to understand him? When he says, that of an hour and an event in the future he is ignorant, how else than by the blankest sophistry can it be alleged that he claims the prerogatives of Deity? It cannot be replied, that he is then speaking as a man, as but a part of himself, for this would be trifling, as no man need disclaim the prerogative of omniscience.

Disappointed as I am, that my critic should so wink out of sight the position on which I build the whole of my argument, I must follow him on some subordinate issues. I have not argued against the Divinity of Christ, for my own belief is that Christ is Divine, that God has imparted to him Divinity. I have asked for a single word of proof that he, or his Apostles for him, demand our worship. One sentence would have satisfied me on that point, but the New Testament cannot furnish one. I remember very well, that, when I was composing my article, I hesitated long upon the doubt, whether I had better attempt any statement of the varieties of speculation, conception, and belief as to the nature and rank of Christ held by Unitarians as secondary to their essential, Scriptural tenet that he was wholly subject to and dependent on God, referring to the gift and endowment of God all that he was and said and did, as one who could do nothing of himself, but had received his commandment from the Father. The essential belief of Unitarians is admirably expressed, both on its positive and its negative side, by a plain statement of St. Paul, to which it would delight us to see our Orthodox friends do justice. It is found in 1 Cor. xv. 27, 28: "All things are put under Christ; but it is manifest that He is excepted which did put all things under him. And when all things shall be subdued unto him, then shall the Son also himself be subject unto Him that put all things under him, that God may be all in all." Knowing very well that, after assuring the Scriptural character of their faith on this point, Unitarians yielded to the speculative instinct which prompted them to form some conception of the rank and nature of the being whom the Supreme had constituted his vicegerent, and knowing also that their speculations covered a wide range, I hesitated, as I have said, whether it were expedient to refer to them at all. I did, however, devote a very small space to them. Of course there are extreme views among them, and these extreme views are mutually inconsistent, and not reconcilable with those which lie between them. Of these my critic allows himself to say, that "Unitarians place Christ anywhere they please in the rank of derived or created existence." If he will allow me to speak in behalf of brethren with some of whom I agree, and with some of whom I differ, I will venture to suggest, that none of them would claim a right to place Christ where they please. They feel at least some measure of the honest and earnest interest of Orthodox persons in trying to reduce the terms applied to Christ to a consistent and exhaustive theory concerning him. Precluded from availing themselves of the conclusion to which the Orthodox leap by skipping over all the passages in which not merely "the human nature of Christ," but Christ himself, is subordinated to God, they are left to construct a theory that shall start from that as a fixed fact. They insist, however, that Christian truth is concerned with Christ in his offices, rather than made dependent upon any speculative view of his nature or rank in creation. They affirm that the Scriptures speak to us of the being, will, and attributes of Jehovah, and present an especial mediator between us and him under the title of Christ, or the Son. It is with this Christ the Mediator that we have to do. We should regard it as but poor presumption to undertake to limit the gifts or prerogatives which God may impart to him, but we do insist that, by the clearest Scripture testimony, all that Christ was, was of the bestowal and endowment of God. Of his own self he could do nothing. This does not mean that of his own self in another or duplex sense he could do everything. The passages of Scripture which lead the Orthodox to assign to Christ a double nature, lead the Unitarians to insist, that, like any other creature of God, he was nothing of himself, while, through the special work and purpose of God in him, he was so endowed as to be a sharer of the Divine counsels. Not a single sentence or line do we find in the Bible, the fair and full meaning of which is not accepted and exhausted by the simple statement of the august truth, that Christ "received from God the Father honor and glory, when there came such a voice to him from the excellent glory, 'This is my beloved Son, in whom I am well pleased.'"

I made but a passing recognition, in a few sentences, of the extreme variations in the speculative opinions held by Unitarians as to the nature and rank of Christ. A cool, rationalizing conception of him, and a fervent, devout, and loving reliance upon him, must of course lead to extremely different views of him. My critic rightly infers, though from no direct statement of my own in that connection, that I hold the highest possible view of the nature and the rank of Christ that is consistent with his subjection to the Being who sent him into the world, and to whom he prayed. But after quoting a few of my sentences, which present the extreme views of Unitarians, and bringing into prominence those which define the loftiest and most revering conceptions of Christ, my critic remarks upon some sentences which he copies from pages 144, 146, and 147.

"And I would inquire, first of all, whether Mr. Ellis has reflected on the inherent absurdity of some of the expressions above quoted. If Christ is not infinite in his nature and perfections, then he is finite. If he is not the Eternal, then he is subject to the limitations of time. And certainly, between the infinite and the finite, the eternal and the temporal, there can be no comparison. There can be no such thing as a created intelligence being *almost equal* in essence with the Supreme. A created being may hold rank above all other orders of created beings, but he cannot '*touch upon* the prerogatives of Deity.' 'The awful vacuum between the loftiest angelic natures and the Supreme, has now a radiant occupant, *who fills the whole of it.*' Is this conceivable? Is it possible? The truth is, if Christ is not God, he is *infinitely less than God*. Between him and God *there is no comparison. There can be none.* Those, therefore, who deny the proper divinity of Christ — however high they may exalt him in the scale of finite intelligence — do really pull him down an infinite distance. They may think to honor him; they may not intend to degrade him; but (if he is what we believe him to be) they do degrade him, and that infinitely. However good their intentions may be, they cannot help it."

I would answer, that all the expressions which I have used as employed by Unitarians for the exaltation of Christ are relieved of any "inherent absurdity" the moment they are referred to the exhaustive summing up of the Apostle in these words: "It pleased the Father that in him should all fulness dwell" (Col. i. 19); the work which God "wrought in Christ when he raised him from the dead, and set him at his own right hand in the heavenly places, far above all principality, and power, and might, and dominion, and every name that is named, not only in this world, but also in that which is to come; and hath put all things under his feet, and gave him to be the head over all things to the Church." (Eph. i. 20 – 22.) "Wherefore God hath highly exalted him, and given him a name which is above every name." (Philip. ii. 9.) Now in these and many other passages the loftiest titles and prerogatives are assigned to Christ, to the being presented to us in the New Testament as our Mediator, who came to lead us, reconciled, to God. And all these exalted honors are attached to Christ as derived gifts. They are never spoken of as self-possessed, nor as given by one of his *natures* to the other of his *natures*, but as bestowed upon him by the sovereign pleasure of the One Supreme God. Some Unitarians, and, if it is proper to add, the writer is one of the class, love to gather from the New Testament all these lofty and transcendent terms of Divine honor attached to Christ, and to fashion from them such conceptions as I have sought to express, and on which my critic comments as above. Now if he finds no difficulty in conceiving of the Messiah as the Supreme God, I am certainly at a loss to understand how he can stumble at any of the expressions which I have used. Will he question the ability of God to communicate, impart, transfer, or divide any of his prerogatives to Christ, to make Christ as "his fellow" almost his equal, to allow him to touch upon the prerogatives of Deity, and to fill the whole space between himself and the loftiest angelic nature? My critic may stumble at these views, but it is a silly trifling with the old bugbear frights of polemics to pretend that Unitarians, in trying to fill out the Scriptural delineations of Christ, "degrade him infinitely." For I must remind my critic again, that Unitarians have a God beyond and above his Messiah, and that we still connect with the Supreme his supremacy.

I have in these remarks anticipated the answer to be given to the next two queries of my critic, as follows: —

"Let it be inquired, secondly, whether the language above quoted does not present us with *two Gods*, — not two persons in the one Godhead, — but *two Gods*. 'Our doctrine gives to us the same God whom they worship, and another being, — yes, *a Divine being besides*.' 'The awful vacuum between the loftiest angelic natures and the Supreme has now an occupant *who fills the whole of it*.' Besides the Eternal Father, there is another being, '*the sharer of his throne*, his *counsellor* and *companion*,' 'touching,' in point of perfection, 'upon *the prerogatives of Deity*.' If here are not two Gods, I hardly know in what language such a doctrine could be exhibited. What have Trinitarians ever written that was so palpably inconsistent with the unity of God as this.

"But I must inquire, thirdly, how the language above used can be reconciled with the testimony of Scripture as to the proper *humanity* of Christ. Our Saviour is expressly called a *man* more than fifty times in the New Testament. He is represented as possessing all the sinless affections and infirmities of a man. He 'grew in wisdom and in stature.' He was hungry, thirsty, weary, and tempted; he ate, drank, and slept; he appeared, lived, suffered, and died as a man. In short, we have as much evidence from Scripture that Christ was a man, as we have that Peter, James, and John were men, or that any human being is referred to or spoken of in the Bible.

"But a mere human body does not make a man. It requires also a *human soul;* not that pre-existent, super-angelic, god-like intelligence of which Mr. Ellis speaks, — but a *human soul*, 'made in all points like as we are, yet without sin.' Without such a soul, Christ could not be a man; and the fulness of Scripture testimony, as to the *fact* of his humanity, is falsified."

Supposing my critic to be as well able as I am to answer his question, whether the Unitarian view does not present us with "two Gods," I leave him to find relief from his perplexity here without my help. As to "the proper humanity of Christ," we receive that as the basis, the medium, the manifestation, through which God wrought his work in Christ. "Christ was found in fashion as a man." This is all that the Scriptures reveal to us about the matter, and to inquire below or beyond it is to inquire in vain.

To meet the claims of candor in allowing an opponent a fair hearing in his own words, I copy the following long extract in continuation of his comments.

"I have spoken of the abundant Scripture testimony as to the fact of Christ's humanity. This testimony is equally explicit, and scarcely less abundant, as to the fact of his Divinity. The names, the attributes, the works, and the worship of the Supreme Being are all, in Scripture, ascribed to Christ. In fact, it is as easy to prove, from the language of Scripture, that Christ is God, as it is to prove that the Father is God, or that there is any God at all.

"A few of the Scripture proofs of the proper Divinity of Christ Mr. Ellis runs over, disposing of them in the briefest manner, much as Unitarians generally have done before him. It is painfully evident, from the manner in which these passages are disposed of by Unitarians, that no additional amount of Scripture testimony would be likely to satisfy them. As these texts are explained away, others might be. Indeed, the same glosses and interpretations that would take the Divinity of Christ out of the Bible, would take it out of the Athanasian Creed, or the Assembly's Catechism, or any other Orthodox formula of doctrine.

"But if Christ is both God and man, — if he speaks, and is

spoken of, in both these characters in Scripture, Mr. Ellis thinks that, in all fairness, we ought to be admonished of this important fact. And so in truth we are. We *are* admonished of it. The Scriptures set Christ before us as both God and man; and now, when we hear him speaking to us, we can easily decide as to the character in which he speaks, from the tenor of his words. When we hear him saying, 'My soul is exceeding sorrowful, even unto death,' — we cannot doubt that he speaks as man. And when we hear him saying, 'I am Alpha and Omega, the first and the last, which was, and is, and is to come, the Almighty,' — we can as little doubt that he speaks as God.

"It is further said, that, of the whole doctrine of Christ, nothing is more plainly set forth in the Scriptures than his *dependence on the Father*, and his *inferiority* and *subordination* to him. And now, strange as it may seem to our Unitarian friends, we accept this statement fully. We believe in Christ's inferiority to the Father. As man, he was essentially and infinitely inferior. And as the constituted mediator between God and men, he was, and is, subordinate to the Father. He taught what he was appointed to teach; he did what he was appointed to do; he suffered what he was appointed to suffer; and all this in perfect consistency with his possessing a *Divine nature*, in which 'he thought it not robbery to be equal with God.'

"Again, it is said, that, by making Christ God, we 'confound him with the Father'; we make him 'identical with God'; and thus 'his prayers must be construed as soliloquies'; and in his intercessions we have 'God interceding with God.' 'We are told of a covenant between two persons, when, in fact, there is but one'; and of 'a mediator between two parties, who is himself one of those parties.' All this, and much more like it, is based on the groundless assumption, that Trinitarians make no distinctions in the Godhead. But do not Unitarians know that we make such distinctions, essential and eternal distinctions? Do they not know that the Bible makes them? 'In the beginning was the Word, and the Word was *with God*, and the Word *was God*, the same was in the beginning *with God*.' 'Glorify thou me with thine own self, with the glory which I had *with thee* before the world was.' The doctrine of the Trinity is the doctrine of *three personal distinctions in one God*. The Son is not identical with the Father, nor the Father with the Son, nor the Spirit with either the Father or Son. In the Scriptures, the Son in his Divine nature often addresses the Father, and the Father the Son. 'Thy throne, O God, is for ever and ever.' 'Glorify thou me,' &c., as in the passage above quoted.

"Mr. Ellis has some strange misconceptions of the Trinitarian doctrine, such as that it 'represents Christ to us as a *fractional part* of the Godhead.' We never before learned that a *spirit* — not even a human spirit, much less the Divine — could be divided into parts. Why should any Theist indulge in such materializing conceptions of the Godhead?"

These suggestions, in the usual strain of Orthodox special pleading, are equally familiar and inconclusive to Unitarians. Most of what can be called argument in these paragraphs will be found to have been anticipated in the essay that is under criticism. As to the assertions made by my critic, they are easily disposed of. There is a great difference between the Divinity of Christ and the Deity of Christ. "The names, the attributes, the works, and the worship of the Supreme Being are" *not* "all in Scripture ascribed to Christ." This cool assumption of the affirmative on a point on which my essay maintains the negative side, is too hasty and unsatisfactory. In a note to the paragraph containing this assumption, my critic makes a Scripture quotation, bearing on an emphatic topic already referred to by me, — the lack of proof that Christ is an object of our worship. He quotes Rev. v. 13, for honors paid "to the Lamb," after worship has been paid to God. And this is the Scripture testimony to his broad assertion above!

Let the reader mark the blank affirmation in the fourth paragraph, that the Orthodox "believe in Christ's inferiority to the Father. As *man*, he was essentially and infinitely inferior!" Indeed! This is a great admission! A man is inferior to God! But was not Christ *as Christ*, in every manifestation and representation of him to us, inferior to God? An Apostle, commending to us the lowliness of Christ, says, that, though divinely furnished by God, "he did not grasp at an equality with God." Yet a Theological Professor is reduced to the strait of quoting these words under a mistranslation which directly inverts the Apostle's assertion, to set aside the whole Scripture testimony that *Christ — not as a man*, but as Christ, the Messiah — was not the Supreme God.

In the fifth paragraph my critic endeavors to controvert a direct argument, by alleging that it "is based on the groundless assumption that Trinitarians make no distinctions in the Godhead." We know they try to do so. But to his question whether we do not know that the Bible makes them, I answer, for one, No!

As to the objection of my critic founded on "fractional parts of the Godhead," I have but to refer him to his own illustration used above, about the tree and its three branches.

A few incidental suggestions close the criticisms which I have followed at such length. I had asserted, on page 150, as of the teaching of Trinitarianism, "that Christ parted with all that in him and about him was not God when he left the earth," &c. My critic answers: —

"Mr. Ellis will be glad to learn that Trinitarianism teaches no such thing. We do not believe that it was 'the flesh alone' which brought 'Christ into sympathy of nature with us.' He had a *human soul* as well as a human body, with all the capacities and sinless affections of such a soul. With his human soul and his glorified body he has gone into the heavens, where he ever liveth — God-man and Mediator — 'to make intercession for us.'"

I am glad of an opportunity to correct here my own error, which I discovered soon after the printing of my article, in saying what I did say about the *teaching* of Trinitarianism on this point. The sentence was but a blundering and inadequate expression of what was in my mind. I object to the Trinitarian view of Christ, that by converting him into God it deprives us of that mediatorial being whom the Scriptures present to us "in our likeness."

To my remarks on page 151, relating to the necessity of some other views of Christ than as an "Example" or "Teacher," my critic replies, that we are in danger of losing him in those precious earthly offices by not recognizing "his proper humanity." I have copied this suggestion, not because I see any force in it, but because my critic seems to have attached importance to it.

He concludes with a comment on my affirmation, that candid Orthodox judges of Unitarians will have less and less reason to say, "*You do not make enough of Christ.*" After expressing a devout hope that this resolution may be faithfully fulfilled, he adds: —

"We cannot utter for our friend a better wish, or a more important prayer, than that he may be led to think more and more of Christ, until he comes to the full realization of him as 'the child born, and the son given'; a human being like ourselves, who is yet the 'Wonderful, the Counsellor, the Mighty God, the Everlasting Father, the Prince of Peace.'"

Fully appreciating, as I sincerely hope I do, the kind, Christian spirit which prompted this suggestion, I cannot but as kindly say to my critic, that such a garbling perversion of Scripture language, for the sake of levelling it against us, is especially offensive to our taste, and utterly ineffective as appeal. A vital, fundamental Christian truth ought not to be made dependent, even for a statement of it, on a mistranslation of a few old Hebrew words, which candid Orthodox scholars are as ready as Unitarians to correct. But when, as a matter of fact, was Christ ever called "the Mighty God, the Everlasting Father"? We must not be robbed of our Christ, by having him substituted for our God.

X.

THE DOCTRINE OF ATONEMENT.

I HAD expected to find the zeal and earnestness of my critic most effectively brought to bear upon a refutation of my statements in the discussion of the great doctrine of the Reconciliation of sinners to God by Jesus Christ. My disappointment strengthens with each reperusal of what he has written, as wholly inadequate to meet the terms of the discussion. No reader of his criticisms could learn from them the substance either of my statements of the Unitarian view, or of my objections to the Calvinistic view, while the point of controversy on which alone I lay stress is not even recognized. I must therefore ask my readers, who may be following me through this reiteration of my argument, to turn back to a few references which I shall indicate. On page 191 I affirmed, in the most explicit and strong language which our mother tongue affords, the following:—

"Unitarianism does not undertake to fathom, or comprehend, or give expression to, all the mysterious influence and efficacy, and mode of operation upon man, and man's soul and destiny, of the sacrificial death of Christ, but is free to acknowledge an unexplained and inexplicable agency in it." Stronger sentences even than this are added, for the sake of presenting with all possible stress my own conviction, that an efficacy is ascribed in the Scriptures to the mediatorial work of Christ, which, as to the method of its operation, is not explained. I wrote: "We are cheerfully willing to admit that God has comprehended influences in the sacrificial death of Christ, which are designed to be efficaciously felt and mercifully availed of by us, without yielding to the solution of our understanding." With warm gratitude I accepted the noble avowal made by the great Bishop Butler, which I quoted on page 192, "that *Scripture has not explained* how and in what particular way Christ's death is efficacious for our pardon." This avowal, from one of the sincerest Christian men and most clear-minded thinkers that ever accepted Orthodoxy in some undefined modification of it, I regard as a rebuke, all the more effective for its gentleness, of those who are so ready with a dogma of their own about God's need of satisfaction, or the demands of his law. After these reiterated acknowledgments of an unrevealed and mysterious element in the mediatorial work of Christ, which are to be found stated or intimated on many of my pages, I defined the Unitarian view as looking wholly man-ward for the operation of these mysterious and inexplicable influences. I wrote on page 193, Unitarianism "maintains that the death of Christ, *so far as its efficacy is distinctly defined* [leaving still the mystery allowed for and unattempted], is instrumental to our salvation through its influence on the heart and life of man, not through its vicarious value with God; and also that revelation does not acquaint us with any *obstacle* in the method of administration which God has established as his government, which prevents his exercising mercy to the penitent, except through the substitution of a victim to law."

Unless now I lack the faculty of expressing what is in my mind, I have plainly conveyed a clear statement of the Unitarian view, and have intimated an objection to a precise theory of an inferential or constructive character, which Orthodoxy interpolates into the Christian system. This theory I have stated on page 199, as affirming "that God, in order that he may exercise mercy towards the penitent, requires or accepts an expiatory offering made by innocence to his own law." Of any possible form, shaping, or announcement of this theory, which shall retain the substance of it, I have avowed my belief, that not a single line or sentence can be quoted in testimony from the Scriptures. The Bible knows nothing of such a theory, and says nothing about it. There is no intimation, not the faintest, that an explanation of what is left in mystery about the efficacy of the mediatorial work of Christ, is to be looked for in the direction of that theory. It is from beginning to end, in every stage of it, and in every element of it, a pure invention of the human fancy, and only by the hardest and most ingenious constructiveness of inference can the parts of it be picked out from the words and imagery of disjointed texts, and tessellated into a doctrinal formula. I have quoted, page 197, the assertion made by Dr. Woods, that "all the influence of repentance results from the death of Christ." But if his whole share in the blessed life of heaven, which we doubt not that excellent divine is now enjoying, had been made to depend upon his quoting a single proof of that statement from Christ, or an Apostle, he would have fallen short of the great salvation. To Dr. Woods applies the censure which I have also quoted from Bishop Butler (page 196): "Some have endeavored to explain the efficacy of what Christ has done and suffered for us, beyond what the Scripture has authorized."

It is for going beyond what the Scripture has authorized, and for trying to force upon it a theory inconsistent with its other teachings, that we object to the Orthodox dogma of the Atonement. We do not object to it, that it makes our forgiveness and salvation to depend upon the death of Christ, nor that it asks us to believe in some mysterious and unexplained efficacy in that mediatorial work. But we do object to that unscriptural and pagan element in its theory, which represents God as looking upon the misery endured by Christ as an equivalent offset, expiation, or substitution for the sufferings of the sinner, and the only method by which God could exercise his attribute of mercy toward man. We hail with gratitude the relief offered us in the writings of some of the most liberal and enlarged minds of existing Orthodox communions, which repudiate the old, barbarous, and vindictive representations once used in setting forth the imagery of the doctrine of the Calvinistic Atonement. But we still encounter a remnant of the old, hideous device, however it be subdued, in the "governmental theory." In exact proportion to the element retained in this theory of the ancient and the substantial Orthodox doctrine, which taught that God's law prevented his exercise of mercy except through the expiatory suffering of an innocent victim substituted for the sinner, — in that same proportion do we measure our opposition to the theory. We insist, that what the Scripture has left unexplained as to the mode of efficacy of the mediatorial work of Christ shall not have the veil drawn from it by the obtrusion of any such theory as this in the place of the mystery. Scripture tells us that Jesus was a victim to the wickedness and prejudices of the Jews. But no earnestness of Orthodox appeal can ever dispose us to believe, that, had the passions of those Jews fallen one whit short of the actual crucifixion of Christ, God, the Father of the human race, could never have forgiven and restored one single penitent sinner of that race through time or eternity.

After this summary of the positive and direct points discussed in my essay, I revert to the criticisms now before me. I find the paper plentifully strewn with those texts from the Epistles, especially from that doubtful Epistle to the Hebrews, which, with their perverted constructions, glosses, and associations, form the staple of an Orthodox argument on this doctrine. One needs not go out of the range of the works of the best Orthodox commentators and expositors, particularly of some who have written within the last few years, for proof of the utter irrelevancy of those texts for the use to which they are adduced. Translate by the term *Mercy-seat* the word mistranslated by *Propitiation*, and connect with it the uses and truths of which the Mercy-seat of the Ark was the symbol in the old Covenant, and the Orthodox theory is lamed in the very start for authenticating itself by Scripture.

Recognizing my allowance of the favorable modifications of the old doctrine, and assuming a defence against me of the governmental theory, my critic says: —

"It supposes that an atonement for sinners was necessary, not merely as a means of bringing them to repentance, but to open a way of salvation for them, when they had repented. It was necessary to sustain the honor, the broken law of God, to vindicate his authority, to satisfy his glorious justice. Or to present the whole in almost the precise language of Paul: a propitiation, an atonement, was and is necessary, '*to declare God's righteousness* for the remission of sins that are past, through the forbearance of God; — *to declare*, I say, at this time, *his righteousness*, that he might be just, and the justifier of him who believeth in Jesus.' Rom. iii. 25."

The reader can hardly fail to note the chasm which divides the assertion of the critic from the assertion of the text, even after he has used the help of false emphasis and italics upon its words. Where is there anything about the insufficiency of repentance, the demands of an insulted law, and the value of substituted sufferings as recognized by God? My critic would say, these come from the text by fair inference. I grant the operation of inference, but deny the fairness of it. The lucid paraphrase of Locke lets in a better light: — "They have all, both Jews and Gentiles, sinned, and fail of attaining that glory which God hath appointed for the righteous. Being made righteous gratis, by the favor of God, through the redemption which is by Jesus Christ. Whom God hath set forth to be the propitiatory or mercy-seat in his own blood [death], for the manifestation of God's righteousness, by passing over their transgressions, formerly committed, which he hath borne with hitherto, so as to withhold his hand from casting off the nation of the Jews as their past sins deserved. For the manifesting his righteousness at this time, that he might be just in keeping his promise, and be the justifier of every one, not who is of the Jewish nation or extraction, but of the faith in Jesus Christ." And in a note this discreet commentator remarks: — "Redemption by Jesus Christ does not import there was any compensation paid to God, by paying what was of equal value, in consideration whereof they were delivered: for that is inconsistent with what St. Paul expressly says here, namely, that sinners are justified by God gratis, and of his free bounty."

The following paragraphs might seem at first sight to contain matter covering the purpose for which it is alleged.

"Mr. Ellis admits that the death of Christ was a sacrifice, 'in the highest and most sacred signification of the word'; but 'a sacrifice *for man*, and not *to God*.' Unfortunately, the Apostle Paul seems to have taken a different view of the matter. 'Christ also hath loved us, and hath given himself for us, *an offering and a sacrifice* TO GOD, for a sweet-smelling savor.' Eph. ii. 5. 'How much more shall the blood of Christ, who, through the Eternal Spirit, offered himself without spot TO GOD, purge your conscience from dead works.' Heb. ix. 14. Also the bloody sacrifices of the Jews — all *typifying*, *shadowing forth*, the sacrifice of Christ — were offered, in every case, *to God*. And the same may be said of the intercession of Christ. This is but the carrying out, the consummation, of his work of Atonement; and yet no one can doubt that his intercessions are addressed to God.

"Mr. Ellis denies — in face of the full and explicit exposition of them given by the Apostles, and especially by Paul in his Epistle to the Hebrews — that the sacrifices of the Jews had any reference to the death of Christ, or anything in them of a typical character. 'Not the most distant intimation is given in the Old Testament, that the ritual sacrifices looked beyond themselves to an anticipation of the sacrifice of Christ. Not a word can be quoted from lawgiver, prophet, or priest, to prove that such a reference was had in view.' We cannot stop to argue the question as to the typical character of the Hebrew sacrifices. If this character is not expressly given to them in the Old Testament, it is in the New. Paul has argued the question sufficiently, both for himself and me.

"Mr. Ellis has another notion respecting the sacrifice of Christ, which is, perhaps, peculiar to himself. Certainly it is very different from that of the New Testament. The doctrine of Paul is, that Christ, the Great High-Priest of our profession, *offered up himself* a sacrifice for our sins, 'who, through the Eternal Spirit, *offered up himself*, without spot, to God.' But Mr. Ellis thinks that he was offered up by his murderers. 'We regard Christ as a victim offered up *by human sin* for human redemption.' 'It was *man*, not God, who made Christ a curse for us.'"

I might ask my critic here a series of questions which he would find it difficult to answer. Thus, for instance, How did he succeed in satisfying himself, against the judgment of the best critics and an overwhelming array of external and internal evidence, that St. Paul wrote the Epistle to the Hebrews? Would he take upon himself the defence of all the forced analogies, accommodations, and fanciful parallelisms by which the writer of that Epistle — so strangely unlike everything which we have from the pen of St. Paul — attempts to conciliate ritualistic Jews to the simplicity of Christ? Again, leaving as of no account what I have said in my Essay in explanation of the class of texts here quoted, does either one of them, do all of them, when their figures are forced into the most literal construction, convey the terms of the Governmental Theory? Is the death of an innocent victim really of sweet-smelling savor to a holy God? Is a sort of Divine suicide really suggested to us by the Apostle as a matter of gracious contemplation in heaven? Is a "purging of our consciences from dead works" equivalent to a satisfying of the Divine law by a vicarious victim? And, once more, if Christ by his own voluntary submission was not made a victim by men, was he, the Beloved Son, really made a curse by God?

I cannot here reargue matters which I have discussed according to my ability, however inadequately, in the preceding Essay. Yet, as I recognize the kindest possible intent in my critic, as well as his firm persuasion that his plea ought not to be without force with me, I will not slight any part of it. In connection with what I have just quoted from him is the following: —

"Mr. Ellis's objections to our doctrine of Atonement are such as these: — First, 'it is not distinctly revealed, nor directly taught in the Scriptures.' He admits, indeed, that, 'by the aid of inference, and construction, and ingenuity, Orthodoxy can make out an argument of considerable plausibility for this theory.' 'A marvellous show of apparent authority may be claimed for it.' Still, it is in his view an unscriptural doctrine. 'Where is there a sentence within the covers of the Bible that can be quoted as explicitly advancing it?' Its believers 'should give us at least one text, which includes all its essential terms.' If by this it is meant, that we have, in no one text of Scripture, a full, scientific statement of the doctrine of Atonement, we admit it. The Scriptures do not abound in scientific statements of doctrine. But if it be meant that the Scriptures do not, in a great many passages, teach the doctrine of Atonement, in *our* sense of the word, — Atonement by the sufferings and death of Christ, 'an offering and a sacrifice to God for a sweet-smelling savor,' — we record our most solemn dissent from such a statement; — a dissent in which we have the concurrence of nine tenths of the Protestant Christian world, including most of the Unitarians of a former age. Mr. Ellis is not ignorant of the numerous passages which clearly enough assert this doctrine; for he cursorily reviews some of them, and endeavors to set aside their obvious import. But the attempt is a vain one. The real meaning shines out too clearly to be obscured by anything short of torture. Professor F. D. Huntington, having quoted the same Scriptures, says: 'Now, as one ponders the singular force, and directness, and agreement of these passages, and very many more of the same import, and marks their cumulative power, as they resound through the New Testament, we submit that it will not be strange if he feels that on those' who deny the Orthodox doctrine 'rests the burden of explaining how, according to the Bible, the death of Christ is *not* the divinely ordained and essential *ground* of human salvation.' 'There is some reason to think that passages like those we have quoted have become comparatively unfamiliar to Unitarian ears, by having been dropped out of Unitarian preaching, under a natural persuasion that they do not harmonize with the Unitarian theory.'"

No! The Governmental Theory of Atonement is not distinctly revealed nor directly taught in the Scriptures. It is for those who place this theory at the very foundation of the Christian system to account as best they can for the fact that they have to use their own ingenuity to construct a formula for expressing it. How is it that, in all the discourses of the Master and of his Apostles, from first to last, not a single sentence was uttered embracing either, much less both, of these two terms of the Theory, — namely, the insufficiency of penitence to win the mercy of God, and the necessity of satisfying an outraged law by the suffering of the innocent, regarded by God as an equivalent by way of substitute for the sufferings of the guilty? But my critic yields the point. I thank him for his candor in affirming what nevertheless could not have been denied. He grants that no one text of Scripture contains a full scientific statement of the doctrine of Atonement, — i. e. of the Orthodox doctrine. Why then should he make a scientific statement of it for us? Confessedly, it must be only by putting together texts, and parts of texts, and by making one's own inferences and constructions a solvent or a cement of them, that this Theory can find terms for its expression. But even then it cannot express all its terms in Scripture language or phraseology. Let this most significant fact be pondered well. Inspiration has not given us the means for stating the Orthodox doctrine of atonement in a formula. Not a single other Christian doctrine can be specified for the expression of which we cannot find in Scripture language an adequate and exhaustive sentence, whether for the simple uses of a child's catechism, or for inscriptions over the most magnificent portals or the most august altars. The mediatorial work of Christ must be expressed in the uninspired speech of men, if we wish to express it by the terms of the Governmental Theory. There is a remnant of the old-fashioned style of controversy in the sentences in which my critic says that I am not "ignorant of the numerous passages which clearly enough assert this doctrine"; and that I "endeavor to set aside their obvious import." The *clearly enough* may signify the evidence which satisfies him without satisfying another. To charge a serious searcher for the truth in the Scriptures with an endeavor to set aside their *obvious import* is to give up one's charity under a momentary testiness at being foiled in an argument. The obvious import of Scripture is what I am seeking, not rejecting. Some Unitarians have doubtless, as I said in my essay, allowed the passages and phrases quoted by Professor Huntington to drop out of their preaching, because Orthodox perversions had connected false associations with their meaning. But other Unitarians have loved to retain them in use, not finding in them a trace of the terms of the Governmental Theory.

The next paragraph challenges my assertion that "the Scriptures do not lay the emphatic stress of Christ's redeeming work upon *his death*, above or apart from his life, character, and doctrine." (p. 184.) My critic, on the other hand, says that fifty years' reading of the Scriptures has shown him that they lay an "emphasis altogether peculiar upon the blood, the cross, the sufferings, and the death of Christ," in connection with the salvation of sinners. He admits the stress that is laid upon the resurrection of Christ, but ventures the assertion, that "the number of passages in which our salvation is referred to the sufferings and death of Christ, compared with those in which it is referred to his resurrection, will be as four to one." I cannot call to mind a single passage in which our *salvation* is referred to the resurrection of Christ. I spoke of his redeeming or mediatorial work as a whole. Any one who wishes may make a count of the passages.

The paragraph which follows will be found to contain a good Orthodox argument against a difficulty of its own raising.

"Mr. Ellis objects again to our view of the Atonement, that it 'fetters God's exercise of mercy, by the restraints of his penal law.' (p. 214.) But the laws are of his own appointment, and he is no more fettered by them than he is by the great law of *justice*, of *right*. It is no restraint of God's moral liberty, that he cannot do wrong; nor is it any restraint upon his mercy, that he cannot exercise it in violation of justice, — to his own dishonor and the detriment of all those great interests which his law protects."

But the actual difficulty is, that the claims of real justice are not met by the method invented by Orthodoxy for relieving the Divine government of the dilemma also invented for it. We do not find any such dilemma recognized in Scripture as embarrassing the Almighty. He has mercy on whom he will have mercy. If he has said, as revelation affirms that he has, that he that confesseth and forsaketh his sins shall be forgiven, — not a word being intimated of any "governmental difficulty" in the way, — we certainly shall leave the Merciful Judge to harmonize his own methods, and shall create no embarrassment for the sake of getting round it. It is hardly fair, however, to meet the assertion, that God may freely forgive the penitent, with the dogmatic affirmation that God cannot do wrong. It is hard, too, to find that mercy, which all through the Bible is represented as the crowning attribute of a God of love, needs an Orthodox invention to secure it from turning to his *dishonor*.

The next point argued by my critic is as follows: —

"Mr. Ellis insists that repentance is not only the sole condition of pardon, but the sole *ground* of it; — that no other ground, no expedient to sustain law, while dispensing mercy, is required or needed. 'Forgiveness on penitence does not, in any case, peril the authority of the Divine law.' (p. 216.) To prove this, Mr. Ellis cites cases in which forgiveness is promised and granted to the penitent, without any referrence to an Atonement as the ground of it. He even says, that one 'single case by which, on the authority of inspiration, full forgiveness was promised on simple repentance, without reference to any implied or reserved condition, would prove that the Divine administration, as revealed to men, did not always recognize this limitation of the prerogative of mercy.' (p. 200.) Now this seems to us a very strange assertion. Suppose forgiveness to the penitent cannot be imparted, except through the efficacy of a provided Atonement, is God bound, in every promise of forgiveness to the penitent, to make a full statement of the ground of such promise? Not at all. As well might we infer, because forgiveness is said to flow through the blood of Christ, without any express mention of repentance, that therefore repentance is unnecessary. 'In whom we have redemption, through his blood, the forgiveness of sins, according to the riches of his grace.' (Eph. i. 7; Col. i. 14.) The truth is, God has stated with sufficient clearness and frequency, both the *grounds* and the *conditions* of pardon under his government, — though not always both together, — and we are not at liberty to set aside either the one or the other."

No other ground for the exercise of mercy on the part of God is recognized in Scripture, than penitence on the part of the sinner. To say that God is not bound, in every case of the exercise of mercy to a penitent, to make known to him a reserved but all-essential condition beside penitence, is to make a supposition of a merely possible contingency to stand as an offset to hundreds of passages which say that penitence insures forgiveness. The subtle distinction between the *grounds* and the *conditions* of pardon is a pure Orthodox invention, a dogmatic device of which the Scriptures know absolutely nothing.

One other matter of extreme importance, in its vital connection with the true Scripture doctrine as to the terms of acceptance with God, is recognized by my critic in the following paragraph: —

"Mr. Ellis thinks the Orthodox are much perplexed about the condition of Jews and heathens, who have died without any knowledge of the sacrifice of Christ. But we feel no such perplexity. We hear of none. We believe with Peter, 'that God is no respecter of persons: but in every nation he that feareth him, and worketh righteousness, is accepted with him.' (Acts x. 34.) But how accepted? Undoubtedly, through the

Atonement of Christ, though he may never have heard of it. The Jew, the heathen, who fears God, and works righteousness, has the *element* of faith in Christ, though not the *form* of it. He has that (as in the case of Cornelius) which *will be* faith, the moment he comes to the knowledge of Christ, whether that knowledge is first imparted in this world, or the next; and he is as really forgiven *for Christ's sake*, as the devoutest Christian. The entire company of the redeemed in heaven, 'of every kindred, and tongue, and people, and nation,' are represented as singing with one voice: 'Thou art worthy to take the book, and to open the seals thereof, for thou wast slain, and hast redeemed us unto God *by thy blood*.'"

I will take the word of the writer as evidence that he himself feels no perplexity on this painful and fearful issue raised by the Orthodox dogma that the terms of salvation are repentance *and* faith in the propitiatory sacrifice of Jesus Christ. But I cannot receive his disclaimer as meeting the terrible perplexity presented by the creed. The pages of this volume contain abundant evidence of the perplexity which consistent Orthodox men have found in disposing of the heathen through the Calvinistic theory. Some of the Orthodox of firmer theological nerves rode over the perplexity by sending the heathen in a mass to hell. On pages 174 and 175, I have quoted good Mr. Flavel's own words to this effect. He has no idea of being "indulgent to the heathen." He maintains the direct "impossibility of their salvation that know not Christ." Heathens, he says, cannot "inherit heaven." He adds: "I know it seems hard that such brave men as some of the heathen were should be damned. But the Scripture knows no other way to glory but Christ, put on and applied by faith. And it is the common suffrage of modern sound divines, that no man by the sole conduct of nature, without the knowledge of Christ, can be saved."

Again, on pages 350 and 351, I have taken notice of the shock caused to many of the Orthodox by the bold assertion of the North British Review, that the heathen will not perish because of their ignorance of the Gospel. I cannot but admire the ingenuity of my critic in his curious device for disposing of the perplexity. The purpose of it is so kindly, humane, and Christian that it must be winked at. In fact, it comes to the same result as does the Unitarian view, though it goes the longest way round to get to it. Faith in Christ as an expiatory sacrifice is essential to the salvation of a penitent, — says the creed. The pious Jew, says my critic, has *the element* of that faith, he has what *will be it* when he has a chance to know it as such. It is a beautiful and a grateful suggestion. Heartily do I thank my critic for it. But still it is a most round-about way for bringing the free mercy of God to bear upon the penitent.

When I wrote the essay with the criticisms upon which I am now concerned, I devoted considerable space to the argument, that the exercise of the Divine prerogative of mercy under the Jewish covenant was not fettered or made dependent upon any express or implied limitation, least of all that limitation which Orthodoxy now imposes upon it. This argument was designed to meet the well-known Calvinistic theory, that the Old Testament sacrifices were typical of the crucifixion, and that the penitents had an anticipatory share, through faith, in the benefits of Christ's death. I should not have then spent such labor on an incidental point, had an essay which has appeared in print this year been available for my use during the previous year. I refer to a most remarkable and significant essay which appeared in the Bibliotheca Sacra for January, 1857, — one of those admirable papers which that valuable periodical has furnished as the fruits of liberal scholarship and the tokens of independent thought in the Orthodox body. The theme of the essay is, — "The Knowledge and Faith of the Old Testament Saints respecting the promised Messiah." The question under discussion is, "What Knowledge had they of him in his peculiar character as an *atoning Saviour*, and what Faith, if any, did they exercise in him as *such?*" The answer is, None at all, of either Knowledge or Faith! The argument is as follows: — "The promised Messiah is never held up in the Old Testament as the object of confidence, faith, or love; nor are the Jews called on to rely personally upon his Atonement for the remission of sins and acceptance with God. Nowhere in the Old Testament is faith in an atoning Messiah proposed or required as a condition, or pardon promised on the ground of it." "The promise of pardon is everywhere made to repentance and reformation, when they are hearty and thorough enough." "We may have our theory, that to know and believe on Christ has, in all ages, been indispensable to pardon and salvation. But the Bible nowhere says that it was so to those who lived before the crucifixion, or even to those now living where the Gospel is not known. Is it not presumptuous for us to have opinions and theories on such a point, not fairly deduced from the revelations of God?"

I must quote two more choice extracts from this excellent paper. "Repentance is a saving grace, as well as faith in Christ. And where one of them, genuine in its character, is exercised, the other infallibly will be, if the subject has the requisite knowledge." "All that can be regarded as moral excellence in the renewed sinner is probably not less clearly indicated by his godly sorrow for sin, and his hearty striving against it, than by the simple act of faith in Christ."

For writing and saying precisely such things as these fifty years ago, Unitarians were charged with opposing and ridiculing missions to the heathen. Compare now the views of Mr. Flavel and other old Calvinists with these "indulgent" views, which have the indorsement of an Orthodox periodical. Let the reader do that, and then he will gratefully thank God for the progress and power of true Gospel light amid dark human speculations.

But a very serious embarrassment still arrests one's thoughts, as he considers that those who yield all that I have just quoted insist, nevertheless, that the propitiatory sacrifice of Christ, whether the fact of it be known or not known, is still the all-essential *ground* of the pardon of a penitent heathen, Jew, or Christian. Most significant is the suggestion which forces itself upon our minds in leading us to ask, If Orthodoxy, in conceding what it does concede to avoid one terrible perplexity involved in its theory, does not run the risk of sacrificing a chief, if not the highest, recommendation of its theory, — namely, the power of motive which it offers to the penitent in displaying and appealing from the willing sacrifice of Christ? The more that Orthodoxy concedes as to the efficacy of Christ's Atonement for those who know nothing of it, the less does it make of that Atonement as furnishing motives to the sinner, while it increases proportionately the stress of value assigned to it for satisfying God, in the way of a substitution. We know and admit the power over the human heart which goes with Orthodox appeals from the cross of Christ. Those appeals turn themselves into earnest and loving motives to penitence and amendment of life. This is the one redeeming influence even of the most harrowing views of the Atonement which have been presented under Roman Catholic or Calvinistic preaching from the crucifix or from Calvary. Sinners have often been induced to forget the hideous representations made to them in the name of God the Father, of his unrelenting demands and his stern vengeance, through force of the gentle and melting sway of the self-sacrificing Saviour over their hearts. It is an incitement, a help to penitence. It furnishes a motive of irresistible might, and one which the heart loves to own and obey without imposing upon it measurement or limitation. This power as a motive comes from the cross of Christ, in that view of it which has its highest and holiest influence to Unitarians. Orthodoxy, too, has won some of the triumphs which it has ascribed to the God-ward view of the Atonement from this irresistible power of motive which goes with appeals to the heart from the cross. Yet this power of appeal from the cross, as furnishing motives for penitence and obedience, of course is restricted to those who actually have knowledge of Christ. The old Jews and the heathen, then, if benefited by the cross, had no help of motive from it, and its entire efficacy in their case must be its God-ward efficacy in their behalf *for* them, not at all *upon* them. It is implied that, at some future time, these forgiven Jews and heathen, who supposed they were forgiven by a simple exercise of God's mercy, will learn that the real ground of their forgiveness was the cross of Christ. The discovery will disclose to them that, while they thought they owed their discharge solely to the clemency of their judge, their debts have, unknown to them, been paid to him by a substitute. The admission being yielded, that millions of human beings may have the whole benefit of the cross without any knowledge of the sacrifice upon it, without any help from motive or gratitude in appeals from it, it must follow of course that in their case the whole necessity for the cross was on the side of God, and the whole operation of it is God-ward. Now, if millions of the human race may thus have the full benefit of the cross without any knowledge or subjective help from it on earth, why is that knowledge or subjective help from it essential to any portion of the human race? Is not this a making the cross of Christ of none effect upon men, to assign all its effect to its operation with God? Why, then, might not the crucifixion have transpired, and the whole world for ever have been ignorant of it? If the mediatorial work of Christ, instead of being a means and medium for manifesting the merciful purposes of God, was the *ground* of the Divine mercy, why was not heaven, rather than the earth, the scene of its display?

As to the Scripture quotation with which my critic closes, I have yet a few remarks to offer. His scholarly attainments would forbid his denying that "the blood of Christ" is simply an idiomatic synonyme of "the death of Christ." Some Orthodox writers of less culture would not admit this etymological fact, because they love to indulge every fancy which associates the cross with an immolation, and turns its blood to the service of a ritualistic purification. But proceeding upon the allowance, which an intelligent reader will not withhold, how does that song of the redeemed afford any support to the Trinitarian, or to the Governmental Theory? How can God be said to have redeemed us to God? Where is there any recognition of the indispensable condition of expiation, or of the Divine demand of a substituted victim, or of God's acceptance of Christ in that character? Much of the most emphatic statement of Orthodox doctrine on this subject, as in opposition to us, is made by a mere blind or catch in words. We are said to fall short of the problem of redemption by giving up "an Infinite Saviour." This is intended by the Orthodox to convey against us a charge of depreciating Christ. But if the charge were really taken by us as meaning anything, it would be that we did not believe in God. We have "an Infinite Saviour," for as Christ, the medium of that salvation taught us, we refer the plan, the method, the grace, and the glory of our salvation to God. We say, in words as intelligible as those quoted from the mystical Apocalypse, "God so loved the world, that he gave his only-begotten Son, that whosoever believeth in him should not perish, but have everlasting life."

This speculative and argumentative dealing with the sacred theme of Reconciliation to God by Jesus Christ, has not been to me a congenial or welcome process. On the contrary, I have found positive pain in bringing the holiest and tenderest of all the precious soul-sacraments of the Gospel under debate as a theory, a dogma. God forgive me, if, in secularizing the theme as the claims of controverted truth seemed to allow, I have brought to its discussion any other than chastened and serious and humble feelings. The meaning of prepositions is one thing. Saving and efficacious faith in Christ is another thing. Accepting thé great text with all three of the meanings of its preposition, I read, "God was BY, IN, and THROUGH Christ reconciling the world unto Himself."

XI.

EXCLUSION OF UNITARIANS FROM CHRISTIAN FELLOWSHIP.

Near the close of my Essay on the Atonement, I had expressed a regret that the rejection by Unitarians of a constructive interpretation or theory of the Orthodox doctrine was made a principal reason for excluding them from Christian fellowship. My critic makes a most kindly reference to this matter, and I doubt not his gentle and earnest words are but an inadequate utterance of the sincerity and full conviction of his heart. But he says that, "while existing differences remain, this lack of fellowship is inevitable." It is impossible that we should "unite cordially and consistently in the most solemn rites and acts of Christian fellowship." I cannot deny my critic the right of addressing the reader in his own words on this point.

"Most gladly would we accept the fellowship of those (or the more serious part of them) who now constitute the Unitarian community in this country. We have longed for it, prayed for it, waited for it; and still we wait. In this community we recognize not a few whom we respect and honor, and whom we are permitted to regard as among our most valued friends. We had hoped that the time was approaching, and near at hand, when those who had gone out from the old Orthodox Congregational churches of New England, and embraced what themselves think is another Gospel, would return. But at present we see little (we are sorry to say it) to encourage such a hope. Accepting the articles before us as a specimen, we see little advance in the right direction (unless it be in the matter of phraseology) beyond what was inculcated thirty years ago. We have the same differences now as then, in respect to the mode of the Divine existence, the natural state and character of man, the person and work of Christ, and the foundation of the sinner's hope; and while these continue, we see not how there can be fellowship, as Christians. We impeach not the sincerity of those who differ from us; we question not the excellence of their moral characters and social virtues; we will treat them not only with courtesy, but kindness, in all the relations and intercourse of life. But until they can sing with us the "new song" which should be sung by all Christians on earth, as we know it will be by all in heaven: 'Unto him who hath saved us, and *washed us from our sins in his own blood*,' — we see not, as was said above, how there can be the fellowship of Christians."

Now I would not be understood as laying any undue stress upon an incidental matter, to which I made a passing reference fully as much under a prompting of regard for Orthodox friends as with a zeal for securing a full Christian recognition for my own brethren. I have noticed in some other quarter a criticism on what I had written, to the effect that, though Unitarians denounced and withstood Orthodoxy, they had a timid longing, a weak and fond craving, to hold an unbroken fellowship with the Orthodox. I do not share that feeling in any form or measure of it which implies a desire of being indorsed by the Orthodox, or of being admitted into their more private or confidential religious associations. On the contrary, I think our present relations are, on the whole, preferable to any such forcing of sympathies and overcoming of mutual antipathies as would enter into the first conditions of such close fellowship. On some matters we could not possibly harmonize. If I may be allowed to say in the mildest terms possible what it seems ungracious to say in any way, I will avow my conviction that Unitarians would find full as much, if not more, embarrassment and hard forcing of sympathy in a full union with the Orthodox, as would the other party to the compromise. A fellowship between the parties would require full as much of concession and charity from the liberal as from the rigid side. As there is no denying the fact, there may be some grace in making the frank assertion, that Unitarians do not like some of the ways and schemes of the Orthodox. We do not like the strictly Orthodox type of character, certainly not till it has been modified, humanized, and liberalized. We deem it harsh, ungenial, narrow, repulsive, not winning, gracious, expansive, or attractive. It is in our view but an inadequate expression of our ideal of a Christian character. We think that the intense concentration by which Orthodoxy makes the whole problem of the universe to turn for each individual upon the means of rescuing *his* soul from the wreck of a doomed world, and from the fate sure to befall his neighbors, has a most direful effect upon the more loving sensibilities of the human heart. Then, too, when we hear the Saviour of the world monopolized, in the boastful arrogance of some confident converts, as "*my* Saviour," as if they were dearer to him than the veriest wretch whom they would scorn, — when we hear this from some whose peculiar favor with God is to human judgment more than doubtful, — we cannot but feel that Jesus is wounded in the house of his professed friends. Nor is it by any means in matters of taste and sensitiveness that Unitarians are thus often repelled by some of the Orthodox. Far otherwise. Grave objections arise as to the policy, the propriety, the rectitude, of what is known among men by the phrase "Orthodox management." We could not heartily accord with some measures which engage often their heartiest zeal. Most seriously, too, do we dissent from their mode of presenting the Gospel, and from their interpretation and application of it. I have allowed myself to write with this frankness merely to convey something of my meaning in affirming that the embarrassment attending a full fellowship between the Orthodox and the Unitarians would by no means be wholly on the side of the former. And still I repeat what I had written as to our regret at our exclusion from "the pale of Evangelical Communion," because of our rejection of "a constructive view expressed in a doctrinal formula." We regret it, as I also said, as much on account of its effect on the Orthodox, as on account of its effect on ourselves. The reason by which this policy, taking the name of conscience for its warrant, justifies itself, is but one of a series of similar reasons used by different Christian sects for vindicating their exclusion of their brethren of other communions. The Orthodox Congregationalist bars out the Unitarian, as we say, simply because of speculative differences about matters which are not vital to belief in the Christian religion, and to a course of life conformed to that belief. The Baptist denies fellowship to the Orthodox Congregationalist, on the ground of his heresy as to the form and subjects of baptism. The Episcopalian stands aloof from all who are outside of his Church, as being really outside of the true Church of Christ. The Romanist draws out the great Gospel net, and, while assorting its contents as under the direction of St. Peter, makes no more account of an Episcopalian, a Baptist, or an Orthodox fish, than of a Unitarian. It must be a strange sight for Him who is walking the waters and teaching from the shore, to see the fish in his great net assuming the office of self-selection and mutual rejection, the office which he reserved for himself!

But this exclusive policy seems more odious to us when practised by our former brethren, because of its more obvious inconsistency in their case with the principles of Protestantism. We maintain, too, that the ground of our exclusion is a matter not so much of belief, as of speculative opinion. We ask our brethren to look at the facts of the case as they appear to the Christian community at large, and then to Roman Catholics, and then to unbelievers, and then to the critics and impugners of Protestant consistency. Here are intelligent and sincere men and women, who avow themselves as believers in Christ, disciples of his, resting all their hopes on his Gospel, and zealous of sharing with other Christians the practical works of Christian benevolence and effort. The simple acknowledgment on the part of such persons, that their speculative views are such as are generally, though vaguely, called Unitarian, is sufficient to put them outside the pale of fellowship. There is something, too, particularly offensive, at times and on occasions, in the way in which the sentence is executed. Unitarians are solicited to aid in every measure of benevolence and enterprise, they are allowed even a silent presence in the gatherings and associations of the elect; but they may not cause their voices to be heard, or their votes to influence any practical work. In the mean while the fact is well known and indisputable, that nominal Orthodoxy shelters an uncounted number of persons who, though when they joined their respective communions they may have sincerely accepted the received tenets so far as they understood them, have been led by thought, inquiry, and experience to adopt essentially Unitarian views. Real but unavowed Unitarianism is tolerated, but an open profession of it is punished.

Our Orthodox friends, however, would misjudge us if they ascribed our feeling on this subject to any poor pique, or any weak desire to receive their countenance. We are affected by their course towards us solely and simply as it violates the consistencies of Christian truth, the harmonies of Christian charity, and the principles of sound Protestantism. Most free are we to acknowledge, with the generous rivalry of Christian esteem, the piety and zeal of those bodies of fellow-believers who repel us. We will institute no boastful comparisons which will exalt ourselves by depreciating them. But still, though severed from their fellowship, we do not feel that we are really cut off or estranged from a true Christian participation with them in common sacred interests. No sectarian edicts of theirs can deprive us of our full share by faith and works in the glory of all their eminent disciples, and in the powerful efficacy of their testimony to truth and righteousness. No decree of the Council of Trent can exclude us from real fellowship of heart with Fénelon and Pascal, and the very sentiment of love which moves us to approve any evangelical work of Orthodoxy makes us really more effective participants in it, than would a right to raise our hands for voting about it. Thus Orthodoxy is really baffled in its excommunicating purpose against us: its pales cannot be driven so deep as to divide heart-sympathies, nor raised so high as to cut off from us either the direct or the reflected light of Christian truth and love. Granting all this, Unitarians might say one word more as evidence that they are not suing for Christian sympathy under any timid or lonely sense of their own peculiar position. Unitarianism has a fold and a fellowship of its own. Collect together the names and services of those who by their own full consent might properly be entitled *Liberal Christians*, and — if we can say it with becoming humility, we will say it boldly — a Christian man or woman may regard the hospitalities of their household as a fair offset to the sectarianism of other Christians which turns them out of doors. We have within our own fellowship all the elements and fruits of a true membership of the Christian Church. We have our traditions and associations, our saints and martyrs, our poems and biographies, our charities and our progressive enterprises. If need be, we can stand a long and a hard pressure from without, and subsist with tolerable satisfaction on our own resources. Our policy must be to yield forbearingly and heartily to every condescending appeal from Orthodoxy which would enlist us in its good works. So far as, in anything that is right, they ask us to co-operate with them, we must cheerfully assent. For the most part, they have, so far, restricted their advances to us to a simple request that we will allow them to sanctify our money given for benevolent uses. Let them have the money freely, and by and by they may think better of the hearts and minds whose feelings and views the gift represents. Even in the words of my critic which have drawn from me these remarks, it will be observed that he admits the sincerity, the moral fidelity, and other religious virtues of some Unitarians. According to the Christian rule, one man has no right to judge another, beyond these qualities, if even within their range. Why then judge us for speculative opinions, and exclude us because of them? The Orthodox certainly would not sever us from their fellowship for the sake of diminishing the chance of our salvation. Is it, then, because they fear to imperil their own?

XII.

CONTROVERTED VIEWS OF SCRIPTURE.

I COME now to the last of the series of critical papers which are engaging my notice. It relates to my Essay upon the Orthodox and the Unitarian Views of the Scriptures. The paper presents but few points to which I need make a particular reply. In its form and tone it seems at first to remonstrate with a considerable degree of earnestness against some of my positions; but when I try to fix an issue with the writer on anything in which he appears to raise an issue with me, I am baffled. The simple truth is, that, like many modern Orthodox writers, he does in fact make all the concessions, yield all the qualifications, and allow all the exceptions, insisted on by Unitarians, though in an indirect and more guarded way. Indeed, had his paper been in print when I wrote, I might have quoted sentences from it, as I have from the pens of other Orthodox men, in illustration of my own positions. I am compelled, however, to add, that, like many of his brethren, he protests against the views of Unitarians on this subject, in a tone and way which indicate an entire misapprehension of our purposes and ruling aims. What we say in opposition to exaggerated and mistaken Orthodox views of the Bible, is construed by them as said in opposition to the Bible. The abatements which we allow or insist upon as required to reduce an old, superstitious, and untenable notion about the Scriptures, are represented as assaults upon the authority of the Scriptures. Now Unitarians ought not to be compelled at this day to define their position touching these preliminaries of a discussion. I ask with all confidence the question, What denomination of Christians has done more than the Unitarians in Europe and in America to authenticate, defend, and interpret the Scriptures in a way to secure the grounds of a strong faith in them, and to keep them sacred for the uses of piety? Have we not the same interest, the same momentous interest, at stake in them with all other Christians? The Orthodox might as well charge us with trying to vitiate the title-deeds of our dwelling-houses, when we are verifying them and securing our tenements from decay and the weather, as charge us with undermining the Scriptures.

Recurring to the fifth Essay in this volume, the reader will note the method and the purpose of the argument there pursued. In brief, it is as follows. When the Unitarian Controversy opened here, there was a prevailing popular view of the Scriptures which was superstitious, exaggerated, and untenable. Biblical criticism came in with the controversy. In the course of their discussions, Unitarians had to suggest as novelties many facts and considerations which have now become quite familiar. They suggested a revision of the translation in some passages, the presence of error here and there, the necessity of allowing for metaphoric or rhetorical language, and, above all, the utter impossibility of holding to and vindicating against reasonable objections the prevailing views of the verbal inspiration and the infallibility of Scripture. These concessions and suggestions Unitarians made, not for the sake of foisting their own views into the Scriptures, not to diminish one whit the support they were supposed to afford to Orthodoxy, but simply and solely in justice to the claims of solemn truth and for the purpose of vindicating the Bible against the cavils of infidelity. So far as concerns the evidence from Scripture texts of the truth of their own views, Unitarians were perfectly willing to take the Bible as it is. But they know very well that the faith of millions in the Bible could not stand if compelled to hold up ignorant and childish superstitions with it. Therefore they insisted upon the concessions and suggestions just referred to. For this, as my argument proceeded to show, they were sharply censured and most grossly misrepresented by many champions of Orthodoxy. I proceeded then to treat at some length of the grounds and the extent of the needful modification of the old popular notion of the Bible, and to prove, as the crown of my argument, that approved Orthodox writers, from whom I quote, now ratify, in the fullest possible way, all that Unitarians demand and insist upon in the substance of their own views of the fallibility of the Bible in some of its contents, and of the necessity of modifying the old notions of its inspiration. If my mind is clear on any point, it is on this, that even some of the essays and works written by Orthodox men, for the set purpose of answering the Unitarian heresies on these subjects, do in fact ratify and indorse those heresies. Professor Stuart himself is quoted by me as an evidence of this assertion, and it is one of which there is overwhelming proof in his own pages, though his concessions to the exigencies of criticism are often made in the most curious and indirect manner.

In the paper before me, the writer claims for Professor Stuart the credit of originating the science of Biblical criticism in this country, and of "diffusing it, inspiring a zeal for it, and impelling it onward." He adds: "Nearly all in New England, and I might almost say in the country at large, who have attained to eminence in this branch of learning, received their first impulse and instruction from his lips." The valuable services of that excellent and devoted man must indeed be acknowledged by every Scripture scholar in the land. His iron diligence, his independence, energy, and conscientiousness, as well as his thorough kindliness of heart, and his entire consecration to the work of his life, will assure for him renewed and ever fresh memorials of gratitude. My own impression, however, from my private reading, has been, that Mr. Buckminster was really, in order of time and in actual outlay of zeal, the first individual to quicken an interest in Biblical criticism. My critic says that Professor Norton was undoubtedly the first Unitarian who gave himself to the science, but Mr. Norton acknowledged his obligations to Mr. Buckminster. My own admission is quoted to the effect that Mr. Norton adopted some extreme opinions, in which Unitarians have not followed him. But if my critic will consult the work to which I have referred on page 398, he will find that a divine of the Church of England, who aims "to reconcile Christian Orthodoxy with the conclusions of Modern Biblical Learning," indorses Mr. Norton to the fullest extent of his heresies, and even goes beyond him.

Exception is taken to an inference from my words to the effect that Unitarians may believe in the doctrine of inspiration in the Orthodox sense. My critic forgets what in other places he has insisted upon, namely, the modifications of their own theories on some subjects which approved Orthodox men allow. I am willing, for one, to say, that I hold views of Inspiration which are taught and indorsed by such authorities. It is a part of my argument to show that the two parties have been brought into essential accordance of theory here. There is an old Orthodox theory and a new Orthodox theory, between which I have tried to distinguish. My critic shall here speak for himself.

"And yet it is evident that Mr. Ellis does not understand the Orthodox doctrine of Inspiration. At any rate, he does not represent it correctly. We do not believe in the inspiration of translators, or transcribers, or interpreters. A translation of the Scriptures is a proper subject of criticism, like any other translation. And the same may be said of a copy or an interpretation. We do not believe the Apostles to have been inspired in all their intercourse and conversation one with another. For we find them often dull, stupid, prejudiced, ignorant, and sometimes disputing one with another. We find our Saviour not unfrequently reproving them; and Paul on one occasion (to which Mr. Ellis refers) withstood Peter openly, because he was to be blamed."

I am not aware that I have affirmed the belief of the Orthodox "in the inspiration of translators, or transcribers, or interpreters." I have implied, however, what is strictly true, that the old popular view of Inspiration left out of sight the fact that there had been fallible translators, transcribers, and interpreters, and proceeded on the assumption that the text of our common English Bible constituted an authority back of which there was no appeal. I wish the reader to mark the very loose allowance made by my critic as to the imperfections of the Apostles. It is one of those back-handed concessions to which I have already referred.

To what is said in the following paragraphs no real objection can be taken, for when the premises required are established, the conclusion may be accepted: —

"It is sometimes said that the Orthodox repudiate reason altogether, and leave it little or nothing to do in matters of revelation. But this is a great mistake. We hold that reason has much to do in this matter. It belongs to reason to decide whether God has made any supernatural revelation of himself to the world; and if so, where and what this revelation is. What books contain it? Have we the right books? If these books are in the original tongues, have we accurate copies? Or if in a translation, is our translation accurate? Does it give the real sense and spirit of the original? And when all these points are satisfactorily settled, what does the language mean? Do we understand it aright? Here are various points of great importance, which are submitted to our reason, and on which it is the province of reason to judge.

"But beyond and behind all these questions, reason, we think, has no right to go. When we have ascertained, to our satisfaction, that any particular book is from God, and that we understand it as God has revealed it, then we are bound by it. It is to us *the word of God*. So far as it goes, it is an infallible rule of faith and life."

We too may say, that "when we have ascertained to our satisfaction that any particular book (and why not add, any part of a book?) is from God, and that we understand it as God revealed it, then we are bound by it." But the contents of such book will always and necessarily claim to enter among the tests of its Divine origin and authority. If we detect manifest errors in it, our conclusion must be that the particular book or part of the book which is fallible, either never came from God, or has been corrupted.

There is much also that is very loose in the following paragraph: —

"We believe that 'all Scripture is given by inspiration of God,' but then there is an important distinction between inspiration and revelation, which Mr. Ellis does not make, and which may relieve him of some of his difficulties. Revelation makes known to us God's truth and will. Inspiration has respect to the assistance afforded to the sacred writers in recording God's truth and will, or in recording anything else which God is pleased to have written in his word. There is much in the Bible that is not revealed truth, or truth in any sense; and yet 'all Scripture is given by inspiration of God.' The speech of the serpent to our first mother was not revealed truth. It was the first and greatest lie that ever was uttered. And yet Moses was as really inspired in recording the speech of the serpent, as he was in recording the Ten Commandments. The books of Job and of Ecclesiastes (to which Mr. Ellis refers) are not all of them revealed truth. They cannot be. And yet the record — at least the original record — may have been divine and infallible. It may have been written, and we think it was, under the inspiration of God."

It is hardly necessary to repeat here, that the intended Scripture quotation at the beginning of the paragraph is but a begging of the question. There is a great difference between the true reading, "All God-inspired Scripture is profitable," &c., and the reading which my critic adopts. There is hardly an appreciable distinction between *revelation* and *inspiration ;* for if anything is communicated by *inspiration*, it must be something that is revealed. Mr. Lee, in his very disappointing work on the subject, labors hard upon the distinction, for which, by the way, in the form of it which he adopts, he is under an unavowed obligation to another.

I am not prepared to admit that Moses was inspired to serve as an amanuensis for a Personage, who, if he has half the power that has been attributed to him, was abundantly able to keep his own records without taking into his disloyal service a penman previously engaged for a worthier Master. As to "*the original record*" of Job and Ecclesiastes being divine and infallible, it is enough to say that we have not got it. I am confident, however, that I rate the value and authority of those books as high as does my critic. He makes a passing reference to a few of the specific cases of palpable fallibility in the contents of the Bible, some of which he thinks have come in through the error of transcribers. They are *in* the Bible, nevertheless. But all these difficulties, he thinks, "may be disposed of in one way or another, without impeaching the truthfulness or the inspiration of the original writers." But how? That is the very question the discussion of which opens the whole fair field of Biblical criticism. On that field dogmatism and unsupported assumption are sure to be worsted. How can any one assume the infallibility of the Bible, as the mass of readers have it, and then fall back on the autographs of the original writers, which are not in our possession?

One example, most comprehensive in itself, of all the principal assumptions and difficulties embraced in this theme, may serve to present all its bearings to us.

The chief argument in proof of the inspiration of the Old Testament is, that the Saviour quoted it as authority. Of course, then, we are concerned to have a most exact report of his very words. The main argument in proof of the infallibility of his Apostles is the Master's commission and promise to them. This inspiration and this infallibility, then, we should expect to find combined in a report of the Saviour's words authenticating the Old Testament.

Now take the three reports which three of the Evangelists give us of an argument from the Saviour's own lips, founded on a quotation from the Old Testament, for the discomfiture of the cavilling Sadducees.

Matthew xxii. 31, 32 gives it thus: "But as touching the resurrection of the dead, have ye not read that which was spoken unto you by God, saying, I am the God of Abraham," &c.

Mark xii. 26 gives it thus: "And as touching the dead, that they rise: have ye not read in the book of Moses, how in the bush God spake unto him, saying, I am the God of Abraham," &c.

Luke xx. 37 gives it thus: "Now that the dead are raised, even Moses showed at the bush, when he calleth the Lord the God of Abraham," &c.

What were the exact words of Christ in this instance? We may say, substantially, the three reports of them convey them to us. But when salvation is often made dependent upon the exactness of verbal renderings of originally infallible statements, — as in the quotation of some other sentences of Scripture, — we must demand unerring accuracy.

Yet the critic affirms that the tendency of my article and its argument, notwithstanding my "solemn asseveration, is to bring the Bible into doubt and suspicion with the great mass of readers." In vain, therefore, I suppose, shall I assure him that I am fully persuaded that the views referred to are the only possible means for *removing the doubt and suspicion* of another large mass of readers. He asks, "What is the use of parading these difficulties, and exaggerating them, so as to make the impression that the Bible is a very unreliable book?" Whoever does what the critic here suggests, I hold, as heartily as he would, to be an unwise, an unfair, and a mischievous person. No one who commits to the Bible such transcendent interests of humanity as I believe to be intrusted to it and dependent upon it, would run the risk of being justly liable to such a charge. It is very easy to discern the difference between a captious, cavilling critic, and a discreet champion of the Bible. Where have I paraded, where have I exaggerated, the difficulties presented, not so much by Scripture, but by Scripture when embarrassed by an artificial and superstitious authority or character? My aim has been to state them in a moderate and cautious way, for the simple purpose of showing that they arise and receive their whole seriousness, as objections of any weight, from the Orthodox theory which assigns to the promiscuous contents of the Bible a divine authority not claimed by them for themselves.

My own strong conviction is, that the Bible carries with it its own warrant for asking our faith in its principal contents. It commends its lessons to the heart and soul of man. The old Orthodox theory of its inspired infallibility would never suggest itself to an intelligent reader of our day, who, with the best training which the other sources of knowledge afford him, should turn for the first time to the perusal of its pages. The hostile criticisms which pick flaws and detect imperfections in it here and there, answer to the superstitious and exaggerated claims which are set up for it by its indiscriminating idolaters. We have no right to tamper with the record, nor to overstate its difficulties, nor to dispute the authority of inspired writers on any points covered by their divine commission. Neither have we any right to speak of everything in that book as having the especial sanction of God. We have no original record from either of the writers. In their present form, to the mass of readers the Scriptures present themselves as sufficiently intelligible and authoritative for all the reasonable uses of faith and piety. To the scholar they present perplexities which he must deal with as best he can. I am happy to close these remarks with an expression of my entire persuasion, that, allowing for our different ways of conveying the positive and the negative elements of our belief on this subject, my critic and myself are substantially agreed.

THE END.

www.ingramcontent.com/pod-product-compliance
Lightning Source LLC
LaVergne TN
LVHW021301110826
845150LV00003B/451

* 9 7 8 1 4 2 5 5 5 9 5 7 1 *